International Sports
Economics Comparisons

International Sports Economics Comparisons

EDITED BY RODNEY FORT AND JOHN FIZEL

Studies in Sports Economics

Westport, Connecticut
London

Cat

Library of Congress Cataloging-in-Publication Data

International sports economics comparisons / edited by Rodney Fort and John Fizel.
  p. cm. — (Studies in sports economics)
  Includes bibliographical references and index.
  ISBN 0–275–98032–4 (alk. paper)
    1. Sports—Economic aspects—Cross-cultural studies. 2. Professional sports—Economic aspects—Cross-cultural studies. I. Fort, Rodney D. II. Fizel, John. III. Series.
  GV716.I58 2004
  338.4'7796—dc22   2003062260

British Library Cataloguing in Publication Data is available.

Library of Congress Catalog Card Number: 2003062260
ISBN: 0–275–98032–4

First published in 2004

Praeger Publishers, 88 Post Road West, Westport, CT 06881
An imprint of Greenwood Publishing Group, Inc.
www.praeger.com

Printed in the United States of America

Contents

Preface

Sports are a worldwide economic phenomenon. Around the world, institutions to govern them and organizations to run them vary significantly. The purpose of this volume is to shed light on this variation. It has also been our experience that economists gathering together from different lands typically spend the first few minutes simply catching up on the facts of institutions and organizations, and often the way in which they thought the world worked ends up being false. If this book accomplished nothing more than presenting the facts of international sports institutions and organizations, that would be enough. But, as readers will discover, it does much more than that. It has been our distinct pleasure to have had a hand in guiding this volume to completion. As editors, we offer just this brief preface since there is so much ground to cover.

The first four sections cover Western Europe, and the leadoff chapters set the tone for issues and comparisons. Bourg notes that the "European model" is an evolving policy choice. The originality and architecture of the European model are in danger, notably the aspects that distinguish it from the American model; that is, the primacy of the sports objective over the economic result. The chapter examines the challenges confronting European policy makers as they decide which economic model to apply to European sports into the future. Szymanski wonders if there even is such a thing as the "European model." The European Commission suggests that there is a distinct European model of sport, and this chapter explores its existence by comparing European and U.S. institutionalized antitrust frameworks.

Gerrard's chapter sets the stage for the labor and competitive balance sections to follow. European soccer faces major problems in maintaining both its sporting and financial viability, as competitive imbalance and rising player costs threaten its existence. In addition to surveying these problems, the chapter considers alternative long-term solutions.

Labor issues in Western Europe deserve their own treatment, and Staudohar sets up a good comparison between those of Western Europe and the United States. Specifically, the chapter compares and contrasts the evolution of free player movement in Europe and the United States. Gouguet and Primault provide history and data analysis on the transfer system. From the perspective of economic theory, they ask, how can the value of a player transfer between two clubs be objectively determined? In turn, the type of system chosen to regulate professional championships in Europe will depend on how that value is determined. The chapter also includes history of transfers and their regulation. Andreff provides an excellent example of one problem that seems constantly to plague policy makers the world over—international talent migration. Beyond the ethical aspect of such transfers, their economic impact is examined from the perspective of the French clubs that import the talent, the home clubs in primarily developing countries, and the governments of developing countries exporting the talent. In a suggestion that already has stirred some controversy, a novel tax approach is offered and compared to Fédération Internationale de Football Association (FIFA's) current transfer regulations.

Nothing is more important to pro leagues than competitive balance—or the lack thereof. Using both smaller and larger markets, Moorhouse effectively sets out the issues in a survey. This contribution uses recent evidence from some of the smaller countries (media markets) of Europe—Scotland, Portugal, and Holland—and some of the larger countries (media markets)—England and Italy—to assess the extent of economic imbalances within and between leagues, to discuss the effectiveness of the policy options currently being touted, and to argue that European soccer requires much more radical solutions if it is to solve its economic and sporting problems. Simmons and Forrest go straight to the heart of the matter to investigate the relationship between wage bills and winning, providing comparisons to the United States. This chapter asks whether a significant correlation between team performance measures and team wage bills is a more prevalent phenomenon in professional sports leagues on one side of the Atlantic or the other. The relationships between team performance measures and team wage bills in the four largest U.S. professional sports organizations (Major League Baseball, the National Basketball Association, the National Football League, and the National Hockey League) and two European soccer leagues (England and Italy) are assessed. Frick and Prinz take a broader empirical look at competitive balance across the rest of Europe, comparing the survivability of recently promoted teams to first divisions across three different TV revenue-sharing arrangements.

The remaining topics for Western Europe are in the last section. Downward and Jackson compare the Premiership form to the Super League. Following the evolution of these two leagues, the chapter compares and contrasts their key features, including the means by which increased commercial pressure produced the Premiership and the Super League as well as the impacts that these developments have had on league structure, competitive balance, club finances, and the labor market. Gratton and Solberg compare and contrast sports broadcasting in Western Europe and the United States. In particular, the increased regulation of European markets and the importance of public service broadcasting channels in Europe have led to a difference in the distribution in the two regions of broadcasting rights between pay and free television. The result is that European consumers pay substantially more for sports broadcasting than their U.S. counterparts. Rounding off the look at Western Europe, and highlighting a unique difference between North American and European forms, Dobson and Goddard examine stock flotation. The chapter presents the history of stock floating in European pro team sports. In addition, event study is undertaken to explain the behavior of team stock prices.

Turning to the rest of the world, Longley explores a truly unique part of the Canadian pro sports system, its Canadian Football League. The chapter focuses on labor restrictions and government sports policy, providing both a historical perspective and an analysis of some of the current economic and policy issues facing the industry.

Owen and Weatherston take on the Southern Hemisphere rugby union's evolution to professional status. The aim of this chapter is to document the changes in the organizational structures that have occurred since the sport's professionalization in Australia, South Africa, and, in particular, New Zealand (all of which are winners of the three Rugby World Cup competitions for national teams held to date), and to compare these with organizational structures in more established professional team sports in other countries.

Aidar, de Ameida, and Miralla present breaking developments governing soccer in Brazil. The chapter covers the new (as of this writing) soccer legislation in Brazil, including talent hiring rules and rules on the acquisition of clubs by investors. The chapter also documents the rise of professional leagues after the new legislation and provides what little data there are on professional teams, turnovers, and wages.

Two chapters cover Japan and Korea. Kawaura and La Croix examine cultural variation in Japan and the United States regarding the rules of baseball. Major League Baseball (MLB) rule alterations are usually adopted by Nippon Professional Baseball within a short period of time. Implementation of the draft, adoption of the designated hitter, and abolishment of the reserve clause are analyzed for possible cultural variation in outcome. Lee covers competitive balance and attendance comparisons in baseball for Japan, Korea, and the United States. These elements are compared across the variety of leagues and their different institutions.

A trio of papers covers Australia. Macdonald and Borland survey seven major sports competitions in Australia. For each competition, three main themes—organization, outcomes, and key policy issues—are examined. Booth turns to competitive balance and the impact of revenue sharing and labor market interventions. This chapter examines the levels of competitive balance in a league composed of win-maximizing clubs under a variety of labor market devices and revenue-sharing rules, making for interesting comparisons with competitive balance levels achieved in other professional sports leagues. The levels of competitive balance achieved in the Australian Football League are compared with the outcomes in major leagues in North America. Finally, Dabscheck looks at the current state of flux in Australian sports, including labor market rules, collective bargaining, and broadcast rights issues in Australian leagues.

Part I
Western Europe: Overall Issues

1

Professional Team Sports in Europe: Which Economic Model?

Jean-François Bourg

INTRODUCTION

From the middle of the nineteenth century onward, Europe designed and structured modern sports. However, until recently—essentially 1995, with the Bosman ruling of the European Court of Justice—sports did not appear as a concern for the community authorities. For example, the Treaty of Rome, signed in 1957, did not have any sports-related measure. The sporting movement, therefore, developed completely autonomously.

However, competitive sports as a spectacle really only entered the European marketplace in the 1980s (Bourg, 2000). From then on, this conversion of administrative sports institutions in the professional sector to traditional economic mechanisms meant that marketed sports were subject to competition law and to the rules of free movement of labor. But this new access to functioning markets by clubs' factors of production (the Bosman ruling for the labor factor and the introduction of stock flotation for the capital factor from 1983 in England, 1998 in Italy, and 2000 in Germany, for example) has jeopardized the sporting and financial balance of championships.

Indeed, this double breakdown—economic and legal—in the previous order has thrown up a major incompatibility: Competition is incapable of regulating the labor market and collective team events; that is, those who oppose the clubs, taking account of the peculiarity of sports competition (Neale, 1964). The uncertainty of the result epitomizes the uniqueness of sports events compared to any other event, giving it its unique character, and the interest that comes from it justifies the market value of the event.

The match is jointly produced by the two teams that face each other. It is probable that the quality of the match depends mainly on the balance of the forces involved. If, as seems safe to assume, winners turn their financial success into success at increasing the future quality of their teams, then their future chances of increasing their on-field success also rise. At the same time, losers are weakened because they must release their best, highest paid players in order to reduce costs since revenues fall with their mounting on-field losses. Hence, the inequality of the teams will be detrimental to the balance of the competition and consequently to interest in the event, including a decrease in the number of spectators and in the television audience, a decrease in the overall takings of both clubs and the league, and the possible appearance of deficits.

In view of this law of increasing and decreasing returns, which tends to segment the championship insofar as resources are concentrated in a small number of clubs to the detriment of others, what regulations can be implemented? The point of this study is to examine how and why the European system of professional team sports does not guarantee the economic coherence of championships, preserve the financial viability of them, or ensure the balance of the competition. Finally, the study asks how the founding principles of European sports model, which distinguish it from the North American model, can be safeguarded.[1] Indeed, the historical and ethical basis for sports competitions in Europe has been the opening of all championships that are linked by a relegation-promotion mechanism, along with the direct and solid links that bind professional clubs together with amateur clubs and regions. It would therefore be advisable to undertake a more normative approach in order to determine which regulatory instruments to implement with regard to the founding principles of European sport as well as competition law.

ARE SPORTS COMPETITIONS BALANCED?

The notion of uncertainty is the very basis of all competition. Therefore, the aim of the institutions managing a championship is to preserve the balance of the clubs involved. Economic literature dedicated to both the necessity of maintaining the uncertainty of the result and to measuring the distribution of the forces involved and identifying the influence of variables of internal competition in a championship is both old and plentiful (see especially El Hodiri and Quirk, 1971; Fort and Quirk, 1995; Rouger, 2000). Through successive contributions, the concept of competitive balance was related to the standard deviation of winning percent in order to supply information about the "health" of a championship. Competitive balance is now commonly analyzed as the ratio of the standard deviation of actual winning percent to the so-called "idealized" standard deviation.[2]

According to this definition, which is widely accepted and used by the scientific community, competition would be all the more fierce if this ratio were close to one, making competition identifiable as being in an idealized situation. On the other hand, the higher this value, the less uncertain the championship would be. Therefore, this indicator enables the development of competition to be measured within the same competition, and the levels of uncertainty of several championships among themselves to be compared. However, no theoretical analysis or empirical approach has determined the efficient level of competitive balance with regard to supporters' expectations. From the statistical point of view, all the teams in a perfectly balanced competition (admittedly an unrealistic hypothesis) would be equally strong, and every match would finish with an equal score. It would therefore be impossible to establish a ranking, and the interest of such a championship would be debatable.

The long-term study from 1981 to 2000 of this ex post assessment of strength distribution in the five main European soccer championships is full of lessons to be learned (see Table 1). Considering the stability over a period of time, and considering it from the least to the most certain—that is, from the French to the Italian championships—the hierarchy of teams was as expected. The position of each country can be explained by the more or less interdependent economic organization, operating mainly through the regulating function of broadcasting rights.

On the other hand, something unexpected was noted: Competitive balance tended to improve during the period, especially after the liberalization of the players' market (the Bosman ruling of December 15, 1995) and the implementation of a new financing model for the major European clubs (1990s). It is interesting to note that France's improvement in homogeneity during the post–Bosman ruling period (1995–1996 to 1999–2000) compared to the pre–Bosman ruling period (1990–1991 to 1994–1995) could be partly explained by the 100 best French players heading abroad after the

Table 1
Competitive Balance in the Main European Soccer Championships (Professional First Division, Averages by Period 1980–1981 to 1999–2000)

Periods	France	Germany	England	Spain	Italy
□ 1995/96 to 1999/00	1.2979	1.3612	1.5028	1.4197	1.5779
□ 1990/91 to 1994/95	1.3731	1.3724	1.4397	1.4194	1.6194
□ 1985/86 to 1989/90	1.2334	1.4036	1.4843	1.5638	1.4084
□ 1980/81 to 1984/85	1.4082	1.5561	1.3656	1.3996	1.4015
□ 1980/81 to 1999/00	1.3282	1.4233	1.4481	1.4506	1.5018

ruling, which was not offset by the arrival of major foreign talent. This impoverishment helped to level downward the teams' potentials, which strengthened uncertainty (eight different championship winners from 1992 to 2002). In contrast, the stability (represented by Spain) of, and above all the improvement (represented by Italy) in, competitive balance during the same period does not reflect the permanent domination of the same group of clubs, the beneficiaries of deregulating the players' market and commercial rights. These teams monopolized access to the national title (four different winners) and to the lucrative Champions League (Real Madrid, F. C. Barcelona, Juventus, and Turin).

Season-by-season observation from 1979 to 2000, as opposed to the previous five-year phase, of the changes in value of competitive balance shows, for example, that competition was more homogeneous in the 1999–2000 season for France (0.9075) and Spain (1.0512). Conversely, the uncertainty of the result was weakest in the 1978–1979 season for England (1.8449), 1979–1980 for France (1.6627), 1982–1983 for Germany (1.7842), and the 1989–1990 season for Spain (1.7598). If the period 1980–1981 to 1999–2000 is divided into two blocks of ten years in order to reduce the impact of a very high or a very low value on the average, an improvement of competitive balance is noted during the 1990 to 1991 sequence in two championships (+4% in Spain and +8% in Germany), and a deterioration of this indicator in three championships (–1% in France, –3% in England, and –14% in Italy). This variation in competitive balance did not seem to bother supporters who, during this period and independently of the variations of this indicator, were increasingly numerous in the stadia. From this point of view, and strictly speaking, since the economic progress of the championships does not seem to have been reduced by the practices of sports leagues, could competition judges accept these restrictive practices in their wish to regulate competitions? We'll return to this issue later in the chapter.

None of the data in Table 1 appear to validate the idea that only a strong regulation of human and financial resources restores team potential and strengthens the unpredictable character of sports results. Indeed, all admit that the European championship market has been operating in a more free-market framework since the mid-1990s.

Therefore, is it necessary to find a new illustration of what has become known as the "invariance principle" (Rottenberg, 1956), according to which the division of talent between clubs would be absolutely identical whether or not restrictions on player mobility or rules about income sharing exist, and this provided that club owners are looking to maximize their profits. Such stylized points appear completely contradicted by reality. On the international level, economic and sporting dualism have been extended by the consequences of liberalizing the players' market, the unequal development in turnover of the various championships, and the lessening importance of solidarity for revenue sharing. The seventy most important transfers in the history of soccer have taken place since the Bosman ruling. Among those, 65% come from two countries (Spain and Italy) and from seven clubs which, by themselves, account for 40% of quarter-finalists from the Champions League (1998–2002), whereas theoretically clubs from fifty-one countries have access to it.

In addition, if it is revenue sharing that enables America's National Football League (NFL)—recognized as the most homogeneous in North America—to be balanced, it means that the maximization of profits hypothesis, which is the basic hypothesis and traditionally accepted over the Atlantic, does not hold (Lavoie, 1997), and that the majority shareholders have other motives (wins, disinterested pleasure, etc.). In this case, majority shareholders could be prepared to accept large financial losses to achieve on-field success.

It is true that a strict view of European clubs as maximizing sporting gains and North American clubs as maximizing profits now appears to be simplistic and artificial. Indeed, the abandonment of the status of a not-for-profit organization and the spread of limited companies as legal support for professional clubs during the 1990s, and the possibility of issuing shares and bonds, of distributing dividends, and of remunerating managers have all considerably changed the way in which European clubs are managed. From now on, good sporting results will not constitute the ultimate aim of team owners. Instead, they are thought of increasingly as a necessary, but not always indispensable, condition for achieving extra-sporting aims (commercial, with merchandising; financial, with listing on the stock exchange; etc.) (Eurostaf, 1998).

This change, along with the study of professional soccer in Europe, is why we can suggest that the idea of competitive balance, as it is currently defined and calculated, does not constitute a comprehensive and totally pertinent indicator for measuring the inequality of team performances. The ratio of the standard deviation of winning percent to the "idealized" standard deviation indeed provides good information about the dispersion of team results, while assessing in what proportions they differ from a situation in which all teams win 50% of their matches. But there is a hole in this measurement (Lavoie, 1997, 98). Let us imagine a very close championship, but one in which, season after season, the same teams finish in the first places and qualify for the playoffs and the European cups. This is the case with most European professional team sports (particularly soccer, basketball, and rugby). For example, 70% of the soccer clubs that qualify for the Champions League remain the same, season after season. Such a stable and persistent domination by certain clubs is not taken into account by this dispersion indicator (see Bourg, 1989, and Bourg and Gouguet, 1998, for an illustration of the stability of clubs traditionally found at the top and the bottom of the table at the end of the season).

Therefore, in order to see in what proportions the winning teams remain winning teams and, conversely, the losing teams remain losing teams, it would be appropriate to use another measurement of repeat appearances at the championship level. The development of such measurements used to analyze National Hockey League (NHL) championships appear to show that the winning (or losing) teams have had more of a tendency to remain winning (or losing) teams more recently than in the past, a finding that would not appear with sporting balance (see Lavoie, 1997, 101).

DOES A EUROPEAN SPORTING MODEL EXIST?

Admittedly, identical principles govern what can be called "the European model" and the "North American model," but operating methods differ greatly by country (see Table 2). The competition between clubs is structured by a pyramid-shaped and close-fitting system of sporting qualification, from the lowest local level to the international level. The result is unity in the sporting movement, the components of which are linked by a continuous mechanism of promotion-relegation. A territorial organization unites a team to a town. The aim of the clubs themselves is to maximize wins while staying within budget since, until the 1990s, the law forbade the distribution of dividends and most clubs do not make a profit. Even more fundamentally, and unlike U.S. leagues, a club's bad sporting results can lead to exclusion from the most prestigious events (the Champions League, the Union des Associations Européennes de Football [UEFA] Cup, the national premiership, etc.). On the other hand, those clubs developing in the second or third division have been able, over the last few years, to reach the national

Table 2
Organization of Professional Team Sports in Europe

Convergences	Divergences
□ ways of access to the competition (sporting)	□ club turnover
□ club aims (sporting gains)	□ weight of taxation and social charges
□ functioning of the championship (open with relegation promotion)	□ budgetary control of clubs
	□ quotation on the stock market
□ system of law (Community competition law)	□ co-ownership of clubs
□ link with amateur sport (organic)	□ ownership of stadia
□ link with a territory (closed)	□ ownership of broadcasting rights
□ functioning of the labour market (free-market)	□ ways of selling and dividing up of broadcasting rights
	□ sporting balance in national and European competitions

Table 3
Competition Factors in Europe (First Division Professional Soccer Clubs)

Characteristics	Germany	England	Spain	France	Italy
Ownership of broadcasting rights	League/clubs	Clubs	Clubs	League	Clubs
Weight of taxation and social chargers	56%	50%	48%	77%	50%
Clubs quoted on stock market	1	20	0	Forbidden	3
Co-ownership of clubs by same shareholder	Up to 49.4%	Up to 9.9%	Up to 5%	Forbidden	Forbidden in same division
Budgetary control of clubs	Yes	No	No	Yes	No
Championship broadcast rights (million Euros, 1999/00)	300	800	300	260	400
Turnover (million Euros, 1999/00)	700	1200	600	600	1000

soccer cup final in their countries, to qualify for the European UEFA Cup, and this in the same capacity as thousands of professional or amateur clubs enrolled for that competition.

Beyond these points, which are common to all European countries, many differences exist (see Table 3). These differences distort competitive balance, so that the best teams of each national championship face each other every year in the same European event, the Champions League, or the UEFA Cup. For example, in countries where budgetary controls do not exist, clubs can recruit and win a European title (as happened recently with the move of Anelka, Figo, and Zidane to Real Madrid for 170 million euros), while at the same time amassing significant deficits. In 2000, Real Madrid won the Champions League, despite liabilities of 230 million euros.

The more free market the criteria, the greater the ratio of broadcasting rights fees earned by the club that receives the most and the club that receives the least: ratios of 1.7 in France, 2.2 in England, 2.6 in Germany, 5.3 in Spain, and 6.3 in Italy (see Table 4). This imbalance is strengthened by the fact that channels broadcast, in preference, the matches of the main clubs to the detriment of the small teams, which are thereby penalized relative to their more successful on-field business partners. For example, during the 2001–2002 French championship, twenty-seven matches of Olympique de Marseille were televised, twenty-four of Paris Saint-Germain, but only two of Guingamp and one of Lorient were televised.

A CRISIS OF TRANSITION?

In fact, if the European system of professional team sports does not succeed in ensuring sporting balance, economic coherence, and financial viability

Table 4

Decline in Broadcasting Pooling Rights in European Professional Soccer (in %)

Criteria Competitions	Solidarity*	Sporting Performance**	Media Performance**	Total
French Championship - division 1				
1998/1999	91	9	0	100
1999/2000	73	27	0	100
2002/2003	50	30	20	100
English Championship - division 1				
(since 1992/1993)				
2002/2003	50	25	25	100
Champions League (Europe)				
1999/2000	16	40	44	100
2000/2001	11	39	50	100
Italian Championship – division 1				
(payment by the meeting)				
2001/2002	0	0	100	100

*Fixed, identical amounts for all clubs, independent of sporting ranking and of the number of matches broadcast or their audience.
**Variable amounts, according to the performance of each club.

in its championships, it is probably because it is experiencing a crisis of transition between two models of financing, which coexist within the same levels of competition.

The traditional European model, Spectators-Subsidies-Sponsors-Local (SSSL), reached its maturity in the 1970s. During the 1980s, and above all during the 1990s, new sources of income appeared and, simultaneously, the relative portion of the old sources declined in team budgets. From then on, the thirty major European clubs have had the Media-Magnates-Merchandising-Markets-Global (MMMMG) structure (see Andreff, 2000). The emergence of this new model translates the combined effects of deregulation, dependence on the financial markets, and economic globalization into professional sports (see Andreff and Staudohar, 2000). Therefore, the shareholders who expect a return on their investment henceforth define the rules of governance of these clubs, and the clubs' factors of production develop strategies on the European and world market. On the other hand, SSSL model clubs, which comprise about 90% of the total, respond to a more "sporting" and national logic, taking into account their financing by supporters and private or public sponsors. The transition from one model to another is justified by the exhaustion of the traditional financing of major clubs, which are facing growing needs linked to the weight of salaries and in their demand to acquire the best talent in order to maximize sporting gains in a market where, with no restriction to limit the effects, competition is very intense.

Clubs adopting the MMMMG model become subject to the assessment and sanction of the markets, especially financial ones, which are interconnected on a global scale. It would lead to clubs behaving in an individualistic way, requiring a situation in which the players' market would be strictly regulated and in which the league would be a stable cartel of clubs. Are we then heading toward a closed European league that brings together in an exclusive and sustainable way clubs converted to the MMMMG model, with clubs of the model SSSL being restricted to their national championships? In fact, what remains is the question of the type of organization model for professional team sports.

In Europe, self-regulation is less and less accepted and used, whereas the North American leagues have practiced it for decades: in 1936 for the draft (NFL), and in 1983 for the salary cap (National Basketball Association). Therefore, it would be appropriate to wonder about the way to preserve competitive balance in Europe. In addition, regulation needs to restore championships to economic coherence and financial viability. And there will be practical difficulties. Regulation aimed at enhancing the uncertainty of results leads to pressures on leagues under competition law and to methodological difficulties concerning relevant geographical areas and sporting structure. Paradoxically, the current application of competition law in Europe leads to a protection of the partners (suppliers, equipment makers, broadcasters, sponsors) and to an economic, financial, and sporting concentration around several major clubs.[1]

THE DIFFICULTIES OF REGULATING EUROPEAN CHAMPIONSHIPS

The Territoriality and Nature of Championships

In North America, the uniqueness of the competition (only one per discipline and only one level of competition), the stability of the members of the league, the access to the league by franchise purchase rather than promotion-relegation all represent key characteristics for efficient regulation. Indeed, the closed nature of the leagues is manifested in external noncompetition (clubs are not in competition with others in a supranatural competition) and in an absence of internal sanctions (qualification or relegation).

The European system of open and linked championships (national/European) complicates the implementation of player market restrictions like the salary cap. Its application solely in one country would amount to handicapping the clubs taking part in European cups facing foreign teams not subject to a cap. A salary cap that is not systematically or consistently applied could be useful in balancing the national championship, but it would compromise the chances of European wins by the best clubs. Let us take the example of France. An annual salary cap of 25 million euros per club (which corresponds to the French average aggregate employee earnings in 2001–2002) would weaken the strength of a club like Lyon in the Champions League, where Lyon already lags behind spending on salary by the major European clubs (50 million euros for Lyon, 100 million for Manchester United, Real Madrid, or Juventus of Turin).

An efficient European salary cap would require homogeneity of fiscal and social law across countries, as well as the elimination of competitive distortion.[3] Consequently, a draft in Europe would undermine the training system, since a list of young talent should be made available to all clubs, penalizing the most effective training centers, which would be "plundered." Clubs would no longer be encouraged to invest in training, since others could benefit from their efforts and they themselves could get their supplies elsewhere. Further, a similar salary cap for all clubs would not put them all in the same position. Therefore, some (Rouger, 2000, 20) suggest two series of adjustments in order to apply an effective salary cap in Europe. First would be to establish a ceiling on the various amounts, weighted according to different fiscal and social pressures in each country. Second would be to establish a tax on clubs taking part in European championships when they exceed the aforementioned ceiling in established for their country. The tax revenue can be used to support clubs developing at the national level. This support for the poorest clubs by the richest would be similar to the Major League Baseball system in North America. But in Europe, the difficulty would come from the fact that the major clubs involved in the two levels of competition (national and European) are obliged to invest enormously in talented players, contrary to North American teams.

The same complication arises for sharing broadcasting rights or instituting a European version of the North American draft. An optimal distribution of broadcast rights fees that encourages balance among teams in the pursuit of a national championship would have implications for the ability of the national champions as they move on into competition for European championships (see the fifth European place of French clubs in 2002, which is the last place of the main soccer-playing nations and has been so for many seasons). Turning to the draft, whereas the training of young people is outsourced to colleges, universities, and minor leagues in North America, this system is internalized in Europe, since the clubs have an obligation to set up and finance their own training centers, from which they recruit by preference.

Competition Law versus Competitive Balance

For the player, the salary cap reduces freedom to enter into a contract with the club of his choice, insofar as the player who, due to the risk of a big reduction in pay if it exceeds the authorized collective ceiling, might find it impossible to leave a club. Mobility could be more or less reduced according to whether a cap would be a soft or a hard cap. The draft represents a sort of barrier to entry into the labor market insofar as access depends on the player's acceptance to sign a contract with a club that he has not chosen and to financial and sporting conditions set by the same club. A refusal would lead to the player's professional disqualification for at least a year.

Any negotiation among the leagues, the clubs, and the players should lead to a collective agreement, which could reduce the concern of competition judges by showing them that competitive balance (statistical notion) and competitive equilibrium (economic notion) are comparable insofar as the dominant position of one of the actors in the market could jeopardize it. Thus, assessing anticompetitive behavior would be carried out according to the rule of reason (case-by-case comparison of the advantages and disadvantages), rather than a per se approach (a priori decision, by nature) (Combe, 2002).[4] And yet, current practice of competition law contributes more to deregulation of than to protection of balance (Rouger, 2000, 229). The competitive equilibrium of a market should no longer appreciate solely according to its nearness to hypotheses of pure and classic competition, but should be considered instead in the light of the actors' strategic behavior.[5]

In the Adidas/National Football (soccer) League affair, the French judges did not take this analysis into account when sanctioning an exclusive sales agreement signed by the league for the supply of equipment to all clubs. Had they taken the points discussed above into account, the judges would have seen that this contract put Adidas in a very favorable position in the sporting goods market and that Adidas could not be exempted from the anticompetitive rules. This being so, there was confusion between the professional sports league and their business partners that contributed to its financing. This decision was legitimate in relation to the workings of the sporting goods market, but the judges did not examine the impact this agreement could have on the balance of the competition. This kind of application leads to a stronger protection for business partners of sports than for the leagues, which are weakened by their desire to organize collective sales and equal distribution of broadcasting and marketing rights in order to balance the competition.

This competitive case law strongly encourages clubs to behave in an opportunistic manner. The major clubs apply pressure, which is often effective in taking broadcasting rights for themselves or having access to the financial markets, by threatening the leagues with legal action for restriction of their own free development before competition judges (see Tables 3 and 4). It is true that, taking into account what is at stake, sporting sanction encourages major clubs to pursue this individualistic behavior. Indeed, access to the market based on sporting criteria weakens healthy clubs, which are penalized by relegation to a lower division. In France, broadcasting rights received from the league are divided by five in case of relegation to the second division, and nonqualification for a European cup leads to a loss of earnings of 10 to 30 million euros. Out of ninety-three clubs that followed each other in divisions one and two from 1980 to 1990, twenty-five had to face three or more changes in competition level; only seven developed in a continuous way in division one. On the other hand, thirty played in division two for only one or two seasons before experiencing voluntary liquidation.

The major clubs do not bear this unpredictability and its economic consequences very well. They also consider that their contribution to the turnover should be higher than that which they receive by means of redistribution or to that which they would receive by marketing these rights themselves.[6] The individual ownership and sale of broadcasting rights has spectacular consequences. The major Italian and Spanish clubs strengthen their domination (Juventus, Lazio of Rome, Real Madrid, and F. C. Barcelona) having at their disposal amounts fifteen times higher than their less prestigious opponents, whose matches are often broadcast only on local channels.

It is therefore paradoxical that respecting anticompetitive rules enable certain clubs to increase their dominant position in the championship, while the professional sports market does not come within the framework of a pure and classic competitive market—the inseparability of clubs' functions of production creating an interdependence in their relationships, and the imperfection of information leading to uncertainty in their environment (the vagaries of sporting results, players' efficiency, etc.). The main objective of a league must therefore be the preservation of sporting uncertainty, while reducing the opportunistic temptations for clubs.[7] Now, noncooperation constitutes a basic rule for sporting competitions. There is therefore a risk of suboptimality if the system is weakly regulated, since clubs naturally behave opportunistically and with scant regard for others.

The danger for competition is all the more important as individualistic behavior accentuates the economic difference between rich and poor clubs (Bourg, 1989; Bourg and Gouguet, 1998, 2001). The strong increase in the standard deviation of the financial competency of clubs stigmatizes their increasingly unequal character as turnover increases.[8] The lack of financial unity in championships, both internally and in relation to others, risks destabilizing even more national and European competitions, despite the fact that it would consolidate the hierarchy.[9]

PERSPECTIVES AND CONCLUSIONS

A more flexible and contemporary application of competition law could help to balance competition that has been damaged by a free-market structure and opportunistic behavior by clubs. To apply such a law, sports bodies must demonstrate to competition judges that maintaining competitive balance requires putting in place restrictive measures on the labor and sporting event markets.[10]

A more collectivist system would preserve both the product and the system, ensure maximum profits, and contribute to the "economic progress" of professional sports. It is the lack of such an approach that makes the current behavior of European sports bodies dangerous. They do not take into account the impact that the economic differences between rich and poor can have on competition.

It goes without saying that aims differ according to the organization of the championship. Unlike the North American leagues that are closed—the reason why sporting results are not a heavy constraint—results are, in fact, the main aim of the open European championships.[11] In North America, the hermetic framework of competition makes the implementation of regulatory tools easier owing to the very fact that it is a matter of a closed economy. This is not the case in Europe, where the interdependence of the championships and their disparity in financial, fiscal, and social terms complicates, or renders useless, any desire for regulation. For some people, only a closure of the leagues would remedy these constraints.[12] Indeed, the mixing of two levels of competition (national and European) gives a considerable economic advantage to those clubs involved in the two levels, compared to those that develop solely within the national championships. The revenues drawn from the Champions League destabilize the national competitions because they, by themselves, are often higher than the total budget of their opponents (between 30 and 40 million euros per year). Therefore, these clubs have a greater capacity than the others to invest in the available talented, which enables them to maintain their supremacy.

This proposal for a closed league would, however, have certain drawbacks. The first would be to weaken the European training system, which is based on openness to competitions and internalized training. The second drawback is the fact that clubs participating in a closed league would release only with great difficulty their best players for national team matches. The third would result in a breakdown of the pyramidal and unitary organization of amateur and professional team sport championships in Europe.[13]

Is it possible, then, to envisage an alternative to the creation of a closed and accessible league, either according to financial criteria (e.g., buying a franchise) or to other criteria (e.g., reputation, European honors, etc.)?[14] The current organization of team sports in Europe is not incompatible with the development of economic solidarity, which could be encouraged via the law on competition.[15] To do this, sports bodies can claim the benefit of a "sporting exception," which would exclude the professional team sports market from the application of articles 39, 81, and 82 of the Union Treaty.

The fear of these sports bodies, inspired by the Bosman ruling, is that competition law would legitimize an overly free-market system, hence favoring individualistic behavior by the major clubs. The major fault of a "sporting exception," which would be granted to professional team sports in relation to the rules of competition, lies in the fact that it does not solve in any way the central problem of regulation. And nothing indicates that the liberalization of the market would not accentuate the economic differences between rich and poor even more. The example of collective bargaining for broadcasting rights is telling: The legal possibility of collective sales is useful, but it is not enough to regulate correctly the competition. Only an egalitarian redistribution of these rights could lead to a homogeneous competition—not a sharing according to the sporting ranking and media exposure of the teams. For, in the latter case, the major clubs would be encouraged to behave in a more individualistic way.

Hence it is preferable to explore the partial and conditional exemptions anticipated in the Union Treaty.[16] Thus, centralized bargaining for broadcasting rights would only be legitimate if it contributes to balancing the competition. Conversely, any distribution not following these lines would be condemned. This updated application of competition law would make it possible to fight effectively against the opportunistic behavior of clubs that is harmful to the balance of the competition.

The well-understood aims of sports bodies (competitive balance in the championship) and of the judges of competition (competitive equilibrium in the concerned markets) would be similar. For the "glorious uncertainty of sport" is not the result of a free-market working of the championships market, but rather the result of a united organization. Over the last few years in Europe, this open debate has shown what is very much at stake in terms of the European sporting system's architecture and the efficiency of the European sporting system, as well as helping to preserve its founding principles. Admittedly, competition law must find a field of coverage in professional sports, but all professional sports cannot be included in this field of coverage.

NOTES

1. This analysis relies on the example of soccer, as it is the foremost professional team sport in Europe and it has the most available statistical data. Other disciplines have seen a similar development, but it has been less intense.

2. This theoretical value is calculated in the following manner (Quirk and Fort, 1992; Fort and Quirk, 1995):

If all the teams are of equal strength, in a hypothetical championship of m matches for each of them, then the probability of winning each match is $p = 0.5$. With x being the number of matches won in a season, the expectation of x is given by:

$E(x) = 0.5\ m$ and the variance of $x\ V(x) = 0.25\ m$.

The percentage of wins out of total matches *w* of each team can be arrived at with:

$$w = x/m$$

when $E(w) = E(x)/m = 0.5 \ m/m = 0.5$ and $V(w) = V(x)/m^2 = 0.25 \ m/m^2 = 0.25/m,$ which gives finally the standard theoretical deviation of the percentage of wins:

$$\sigma w = 0.5 \ \sqrt{m}.$$

3. It must be remembered, too, that the area covered by the European Union (fifteen countries) is much smaller than that managed by UEFA (fifty-one countries), which represents the territory of the European Cups.

4. Anticompetitive rules may be inapplicable to a particular league practice if the contribution of that league practice to economic progress offsets any threats to competition or if statutory instruments have already made the practice legal. The impossibility of implementing this second method comes from the fact that no European Community measure legitimizes European sports bodies, whose existence and monopoly are only recognized by the international sports federations.

5. From this point of view, the theory of contestable markets makes a contribution, while showing that, to be competitive, a market is not necessarily the place where a large number suppliers and applicants meet. The fact that entering the market or leaving it can be carried out immediately, with no special costs, is more important.

6. Olympique de Marseille claims 50 million euros from the league, which is six times more than its current share. The club reckons that it could obtain this amount if it sold its broadcasting rights itself. The key to sharing out has developed in this way: 91% of TV revenue was equally shared in 1998–1999, as against 50% in 2002–2003, with 30% being distributed according to final position and 20% according to three criteria (sporting performance of the club over five years, the number of televised matches, and the exterior filling rate).

7. The opportunism of the actors becomes widespread within the framework of noncooperative games with partial information (see the "prisoner's dilemma").

8. In 1998–1999, the standard deviation in the French second division was 16; that of the first division was 100 (Rouger, 2000, 268).

9. Many econometric tests on professional soccer have shown the positive relationship that unites the financial competency of a club with the possibility of its obtaining good sporting results. During the 1997 to 2002 seasons in the Champions League, 80% of the teams reaching the final stages were the same, and all were among the twenty richest clubs in Europe. The three largest budgets have even won all the recent (as of this writing) Champions League finals: Manchester United (1999), Real Madrid (1998, 2000, 2002), and Bayern Munich (2001).

10. Similar to what has been carried out in the United States since the 1960s.

11. We have seen that the dichotomy—profit maximization constrained by sporting results (North America), and sporting results maximization constrained by budgets (Europe)—was simplistic and did not take into consideration the legal and economic permutations of European professional team sports.

12. See Hoehn and Szymanski (1999, 231), who have attempted to organize rationally a European soccer league, including four conferences of fifteen clubs each from twenty-eight countries.

13. This argument has a relative impact insofar as currently, the weakest clubs never, or very rarely, participate in the battle to win the national title or for qualification for European competitions. In actual fact, there is therefore a sporting dualism.

14. See Primault (2001), for an outline of a mixed system with a semiclosed European league, renewable every three years, in part with clubs from national championships.

15. See the major decisions of U.S. case law, which exempted from antitrust laws certain restrictive rules in baseball (1922, 1953, 1972), in football (1974, 1977), and in basketball (1975) based on the rule of reason and not on the per se approach (Staudohar, 1999; Rouger, 2000).

16. Theoretically, the setting up of means of regulation, even anticompetitive, is possible if these means contribute to the economic progress of championships and if their purpose is to distribute better the profits resulting from them; in other words, if they have regulatory effects on the balance of competition.

2

Is There a European
Model of Sports?

Stefan Szymanski

Soccer is not as American as baseball, hot dogs, apple pie and Chevrolet.
. . . Never was, never will be.
                    —Sean Coughlin (*Asheville Citizen Times*, South Carolina)

The American model . . . in no way corresponds—legally, culturally, or even
socially—to the European model.
                    —D. Primault and A. Rouger (1999)

INTRODUCTION

There can be little doubt that when Europeans talk of a European model of
sports, what they mean is a model that is distinctively un-American. When
the European Commission published its document *The European Model of
Sport*, they spoke of a distinction between the "East European" model of
the former Communist bloc and the "West European" model of the region's
mixed economies. But the East European model is dead, and no one wants
to revive it. When looking to the future, the Commission sees either the
continuation of Europe's mixed economy model or a convergence with an
American model. Nor is the Commission alone. Primault and Rouger (1999),
quoted above, Andreff and Staudohar (2000), and Hoehn and Szymanski
(1999), among others, all identify significant differences between European
and American sports models, and question whether convergence is likely or

desirable. Fort (2000) offers a dissenting voice, claiming the differences are more apparent than real, but even he argues that Europeans should see the future evolution of European sports through the lens of American experience, implicitly accepting that the European experience is different from the American one.

This chapter sets out to address three questions:

1. Why has the European experience differed from the American?
2. How should we characterize the differences that currently exist?
3. In light of the changes that appear to be driving European sports today, which can be pejoratively labeled as "commercialism," is convergence with an American model inevitable?

WHY HAS THE EUROPEAN EXPERIENCE DIFFERED FROM THE AMERICAN?

In every culture humans engage in sports. However, the form that sports take is often dictated by the preoccupations of that culture. To put it another way, human beings choose to engage in sporting activities in ways that enhance their own sense of well-being, and what it means to be well is something that varies by culture.

The practice of sports in modern industrialized nations bears little relation to the organization of sports in other cultures. Even the modern Olympic Games, revived by Baron de Coubertin at the end of the nineteenth century in conscious emulation of the ancient Greeks, bear little relation to their progenitor. Most obviously, the first Olympics, like almost all premodern sports, were a religious activity, whereas modern sports are almost entirely secular. Guttman (1994) identifies a number of other characteristics that distinguish modern sports from their precursors. These include bureaucratization (keeping records, establishing hierarchies for the administration of competition and rules) and routinization (regularizing competition to facilitate comparison among results).

Formalized sports emerged in the last two centuries among the nations of Europe and in the United States, and they have produced forms of sporting competition that have few parallels in any other culture, living or dead. Almost all "modern sports" were formalized somewhere between 1840 and 1900, for example, baseball (1846), soccer (1848), Australian football (1859), boxing (1865), cycling (1867), rugby union (1871), tennis (1874), American football (1874), ice hockey (1875), basketball (1891), rugby league (1895), the Olympics (1896), and motor sports (1895).[1]

Historians (see, e.g., Mason, 1980; Vamplew, 1988) have argued that the process of formalization of sports mimicked the formalization inherent in industrialization and urbanization (timekeeping, routinization). The process of standardization and the creation of interchangeable parts were key steps in the development of industrialization, and so too was the standardization of sporting competition a key to the development of modern sports. It does not seem to be a coincidence that most of this development took place in an urban, industrial setting, nor that the development of most sports occurred in the leading industrial nation of the nineteenth century.

Industrialization has had two great consequences for the modern world. The first has been the mass production of goods and services for sale to consumers, and the second has been the mass production of the means of destroying consumers by what we now call the military-industrial complex. These two great enterprises were prosecuted with extraordinary vigor in the nineteenth and especially the twentieth century, and behind both the state wielded significant influence at every stage. In particular, military activities in the modern era have been primarily initiated and coordinated by the state.[2] State involvement in the production of goods and services for consumption has been less enveloping. In the Anglo-Saxon economies of the United States and the UK, private enterprise and the market have always played a significant, usually dominant, role. In the rest of Europe (and Japan), the state has played a larger role, but private enterprise still has contributed significantly, giving rise to what is generally known as the mixed economy. Furthermore, since the 1980s and the collapse of European communism there has been a trend away from state control toward private ownership and the rule of the market. Nonetheless, in much of Europe the state remains a dominant player in the economic field.

Like industrialization, sports, in their evolution, have offered two faces to the world. Much of modern sports developed out of nineteenth-century military imperatives of the emerging nation-states, and in those countries the state has retained until today a significant role in the organization of sports. But sports are also entertainment, and their development as such has been driven largely by market-oriented economies.

War, Sports, and the State

"The battle of Waterloo," the Duke of Wellington is supposed to have said, "was won on the playing fields of Eton." True or not, no quotation can better illustrate the nineteenth-century perception that modern sports had a fundamental role to play in maintaining an efficient military power. The English public school movement of the early nineteenth century, associated with educationalists such as Matthew Arnold, embraced a new ideology of education based on sports, health, and discipline to breed an elite capable of governing an empire. This movement created a generation of British men (and some women) who treated the playing of cricket, and soon soccer, as part of a normal active life. However, this was a generation of players, not performers.

This model of sports emerged in free-market Britain without any explicit direction by the state. Theorists in continental Europe, however, did envisage a role for the state. Although the practice of modern sports is distinctive compared to the practice of sports in other cultures, European thinkers drew heavily on classical Greek ideals when considering the motivation for participating in sports. To the ancient Greeks, physical exercise was a part of the normal activity of the male citizen, ensuring his readiness to serve the city-state in times of war. European thinkers adopted this rationale. Some, such as Rousseau, went further still and argued that exercise was a critical element in the preparation of children for citizenship. Advising on the design of the Polish government (1772), he argued, "In every school a gymnasium, or place for physical exercise, should be established for the children. This much-neglected provision is, in my opinion, the most important part of education, not only for the purpose of forming robust and healthy physiques, but even more for moral purposes." Indeed, in Rousseau's scheme, exercise was not merely for pleasure.

> They should not be allowed to play alone as their fancy dictates, but all together and in public, so that there will always be a common goal toward which they all aspire . . . for here it is not only a question of keeping them busy, of giving them a robust constitution, of making them agile and muscular, but also of accustoming them at an early age to rules, to equality, to fraternity, to competition, to living under the eyes of their fellow-citizens and to desiring public approbation.

Friedrich Jahn (1778–1852) founded the gymnastic "Turnen" movement in Prussia in the early nineteenth century, and he is credited with the invention of gymnastic exercises such as the parallel bars, the horizontal bar, the rings, and the pommel horse. But this was not sports for entertainment, nor even for the pleasure of competition. Jahn was driven by the need to improve the physical quality of Prussian soldiers following their defeat by Napoleon at the battle of Jena (Seners, 1999). The success of this movement spread to other countries, most notably France, where Francisco Amoros (1770–1848) was responsible for opening the Ecole Normale de Gymnastique Militaire in 1852 (Seners, 6). In 1873 the Union des Societes de Gymnastique de France was founded as a governing body specifically as a response to defeat by Prussians at Sedan (Arnaud, 2000, 15). Thus some sports developed in the nineteenth century as part of the state's drive to improve military performance. Clearly this led to excesses, as the European Commission acknowledged when it referred to the use of sports by the fascist regimes of Nazi Germany and Mussolini's Italy (European Commission, 1998, 10).

The connection between war and sports in the nineteenth century ensured that the European states would play a leading role in the evolution of sports. Even when militarism had been discredited, the state's role did not disappear. Instead, its apparatus was turned toward the promotion of other benefits that sports might produce for the state and society.

In addition to enhancing military preparedness, Houlihan (1997) identifies five further reasons for government involvement in sports:

1. Social regulation on moral grounds (e.g., regulation of blood sports)
2. Concerns for the general level of health and fitness
3. Sports as a motor of social integration
4. Sports as promoter of international prestige
5. Sports as a promoter of economic regeneration

The European Commission has reviewed the role of European governments in sports and a brief summary of the roles and responsibilities of each of the member states can be found at http://europa.eu.int/comm/sport/info/structures/a_struct_en.html. These statements give a clear idea of the degree of state direction involved.

France

The Ministry of Youth and Sports and the Ministry of Education are responsible for most physical and sporting activities. The Ministry of Youth and Sports is responsible for promoting all forms of sporting activities for all age groups, for the management and supervision of State aid support to sports groups and for defining and implementing training schemes for voluntary or professional sport leaders. The Ministry exercises its responsibility through regional Youth and Sports Offices and offices of the "départements."

Greece

The General Secretariat for Sport is primarily responsible for the financial and scientific support of top sport in collaboration with the sports federation and the scientific sports centres and for the financial support and organisation of Sport for All on central as well as local level in collaboration with the local authorities, the clubs and other sports institutions. For the implementation of its sports policy, the General Secretariat for Sport collaborates with the following Ministries: the Ministry of National Education and Religion, the Ministry of National Defense and the Ministry of Public Order.

Italy

While the CONI [the national Olympic Committee, licensed directly by the state] has the task of encouraging and organizing sports activities at all levels, the so-called "vigilance" is led by the Presidency of the Minister's Council, under the responsibility of the Deputy Prime Minister through the "office for liaisons with sports bodies." The same office is also entrusted with some administrative functions concerning extraordinary funding programmes for sports facilities.

The State has a complementary role in promoting through the Regions and Local Authorities the necessary conditions for citizens to participate freely in their favourite sports.

Spain

According to the Sports Law of 1990, the Higher Sports Council (CSD) is the central body responsible of public administration responsible for Sport on the national level. It is an autonomous body controlled by the Ministry of Education and Culture.

Finland

The general management and supervision of sport is the responsibility of the Ministry of Education. Physical cultural matters are handled by the Youth and Sport Department of the Ministry of Education. The National Sports Council (NSC) is the expert body for advising the Ministry of Education on sports affairs. It has three divisions: the Sports Science division, the Sports Policy division and the Special Group division.

The relationship between government and sports in the United States is significantly different from the relationships in Europe suggested by these statements. The U.S. government claims no overall responsibility for sports either at the federal or state level, although it does take some responsibility for enhancing opportunities for participation in physical fitness and sports through organizations such as the President's Council on Physical Fitness and Sports (PCPFS). However, the purposes of such interventions are strictly limited as can be seen from documents such as Executive Order 13265 of June 6, 2002, setting up the PCPFS. Its purposes are to "expand national interest," "stimulate and enhance co-ordination," and "expand availability of quality information."

One way to contrast the state's involvement in European sports with the American approach is to consider the subject matter on one of the most influential texts on the economics of sports, Roger Noll's *Government and the Sports Business*, published in 1974. First, it is worth noting that this book was primarily concerned with the way in which privately owned teams organized sports markets rather than with government involvement. To the extent that the book did consider the state's participation, it did so by examining the role of government legislation or the courts in restraining abuses of monopoly power. In Chapter 12, Noll considered U.S. Senator Marlow Cook's 1972 proposal to establish a federal agency "to regulate sports broadcasting arrangements, drafting procedures, the sale and movement of franchises and the limitations on competition for players." Needless to say, such thoroughgoing federal regulation did not materialize.

Thus, one contrast between the historical experience of Europeans and Americans in relation to sports concerns the role of the state, significant in the former, relatively insignificant in the latter. But this is not the only source of historical differences.

Sports as Entertainment

The historical development of sports in nineteenth-century Britain and the United States has much in common. State involvement in Britain was as limited as in the United States, and sporting competition emerged along private lines, first as amateur sports organized for the benefit of the players. As modern sport developed, however, sporting events increasingly attracted spectators, and businesspeople saw an opportunity to turn a profit.

Despite these similarities, however, some British and American sports developed distinctive institutions as early as the nineteenth century.[3] In particular, the dominant team sports, in addition to involving very different athletic skills, have developed distinctive rules and regulations. This is most easily illustrated by considering the development of the archetypal American and British sports, baseball and soccer.

Baseball

Seymour (1971), the authoritative early baseball historian, makes it clear that the structure of the National League created in 1876, and the foundation of organized baseball, emerged as a consequence of the free-for-all that was undermining interest in the new national sport. From the end of the American Civil War, interest in the game spread rapidly across the country, with teams and competitions proliferating and vying to attract spectators. The barnstorming teams of this era crossed the country in search of opponents, relying on winning-record driven reputations to generate income. The natural equilibrium of this free-entry dynamic game is (a) barnstorming teams attract support as long as they are winning and then collapse when they lose (a rational bubble), (b) team owners dissipate all the rents in competing to hire the best talent, and (c) the opportunities for gambling on the records of individual teams generate match fixing.

The founders of the National League perceived this to be an unstable equilibrium that would result in the loss of spectator interest in the game, as well as being an unsatisfactory equilibrium for team owners. Thus the National League was a deliberately elitist affair, intended to invest the members with a stake in its long-term success (to combat short-run incentives for match fixing), to create exclusive territories (the incentive to invest in local markets), and to establish monopsony rights over the players (the reserve clause). The extraordinary success of this model made it not only the basis for the national sport of the United States but also for the other North

American team sports (football, basketball, and ice hockey). America exported this model to other countries (e.g., baseball in Japan and Mexico, basketball in Australia) and to sports in other countries influenced by the United States (e.g., Australian rules football in the 1970s). In particular, although other team sports in the United States developed new organizing principles (e.g., the draft in football or the salary cap in basketball), these principles were largely integrated into a common framework that characterizes each of the major sports.

Soccer

The creation of the Football League in England in 1888 had similarly momentous implications for this national pastime in nations that adopted the British model of league organization (see Inglis, 1988, for full details). The Football League was formed by a group of teams that belonged to an all-encompassing governing body, the Football Association (FA), founded in 1863. As well as laying down the rules, the FA administered its own successful club competition, the FA Cup, and organized international representative matches against other countries using club players.[4] Unlike the founders of baseball's National League, the founders of the Football League did not break away from the existing structures, but worked inside them. This meant that (a) the Football League never attempted to become an exclusive institution, but set out to admit all the major team into its ranks, and (b) League teams accepted from the beginning the practice of releasing star players to represent, without compensation, their country in international competition (although this has become increasingly controversial).

As soccer spread rapidly around the globe and other nations adopted the British system, a distinctive organizational structure evolved, involving:

1. An overarching governing body responsible for the rules and organizing highly successful competitions (e.g., the World Cup, the European Championship) independent of domestic league authorities
2. A domestic league system incorporating promotion and relegation[5]
3. A system in which star players are paid employees of clubs and compete for them primarily in league competition, but are also representatives on the national team whose success is usually seen as even more prestigious

This system applies not only to soccer worldwide but also to a number of other team sports, mostly in Europe where the soccer system is dominant (e.g., rugby union and basketball in Europe).

Sporting Plurality

Perhaps the greatest institutional difference between Europe and the United States lies in the plurality of national leagues in the former and the monopolization of the highest level of competition in the latter. Although competition among rival leagues has characterized part of the history of North American sports, in most cases competition at the league level has not survived long. Fans are drawn to the best competition; competing head-to-head to attract talent has driven down profits to the point where either leagues have folded or mergers have occurred. The close substitutability of rival major leagues in the eyes of consumers has thus been the driving factor toward establishing dominant major leagues in each of the North American team sports, particularly in the television age.

European experience is different for the simple historical reason that consumers have much more rigidly defined regional loyalties. These are associated with national territories, and as a result the national leagues of Italy, Spain, Germany, and England are seen as only imperfect substitutes. Although competition for player services is intense, it has not brought about league bankruptcy or mergers (even for relatively small European nations such as Belgium, Denmark, or Greece) because consumers have tended to remain loyal to their national leagues. Some writers, such as Fort (2000), have pointed to the regional loyalties associated with college sports conferences in the United States. In some regions, these local rivalries tend to dominate almost all interest in sports. Nonetheless, it remains true that the dominant sporting series in the United States, at least from a commercial point of view, are those that are organized on a national (Europeans might say continental) level.

HOW SHOULD EXISTING DIFFERENCES BE CHARACTERIZED?

In this chapter we will focus primarily on professional team sports, largely since this is where the greatest differences between the European model and the American model are to be found. When it comes to golf or the Olympics, it might conceivably be said that there already exists a global model, which subsumes both European and American practice. The similarities, at least, seem much more striking than the differences.

In professional team sports, however, the differences appear much greater. Table 1 is an attempt to draw a systematic comparison of the differences.

Consumer Preferences

Consumers differ in what they want from sports within both Europe and the United States, so it would not be impossible to imagine that systematic differences existed between the regions. On the other hand, is there any reason to think, a priori, that Europe contains more of a particular type of consumer than the United States?[6] This is a very difficult question to answer,

Table 1
Professional Team Sports in the United States and Europe

	United States	Europe
Consumer preferences	Limited regional segmentation	Significant consumer loyalty to regional leagues
Governance	Organizational independence of the domestic major leagues	Integrated governance structure within a global hierarchy and national leagues subordinate to national associations that participate in international competition using league players
Entry and exit	A fixed number of teams	Mobility of teams through the system of promotion and relegation
	Entry through the sale of expansion franchises	Free entry for new teams at the bottom of the hierarchy, but promotion on sporting merit only
Exclusivity	Exclusive territories and franchise mobility	Non-exclusive territories
Labour market rules	Draft rules giving teams monopsony rights in player acquisition	Competitive labor markets at the entry stage, no draft
	Roster limits	No roster limits
	Low player mobility and limited player trading, especially for top stars	High player mobility and trading for cash, especially for top stars
Unions	Collective bargaining over player conditions	Limited unionization or collective bargaining over player conditions
Collective selling	National broadcast rights (exempted from antitrust)	Limited collective sale of national broadcast rights (no antitrust exemption)
	Collective sale of merchandising	No collective sale of merchandising
Ownership restrictions	Restrictions preventing the stock market flotation of clubs	Limited restrictions on the stock market flotation of clubs

principally because, on each continent, the existing arrangements are weighted toward different consumer groups, whereas the question asks whether consumers would respond differently when offered the same product. Take for example one of the most notable differences between consumers of U.S. team sports and European soccer consumers: hooliganism. Hooliganism, involving the smashing of stadium facilities, fighting between rival gangs of supporters, terrorizing the local population, and other excesses, is commonplace in Europe but fairly rare in the United States. However, there are many factors that encourage hooliganism in Europe and many that discourage it in the United States. In Europe, fans typically travel to away matches, partly because the distances are usually much shorter than in the United States, creating an opportunity for confrontation between rival fans. Before the 1990s, stadium facilities in Europe were much worse than in the United States, with limited opportunities to buy food or drinks other than alcohol, poor seating or standing only, poor protection from the weather, and very low prices. Moreover, in this period policing was very lax and penalties limited. The problem of hooliganism has declined (but not disappeared) due to better facilities, better policing, and harsher penalties. Would the hooligan element have emerged in the United States if the treatment of fans had been similar to that in Europe? It is at least possible.

The difficulty of knowing whether the preferences of fans reflect differences in culture or differences in habits affects every aspect of sports. For example, Kahane and Shmanske (1997) found that, all else being equal, teams with more stable team rosters enjoyed higher attendance. Fans appear genuinely to prefer team stability. There is no evidence of any such preference among European soccer fans. But player trading has been part of the fabric of soccer since the nineteenth century. And in the highly regionalized markets of Europe, player trading nowadays gives fans the opportunity to see international stars with whom they are familiar from international representative matches they have seen on the TV (e.g., the World Cup). If three-quarters of the best talent in baseball played outside the United States, and this talent was on show at a Baseball World Cup, might not Americans find the notion of player trading more appealing?

The most important difference in preferences that exists concerns regional loyalties. Historically, fans only paid attention to domestic league competition. The World Cup did not start until 1930, and international competition among clubs did not start until the advent of the European Cup in 1956. It is arguable that international competition only really became important when the quality of TV pictures reached a level where the viewing experience of soccer achieved broad appeal, possibly during the 1970s. Since then, interest in international competition has increased considerably. Within Europe, this has meant that the European Cup, now called the Champions League, has achieved a level of popularity that is comparable to domestic soccer. However, it remains true that fans tend to watch matches involving domestic teams. For example, in the 2000–2001 season, fifteen of the seventeen Champions League matches broadcast in England on free TV involved English teams (even if in some cases a majority of players were from overseas), and the other two matches had below-average ratings, even though one was a semifinal and the other the final.[7] However, regional loyalties also exist in the United States, and in most regions it is mainly the local baseball team that attracts the lion's share of the TV ratings, so perhaps the differences are not so great.

The most interesting questions, however, are these. Currently fans in Europe follow two main competitions—the domestic league and the Champions League. Would an enlarged Champions League be strong enough to significantly reduce interest in domestic competition? And, if the big teams abandoned the domestic leagues to play only in the Champions League, would domestic leagues wither?

Governance

The possibility of this eventuality has been much discussed in Europe, and proposals for a breakaway European Super League have existed since at least 1988. Private sector broadcasters have been the driving force behind these proposals (e.g., companies such as Mediaset in Italy, part of the business empire of Silvio Berlusconi, currently prime minister of Italy), since they perceive a Super League, featuring the top playing talent in Europe, as being more attractive than domestic soccer, where each league has a small number of good clubs and a lot of mediocre ones.

If consumers would be interested in such a league, why hasn't it been created? There are two answers to this question. The Champions League, which currently involves playing up to seventeen matches in a season, already represents a small-scale version of a Super League. Moreover, this championship has been expanded in recent years precisely when it appeared that the clubs were reconsidering the feasibility of a breakaway league.

However, the current league structures involve considerable difficulties for the clubs, not least of which is a match schedule of up to sixty games in a ten-month season, which many experts believe places too much strain on the players. Squad sizes have expanded, but this has meant that big clubs have been unable to field their best players in all matches, undermining performance in all competitions. It is clear that a shorter schedule would be in the interest of the bigger clubs, and this is precisely what a well-run Super League could offer.

One reason why a Super League has not been created is the governance structure of European soccer. The European Commission talks of the pyramid structure, with clubs at the base, regional associations above them, national associations above them, and international governing bodies at the apex. Although clubs may be willing to break away from these structures, players may be reluctant to move to new leagues. If, for example, national associations refused to recognize the new leagues, players might be disqualified from representing their national team, a privilege they would be unwilling to forgo, both out of loyalty and financial interest.[8] How real this threat may be, however, is open to debate. In 2000, European basketball clubs set up their own breakaway league, the Euroleague, in competition with the Suproleague run by the International Basketball Federation (FIBA). Yet when FIBA called on the national associations to sanction the Euroleague clubs, they refused. However, the soccer associations of Europe wield enormous political power,[9] particularly through their role in granting the right host the two major international representative tournaments, the World Cup and the European Championships. Politicians might well be inclined to back the associations against the clubs.

This point highlights another interesting feature of the pyramidal structure in Europe. In the United States, the major leagues, which are controlled by the clubs themselves, promote the single tournament involving the clubs. The soccer associations of Europe not only sanction league competition, which in most cases they also sponsor, but they also promote a variety of other tournaments. These might be lower level club competition, their own knockout club competition (e.g., the FA Cup in England), amateur competitions, and, most important, international representative competition. Thus, for example, when Sepp Blatter, the chairman of Fédération Internationale de Football Association (FIFA), the worldwide soccer governing body, proposed the introduction of a biennial championship (instead of quadrennial), he was proposing the extension of a competition that would generate increased income from FIFA but would also likely reduce the time available for club competition and increase the amount of time during which the clubs would have to release their contracted players (without compensation). Conflicts of interest such as this, unknown in the United States, have arisen in basketball, international motor sports (the governing body, the Federation Internationale de L'automobile, or FIA, sanctions the organization of Formula One and in exchange claims ownership of the broadcasting rights), rugby union, and cricket.

Entry and Exit

Most observers agree that the system of promotion and relegation, which enables strong performing teams from lower levels of competition to enter senior leagues and replace the worst performing teams in the higher division, is a distinctive feature of the European model of sports (e.g., European Commission, 1998; Andreff and Staudohar, 2000; Primault and Rouger, 1999; Hoehn and Szymanski, 1999). Noll (2002) and Ross and Szymanski (2002) suggest that this mechanism would be a suitable means of dealing with the widely perceived problem of major leagues' monopoly power in the United States.[10]

Several distinctive features of the promotion-and-relegation system should be noted:

- It reduces clubs' ability to extract rents through the threat of relocation because (a) clubs cannot be sure of their continued presence in the major league, and (b) alternative locations do not need to attract a team to enter the major league; they can invest in seeing their own local team promoted.
- It appears to reduce the variance of within-season win percentages. Kipker (2000), Forrest and Simmons (2002), and Szymanski (2003) have noted that the standard deviation of win percentages relative to the idealized standard deviation[11] seems much smaller in European soccer. This is because teams cannot afford to give up trying even when they are out contention for the title, and indeed the weakest teams must try hardest to avoid relegation, which is a significant source of interest for the fans.
- It appears to undermine profitability. Again, several authors have noted the seemingly much lower rates of profit reported by European clubs. Fort (2000) attributes this to a failure to distinguish economic from accounting profits. However, from a theoretical point of view we would expect that profits would be lower in a system of promotion and relegation than in a closed one (i.e., where entry is only possible with the consent of the incumbents), just as we would expect, all else being equal, profitability to be lower in a market with free entry than one in which significant barriers exist.
- It promotes uncertainty. This may add to the interest of the consumers in the short term, but in the longer term may undermine the incentive of owners to invest in facilities. It is reasonable to argue that in general the facilities of the major leagues in the United States are of higher quality than most European soccer stadia, which is not surprising given the staggering level of municipal subsidy in the United States (see, e.g., Siegfried and Zimbalist, 2000). Arguably, closed leagues produce overinvestment and open leagues underinvestment, although this is an area that deserves more detailed research.
- It can lead to highly inefficient outcomes. It is possible with promotion and relegation that a team from a major European city such as Rome or Paris could end up with no teams competing in the major leagues, while poorly supported small towns play at the highest level. Heartening as such David and Goliath stories may be, there can be little doubt that erratic outcomes like this will significantly reduce overall welfare. However, this threat should not be overstated. First, the biggest teams tend to be those that are most infrequently relegated. Second, because there is no territorial exclusivity, large cities tend to have several teams (e.g., London usually has four to six teams in the top division, with a further six to eight eligible for promotion).

Exclusivity

Territorial exclusivity is unknown in Europe, but it is a feature of all major leagues in the United States. The issue is in fact very closely connected to promotion and relegation. The desire to protect geographical territory is motivated by the same argument as that in favor of a closed league—to pro-

tect the investment incentives of the owners. The argument in favor of unlimited entry is likewise one of promoting competition, eroding rents, and
providing incentives to deliver what the consumers want.

Labor Market Rules and the Unions

As was observed above, the original rules controlling the movement of
players in baseball (the reserve clause) and soccer (Retain and Transfer) were
in fact very similar. Moreover, with the aid of the courts, player unions have
been successful in both regions in undermining these restrictions. However,
here the similarities end.

On both continents it is perhaps fair to say that unions were relatively weak
until the 1950s. In both cases early attempts to challenge the restrictions were
rejected on the grounds that players had a choice not to sign the contract.
However, by the 1960s legal opinion was turning against these restrictions,
and forms of free agency emerged in England as early as 1963 and in the
United States by 1976. (For the history of these changes see Staudohar,
1996, on the United States; Szymanski and Kuypers, 1999, Chapter 4, for
the UK.)

However, the response in the United States to the emergence of player
unions was to reach collective bargaining agreements, a process aided by the
antitrust exemption granted to such agreements. In effect, the teams were
able to sustain restrictive agreements among themselves by writing them into
the collective bargaining agreement in exchange for concessions to the players. Examples of agreements that are sustained by this practice include the
draft system, the salary cap, arrangements relating to roster limits, and the
right to call up players from the minor leagues.

Unions in Europe, without the protection of an antitrust exemption, have
in general held a much weaker position. Moreover, the players have shown
limited enthusiasm for ceding negotiating powers to the unions, perhaps in
part because the fragmented system of Europe gives any one league in
Europe significant outside options if they cannot reach agreement with the
domestic union. Although an embryonic pan-European players' union exists,
the enormous differences in labor market practices across the Continent
militate against international solidarity.

At various times the leagues have tried to restrict the international mobility of players, but mobility has in fact increased significantly over the past
thirty years. The European Union itself has played no small role in opening
the European labor market, and freedom of movement of labor is one of
the key articles written into the Treaty that defines the European Union. This
article was invoked in 1996 in the famous Bosman case, which held that the
traditional system by which players were traded by clubs for cash had to be
significantly liberalized, effectively creating free agency for all players by the
time they reached the age of twenty-three. Player trading has always been

an integral part of the European system, much more so than in the United States where player trades, especially for cash, have been increasingly discouraged over recent years. One reason for this difference may have to do with promotion and relegation. Promoted teams entering a higher level of competition must be able to acquire players quickly if they are to compete, while relegated teams that can expect to generate a much lower income need to be able to reduce their costs quite rapidly. Without a well-developed player trading system it is hard to see how the promotion-and-relegation system could work smoothly.

Collective Selling

In the United States, the 1961 Sports Broadcasting Act exempted from antitrust prosecution collective selling by leagues of sponsored telecasts. Although the scope of this exemption is less broad than some European sometimes imagine, there is no general exemption in European law, and several countries have enforced individual selling (notably Italy). (See also Note 8.)

Ownership Restrictions

In Europe, there have been few restrictions on the right of owners to sell their clubs, although some jurisdictions, such as France, have imposed some limitations. As a result, a number of clubs, especially in the UK, floated on the stock market in the 1990s. In the United States, stock market listing has been prohibited in most of the major leagues. Cheffins (1998) provides an interesting discussion of the motivation for this attitude toward the stock market.

IS CONVERGENCE WITH AN AMERICAN MODEL INEVITABLE?

"There is a European Model of sports with its own characteristics. This model has been exported to almost all other continents and countries, with the exception of North America. Sport in Europe has a unique structure. For the future development of sport in Europe, these special features should be taken into account" (European Commission, 1998, 5). This chapter has attempted to outline these differences and the historical accidents that caused the two different models to evolve. The European Commission, however, was prepared to pose a further question: "Is there any advantage for Europe in moving toward the US model of sport?" (10).

This question arose for the European Commission primarily because of the proposals to create a Super League in soccer and the increasing tensions between the major clubs and the governing bodies. The tension itself has been largely driven by the extraordinary growth in the value of broadcast rights that occurred during the 1990s (in 1986 live broadcast rights for top

English soccer sold for £3 million per year; by 2001 they were worth in the region of £500 million). Not only did this shift create tension within the organization of European soccer, it also forced the antitrust authorities to consider the validity of collective action in sports, an issue that has been addressed in the United States for the past fifty years.

The Commission's questioning reflects a current of European public opinion that regrets the incursion of commercialism into sports (this is perhaps the position of Primault and Rouger, 1999). For these purposes commercialism is symbolized by the increasing importance of TV and TV money. Other aspects include the objective of the clubs (profit rather than success), the nature of club ownership (in particular stock market flotations), increasing sponsorship, and increased marketing. Many of these innovations are perceived to come from the United States. For example, it is well known that European clubs have looked to their U.S. counterparts to learn how to develop their merchandising operations. Hence commercialization is equated with Americanization. Commercialization is therefore also seen as being likely to produce competition reforms along American lines: closed competitions, franchises, and so on.

Rather than accept the inevitability (or desirability) of market forces, opponents of commercialism advocate structured intervention on the part of the state to preserve institutions. And indeed proponents of such actions would argue that all markets are in reality regulated (even the stock market); the issue is not to minimize regulation, but to optimize it. The difficulty, of course, is not with the logic of this view, it is a matter of precise interventions that are advocated, and it is important to state that opponents of commercialism do not share a unified view of what should be done. Each individual tends to have different sticking points. These might include opposition to

- Rescheduling matches to suit TV audiences
- Restructuring competitions to increase the exposure of the largest clubs
- Sponsorship logos on sportswear
- Distribution of soccer profits to shareholders
- Stock market flotation of clubs
- The use of larger incomes by larger clubs to establish dominance
- The increasing share of matches played in European rather than domestic competition
- Increasing ticket prices
- Migration of the best players to the richest clubs, particularly on an international scale

Interestingly, almost all of these objections are voiced in one form or another by fans in the United States (for example, sponsorship logos on sportswear seems much more detested in the United States, where it is rare, than it is in Europe, where it is commonplace). Many fans in the United

States also advocate a regulated solution to the problem and, as the earlier quotation from Noll shows, such ideas have occasionally surfaced in Congress. What is different about the United States is (a) the mechanisms for imposing a regulated solution do not appear readily at hand—if such a solution were to be espoused a whole new apparatus would need to be created—and (b) the establishment seems skeptical about the feasibility of such intervention.

Regulation in Europe seems a more plausible option. There is a long history of intrusive regulation in all aspects of social activity, and in many European states it is widely perceived to be a success.[12] Given the existence of strong governing bodies in European sports, many perceive there to be a ready avenue for preserving existing structures and preventing breakaway leagues. However, this is not to say that advocates of intervention have been wholly successful in limiting change. One clear bellwether of change is the position of sports within the Treaty that governs the European Union (currently the Treaty of Amsterdam, formerly the Treaty of Rome). The Treaty makes no explicit mention of sports, and, as a result, the authorities have been obliged to treat sports as an ordinary commercial enterprise in relation to issues such as the free movement of labor or the collective selling of broadcast rights. It is true that courts have recognized, on a rule of reason, the special nature of sporting competitions, but per se exemptions from antitrust scrutiny, for example, would require a Treaty amendment. Several sporting bodies attempted to obtain just such an exemption at the end of the 1990s and failed. This means, for instance, that as things stand, the governing bodies would have limited legal powers to prevent a breakaway league, as was shown in the case of FIBA and the Euroleague.

Economists tend to get caught in the middle of this debate. On the one hand, economists on both sides of the Atlantic have been apt to argue for fairly strict interpretation of the antitrust laws in relation to activities such as collective selling, judging that consumer interest will tend to be better served by competition. Taking an economic position on closed versus open leagues is much more difficult. From an economic perspective, the debate should focus on issues such as the feasibility of entry, by teams or by entirely new leagues, the effect on rent dissipation, the incentives to invest, the economic distribution of benefits, and so on. In reality, however, these issuers have been drowned out by the emotional debate about traditions. This fact is perhaps inevitable, but it may also be fair to say that economists have failed to present any detailed reasoning on the pros and cons of alternative systems, so it may not be surprising that they have been marginalized.

NOTES

1. All of these dates are subject to controversy, but although earlier versions of these sports may have existed, few had official rulebooks before these dates. The only

clear exceptions are golf, cricket, and horse racing, for which rules and clubs existed from the mid-eighteenth century.

2. Armed insurrection, in the form of revolution and terrorism, are the exceptions to this rule.

3. This is not true for all sports; some, such as golf and tennis, have recognizably similar institutions.

4. The first FA Cup final and the first international match (Scotland versus England) both took place in 1872.

5. This is a structure in which, at the end of each season, clubs affiliated with the governing body are eligible for promotion from a given league division to its immediately senior division on the basis of league ranking and are subject to relegation to the immediately junior division on the same grounds.

6. Fort (2000) asks a similar question, and the answers here are similar to his.

7. Comparing the two semifinals, the one with the English participant attracted 7.6 million viewers, whereas the one without any English team attracted only 5.5 million (17% fewer).

8. Players are paid little to appear, but they can sign lucrative sponsorship and endorsement deals if they play for the national team. Clubs, by contrast, receive no compensation at all for releasing their players, which they are obliged to do by the national associations.

9. For example, in 1997 the German competition court held that collective selling of broadcast rights to European (UEFA) Cup matches involving German clubs by the German Football Association (DFB) was illegal. In 1998, however, the DFB was able to obtain an antitrust exemption from the German Parliament.

10. The alternative that has been suggested is breaking up of the major leagues. See, for example, Ross (1989) and Quirk and Fort (1999).

11. Assuming every team always has a 50% probability of winning.

12. For example, the French public is proud of the French state railways. The employees went on strike when the government suggested privatization, but rather than complain about the disruption, the French public backed the strikers.

3

Still Up for Grabs? Maintaining the Sporting and Financial Viability of European Club Soccer

Bill Gerrard

INTRODUCTION

Europe remains the heartland of soccer, the one truly global team game. European domestic clubs and the national representative teams are the dominant force worldwide both in terms of sporting success and financial size. The only long-term challenge to European soccer hegemony has come from South America, but that challenge in recent years has been largely limited to the success of Brazil and Argentina in the Fédération Internationale de Football Association (FIFA) World Cup tournament. The leading South American domestic clubs, once on a sporting par with their top European rivals, now lag behind as poor economic conditions both within the national economy and within the domestic soccer leagues have forced many of the best South American players to move to European clubs. For example, just over two-thirds of the Brazilian and Argentinean 2002 World Cup squads currently play for Europe domestic clubs. Likewise, emerging soccer nations from Africa and Asia have enjoyed success in recent World Cups, but their best players too are joining the "muscle drain" (Andreff, 2001), migrating to European clubs.

Yet, despite the obvious sporting and financial strengths of European soccer, it faces major problems in maintaining both its sporting and financial viability. The cash-rich environment of professional soccer created by the huge growth in the value of its media and other image rights has dramatically increased the revenue potential of the leading domestic clubs. But the high industry revenue growth also has created greater divergence in financial size between and within leagues. The inevitable consequence of greater revenue divergence is that competitive balance is undermined, threatening the long-term sporting viability of both domestic and cross-border tournaments. In addition, the advent of Bosman free agency has significantly shifted relative bargaining power toward the star players, generating an inflationary spiral that threatens the financial viability of European club soccer. Unsustainable levels of player wage costs have pushed many clubs across Europe to the brink of bankruptcy. In England, for example, several clubs have gone into voluntary administration (the equivalent of Chapter 11 bankruptcy in the United States) in recent years, particularly following the collapse of the Football League's TV contract with ITV Digital in 2002.

The aims of this chapter are to provide a survey of the current sporting and financial problems of European club soccer and to consider proposals suggested as possible long-term solutions, particularly tournament restructuring and salary caps. It is argued that appropriate tournament restructuring is the only viable long-term means of maintaining a high degree of competitive balance within European club soccer, provided that sufficient active fan support for the new tournament formats can be achieved. It is also argued that a salary cap is likely to be infeasible in European club soccer given the size, diversity, and openness of its structure. It is concluded that club licensing and wage benchmarking and disclosure provide more practical alternatives for enhancing the financial stability of European soccer clubs.

The chapter begins with a discussion of the two fundamental structural differences between European soccer and North American major leagues. The next section focuses on competitive balance within European domestic soccer leagues and cross-border club tournaments. This is followed by an exploration of the nonsustainable rate of player wage inflation that has resulted from the introduction of Bosman free agency. The chapter concludes with a discussion of tournament restructuring, salary caps, and other current proposals for maintaining the long-term sporting and financial viability of European club soccer.

THE FUNDAMENTAL STRUCTURAL CHARACTERISTICS OF EUROPEAN SOCCER

The Merit-Hierarchy Tournament Structure

There are two important features of tournament structures in North American professional team sports. First, tournaments are organized as a fixed hierarchy in that the tournaments at different levels of the sport are entirely independent, with no movement of teams between these tournaments. There is no promotion and relegation between the major and minor leagues or between the different levels of the minor leagues. Second, at the major-league level, there is a single tournament consisting of a regular season followed by playoffs, and, in the case of baseball and ice hockey, the tournament is cross-border, involving both U.S. and Canadian teams. In contrast, European soccer is structured as a merit hierarchy, with promotion and relegation of clubs between leagues (and divisions within leagues) on a season-by-season basis determined by sporting performance (although in exceptional cases clubs have been relegated for a breach of league rules). Furthermore, clubs participate in several tournaments scheduled concurrently. Typically, professional clubs participate in domestic league and cup tournaments, with the leading clubs also participating in one of the Union des Associations Européennes de Football's (UEFA's) two European cross-border club tournaments, the Champions League and the UEFA Cup. The European club tournaments maintain the merit-hierarchy structure, with entry determined on the basis of success in the domestic league and cup competitions.

The merit-hierarchy tournament structure is a fundamental feature of European soccer. Soccer's governing bodies often claim that a merit hierarchy is an essential prerequisite for the legitimization of tournaments, but the claim still awaits serious empirical scrutiny. Merit hierarchies can provide enhanced incentive effects, with prizes for successful teams (i.e., promotion and entry to European tournaments) as well as punishments for the most unsuccessful teams in the form of relegation to lower quality, lower revenue league tournaments. A wider range of rewards and punishments can encourage greater fan interest. For example, within the top division in any domestic league there is competition between the stronger teams for the championship and European qualification, whereas the weaker teams compete to avoid relegation to a lower division. Unlike a fixed hierarchy with no relegation, fan interest can remain high for unsuccessful teams, with contests against other unsuccessful teams taking on added significance, the so-called "relegation battles." However, the incentive effects of merit hierarchies can be undermined by divergent revenue growth that reduces the likelihood of promoted teams competing effectively in the higher level tournament and increases the likelihood of relegated teams dominating the lower level tournament.

The Player Transfer System

Contest legitimacy in team sports requires some minimum degree of player-team allegiance that prevents players from appearing for more than one team in the same tournament. Hence all team sports have some form of registration system that ensures that players can only appear for one team at any point in time. A player registration system necessarily regulates the movement of players between teams. The key issue is whether or not these regulations are purely temporal controls, restricting player transfers during the scheduled tournament. Examples of temporal controls include transfer windows and transfer deadlines. More wide-ranging transfer regulations that go beyond merely limits on the timing of player transfers are economic controls, which limit the ability of players to bargain with all of the potential buyers of their playing services. Free agency represents a player market that has no economic controls, with out-of-contract players able to negotiate with any team. Player reservation systems such as the draft and the reserve clause represent economic controls, with teams allocated exclusive rights to negotiate employment contracts with individual players.

European soccer has a very specific form of economic control on player transfers, namely, the payment of transfer fees. A transfer fee is a cash payment by a player's new club to the former club in order to purchase the exclusive rights to register the player (and, by implication, the exclusive rights to that player's services in club tournaments). These transfer fees can be very high. For example, the world record transfer fee is £47.2 million ($71 million) paid in July 2001 by Real Madrid of Spain to Juventus of Italy to obtain the rights to registrar the French international player Zinedine Zidane.

The operation of the player-transfer market in soccer has changed considerably in recent years. Originally, a retain-and-transfer system operated, which gave clubs the exclusive right to retain a player on terms at least as good as the previous contract (Sloane, 1969). Players had no rights to request a transfer and could only move to new club if their current club sanctioned the transfer and received an acceptable transfer fee. The retain-and-transfer system was progressively relaxed from the 1960s onward, with players gaining increased rights to request a transfer, but transfer fees remained payable irrespective of whether the player was still under contract.

Following the Bosman ruling in 1995, the transfer market in soccer has been radically reformed. A Belgian professional soccer player, Jean-Marc Bosman, successfully challenged the legality of the transfer system in the European Court of Justice. The Court ruled that the payment of transfer fees for out-of-contract players moving between European Union (EU) member states contravened the Treaty of Rome. It also ruled that restrictions on the number of foreign EU nationals that clubs could sign and/or play also contravened the Treaty of Rome. Initially, the Bosman ruling created international free agency within the EU, with out-of-contract players able to move freely to clubs in other EU leagues without payment of transfer fees. The only exception was for players under the age of twenty-four, for whom transfer fees were payable in respect of the training costs incurred by clubs. Eventually, the Bosman ruling was applied to the rules governing domestic transfers. Thus, as a consequence of the Bosman ruling, there is now free agency throughout European soccer, with out-of-contract players able to move to new clubs on free transfers (i.e., no transfer fees payable). Transfer fees do remain payable as compensation for early termination of contracts and training costs. The position has remained virtually unchanged following the recent revision of FIFA's rules for international transfers in response to further EU scrutiny of the rules (Gerrard, 2002). FIFA's revised transfer rules include a detailed formula for the calculation of training costs and their distribution between clubs responsible for the player's training. Players have also acquired greater rights to terminate their contracts early.

COMPETITIVE BALANCE IN EUROPEAN SOCCER

The Importance of Competitive Balance

The economic value of a sporting contest in any given potential market is likely to depend on four qualitative characteristics of the contest: contest legitimacy, playing quality, uncertainty of outcome, and contest significance. Contest legitimacy has several dimensions. Daly defines contest legitimacy as "the degree to which a league's fans perceive that the contests are fair and beyond manipulation and that the teams and players involved are doing their best to achieve athletic victory" (1992, 17). Individual contests must be perceived as involving two independent teams that are both truly competing to win the contest within the laws of the game. But contest legitimacy goes beyond the requirement that teams engage in true and fair sporting competition. It also requires an open-structured tournament allowing freedom of entry within its spatial domain to all teams that have the potential ability to win the tournament. This requirement ensures that fans perceive the tournament outcome as decisive. If tournament entry is based on administrative criteria other than recognized spatial boundaries, the tournament winner may not be perceived as a legitimate sporting champion. The contest legitimacy of tournaments is also likely to be path-dependent. Established tournaments, by virtue of their survival, have developed a reputation as being legitimate, with true and fair sporting contests and open entry. This structure provides a substantial barrier to entry of rival tournaments operating within the spatial domain of an existing established tournament.

The economic value of individual contests and tournaments also depends crucially on the playing quality of the teams. Gate attendance and TV demand is greater for contests at the top of any tournament hierarchy by virtue of these contests involving the best players. The other key determinants of the economic value of sporting contests are contest significance and uncertainty of outcome. Contest significance refers to the importance of an individual contest in relation to the outcome of a tournament, and it is affected by the tournament structure. Ceteris paribus, individual contests have greater significance in elimination tournaments compared to round-robin tournaments. Contest significance also depends on the "stage" of the tournament and the extent to which its outcome remains uncertain. In round-robin tournaments, individual contests between teams that are still in contention can effectively become elimination games, with the losers dropping out of contention.

Contest significance is also affected by uncertainty of outcome in tournaments. Uncertainty of outcome refers to the degree of individual contest and tournament predictability. Uncertainty of outcome reflects the competitive balance of teams participating in a tournament. Formally, competitive balance refers to the shape of the probability distribution of the likelihood of teams winning the tournament. Competitively balanced tournaments are characterized by several teams with approximately equal probabilities of winning. In contrast, dominated tournaments are characterized by a small number of teams with high probabilities of winning. Competitive balance depends primarily on the distribution of playing talent across teams, which, in turn, depends on the relative economic size of teams. The economic migration of players on the basis of maximizing marginal revenue products necessarily results in the best players moving to the big market teams with the highest potential revenues.

Maintaining sufficient uncertainty of outcome is often seen as a necessary requirement for the long-term sporting and financial viability of tournaments and requires that tournament organizers foster a relatively high degree of competitive balance. Tournament organizers have four broad types of policy instruments available, allowing intervention at different stages in the causal chain. The most outcome-proximate type of instrument is to impose direct restrictions on the economic migration of players through, for example, some form of player reservation system. Alternatively, organizers can intervene in the player market more indirectly by attempting to influence the pattern of economic migration through restrictions on the incentives to move through, for example, maximum wages and salary caps. A less outcome-proximate approach than intervening in the player market is to redistribute team revenues to bring about greater revenue equality through, for example, sharing of gate revenues and centralized selling of media and other image rights. Finally, the most fundamental form of intervention is to restructure the tournament itself to ensure that tournament membership is restricted to teams of relatively equal economic size. Such fundamental restructuring involves the elimination of small market teams through either termination (as, for example, currently under consideration by Major League Baseball) or exclusion by the creation of "super leagues" consisting of big market teams drawn from existing separate leagues.

Rottenberg's invariance proposition casts doubt on the likely effectiveness of player reservation systems and revenue redistribution (Rottenberg, 1956). The invariance proposition, an application of the Coase theorem, states that the equilibrium distribution of playing talent across teams is unaffected by the allocation of the property rights over the revenue streams, provided that teams and players are wealth maximizers. This suggests that only tournament restructuring and restrictions on player market incentives (e.g., a salary cap) provide viable interventions to enhance competitive balance. In their comprehensive review of cross-subsidization schemes currently used by leagues, Fort and Quirk (1995) conclude that an enforceable salary cap is the only scheme that can improve competitive balance while maintaining the financial viability of small market teams.

The Distribution of Sporting Outcomes in European Soccer

Competitive balance is an ex ante concept and, therefore, difficult to measure directly. Hence, most of the empirical evidence on competitive balance has usually been provided either in the form of the ex post distribution of sporting outcomes or the distribution of the economic size of teams. Little evidence exists on the distribution of playing talent because of the inherent difficulties in measuring it.

In terms of sporting outcomes, empirical evidence on competitive balance is characterized by a wide range of alternative measurements. This is inevitable given the term *competitive balance* has become a catchall for the different aspects of outcome uncertainty and contest significance. Ultimately, the appropriateness of specific measures depends on the objectives of the analysis. In the case of the current study, the concern is with whether or not domestic leagues and cross-border tournaments in European club soccer are dominated and becoming more dominated by the big market teams (and, in the case of cross-border tournaments, by the big market teams from the big market domestic leagues). Thus, the appropriate measures of competitive balance in terms of sporting outcomes are those specifically relating to the distribution of end-of-tournament successful outcomes, such as the concentration of championship titles and bottom four finishes.

Competitive Balance in the Top Divisions of Domestic Leagues

Table 1 provides evidence on the historic concentration of championship titles in sixteen leading Western European soccer leagues. These leagues can be broken down into three groups: highly competitive, competitive, and dominated. The highly competitive leagues such as those in Germany, France, and England have a wide dispersion of championship titles across teams, with the average relative frequency of championship success for the top two to three teams in the range of 12% to 16%. By contrast, the top two or three teams dominate the domestic championship in countries such as Turkey, Greece, Portugal, and Scotland. Only four teams have ever won the Turkish championship. In Portugal, Benfica, FC Porto, and Sporting Lisbon have won all but two of the league championships. Similarly, in Greece, Olympiakos, Panathinaikos, and AEK Athens have won all but six championships. The most dominated domestic league in Western Europe is Scotland, the second oldest elite soccer league in the world, where the two "Old Firm" clubs, Rangers and Celtic, have won over 82% of the 105 league championships. The average relative frequency of championship success for the top teams in the dominated leagues is in the range of 29% to 41%.

Table 1

Concentration of Championship Titles, Leading Western European Leagues

League	Concentration of Championship Titles		
	H-Index	CR(2)	CR(3)
Highly Competitive			
Germany	0.076	28.9%	36.7%
Denmark	0.087	28.1%	38.2%
England	0.087	31.1%	42.7%
France	0.096	28.6%	41.3%
Sweden	0.099	29.9%	43.0%
Competitive			
Belgium	0.121	37.4%	48.5%
Switzerland	0.121	40.4%	51.0%
Holland	0.130	42.3%	55.8%
Italy	0.137	42.0%	55.0%
Norway	0.148	43.6%	58.2%
Dominated			
Austria	0.201	57.8%	68.9%
Spain	0.241	62.0%	74.7%
Turkey	0.275	64.4%	86.7%
Greece	0.326	74.2%	90.9%
Portugal	0.335	70.6%	97.1%
Scotland	0.349	82.4%	86.2%

Notes: H-Index: Herfindahl index. CR(2): share of top two clubs. CR(3): share of top three clubs.
Source: *Rothmans Football Yearbook* (various editions); author's calculations.

The biggest domestic leagues in European soccer are England, France, Germany, Italy, and Spain (known collectively as the "Big 5"). With the exception of the Spanish league (dominated by Real Madrid and Barcelona), the Big 5 leagues historically have been highly competitive. However, the evidence suggests that certain teams are tending to dominate these leagues more often than in the past. The average Herfindahl index for the concentration of championship titles for the 1992–1993 to 2001–2002 seasons was 0.332, compared to a historic average in the Big 5 of 0.127. The difference is statistically significant at the 5% level.

Table 2 provides a more detailed examination of the recent trends in competitive balance of the Big 5 domestic championship race by comparing outcomes in seasons 1992–1993 to 1996–1997 and seasons 1997–1998 to 2001–2002. The evidence is somewhat mixed. There is no general increase between the two subperiods in the concentration of championship titles as measured by the Herfindahl index, but concentration levels are high relative to historical averages. However, there is only a very small, statistically insignificant increase in the gap between the winners and runners-up as measured by the points percentage (i.e., points won as a percentage of the maximum available points). Thus championship races appear to be remaining close, with the gap between the winners and runners-up the equivalent of one win (= 3 points) and a tied game (= 1 point). There is some evidence to suggest that there is a trend toward greater predictability of the top four places in the championship as measured by the adjusted Herfindahl index, but the increase between the two subperiods is statistically insignificant. The average points percentage of the winners has increased from 60.8% to 69.1%, which is statistically significant at the 5% level. This result suggests a widening gap between the winning club and the average top division club, which is particularly noteworthy since the average size of the top division has decreased in England, France, and Spain, implying that the average top division club is stronger in the later subperiod.

Table 2
Competitive Balance in the Top Division, Big 5 European Leagues, 1992–2002

League	H-Index		H-Index (adj)		Points %		Points % Gap	
	Titles		Top Four		Winners		2nd Place	
	92-97	97-02	92-97	97-02	92-97	97-02	92-97	97-02
England	0.680	0.520	0.620	0.800	69.6%	72.8%	4.95%	6.49%
France	0.200	0.200	0.620	0.500	60.4%	66.5%	6.67%	2.75%
Germany	0.360	0.440	0.580	0.680	54.9%	69.0%	2.16%	3.73%
Italy	0.520	0.280	0.720	0.580	61.0%	71.0%	5.29%	1.96%
Spain	0.360	0.280	0.620	0.720	58.1%	66.1%	1.83%	6.84%
Average	0.424	0.344	0.632	0.656	60.8%	69.1%	4.18%	4.35%

Notes: H-Index (adj.): Herfindahl index/maximum possible Herfindahl index. The maximum Herfindahl index is 0.25 if the same four teams finish in the top four every season.
Source: Rothmans Football Yearbook (various editions); author's calculations.

Competitive Balance in Cross-Border Club Tournaments

Table 3 shows the distribution of the domestic league affiliations of the winners of the Champions League (formerly known as the European Cup), the premier European cross-border club tournament organized by UEFA. The tournament has been dominated throughout its history by teams from the Big 5 leagues, with the exception of two periods, 1966 to 1975 and 1986 to 1990. The first period saw the emergence of Dutch soccer as a global power. Two Dutch clubs, Feyernoord (1970) and Ajax Amsterdam (1971–1973), won the European Cup for four successive years in the early 1970s, and the Dutch national team finished as runners-up in both the 1974 and 1978 FIFA World Cup tournaments. The period 1986 to 1990 coincides with the English teams being banned from European club tournaments following crowd violence at the 1985 final. Prior to this period, English teams had dominated the tournament. Overall, the Big 5 leagues have provided 75% of the tournament winners. Indeed, it should be more properly called "Big 4" domination since only one French club, Olympique Marseille, has won the tournament and was subsequently stripped of the title following allegations of match-fixing.

The domination of the Big 5 leagues has become even more pronounced following the change in the Champions league format allowing multiple entries from leagues, with the number of clubs from each league based on the previous European record of clubs from that league. As can be seen in Table 4, the clubs reaching the semifinal stage of the Champions League are almost always from the Big 5 leagues. Since 1999, only one club from out-

Table 3
Domestic Affiliation of European Cup/Champions League Winners, 1956–2002

League	1956-65	1966-75	1976-85	1986-90	1991-02	Total
England	0	1	7	*	1	9
France	0	0	0	0	1**	1
Germany	0	2	2	0	2	6
Italy	3	1	1	2	2	9
Spain	5	1	0	0	4	10
Other	2	5	0	3	2	12
Big 5 Share	80.0%	50.0%	100.0%	40.0%	83.3%	74.5%

*English teams banned from tournament following crowd violence at 1985 final.
**Olympique Marseille (France) subsequently stripped of title.
Source: *Rothmans Football Yearbook* (various editions); author's calculations.

Table 4
Domestic Affiliation of European Cup/Champions League Last Four, 1992–2002

League	1992/93 - 1996/97	1997/98 - 2001/02	1992/93 - 2001/02	Top 10 Teams
England	1	3	4	Manchester United (3)
France	4	1	5	Monaco (2)
Germany	2	5	7	Bayern Munich (4); Borussia Dortmund (2)
Italy	5	2	7	Juventus (4); AC Milan (3)
Spain	1	8	9	Real Madrid (4); Barcelona (3); Valencia (2)
Other	7	1	8	Ajax Amsterdam (3)
Big 5 Share	65.0%	95.0%	80.0%	

Note: Number of last four appearances of top teams shown in parentheses.
Source: *Rothmans Football Yearbook* (various editions); author's calculations.

side the Big 5 has reached the semifinals. And just as the domestic leagues are becoming more dominated by specific clubs, so too is the Champions League. Ten clubs account for 75% of the semifinal places since 1993, with Ajax Amsterdam the only non–Big 5 club. The huge financial rewards accruing from success in the Champions League further cements the position of dominance of these clubs in their domestic leagues and the Champions League. A dynamic process of cumulative causation has been created at the European level resulting in a dominant core of big league, big market clubs, with a large periphery of smaller market clubs that have a negligible probability of success in the Champions League.

The Distribution of Playing Talent in European Soccer

The dominance of the Big 5 leagues suggests that the top playing talent is migrating toward these leagues. A snapshot of the migration patterns of top soccer players is provided by an analysis of the domestic league affiliations of thirty-two national team playing squads that competed in the 2002 FIFA World Cup finals. The finalists were drawn from all of FIFA's six confederations, with the geographic distribution of teams reflecting their sporting status in the soccer hierarchy. Western Europe had the largest representation with eleven teams, including the Big 5. National playing squads are based on the nationality of players, not their domestic league affiliations. Each team had a squad of twenty-three players, so the analysis covers a total of 736 leading players from around the world. The breakdown of domestic league affiliations of these players is given in Table 5.

The pattern of player migration is determined by two principal factors: the soccer status of the player's national team and the economic status of the player's home league. The Big 5 leagues have the highest economic status and, hence, attract most of the top players. Just over 48% of the players were registered for clubs playing in the Big 5 leagues. All of the players in the Big 5 national squads play their domesticsoccer in the Big 5 leagues. In the case of the national squads from the other established soccer powers in

Table 5
Domestic League Affiliations of 2002 World Cup Finals National Squads

Domestic League Affiliation	Western Europe: Big 5	Western Europe: Other	Eastern Europe	South America	Africa	Rest of the World	All
Home	91	49	31	51	24	128	374
Region	24	89	0	6	1	5	125
Overseas	0	0	61	58	90	28	237
Total	115	138	92	115	115	161	736
Big 5							
England	32	43	7	3	12	10	107
France	6	5	3	5	32	2	53
Germany	23	7	17	3	4	4	58
Italy	28	12	7	21	7	3	78
Spain	26	4	4	16	5	3	58
Total	115	71	38	48	60	22	354
Home Share	79.1%	35.5%	33.7%	44.4%	20.9%	79.5%	50.8%
Big 5 Share	100.0%	51.5%	41.3%	41.7%	52.2%	13.7%	48.1%

Source: The Guardian World Cup 2002; author's calculations.

2002 World Cup Finalists
Big 5: England, France, Germany, Italy, Spain
Other Western Europe: Belgium, Denmark, Portugal, Republic of Ireland, Sweden, Turkey
Eastern Europe: Croatia, Poland, Russia, Slovenia
South America: Argentina, Brazil, Ecuador, Paraguay, Uruguay
Africa: Cameroon, Nigeria, Senegal, South Africa, Tunisia
Rest of World: China, Costa Rica, Japan, Mexico, Saudi Arabia, South Korea, United States

Europe and South America, and the newly emerging soccer nations in Africa, around 40% to 50% of their players play in the Big 5 leagues.

In contrast, only about 14% of the players in the other seven finalists play in the Big 5 leagues. African players have the greatest propensity to migrate to leagues outside their home/regional area. Only 21% of African World Cup players play in African domestic leagues, which reflects the growing soccer status of African players but the low economic status of African leagues.

Within the Big 5 leagues, England emerges as by far the largest net importer of playing talent, both from other Big 5 countries as well as elsewhere in the world. Germany, Italy, and Spain are small net importers of Big 5 talent but are significant importers of talent from elsewhere. France is unique in the Big 5 as the only net exporter of talent to the other Big 5 leagues. Only six players from the Big 5 World Cup squads play their domestic soccer in the French league. The poor performance of French clubs in the European Cup/Champions League reflects the loss of playing talent to the other Big 5 leagues.

The Distribution of Economic Resources in European Soccer

The dominance of the Big 5 leagues in European tournaments and the players market reflects the underlying concentration of economic resources in European club soccer. This economic concentration is clearly evident in Table 6, which shows the gross revenues of the top divisions in the Big 5 and six other European leagues. Revenue divergence is and still increasing as the Big 5 leagues grow faster than the other leagues. In 1997, the Big 5 accounted for 84.2% of the total revenue in the selected European leagues. By 2000, this share had increased to 85.6%. The average league revenue in the Big 5 was £878 million in 2000 compared to £123 million in the smaller leagues.

The huge revenue divergence across European soccer leagues creates an equally huge divergence in wage expenditures, resulting in the dominance of the Big 5 in the player market. As shown in Table 7, the divergence between wage expenditure by clubs in the Big 5 leagues and those in smaller leagues is increasing rapidly. In 1997, the average league wage costs in the Big 5 were almost three times greater than in midsize leagues such as the Netherlands and Scotland. By 2000, the corresponding ratio had grown to close to four.

THE FINANCIAL VIABILITY OF EUROPEAN CLUB SOCCER

The long-term prosperity of professional sports leagues requires the maintenance of both sporting and financial viability. Given that the major cost in all professional sports is athletic remuneration, it follows that financial viability requires that wage costs remain sustainable relative to revenue. There

Table 6
Top Division Revenues, Selected European Leagues, 1996–2001 (Euro Millions)

	1996	1997	1998	1999	2000	2001
England	575	771	966	1,113	1,283	1,556
Italy	452	551	650	714	1,059	1,151
Spain	323	524	569	612	758*	939*
Germany	373*	444	513	577	681	880
France	277	293	323	393	607	644
Netherlands		147	162	179	235	
Scotland		137	155	178	215	
Portugal		92*	102*	114	127	
Denmark		42	53	54	59	
Norway		33	50	54	54	
Sweden		32	33	41	47	
Total						
Big 5	2,000	2,583	3,021	3,409	4,388	5,170
Other		483	555	620	737	
All		3,066	3,576	4,029	5,125	
Growth Rates						
Big 5		29.2%	17.0%	12.8%	28.7%	17.8%
Other			14.9%	11.7%	18.9%	
All			16.6%	12.7%	27.2%	
Big 5 Share		84.2%	84.5%	84.6%	85.6%	

*Estimates.
Source: Deloitte & Touche (2002); author's calculations.

are two conditions for the sustainability of wage costs: (1) the wage-revenue ratio must not exceed the threshold level consistent with the overall minimum financial target of clubs; (2) wage growth must not exceed revenue growth in the long term.

The wage-revenue ratios for the top divisions in selected European leagues are presented in Table 8. Two clear trends emerge. First, there has been a general tendency for wage-revenue ratios to increase since 1996, both in the

Table 7
Top Division Wage Costs, Selected European Leagues, 1996–2001 (Euro Millions)

	1996	1997	1998	1999	2000	2001
England	270	363	506	648	794	933
Italy	256	317	417	512	660	868
Spain	171	230	303	342		
Germany		206	261	296	366	440
France	161	178	222	273	324	414
Netherlands	61	91	120	142	163	
Scotland	57	89	89	118	142	
Portugal				81	114	
Denmark		18	24	28	31	
Norway		21	27	31	36	
Sweden		19	23	27	31	
League Averages						
Big 5	214.5	258.8	341.8	414.2	536.0	663.8
Mid-Sized	59.0	90.0	104.5	113.7	139.7	
Small		19.3	24.7	28.7	32.7	
Big 5 Relative to Mid-Sized		2.88	3.27	3.64	3.84	

Source: Deloitte & Touche (2002); author's calculations.

Big 5 and the smaller leagues. Second, the wage-revenue ratios are gener-ally higher in the smaller leagues.

The recent increase in wage-revenue ratios is the consequence of two structural changes in the player market: greater internationalization follow-ing the abolition of limits on the number of foreign players, and the intro-duction of Bosman free agency. The greater internationalization of the player market has led to very significant migration of top international players to the European domestic leagues as evidenced in Table 5. Increased player quality will lead to higher wages, ceteris paribus, but the impact on wage-revenue ratios is ambiguous since revenues are also likely to increase through higher demand. (The relative magnitude of the wage and revenue effects of increased player quality depends crucially on the corporate objectives of the

Table 8
Top Division Wage-Revenue Ratios, Selected European Leagues, 1996–2001

	1996	1997	1998	1999	2000	2001
England	47%	48%	52%	58%	62%	60%
Italy	57%	58%	64%	72%	62%	75%
Spain	53%	44%	53%	56%		
Germany		46%	51%	51%	54%	50%
France	58%	61%	69%	69%	53%	64%
Netherlands	56%	62%	74%	79%	69%	
Scotland	49%	65%	58%	66%	66%	
Portugal				71%	90%	
Denmark		56%	45%	52%	52%	
Norway		50%	53%	57%	66%	
Sweden		58%	70%	66%	66%	
League Averages						
Big 5	54%	51%	58%	61%	58%	62%
Other	53%	58%	60%	65%	68%	

Source: Deloitte & Touche (2002); author's calculations.

clubs; that is, wealth maximization or win maximization.) The introduction of free agency would be expected to lead to wage growth in excess of revenue growth during the transitional adjustment to a higher equilibrium level of wage-revenue ratios based on the structural change in relative bargaining power in favor of the top players.

The impact of Bosman free agency on the wage-turnover ratio (assuming that player quality effects are neutral) is analyzed in Table 9 using the Football Association (FA) Premier League, the top soccer league tournament in England. In order to control for the changing composition of the league and the transitional economic adjustments arising from promotion and relegation, attention is focused on the fourteen clubs that were continuous members between seasons 1993–1994 and 1999–2000. These clubs de facto acquired and utilized sufficient playing talent to avoid relegation and, hence, should be representative of the average top division effect of Bosman free agency on wages. The clubs have been split into two groups of seven based

Table 9
Revenue and Wage Growth, FA Premier League, "Continuous" Members, 1994–2000

	Larger Clubs	Smaller Clubs	All
Revenue Growth			
1994-1996	16.2%	17.9%	16.7%
1996-2000	24.0%	20.5%	23.0%
Wage Growth			
1994-1996	22.1%	17.9%	20.6%
1996-2000	33.0%	31.0%	32.3%
Wage Gap			
1994-1996	+5.9%	0.0%	+3.9%
1996-2000	+9.0%	+10.4%	+9.3%
Wage-Revenue Ratio			
1994	37.7%	54.5%	42.6%
1996	41.6%	54.5%	45.4%
2000	55.1%	76.0%	60.8%
Marginal Wage-Revenue Ratio			
1994-1996	52.8%	54.5%	53.3%
1996-2000	64.9%	95.4%	72.7%

Source: Deloitte & Touche (various editions); author's calculations.

on their revenue size. All seven "larger" clubs had larger revenues in every year than the "smaller" clubs.

In the three years prior to the introduction of Bosman free agency, the average annual wage gap (i.e., the difference between wage growth and revenue growth) was zero for the smaller clubs, with wage-revenue ratios remaining constant at 54.5%. In contrast, the larger clubs had an average annual wage gap of 5.9%, with wage-revenue ratios growing but remaining significantly lower than those for the smaller clubs. After 1996, the situation changed markedly. The average wage gap increased to 9% for the larger clubs and 10.4% for the smaller clubs. By 2000, the wage-revenue ratios for the smaller clubs had increased to 76%, compared to 55% for the larger clubs.

Table 10
Top Division Operating Margin, Selected European Leagues, 1996–2001

	1996	1997	1998	1999	2000	2001	1996-2001
England	15.0%	18.5%	16.5%	10.3%	6.9%	8.6%	**11.6%**
Italy	-0.7%	1.5%	-5.5%	-16.0%	-4.3%	-18.8%	**-8.9%**
Spain	-7.1%	3.6%	-21.8%	-27.8%			**-8.0%**
Germany		8.3%	5.3%	8.1%	5.1%	9.9%	**6.7%**
France	1.8%	-2.4%	-14.2%	-17.8%	5.9%	-6.4%	**-4.8%**
Netherlands		4.8%	-10.5%	-26.3%	-9.4%		**-10.9%**
Scotland		13.9%	-1.9%	-4.5%	-7.4%		**-1.2%**
Denmark		-11.9%	-11.3%	-25.9%	-27.1%		**-19.7%**
Norway		-9.1%	0.0%	-5.6%	-5.6%		**-4.7%**
Sweden		0.0%	-21.2%	-12.2%	-14.9%		**-12.4%**

Source: Deloitte & Touche (2002); author's calculations.

The overall wage gap increased from 3.9% to 9.3%, implying that the structural impact of Bosman free agency on player wage inflation was 5.4% annually.

The consequences of the high and increasing wage-turnover ratios on the operating performance of the top divisions are shown in Table 10. Over the period of 1996 to 2001, only two leagues achieved positive operating margins, England and Germany. The position is likely to worsen as wage-revenue ratios continue to rise, necessitating a period of major financial retrenchment that is likely to exacerbate the economic and sporting divergence between the big market, big league clubs and the smaller clubs.

MAINTAINING THE VIABILITY OF EUROPEAN CLUB SOCCER

European club soccer faces two major threats to its viability. First, the increasing dominance of the big market, big league clubs is undermining the sporting viability of both domestic and European club tournaments. Second, excessively high wage growth relative to revenue growth threatens the financial viability of all clubs. The governing bodies have four possible types of policy interventions: player transfer restrictions, salary caps (and other direct wage controls), revenue redistribution, and tournament restructuring. Economic theory (i.e., the invariance proposition) suggests that player transfer restrictions and revenue redistribution are unlikely to improve competitive balance. Furthermore, both of these types of policy intervention run counter to the prevailing trends within professional team sports over the last thirty to forty years. The player market in European soccer has become much less restrictive, particularly since the Bosman ruling, in line with the general movement in the EU toward the establishment of single markets. The recent changes in the FIFA rules for international transfers represent a further movement toward free agency by allowing players to terminate their contracts early for due sporting reason. The reintroduction of restrictions on player transfers is not a legally viable option. Increased revenue redistribution is likely impractical. Big clubs are opposed to revenue sharing arrangements and have progressively limited or abolished the sharing of gate receipts in league tournaments. Significant revenue redistribution still exists in those leagues that have retained the collective selling of TV rights. But such arrangements are under threat both from the big clubs as well as the competition authorities. Unlike North American major leagues, there is little centralized league control over other image rights and merchandising.

Given the lack of theoretical justification as well as the political and legal barriers to player transfer restrictions and revenue redistribution, attention has focused on salary caps and tournament restructuring. UEFA formed a task force to investigate the introduction of a salary cap. In its final report, subsequently endorsed by UEFA's executive committee, it stated that the introduction of a salary cap is not feasible due to the openness and economic diversity of European soccer and the problems of enforceability (UEFA, 2000). Although UEFA would welcome a joint approach by the Big 5 leagues to the creation of a cross-border salary cap, it seems highly unlikely that the leagues could reach agreement on the objectives, design, policing arrangements, and sanctions necessary for an effective salary cap. The G14 group of top clubs has agreed to introduce a salary cap (player wages not to exceed 70% of turnover), but this is a voluntary arrangement with no sanctions and motivated purely by financial concerns (i.e., control of wage costs), not the enhancement of competitive balance. UEFA's current approach to maintaining the financial viability of the clubs competing in its tournaments is the introduction of a club licensing system setting minimum sporting and financial requirements for participating clubs. In particular, from the 2003–2004 season onward, clubs will be required to provide an audited financial budget to show that they will be able to meet their financial commitments over the following twelve months. UEFA has also endorsed the development of wage-benchmarking systems within domestic leagues to facilitate improvements in the market information available to clubs. The FA Premier League and the Scottish Premier League already operate wage-benchmarking systems.

The only practical solution to increasing dominance in European club soccer is tournament restructuring. Two alternative types of proposals have been suggested: a European Super League and regional leagues. The proposal for a European Super League uses the North American major leagues as its model and seeks to create a competitively balanced league comprising the big market clubs across Europe. Such a league would represent a breakaway from the existing merit-hierarchy structure, with no automatic promotion-and-relegation mechanism. This is the type of structure advocated by Hoehn and Szymanski (1999), who propose the creation of four regional conferences. The G14 clubs have actively discussed a European Super League and, indeed, the Italian media group, Mediaset, tabled specific proposals in 1998. However, to date, UEFA has successfully forestalled such proposals by restructuring its own tournaments. The Champions League has replaced the European Cup. Whereas the European Cup was a pure elimination tournament, the Champions League has two phases of round-robin matches. Clubs that qualify for the first two rounds are guaranteed a minimum of twelve matches. UEFA is currently considering restructuring the UEFA Cup to include a round-robin component. Given these reforms to UEFA's own tournaments, there no longer seems to be any real desire on the part of the top clubs in the Big 5 leagues to abandon their financially lucrative domestic leagues in order to compete in a breakaway European Super League.

However, the restructuring of UEFA's own tournaments has exacerbated the problems of domination. The big market, big league clubs dominate the Champions League, and their enhanced revenue streams from European participation serve to reinforce their domestic domination. The domination of European tournaments by the top clubs from the Big 5 leagues has particularly affected the big market clubs from the smaller leagues. The big clubs from the Netherlands, Portugal, and Scotland as well as Eastern Europe have been successful historically in European tournaments but now find themselves unable to compete effectively with the top clubs from the Big 5 leagues, prompting consideration of the formation of regional leagues. For example, several of the leading clubs from the smaller Western Europe leagues have been discussing the formation of an Atlantic League. The two leading Scottish clubs, Celtic and Rangers, have been prime movers in these discussions. These two clubs have also expressed interest in participating in the FA Premier League in England. UEFA and its member associations have expressed strong opposition to any such cross-border developments outside the established European merit-hierarchy structure. However, restructuring existing tournaments to create an intermediate tier between the European and domestic level provides the only feasible long-term solution to the increasing dominance of the big market, big league clubs while retaining a merit-hierarchy structure. Without this kind of structural change, European club soccer will no longer be "still up for grabs" in a sporting sense, and its economic value may diminish accordingly.

Part II

Western Europe: Labor Issues

4

The European and U.S. Sports Labor Markets

Paul D. Staudohar

INTRODUCTION

Soccer in Europe and baseball, football, basketball, and hockey in the United States are more than just games. They are big businesses with millions of fans, rich television contracts, and championships that make headline news. Stakeholders in these sports—especially owners and players—are often lavishly rewarded. With so much money to divide up, the rules regulating the operation of the labor market are of paramount importance. Each side is seeking to maximize its economic return, trying to obtain as large a piece of the total economic pie as possible.

Distributive outcomes are determined by the power that each side has to influence the bottom line. In earlier times, in both Europe and the United States, players had little power to influence economic results. They had to deal with teams that had exclusive rights to their services in what economists call a monopsony—one buyer for their labor. Players could only move from one team to another if they were sold, traded, or released by their club. Unable to sell their services to other bidders in the labor market, players were in a weak bargaining position.

But all that has changed. Today, players on both sides of the Atlantic have opportunities to move freely from one club to another, selling their services to the highest bidder. This chapter examines the evolution of key rules affecting the player labor market and what the changes mean to principals such as leagues, owners, players, and regulatory bodies. The focus of the chapter is mostly on Europe, because of important recent changes there.

FREE AGENCY IN THE UNITED STATES

Teams in the various American sports are organized into leagues. Operating as joint ventures or cartels, leagues control the right to present games in particular geographic areas. Teams that form the leagues have monopoly rights to stage sporting exhibitions in their exclusive territories. The first league to survive to the present day is the National League in baseball, formed in 1876. One of the ideas behind this league was to consolidate team owner power and prevent players from "revolving," or moving freely from one team to another. As an antidote to revolving, owners developed the reserve clause. This clause was a provision in the standard player's contract in which the club reserved the right to the player's services, and it provided the club with the option of renewing the contract for a year beyond its duration. Although only a year was specified, the reserve clause was assumed to bind the player to the club for as long as the club wished to retain the player's services.

In 1885, the first American sports union was formed. Called the Brotherhood of Professional Base Ball Players, its main objective was to obtain labor market freedom for players. But this and other early unions in baseball were unsuccessful in achieving free agency (for discussion of these unions, see Staudohar, 1996, 2000). It wasn't until 1974 that a crack appeared in the owners' shield. Jim "Catfish" Hunter, a star pitcher for the Oakland Athletics, had agreed with owner Charles O. Finley that Finley would pay $50,000 of Hunter's compensation (half his total salary) into an insurance trust. Finley, who was in the insurance business, later discovered that the deal did not provide him with the tax advantage he expected, and therefore he failed to make timely payment into the trust.

Two years earlier, Hunter's union, the Major League Baseball Players Association, had negotiated a collective bargaining agreement on behalf of all players providing for arbitration of grievances. Arbitration means that a dispute is submitted to a neutral outside person who makes a decision that is final and binding. Because Finley failed to comply with the terms of the contract, Hunter brought the grievance to his union. The union then brought the matter before arbitrator Peter Seitz. The arbitrator found in favor of Hunter, which had the result of invalidating his contract and making him a free agent. Hunter proceeded to sign a five-year contract with the New York Yankees for $3.75 million.

The astounding jump in Hunter's salary showed the power that a high quality player had in the labor market. But Hunter's was an isolated case, so his victory did not translate immediately to other players.

In 1975, however, two other players used arbitration to break the reserve clause. Andy Messersmith, a pitcher for the Los Angeles Dodgers, and Dave McNally, a pitcher for the Baltimore Orioles, each played for a year for their teams without signing a contract. They claimed that their clubs, under the language of the reserve clause, could not extend the contract beyond a year, so they were free agents. Arbitrator Peter Seitz took a literal view of the language and agreed with the players. This decision broke the monopsonistic hold that owners had on players and led to a 1977 agreement stipulating that players are eligible for free agency after six years of major league experience. This six-year rule continues to apply to the sport.

The notion of perpetual reserve clauses in football, basketball, and hockey was later struck down by court decisions. Like baseball, the other sports reached agreements with their unions to establish rules for achieving free agency. Football has the most liberal arrangement, with National Football League players able to become free agents after only four years. In the National Basketball Association (NBA), teams can keep a player for up to five years. There is a minimum three-year contract length for rookies, with clubs having the option of renewing for a fourth year and a right of first refusal in year five (allowing it to match the offer made to the player by another club).

Hockey has the least generous free agent terms for its players. National Hockey League (NHL) players aged twenty-five to thirty can become free agents, but movement to other teams is sharply restricted by draft choice compensation that must be paid by teams based on the following schedule:

Below $400,000: none
$401,000 to $550,000: third-round pick
$551,000 to $650,000: second-round pick
$651,000 to $800,000: first-round pick
$801,000 to $1,000,000: first- and third-round picks
$1,000,001 to $1,200,000: first- and second-round picks
$1,200,001 to $1,400,000: two first-round picks
$1,400,001 to $1,700,000: two first-round picks, one second-round pick
Over $1,700,001: three first-round picks
Each additional $1,000,000: additional first-round pick, up to five

With NHL salaries averaging nearly $2 million, the compensation penalties are so steep on restricted free agents that relatively few good players move from their teams. Once a player reaches age thirty-one and has four years of NHL experience, he can become an unrestricted free agent who can sign with another team without penalty. Under rare circumstances a top quality player can become an unrestricted free agent before age thirty-one. In 2001, for example, twenty-seven-year-old Martin Lapointe of the Detroit Red Wings achieved free agency because he was a ten-year veteran who had never been a free agent and his salary was less than the league average (Cazeneuve, 2001).

The rules governing the American system of free agency are well established in the four major sports, having been determined through collective bargaining between owners and players' unions. When negotiated agreements expire, rules are subject to change. In Europe, the system has also evolved over the years, but only recently have players gained significant opportunity to freely change teams. Unlike the American system, where arrangements are set through collective bargaining between the owners and players, in Europe the government and soccer associations have taken the lead in setting the rules for player transfer.

FREE AGENCY IN EUROPE

In 1885, soccer was made professional in Great Britain by the game's ruling body, the Football Association (FA). Three years later, the Football League was formed. The first union of professional soccer players was the Association Footballers' Union in 1897, which later became known as the Players' Union. After dying out for lack of interest, a reconstituted union was formed in 1919, which eventually became known as the Professional Footballers Association (PFA).

A maximum wage was paid to soccer players in Britain from the outset of professionalism until 1961. The top wage (what we would call today a salary cap for individual players) was only £20 when the players' union finally abolished it.

Similar to the reserve clause in America, restrictions on player movement were imposed from the start of professionalism in Britain. Known as the "retain-and-transfer system," it was based on the idea of a player's registration. Only a player registered with the FA could play professional soccer, and only a soccer club could hold registration. Once a player registered with a club he could move to another club with only his current club's permission (Szymanski and Kuypers, 1999, 99).

British soccer players won a limited form of free agency in 1963, when the old retain-and-transfer system was partly struck down by the courts. Three years earlier, player George Eastham of Newcastle United had sought release from his contract. After repeated refusals, he left the club and took a job outside soccer. Because he was unable to arrange his release from Newcastle, Eastham wrote the league to ask its permission to transfer to another club. The league declined to grant permission because it concluded that the matter was entirely between the player and his club. The PFA decided to challenge this determination in court as an illegal restraint of trade under English law. In late 1960, Newcastle relented and sold Eastham to the Arsenal club, but the suit continued on principle. The ruling from Judge

Wilberforce found that the retain-and-transfer system was "an unjustifiable restraint of trade" (Harding, 1991, 283–287).

But Judge Wilberforce's 1963 decision did not entirely strike down the retain-and-transfer system. He dismissed Eastham's claims for damages against Newcastle United, and clubs continued to retain control of players and transfer arrangements, but without placing unacceptable ties on a player seeking transfer. Clubs transferring players under their control continued to receive transfer fees. The system was modified by an agreement late in 1963 in which clubs had one option to renew a player's contract on terms no less advantageous than under the old contract and for the same period, unless otherwise agreed. If the club declined to exercise the option period the club could offer to renew again. If a player was unhappy with the team's proposal, a tripartite arbitration board called the Independent Tribunal would set a transfer fee. The results of this change were an increase in voluntary player movement from one team to another and and an increase in player bargaining power (Harding, 1991, 295). Salaries for all players rose by 54% between 1960 and 1964 (Szymanski and Kuypers, 1999, 95).

The system was again modified in 1978 when the English clubs agreed to allow players free agency at the end of their contracts, subject to compensation from the club that signs a player to his old club. This led to further rapid compensation increases, as wages tripled in the League's first division between 1977 and 1983 (Szymanski and Kuypers, 1999, 95). But the fact that compensation had to be paid meant that players were less than free to move.

Until the early 1960s there was no need for player agents in Britain because player pay was restrained by the salary cap and lack of opportunity to move to other teams. With the elimination of maximum wages and the introduction of limited free agency, players turned to agents for assistance in salary negotiations and handling investments.

The role of player agents in Britain is similar to that in the United States. Agents at first were intensely disliked and resisted by teams, but later gained acceptance. Some clubs even prefer certain agents with whom they have reached favorable agreements. As in the United States, agents' negotiating skills have produced dramatic increases in player earnings. The problem of agents improperly signing up players while in amateur status is more characteristic of the United States than Britain, where players become professionals at earlier ages. In 2001, Manchester United agreed to pay the club Preston North End the equivalent of $195,000 for the rights to a twelve-year-old soccer prodigy named Daniel Rowe (*Sports Illustrated*, 2001). Such an event would be impossible in the United States.

Agents on both sides of the Atlantic have occasionally engaged in investment programs on behalf of players that have cost them dearly. Agents in Britain are prohibited by Football League rules from arranging transfers from one club to another or renegotiating existing contracts (Flynn and Guest, 1994, 207). These restrictions do not apply in the United States. Although solicitors and accountants represent players in Britain, agents there are more likely to be former players. In the United States, the role of attorney and agent is commonly combined in one person.

In the United States, fees for agents who negotiate player contracts are about 3% to 5% of the total. In Britain, fixed fee arrangements are more common. These arrangements are gaining some acceptance in the United States, especially in the NBA, a result of the 1999 collective bargaining agreement that imposed limits on individual player salary increases.

The FA has proposed licensing of agents. Agents in the United States are licensed and regulated by the players' unions. Another difference is that several American states have laws that regulate agents, requiring posting of bonds and stipulating proper behavior.

BOSMAN CASE

Unification of Europe began in 1957, when the Treaty of Rome linked Belgium, France, Italy, Luxembourg, the Netherlands, and West Germany, committing these countries to elimination of barriers to free trade. Article 48 of the Treaty provides for free movement of labor, and although many restrictions were removed, there was little progress toward integrating labor markets. In 1987, the Single European Act resolved to create a unified market in labor, commodities, and capital by 1992. Over the years other countries were added to the European Union (EU), bringing the total to fifteen.

In 1990, a young law school graduate from Belgium named Jean-Louis Dupont happened to meet through his girlfriend a local soccer player named Jean-Marc Bosman. Bosman was in a jam because his Belgian team refused to release him to a team in France unless the French paid about 9 million Belgian francs (about $208,500) in transfer fees. Because the French team refused to pay, Bosman was unemployed. In European soccer, teams do not trade players as they do in the United States; instead, players seek to arrange their own movement, typically through the assistance of an agent.

Dupont filed suit on Bosman's behalf and the case went on appeal to the highest court in the EU, the European Court of Justice in Luxembourg. The result was the European counterpart of the arbitration award on free agency in American baseball and the court cases in football, basketball, and hockey. In 1995, the court ruled that the player transfer system and restrictions on the maximum number of foreign players on a team were illegal violations of article 48 of the Treaty of Rome (Andreff and Staudohar, 2000). Prior to this decision, players were not free to move from one club to another because transfers could occur only if two clubs agreed on a transfer fee to the club losing the player. This limitation on mobility kept salaries relatively low. Also changed in the Bosman case was the 3 + 2 rule, a quota system allowing only three foreign players on a team in a national league, plus two other foreigners if they played in the host country for five years without a break.

The Bosman case has had significant implications for player salaries, player movement, and club finances. When a top quality player whose contract has expired leaves his club for a larger market team, his former smaller market team is no longer rewarded with a transfer fee. This change has caused an increase in the marginal cost of talent for small market teams and has motivated those teams to sell their players before their contracts expire, resulting in a decrease in team quality (Ericson, 2000). The increase in player mobility is illustrated by data from Dobson and Goddard showing that in 1979, 22 percent of all British soccer players had been with their clubs for more than five years, but by 1999, only 12.8 percent had done so (Dobson and Goddard, 1995, 198).

Another outgrowth of Bosman is that it has been extended to countries outside Western Europe. Attorney Jean-Louis Dupont also litigated a case involving Tibor Balog, a Hungarian player who wanted to sign with a club in Nancy, France. Balog's contract with Belgium's Royal Charleroi Sporting club had expired, but that club demanded a transfer fee of 5 million Belgian francs, which the French didn't want to pay. In 1998, a Belgian district court ruled in Balog's favor. Subsequently, the Fédération Internationale de Football Association (FIFA), the world's governing body for soccer, extended the Bosman ruling to cover all players working in the European Economic Area, regardless of their nationality (Shishkin, 2001b). In addition to Bosman, the collapse of communism has attracted players from Eastern Europe to higher-paying Western European leagues.

Table 1 shows that there has been a substantial increase in the number of non-British players in the FA Premier League and Football League since about the time of the Bosman decision. This shift indicates that in at least one country Bosman's elimination of the 3 + 2 rule has had a pronounced effect.

Table 2 shows the post-Bosman average wages for British soccer clubs. With transfer fees eliminated for out-of-contract players, they now have increased freedom of movement and greater bargaining power. However, not all the wage inflation shown in Table 2 is attributable to Bosman, as club revenues from television also increased during the period covered. But Bosman made it more possible for certain players to capture a larger share of the pot.

The Bosman case refers only to players whose contracts have expired. When players still covered by a contract moved to other teams, their original teams continued to demand and receive transfer fees, and these fees increased rapidly. For example, in 1999, Nicolas Anelka moved from Arsenal to Real Madrid for a fee of $35.7 million, and Christian Vieri went from

Table 1
Non-British Soccer Players

Division	1995-96	1999-2000	Percent Increase
Premier League	57	167	192
Division One	44	123	179
Division Two	33	64	93
Division Three	12	30	150
Total	146	384	163

Source: Football Association and Other English Football Authorities (2001).

Lazio to Inter Milan for $50 million. In 2000, Herman Crespo moved from Parma to Lazio for $54.1 million, and Luis Figo went from Barcelona to Real Madrid for a transfer fee of $56.1 million (*Los Angeles Times*, 2000). Then, in 2001, French star Zinedine Zidane transferred from Juventus to Real Madrid for a fee of $64.5 million. The magnitude of these fees hastened the end of the post-Bosman transfer system.

Table 2
Average Wages in British Soccer, 1994–1999 (Thousands of Pounds)

Year	Premier League	Division One	Division Two	Division Three	All
1994	5,312	2,541	1,096	743	2,397
1995	6,568	2,485	1,256	788	2,735
1996	8,494	3,263	1,324	941	3,289
1997	10,905	3,768	1,734	1,051	4,080
1998	15,222	5,605	2,179	1,201	5,653
1999	19,545	5,343	2,861	1,302	6,729

Source: Deloitte & Touche (1999, 2000, cited in Dobson and Goddard, 2001, 97).

BEYOND BOSMAN

In 2000, the EU's executive arm, the European Commission (EC), proposed that clubs should no longer demand transfer fees of any kind, even for players under contract, because to do so would be an illegal antitrust infringement on players' freedom in the labor market. Spearheading this determination was Mario Monti from Italy, the EC's antitrust commissioner and a former economics professor. Infringement proceedings were filed by the EC against FIFA.

In August 2000, FIFA president Sepp Blatter accepted that the EC was right and that clubs could no longer demand fees for their players. Blatter, however, seeking to retain at least some restrictions on player movement, made a counterproposal to the EC that "developmental fees" would be demanded for players between the ages of eighteen and twenty-four. This fee was intended to compensate small market clubs after young players whom they had invested money in moved to larger market clubs. Still, a player over age twenty-four, like Figo or Zidane, would be able to leave his club as often as once each year with no transfer fee, which would wipe out any balance sheet value for such a player to his former club and lead to a salary explosion among players in the top clubs.

The EC's stance and FIFA's relative acquiescence caused a firestorm of controversy. Particular opposition came from the Union des Associations Européennes de Football (UEFA), which sought to pull down FIFA's white flag. Lobbying by UEFA's leaders, President Lennart Johansson of Sweden and Chief Executive Gerhard Aigner of Germany, plus representatives from other Western European governments, resulted in a decision at the EU summit meetings in December 2000 that sports are a special case and should get concessions from antitrust law (*The Economist*, 2001).

Also involved in the negotiations was the Federation Internationale des Associations de Footballeurs Professionnels (FIFPro), an international federation of soccer groups formed in Paris in 1965 by representatives of the French, Scottish, English, Italian, and Dutch players associations. FIFPro was designed to coordinate the activities of the different players' unions and to promote the interests of professional soccer players throughout the world, objectives that continue to the present. In recent years South American players associations have joined FIFPro (Argentina, Brazil, Chile, Venezuela, Uruguay, and Peru) as well as players unions in Eastern European and African countries. As of this writing, the general secretary of FIFPro was Theo van Seggelen, and the president was Gordon Taylor, longtime head of the PFA in Britain.

FIFPro took part in the discussions between the EC, FIFA, and UEFA, and was closer to the EC's initial position of prohibition of all restrictions on player transfers. A key proposal of FIFPro was that imposing transfer fees based on the costs incurred by clubs in training and developing players not be used as a method to restrict young players from moving. Instead, it recommended free movement for players worldwide, addressing concerns over competitive balance and training of young players through "solidarity pools" operating at both the national and international levels. Placing at least 10% of all player transfer fees into the pools and then distributing the money to smaller clubs would fund these pools. The other negotiating parties were not receptive to some of FIFPro's ideas, including the solidarity pools and the concept of international collective bargaining involving players associations. Consequently, FIFPro decided to drop out of the negotiations.

As negotiations continued, the EC modified its position somewhat, accepting the ideas that player contracts should be based on national labor law, and transfer fees, if any, should be based on objective criteria linked to training costs incurred by the selling club. But it continued to maintain that, under labor law that is applicable to them, FIFA, UEFA, or any other body lacks the legal basis for restricting the contractual freedom of players and clubs.

FIFA and UEFA maintained that transfer fees redistribute money from wealthy clubs, which buy talented players, to smaller clubs, which train these players before they become famous. Complete free agency would cause players to jump clubs, causing instability in the game, and would be a disincentive for investment in the development of young players (Shishkin, 2001a). There was also a risk, recognized by the discussants, that total abolition of transfer fees would cause the larger clubs to divert funds from the transfer fee budget to the wages budget, causing top players and clubs to get rich at the expense of small clubs, which may be driven out of business by market forces (Football Association and Other English Football Authorities, 2001).

THE NEW AGREEMENT

On March 5, 2001, FIFA, UEFA, and the EC agreed in Brussels to new rules for governing the player transfer system. As a result, the EC's pending infringement proceedings against FIFA were dropped. The new rules provide that all players who have reached the end of their contracts are free to move throughout the world, subject only to the provisions concerning training compensation. The rules recognize that training takes place between the ages of twelve and twenty-three. Training compensation is due on transfers up to the age of twenty-three for training incurred up to the age of twenty-one. Compensation is due each time a player changes clubs up to the time that his training and education are complete. If, for instance, a player moves before the age of twenty-three, his original club will get training and development costs. Unless the clubs agree on costs, they will be worked out by a fixed formula. If a player was with more than one club during his training period, his transfer may result in payment to multiple teams.

The agreement provides for a five-year limit on contracts and allows one transfer period per season when players can change teams. There is a three-year minimum for multiyear contracts for players under age twenty-eight, and once past twenty-eight, players must honor long-term contracts for at least two years. For instance, a player under twenty-eight years old who signs a five-year contract must fulfill at least three years or be subject to penalty for breach of contract. The penalty for breach could be a suspension of up to six months.

A system of arbitration is established, but not so as to preclude the right to seek redress before a civil court. A player or club may submit a dispute (e.g., breach of contract, training compensation fees, discipline) to an independent mediator. If no settlement occurs after a month, either party can bring the dispute to FIFA's Dispute Resolution Chamber, composed of equal numbers of members selected by players and clubs, and an independent chairperson. Rulings of the chamber are appealable to the Football Arbitration Tribunal, another tripartite board.

If players fail to observe the terms of their contracts, they are subject to fines and suspensions. There is a "grandfather clause," so that the new rules, effective in the 2002 season, apply only to contracts concluded after adoption of the rules. The rules were formally adopted at a special FIFA congress in Buenos Aires in July 2001.

Meanwhile, following the announcement of the new agreement in March, FIFPro filed suit in a Belgian court against the agreement, noting that the suspension of players who unilaterally break their contracts violates EU labor law. Litigation could take some time to fully resolve, but it will be difficult for FIFPro's challenge to be successful because the agreement involves the highest authorities in law and the sport, and it was reached in order to achieve compliance with EU antitrust law.

As intended, the new rules will cause greater movement of players among teams. They should, however, reduce the number of multimillion-dollar transfers. Clubs will continue to purchase players but will be more likely to wait until the players' contracts have expired. Generally, transfer fees should moderate. But the salaries of superstar players will likely increase significantly. These players will probably insist on one-year contracts (the minimum length), so that clubs will have to renegotiate every year to prevent them from moving. The arbitration system is a good idea, but, in the event of an unfavorable ruling, it could be undermined by either side appealing to their national courts.

How well the smaller clubs fare under the new rules will depend on the generosity of the training fees they receive. Given their opposition to change in the transfer system, motivated by self-interest, it is unlikely that smaller clubs will prosper generally. Financial pressures may cause more of these clubs to go out of business, although small clubs that are successful in developing famous players could do quite well.

What about the impact on sporting equality? There is apt to be little effect. Regardless of the transfer system, the best players tend to go to the richest clubs. In the United States, before free agency, rich clubs like baseball's New York Yankees were successful because they could trade for or buy talented players. Under free agency, the Yankees have the financial resources to ac-quire attractive players leaving other teams. The main difference between a monopsony situation and one of free agency is that in monopsony the eco-nomic rents (profit from use of players) accrue to the clubs, whereas under free agency they are captured by the players. A transfer system cannot over-come the fact that clubs have inherently different levels of financial capability in the market for players.

To achieve sporting equality it is necessary to pool revenues, and the model example of this is the National Football League (NFL) in the United States. All television revenues in the NFL are from national (not local) sources and are shared equally by the teams in the league. Thus, the small market Green Bay Packers receive the same television revenues as the big market New York Giants. Also, gate receipts in the NFL are shared 60% for the home team and 40% for the visiting team. These arrangements for revenue sharing keep teams on the same financial level, so that they can effectively compete for free agency players.

In European soccer there is less sharing of television revenues; the richer clubs keep the lion's share. These clubs also benefit greatly from higher at-tendance, sponsorships, sale of club merchandise, and sale of stock to the public, putting smaller clubs at a competitive disadvantage. The rich-poor disparity likewise crops up in American baseball and has contributed to the work stoppages that have plagued that sport, as small market teams seek fi-nancial relief. Player strikes are one problem that Europe has avoided, but this could become a problem in the future with the internationalization of soccer rules and an international players' union demanding changes.

5

Economic Analysis of the Transfer Market in European Professional Soccer

Jean-Jacques Gouguet and Didier Primault

INTRODUCTION

In soccer, the transfer fee is the financial amount that accompanies a player transferring from one club to another. Currently, the basic problem is to understand why transfer fees exist and how to determine their size. These issues have become fashionable (again!), following the European Commission's demands for reform, if not abolition, of the transfer system. This conflict between the Commission and the international soccer authorities coincides with media coverage of historically large transfer fees paid as several stars move between prestigious clubs (for example, Real Madrid, PSG, and Manchester United).

In order to throw light on the debate relating to the legitimacy of such sums, or even their influence on the balance of competition, it seems necessary to return to economic theory (Gouguet and Primault, 2001–2002/2003). Returning to theory aids in correctly describing how to objectively determine the value of a player's transfer between two clubs. The type of system put in place to regulate professional championships in Europe depends on the determination of these values.

THE ECONOMIC BASIS OF TRANSFER FEES

There are two approaches to the economic analysis of transfer fees. The cost-based approach elicits the user value of the player. The talent-based approach determines the value of a player as one would determine the value of a painting. Using these approaches demonstrates that there can be a discrepancy between player value and price. Further, the market failures that follow from a segmented player market become apparent.

The Cost-Based Approach

It is possible to assimilate the transfer fee into the user value of the player. This value can be calculated at the club level in a classical examination of labor value, or at the player level in a neoclassical examination of utility value.

From the perspective of the soccer club, it is the owners who invested in soccer, who took the risks. The club owners could therefore consider themselves to have every right to recover the total of their contribution. From this perspective, it is reasonable to seek a transfer fee equivalent to the player's user value to the club. It is assumed in this case that the club holds the player under contract.

On the other hand, if the player is completely free to use his abilities, one could look for the theoretical basis of player demand in G. S. Becker's theory of human capital. The rational player invests in human capital in order to optimize the overall return of his asset portfolio (monetary, financial, real, and human). In order to do this, he carries out a standard calculation of opportunity cost; that is, the capitalized cost of the human capital acquisition must be inferior to the converted sum of the anticipated income.

For soccer players, training is the primary means of increasing the stock of human capital. Following Becker's prescription in the soccer case, the player invests in training until the capitalized cost of this investment (the income from work forgone during training, the time spent studying, and school fees) is equal to the capitalized income due to the training being completed.

Whether one applies labor value or usefulness value, the economic basis of transfer fees can always be found in the use value of the player. Of course, how to measure such a value still remains a question. It is at this level that economic analysis becomes more difficult, and it has to be recognized that there is a distinct lack of work on human capital accumulation in sports.

The Talent-Based Approach

Under the talent-based approach, the value of the transfer fee lies in the quoted value of the player, just as the value of a painting lies in the quoted value of the painter. The problem is to determine such a quoted value relatively objectively. In the field of art, econometric studies carried out by analyzing multiple regressions have given convincing results (Pommerehne and Frey, 1993). Four determining factors in the value of an artist and his or her work have appeared:

1. The number of exhibitions already had and the number of prizes received
2. The time passed since the first exhibition
3. The flexibility of the artist
4. The price of previous sales

As far as we know, the talent-based approach is rare in sports (Dobson and Gerrard, 1997), but the econometric tests that have been performed confirm the results obtained in the field of art. The variables to be employed include the number of years spent at the top level, the list of sporting honors, the player's position, and player flexibility, age, and nationality. On this basis, it should be possible to establish a quoted value for players that could be used to calculate the transfer fee.

Until recently, the quoted value of players has been left to the market, which would not necessarily be a bad solution if the labor market in professional sports, generating transfer fees, were functioning correctly. But, through the rest of this chapter, we argue that such is not the case. Talent intervenes in a decisive way in determining the relative value of players, but other elements distort player transactions, yielding discrepancies between price and value of players. This opens a debate. Should the task of ascertaining quoted values be left to the market or to an independent external regulator?

Player Market Segmentation

The consent to pay by the purchasing club and the consent to receive by the selling club create a deep rift in the transfer fees for two types of players—the stars and the rest. The existence of this segmentation leads, in turn, to our assessment that there are failures in the labor and transfer market. These market failures drive a wedge between player price and value.

The purchasing club forecasts expected future receipts based on the acquisition of a player. Adding the player strengthens the team, making it more competitive. Many examples can be given of clubs that have recruited a well-known, fully mature player who has proved himself. In addition, there are revenues directly linked to the player himself. Every player contributes to merchandising revenue, gate revenue, the value of TV rights, and sponsoring contracts. Estimation of these values has been a mainstay of sports economists in the United States (a synthesis is in Fort, 2003). But the more numerous factors and relationships that determine marginal revenue product in the open leagues of Europe complicate the analysis.

Moving on to the consent to receive from the selling club, three main factors come into play. First, the assessment of this consent is based on the capitalized sum of the investments made by the selling club in training, care, and improvement of the player. Second, the club estimates the amount of net losses associated with the departing player, as much from the sporting point of view as the financial one. Third, the club estimates the cost of replacing the player. All of these enter into the amount the selling club will be willing to receive from the purchasing club.

The agreements reached by selling and receiving clubs have created a deep segmentation in the soccer players' labor market between the stars and the rest, and the already-mentioned discrepancy between value and price must be assessed from this perspective. From a quantitative point of view, it is known that the professional soccer players' labor market can be broken down into two radically different segments (Bourg and Gouguet, 2000). In France, for example, there is a primary market made up of forty star players who are the talk of the town. The secondary market is made up of 350 anonymous players whose status with their club is relatively more precarious.

The consequences of the Bosman ruling on transfer fees and the wage bills of major clubs are most apparent among the star players. Since this is a recent change, and only overall trends are generally known, studies are necessary to clarify the nature of transfer fees. For example, out of a total of 342 transfers during the 2000–2001 season in France, 144 were carried out within the country and 198 occurred abroad, of which ninety-three players entered and ninety-four players left (the difference in eleven players is due to temporary transfers). It would be interesting to delve into the overall figures by club and by player in order to assess the degree of concentration of the bulk of transfers.

The richest clubs find and buy the best players in an exaggeratedly competitive environment. So it is that teams in the smaller, poorer leagues are used as reserves (as in the minor leagues in the United States) for teams in the largest, richest leagues. This helps us to understand the very large interclub "dualization" that has been operating in Europe for several years, particularly in the G14. Dualization among the G14 has led to a push for the creation of a sort of European Super League.

The talent-based approach to the determination of transfer fees is insightful regarding the inflationary tensions in the star segment of the labor market. Three variables appear to exert a decisive influence on the level of transfer fee: player position, nationality, and age. Our review of press reports shows that, of the seventy transfer fees that led to the highest level negotiations, forty-eight were forwards and sixteen were midfielders. Defenders and goalkeepers were the distinct minority (five and one, respectively). Player nationality appears to explain transfer fees in the sense that "nationality" indicates the evolving success the players' national teams. It is worth mentioning the case of French players, who were absent from international rankings a dozen years ago but in high demand since their recent victories in the World Cup and European Championship. Six French players are now on the list of the top seventy record transfer fees, all having made their appearance since 1998 (Gouguet and Primault, 2001–2002/2003). Age enters into the equation insofar as speculation appears strongest about young players.

In theory, then, the foregoing enables an understanding of the level of transfer fees, as well as player market segmentation. What remains to be explained is why, for star players, there is a discrepancy between player value and price. Our assessment is that failures in the market for stars lead to discrepancies between their value and the prices actually paid to obtain them. It is this discrepancy that fuels debate concerning the highest transfer fees, deemed too high by some observers.

Market Failures

If the market functioned competitively with perfect information, one could be confident that the player's market price reflected his true value. The leveling out of clubs' consent to pay and to receive would allow a "fair" price to be fixed, if it were determined on an objective basis (by cost and talent). However, the market is often imperfect, owing to the presence of external factors such as imperfections in the nonsporting value of players, imbalance of information, and imperfect information regarding speculation on young players.

Sporting Value—Economic Value

The revenue structure of the best-paid athletes on the planet clearly shows that they live as much on their image as on their work (see the graphic in Bolotny, 2002). Clubs have also absorbed this aspect. Nowadays, they recruit talented athletes who are also vehicles for communicating the club's brand name. The value of a player cannot be reduced to simply sporting value, as this represents only a part of that player's total economic value to a club. It is understood that the nonsporting value of a player is going to depend on many factors that are very far from being perfect. Everything depends, therefore, on the size of the risks that the clubs wish to take (buyers or sellers).

Information Imbalance

The best players and their representatives have great power in the market. Furthermore, players are in possession of information that owners do not necessarily receive. Under such conditions of asymmetric information, it is very difficult to determine the marginal revenue product of each player.

The Speculative Dimension of Transfer Fees

There also is a speculative dimension to transfer fees that applies mainly to young unrecognized players. A simplified portrayal casts clubs as betting on the transition of young players from hopefuls to stars. So it is that many young players from French training centers leave to go abroad to highly paid championships (Italy and England, mainly). Speculation can also play a part in including very high termination clauses with the aim of making financial gain.

Here, too, more study would be necessary to pinpoint these discrepancies between player value and price in order to suggest some instruments for market regulation. Likely targets for regulatory intervention include the frequency of transfer, the anticipated breaches of contract, and the development of transfer fees for the same player over a period of time.

From these simple criteria, it seems to us that we should be able to pinpoint the anomalies. One would then be in a position to assess the magnitude of doubtful transactions. Doing so is all the more important because in the presence of market failure, the competitive balance of championships is threatened. Market regulation is necessary.

REGULATION OF THE TRANSFER MARKET

In this section, we present the regulatory approaches in the European Union (EU) toward free movement, team stability, and integrity in competition. Then, a critical analysis of EU regulation explores the legitimacy of the transfer fee system and the necessity for finding compromise between clubs and players. Finally, a bolder approach to regulation is offered along with its impacts on the labor market and income splitting.

Current Status of the EU Agreement on Transfer Fees

We would like to assess, in the light of theoretical contributions that have been presented, the content of the agreement on transfer reform between the European Commission and interested parties, signed on March 5, 2001. We will content ourselves with recalling the most important principles that, according to Viviane Reding (member of the European Commission), can be summed up in the following way (for Reding's characterization, see Gouguet and Primault, 2001–2002/2003): how to guarantee, at the same time, the free movement of players, team stability, and the integrity of competitions (sporting balance)? The Commission worked out this difficult compromise, which took more than two years of negotiation (December 1998–March 2001) with the concerned parties before it was signed.

Five major themes structure the eleven principles of the agreement that followed discussions between the soccer authorities, the European Commission, and the players' representatives (Gouguet and Primault, 2001–2002/2003). The elements of the agreement, which were restructured during the summer after the final negotiations, were integrated into Fédération Internationale de Football Association (FIFA) regulations at the congress that took place in Buenos Aires on July 5, 2002.[1] The five major themes are:

1. Protection of minors
2. Better payment for training
3. Stability of favored contracts
4. A solidarity mechanism
5. A specific authority for managing disputes

It would appear that all possible approaches to the value of transfers developed in this chapter are more or less included in the five major themes. But some further explanation is worthwhile.

The value based on training costs is fully recognized, and a series of compensation systems is even planned to highlight the role of small clubs, the primary source of professional players' training. It remains to perfect the technical details of calculating training compensation. Such a calculation rests both on validated theoretical bases (human capital theory, status theory, and efficient salary theory) and on recognized methods of economic calculation (present value, productivity, and total economic value). Further study is necessary.

In case of negotiated breach of contract and with the agreement of the club, there will be a transfer indemnity, justified primarily by wage theory. The compensation should rest, according to FIFA, on objective criteria: total salary, remaining length of contract, and total compensation of previous transfers. Here again, all of this would merit development, as much theoretical, on the user value of the player as empirical on the details of criteria behind the calculation.

Whether calculating training compensation or the negotiated transfer fee, a half-hearted reference to the talent-based approach is made. But it must be recognized that this method is not really clarified, either as to content (criteria to be retained in order to define talent) or to organization. But such a clarification could establish the quoted value and therefore the players' ranking as an alternative to market outcomes.

Critical Analysis

Of course, the first question to be asked is: What is the legitimacy of transfer fees? The answer certainly comes from the idea one has of sports and, in particular, the thorny question of the sporting exception. Is the soccer player an employee like any other, with total freedom to change employer?

For some (Federation Internationale des Associations de Footballeurs Professionnels [FIFPro]), for the player to regain freedom of movement, it would be enough for the new club to pay an amount equivalent to the wages owed to the club that has been left. For others (FIFA, Union des Associations Européennes de Football [UEFA]), the player must not unilaterally breach his contract, for fear of harming competitive balance. This is the point of view that the Commission accepted, while suggesting sanctions in case of unilateral breach and offering to control the transfer compensation in case of negotiated breach.

Whatever the opposing points of view, the transfer fee has never been called into question because it well expresses the attempt to reconcile an increasingly invasive industrial economic logic and the necessity of respecting a sporting logic. The latter is especially important because, without it, the spectacle that is the source of the profit will be killed. The foregoing signifies that it is only with difficulty possible to abolish the transfer system, which, contrary to what had been traditionally written, has a genuine usefulness and which rests on an unquestionable economic logic (Gouguet and Primault, 2001–2002/2003).

On the one hand, the transfer indemnities constitute a way of internally financing autonomy in the sporting sector. This system is not perfect, as the preceding discussion makes clear, but nobody at the present time offers a viable alternative. It is very easy to replace a so-called arbiter with another without really being able to predict any new pernicious effects (black markets and wage inflation). On the other hand, it is difficult to accept the comparison made by the Commission between (1) mutually agreed club transactions fixing the amount of the transfer fee and (2) an "arrangement." It is in the name of this argument for the nonrespect of competition rules that the Commission proposed the abolition of transfer fees for a time. However, nothing is more competitive, and at an international level, than the negotiation for the transfer of a star.

The supply of talent is very limited at the star level, and the demand of clubs is increasingly strong owing to the financial stakes. Hence transfer fees have seen an exponential growth. Whereas this phenomenon leads us to think about regulation, abolition is another thing altogether. We find again the traditional discrepancy mentioned in Smith, Ricardo, or Marx between value and price. The price of transfers is diverging significantly from their real values because of current market conditions. It is therefore a change in the functioning of the market that is the aim, and that will occur by looking for a balance of power between the concerned parties.

The Necessity of Finding a Compromise

It must be recognized that the Commission has greatly appreciated the importance of compromise. Viviane Reding, in the period after the agreement of March 5, 2001, correctly declared it was better to have a negotiated solution than an imposed solution. Even with imperfections, negotiating an agreement has allowed the Commission, FIFA, UEFA, FIFPro, and Professional Leagues the chance to meet for discussion, which has allowed the most difficult-to-reconcile points of divergence to emerge. Take the example of the professional players' union reaction to the reform. Eventually, the clubs emerged strengthened, but portions of the reform were removed from the final negotiation, judged too radical. The players' position was basically structured around a double opposition to the training compensation, which was judged too high, and to the system of sporting sanctions in case of unilateral breach of contract.

The union declared itself in favor of total freedom for players and of a transfer system based on the payment of the salary owed. In backing its demands, the union explained that FIFA and UEFA had to submit to the injunctions of the G14. The reform that has been put in place is therefore the result of the predominance of industrial logic that nowadays structures soccer. Finally, the complaint lodged by FIFPro was withdrawn after the players were successful in the suit.

Transfer reform is only in its initial stages. Agreement about several major principles has begun with difficulty, and the concrete details of methods have advanced a little (calculation of compensation, dispute, and staged solidarity), but much remains to be done. It is the responsibility of the actors in soccer to continue the dialogue. Transfer fees are affected by divergent positions among all actors—clubs, unions, agents, leagues, and players. Behind their bargaining, we find again the attempt to reconcile demands for both balanced sporting competition and equitable economic competition.

Toward More Audacious Elements for a Solution

The Labor Market

The primary labor market consideration is the free movement of players. The consequences of the Bosman ruling on club wage bills are now well known. In the same way, transfer reform risks raising players' salaries once again. Indeed, given that star players enjoy great power in the segmented labor market, restrictions imposed on transfer fees would inevitably lead to a substitution effect between amounts devoted to transfers and amounts devoted to salaries. Similarly, the increase of freedom in that category of players, along with the ruling, has rocketed salaries and transfer fees upward.

Different proposals need to be discussed concerning (1) regulating the labor market by finance, (2) improving the quality of information about the labor market, and (3) regulating the distribution of talent in the market. For the first proposal, three main elements occur to us. First, supervisory management committees, after the French model, could be implemented in all of Europe in order to avoid speculative drifts or threats to competitive balance of the Real Madrid kind. But such an attempt would come up against a complex system that brings into play a wide variety of countries and systems. Second, setting up stricter ethically based rules for agents and clubs would be a step in the right direction (agent licences and club licences). Finally, establishing an American-style salary-cap system could be explored further. But it is difficult to apply this type of cap to European interlinked championships. In addition, the total financial control by sporting authorities that exists in American-style "closed leagues" is missing in Europe.

A number of actions could improve the quality of labor market information:

- Transparency of information in order to avoid the development of an underground economy.
- Movement of information between clubs in order to limit the power of players' agents in the market.
- Refinement of market assessment tools by clubs such as strengthening skills and staff in charge of recruitment (American-style scouts).
- Creation of better performance assessment tools, following the example of what is done with statistics in basketball, and without any delusions concerning the possibility of totally reliable tools in this field.

Similarly, a variety of actions can be taken to regulate the distribution of talent in the market:

- Any liberalization of the labor market favors concentrating talent in the biggest clubs, which can then use their financial power. But, in this instance, restricting the transfer fee, leading to salary inflation, would maintain the richest clubs' power to attract talent. Therefore, nonfinancial tools have to be considered.
- If the Americans have devised their own systems (draft, for example), France has preferred the protection of the training club. This solution appears pertinent with regard to the history and culture of European countries. The system must be adapted to respond to new demands (a better respect of the freedom of young players, improvement of the facilities for the integration or reintegration of young people who haven't experienced success).
- The obligation to develop a certain number of players trained in the club could constitute a nondiscriminatory substitute for the former nationality clauses.

Revenue Sharing

All authors, whether American or European, recognize that revenue sharing is certainly the most efficient system for moving toward competitive balance. The way opened by the new FIFA regulations, intended to favor solidarity between the soccer-playing elite and the soccer-playing masses, is an interesting version of revenue sharing. The plan is to distribute 5% of each transfer fee to the different clubs that trained the player. However, since this measure is not intended to reestablish competitive balance, taxing the increase in value made on transfer fees could be considered in order to establish a fund for regulating competitive balance.

But, above all, the debate concerning transfer fees cannot be separated from a more general debate about the ownership of television rights as well as competition methods and the place of national teams. Quite the contrary to this observation, it would appear that in Europe we are distancing ourselves from such a debate. In particular, the richest clubs are looking for the individualization of TV rights.

CONCLUSION

We have tried to clarify, with recourse to economic analysis, the current organization of transfer fees for soccer players as well as the effects that the current organization has on competitive balance. Despite many complementary studies that would be necessary in order to improve any future decision making, several conclusions emerge here.

Since professional sports can be considered tantamount to an industry, the regulation of player movement is left to the free functioning of the market, which determines the levels of transaction. We have clearly shown that the imperfections of such a market largely explain the existing discrepancy between the value and price of certain players. It is necessary therefore to regulate such a market.

The last reform of the transfer system, initiated by the Commission, got it right by guaranteeing better stability of competition while starting to institute a series of solidarity mechanisms. Effort should, however, continue in this attempt to regulate the entire system because of the growing power of certain clubs and star players. Allowing this power to continue risks either distorting competitive balance or moving Europe toward American-style closed leagues.

Finally, reform of the transfer system should make us think of an overall approach to sports and, in particular, to include the relations between professional and popular sports. The value created at the level of the first comes in part from the second, which therefore merits being remunerated. From this perspective, the new transfer system could serve to defend a sporting ethic that is always put in danger by market appetites.

NOTE

1. FIFA regulations for the status and transfer of players and regulation governing the application of the regulations for the status and transfer of players.

6

The Taxation of Player Moves from Developing Countries

Wladimir Andreff

INTRODUCTION

Talented athletes from developing countries are increasingly moving away from their home countries toward North American and West European professional leagues. The clearest cases in point are North American baseball and basketball leagues. Ice hockey would be added if we included Eastern Europe among the less developed world. But the major West European professional sport that attracts Third World players is soccer. Weak performances and lower comparative wages provide a negative incentive to the most talented players and trigger their move away from their countries of origin. Such a "muscle drain" (by analogy with the well-known brain drain from the Third World) is becoming of concern since it is affecting some players under the age of eighteen involved in international transfers. The concern deepens when the transfer of teenage players proceeds with illegal means and clandestine deeds used by outlaw players' agents. Such misdeeds produce market distortions and lead to an inefficient international allocation of talent. Most young players from developing countries are transferred at a fee that is too low relative to the efficient fee. The waste of talented resources is even more obvious when an unsuccessfully tested young player is abandoned by a European professional club as an illegal migrant without assistance or even a return ticket to his home country. In such cases, no matter how low is his education and training cost, it is not covered by the market mechanism. In these circumstances, the young player, his nursery club, and his home country bear the cost of this economic inefficiency, the former two usually having invested in his education and training.

This chapter is, in some sense, a position paper since it assumes that the winners from these distorted international transactions, the professional clubs and the players' agents, should compensate the losers, the young players, the nursery clubs, and the home countries. However, the winners have no good reason to willingly compensate the losers. On the one hand, young players in the Third World, their parents, and their nursery associations usually cannot afford to sue professional team owners and players' agents abroad. On the other hand, they lack accurate information about the international players' market and the required bargaining power to act themselves as agents. Further, weak or absent players' unions in home countries leave the player with little bargaining power against a European club. Thus, intervention is required to do what players, parents, and nursery clubs cannot. The market should be regulated to reduce illegal market distortions that damage Third World players. The only way out seems to be an international intervention with the aim of restricting teenage player movement from developing countries.

The next part of the chapter suggests a tax approach to "throw sand in the wheels of the international labor market" for teenage players. Its feasibility is briefly assessed along with some hindrances likely to arise. Our suggested taxation is then compared with the rules adopted by the Fédération Internationale de Football Association (FIFA) in September 2001 to come to grips with international transfer of soccer players. Whatever the most efficient regulation, it should be completed with a stronger and worldwide supervision of players' agents.

ECONOMIC UNDERDEVELOPMENT AND SPORTS: THE CONTEXT OF A MUSCLE DRAIN

In sixteen less developed countries (LDCs) surveyed by the UN Educational, Scientific and Cultural Organization (UNESCO), athletes were found to leave their country as soon as their sports performance reached an international standard (Souchaud, 1995). This muscle drain is disappointing for the local coaches and sport teachers. The best African basketball players migrate, sometimes changing their citizenship. In many professional sports, developing countries and former Soviet economies are utilized as nurseries for sporting talent and provide a huge pool of labor. In French professional soccer, African players have, every year, provided a substantial percentage of the total labor force (see Table 1). The wage gap between the African and French player markets is between one to ten and one to twenty (de Brie, 1996). Soccer players in Cameroon earn premiums and bonuses between $6,000 and $14,000 per year, well over the domestic average wage, but considerably lower than the average income of a French player. The French

Table 1
Participation of African Players in French Professional Soccer, 1955–1998 (in Percentage of Total Number of Players Involved)

Players from:	1955	1960	1970	1980	1990	1998
North Africa	6.0%	6.0%	0.8%	3.0%	2.5%	3.0%
Sub-saharian Africa	0.7%	6.0%	1.4%	2.5%	8.0%	15.0%
Total	6.7%	12.0%	2.2%	5.5%	10.5%	18.0%

Source: Vierne (1998).

(or any European) overall minimum wage is well over the average income of an African soccer player in his home country, hence a young player is always attracted by the dream of being hired by a European club, even if he has to wander meanwhile in the labor market.

Latin American countries are also suffering from a muscle drain. Fifty-four percent of all the professional players in Brazilian soccer are earning no more than the legal minimum wage of 120 reals (roughly $90) per month. The top 9% best paid players were in 1997 earning over $1,400 per month. The same year, Ronaldo (Inter Milan), Denilson (Betis Sevilla), Roberto Carlos (Real Madrid), and Rivaldo (FC Barcelona) were said by *Business Age* to earn collectively over $140 million per year. Such a wage gap is strong incentive for African and Latin American players to leave their home country for the European market. From 1989 to 1997, 2,084 Brazilian football players migrated to foreign professional clubs all around the (developed) world, in particular to Italy, Spain, Portugal, France, and Japan. All these transfers have been reckoned by the Brazilian Football Confederation to yield roughly $500 million to Brazilian clubs. The same tendency to "drain muscles" from developing countries is observed in other sports.

In soccer, player mobility is now an established international phenomenon. The best players from developing countries are attracted to the European leagues in order to maximize their economic returns. Inevitably, their home countries are suffering a muscle drain as a consequence of their own success in producing players of an international standard. Table 2 provides some evidence of the muscle drain, showing the geographical distribution of players' domestic affiliations for the five African nations that qualified for the 2002 World Cup finals in Japan and South Korea. Only 21% of the players were affiliated with teams in their home domestic league, and only three out of twenty-three players on the Senegal squad were not affiliated with French teams.

In addition to the aforementioned wage gap, the muscle drain is triggered by the low level of sports development in Third World countries (Andreff, 2001, 2002a). A UNESCO survey (Souchaud, 1995) stresses that once exposed to physical education at school, the duration of exposure will have a

Table 2
Geographic Distribution of Domestic Team Affiliations, African 2002 World Cup Players

Domestic Team Affiliation	Cameroon	Nigeria	Senegal	South Africa	Tunisia	Total
Home country	-	2	1	7	14	24
Africa	-	-	1	-	-	1
England	4	4	-	3	-	11
France	7	3	20	-	2	32
Germany	1	-	-	2	1	4
Italy	3	-	-	1	3	7
Spain	4	1	-	-	-	5
Other European	3	11	1	10	3	28
Rest of World	1	2	-	-	-	3
Total	23	23	23	23	23	115

deep influence on developing athletic practice among children and teenagers. Of the surveyed developing countries, one had no physical education scheduled in primary school, three had scheduled one hour per week, and the others between two and three hours per week. In secondary school, physical education was scheduled two to four hours per week in all countries. The problem is that the hours supposedly devoted to physical education are often never fulfilled, mainly due to a shortage of physical education teachers. In most developing countries, the ratio of sports participation is usually below 1% of the population. The ratio of coaches to sports participants is very low since most coaches are not satisfactorily paid and volunteers cannot compensate for the coach shortage.

Although in many developing countries the government is the main sponsor and patron of sports (Kidane, 1996), subsidy levels are too low to secure sports activities all year long. State budgets are low, absolutely, and municipalities' sports budgets also are limited. In most developing countries, there are no sports facilities, and in those countries with facilities, overcrowding is a problem. Among the developing countries surveyed by UNESCO, one has no stadium capable of hosting a big sporting event that would conform to international rules and norms. Most domestic sports events are organized in the capitals of LDCs simply because, in each country, the capital is the only city endowed with appropriate and well-maintained sport facilities. This limitation explains why so few world sport events are located in Third World countries. Only six out of eighteen soccer World Cups have been organized in the most advanced Latin American countries (see Table 3). There has never been a World Cup in Africa, the Middle East, or Central or South Asia, despite repeated and unsuccessful applications by Morocco, and one by South Africa (for 2006). About thirty developed countries handle the

Table 3
The Location of the Football World Cup (Mundial)

Year	Country	Year	Country	Year	Country
1930	Uruguay	1962	Chile	1986	Mexico
1934	Italy	1966	England	1990	Italy
1938	France	1970	Mexico	1994	United States
1950	Brazil	1974	Germany	1998	France
1954	Switzerland	1978	Argentina	2002	Japan, South Korea
1958	Sweden	1982	Spain	2006	Germany

organization of approximately 95% of all international and world sports events per year. The rest of the world, some 170 developing countries, host no more than 5% of the big sports events.

Last, but not least, poor economic and sports development translate into poor performances at international sports events. Several studies have determined that economic development is a major determinant of Olympic successes (Grimes, Kelly, and Rubin 1974; Levine 1974; Elmandjra 1984; Fatès 1994; Bernard and Busse, 2000). Andreff (2001) regressed GDP per capita and population against the number of medals in a sample of countries participating in (1) the 1996 Atlanta and 2000 Sydney Olympic Games and (2) the Winter Games since their inception up to Nagano in 1998. Based on an ordered-logit model, both explanatory variables significantly increased the probability that a country would switch to a higher class of medals won.

Turning now to soccer's World Cup, the winner has always been from either a developed country or one of the three most advanced Latin American countries: Argentina, Brazil, and Uruguay. Several African countries do not even participate in the World Cup because they fear having to pay a fine in case of withdrawal. The overall context of sports underdevelopment does not provide a strong incentive for talented players to stay in their home country even if a professional championship does exist there.

INTERNATIONAL TRANSFERS OF TEENAGE PLAYERS FROM DEVELOPING COUNTRIES: THE JUNGLE OF THE BUSINESS WORLD

Many problems are associated with the muscle drain. First, it undermines the sporting substance of developing countries. Second, it diverts the most talented athletes, those few who have had the opportunity to benefit from the rare domestic coaches and sport facilities. Third, in some cases, it erodes the capacity of the home country to use its most talented athletes in international competition, partly explaining the poor performances of developing countries in world sports events. For instance, soccer players from Africa (namely Cameroon, Nigeria, and Ivory Coast) were not released by their (European) professional clubs for selection to their domestic national teams to play in matches of the 22nd African Cup 2000 (177 out of the 352 registered players were playing in European clubs at the time). The African Cup is nicknamed the "cattle fair" because a number of well-known European club managers, coaches, and players' agents attend it with the objective of recruiting talented players. At the Sydney Olympics, Cameroon, Nigeria, and Morocco had to compete without some of their star soccer players, in spite of FIFA rules compelling clubs to release players selected for national teams.

With the emergence of fifteen- to seventeen-year-old player championships in Africa, international transfers have increasingly affected players under sixteen. In the late 1990s, an increasing number of African players under sixteen were tranferred to European clubs. Most young players transferred to European professional clubs ultimately do not sign a contract and then are left aside, cut off from their family, their friends, and their home country, with no source of income and no assistance. The Bosman case fueled these tendencies by creating an unregulated world market for very young talented players, sometimes referred to as a "market for slaves," "child trade," or "trafficking of human beings" (Tshimanga, 2001). Clubs in home countries cannot impede these transfers and are either hardly compensated or not compensated at all.

Professional clubs do benefit from transferring talented young players from the Third World. Since the Bosman case, European clubs are facing a dramatic increase in the transfer price of European players in a unified labor market. Talented young players "imported" from developing countries can offer an interesting substitute in the face of rising prices in the European market. For example, in 1996, when labor regulations in Belgium fixed the minimum soccer wage at 43,000 Belgian francs (BF) per month, about 1,075 euros, Georges Mouandjo from Cameroon was transferred to RAEC Mons with a contract stipulating a monthly wage of 6,000 BF, or 150 euros. The Italian soccer player union contends that a contract for a talented Italian junior player can be up to 4.5 million euros, whereas the average for an African junior player is roughly 4,500 euros. In particular, young Third World players yield a better return to the club when they are able to improve (or to contribute to improving) its performances in the professional championship and attract more spectators in the stadium. From scattered data, it seems that European professional soccer clubs adding Latin American and African players to their squads are well off both in terms of their gate receipts and their rankings in the various European professional championships. In England, talented non-European players are assumed to make the game more appealing by upgrading the tactics beyond the classical British "kick and rush" (Mignon, 2002).

On the other hand, once hired, a talented young player from Africa or Latin America can after a time be sold again[1] by the "importing" club to another one at a higher price on the European labor market. For instance, the Guinean teenage player Oularé was recruited by the Belgian club of Genk for 100,000 euros and transferred two years later to a Turkish club for 5.75 million euros.[2] Manchester United apparently has a partnership agreement with the Belgian club of Antwerp, according to which the latter is to recruit and train non-European young players, to obtain their Belgian citizenship, and then to transfer them to Manchester. A similar agreement links the Belgian soccer club Germinal Ekeren to the Dutch club Ajax Amsterdam.

Talented teenage players in developing countries are either enrolled in clubs affiliated with their home country's national soccer federation or are playing for nonaffiliated sports associations that recruit nonaffiliated players for their squads. In moving their players to foreign (European) markets, affiliated clubs either bargain directly with foreign clubs or rely on player agents with solid foreign club contacts. However, affiliated clubs are under the supervision and regulation of the national federation regarding the international transfer of players, whether the player is a minor or not. National federation affiliation does not secure that transfers from Third World countries will come across through perfectly legal channels,[3] but it will diminish the probability of resorting to clandestine or illicit recruiting agents.

On the other hand, for players in nonaffiliated associations in their home country, the only way for an international transfer is through an underground labor market characterized by clandestine networks of player agents. The great bulk of players under eighteen transferred from developing countries come via this illicit market. No exit letter from a federation is required, and teenage players can leave the country with a tourist visa. Since neither the nonaffiliated association nor the clandestine agents are governed by a national federation, players are not protected from the possible predatory behavior of outlaw agents. The worst situation emerges when a player, with his family, enters the market and is eventually trapped in the network of illegal player agents connected with European professional clubs.

This issue of international transfers of talented teenage players from developing countries is not a marginal or negligible one. In Italian soccer, 2,273 foreign affiliated players over sixteen have been imported through illicit channels, and their affiliation and position have been straightened out afterward. Moreover, 4,809 foreign minor players, primarily citizens aged six to sixteen from Latin American countries, Cameroon, Nigeria, and Sierra Leone, have been found in Italian soccer clubs. In the Netherlands, thirty-six soccer clubs have been sued by the immigration office for illicit importation of twenty-six players, including eighteen minors from Latin America and seven from Ghana and Sierra Leone in Africa (Tshimanga, 2001). A report to the Italian Senate states that 5,282 non-European players under sixteen were employed by amateur soccer clubs, often subsidiaries of major clubs playing in Calcio (division 1).

Some individual stories have also surfaced in the sports news. In Belgium, Sonny Nwachukwu from Nigeria was tested in 1992 by the club of Genk and started playing with the professional squad without a contract. Afterward, he was transferred to Germinal Ekeren, and then to Tielen, still without signing any contract and playing for minimum wage. Khalilou Fadiga from Senegal (then a naturalized Belgian), now a star player in France (AJ Auxerre), has reported to the press that he had been conned by one players' agent when he was transferred from a club in Liège to a club in Lommel. Serge Nijki Bodo from Cameroon was approached by the Belgian soccer club La Gantoise (division 1) when he was seventeen and started training with the professional squad even though he had not signed a contract. After a while, the coach asked him to contact Racing de Gand (division 3), for which he signed a sheet of paper (not an official contract) in Flemish, a language he could not understand, covering only his accommodation without any wage at all. Then he signed an exclusive contract with an agent who charged 50% of his future income. The agent introduced Bodo to FC Malines and to the Denderleeuw club. In both cases, an excessively high transfer fee requested by the agent ended negotiations without a contract. The story was the same for Luciano Djim from the Centrafrican Republic, after he decided to join Sporting de Charleroi in Belgium.

Problems were so prevalent in Belgium that, in November 2000, fifteen young African players, most of them minors, lodged a complaint in Brussels and Antwerp courts against all the Belgian professional clubs and players' agents. They were complaining about a "trade of human beings" since, after being unsuccessfully tested and thus not hired by professional clubs, they had been abandoned by both clubs and players' agents. Once in that situation, as minors without either a labor contract or a return ticket to their home country, they became de facto illegal migrant workers in Belgium.

In France, the same story applies to Serge Lebri from Ivory Coast and Issiaga Conde of Guinea. Lebri unsuccessfully tested with FC Nantes and, at the age of fourteen, he had neither money nor a ticket home. He kicked around as an amateur until August 1999 when he was found to be without a French ID and expelled back to Ivory Coast. Returning to Africa that year, he enrolled with FC Africa Sports in Abidjan with no chance to return to Europe as a professional player. In 1998, Conde was invited to join the Nîmes Olympique squad (French division 2) at the age of sixteen. Immediately after his arrival at the club, the team managers confiscated his passport. He still negotiated (unsuccessfully) with Toulouse FC (division 1). After he was found to be without a French ID in October 2000, he was put in jail and sentenced to be expelled back home. But in Conde's case, for the first time in France, an African soccer player sued a soccer club (Nîmes Olympique) for illegal work and incitement to an irregular stay in France. French Minister for Youth and Sports Marie-George Buffet intervened on his behalf, arranging it so that he was not expelled. She had already been deeply shocked by the Lebri episode and did not want to face a second case. An official report (Donzel, 1999) has determined that Africa is the primary source of foreign teenage soccer players abroad for French clubs. An update shows that, for the season 1998–1999, fifty-eight non-European young players were under a contract with French clubs, including fifty African citizens; in 1999–2000, there were ninety-six African players out of the total of 108 non-European players.

In Italy, the Arezzo soccer club has been sanctioned for having recruited one player from Ivory Coast and four Argentine players, all under fourteen, without paying a penny out of the 133 euros promised to their families. This is only one example of "baby-calciatore" or "soccer children," between ages twelve and eighteen, torn by Italian professional clubs from their families in Latin America and Africa. In 1998, only twenty-three out of 5,282 non-European teenage players benefitted from a labor contract signed in due terms. In fact, the prestigious Juventus Torino FC initiated the whole business of international transfer of teenage players in 1991 by tearing three players, between the ages of thirteen and fifteen, from Ghana, with the aid of Domenico Ricci, the head of African Football Management, a player management agency. These three players were Osei "Sammy" Kuffour (now a star player in the German Bundesliga), Emmanuel Duah, and Mohamed Gargo, and not one of them ever played with the Torino professional squad. Instead, they were immediately transferred at a profit to the German club Bayern Munich (Kuffour), to Udinese (Gargo), and to another Italian club (Duah). Since then, Domenico Ricci has mediated over thirty-five transfers of Ghanaian teenage players to clubs throughout Europe. More than ten years after the first deal, the (sometimes legally questionable) international mobility of Third World teenage soccer players still remains unregulated.

No money accrues to either the national soccer federation or the nursery association when teenagers transfer internationally from nonaffiliated associations in their home country. As to transfers of players from affiliated clubs, a dumping price on the European labor market means a low transfer fee, which often does not even cover the education and training cost of the transferred player. And players' agents usually take the lion's share in the transaction with a high percentage (in any case higher than 20%) charged on the transfer fee and/or on the first wages earned by players.

A "COUBERTOBIN TAX" TO REGULATE INTERNATIONAL TEENAGE PLAYER MOBILITY

In 1978, Nobel Prize–winning economist James Tobin recommended a tax on foreign exchange transactions that "will throw sand in the wheels of international finance" and put a brake on excessively swift, short-term capital movements in world financial markets (Tobin, 1978). On the other hand, Pierre de Coubertin wished all the countries of the world to participate on equal footing in the Olympic Games. How is it possible to reconcile Coubertin's idea with the harshness of budget constraints in developing countries? Outlined below is a solution (not a panacea) that is likely to alleviate, along with some of the financial problems of developing countries, the aforementioned problem of muscle drain. Since the Tobin tax, as noted by Schulze (2000), is targeted at restricting short-term speculation, it must be redesigned to adapt to our purpose, a "Coubertobin tax," if you will.

Tobin was thinking, in 1978, of a multilateral and uniform tax that would be levied on all short-term foreign exchange transactions. In reducing the return on any foreign investment, the Tobin tax isolates the domestic interest rate from variations in the foreign interest rate. Thus, it would enable a country to implement an autonomous monetary policy and to slow short-term capital transfers. In more recent presentations (Eichengreen, Tobin, and Wyplosz, 1995), the Tobin tax is supposed to achieve three tasks: (1) increase the autonomy of monetary policy, (2) diminish exchange rate volatility, and (3) provide a source of revenues. It has been suggested that these revenues may help Third World countries redeem their foreign debt. Another purpose could be to use tax income for a sort of Marshall Plan in favor of developing countries. In 1998, Tobin even mentioned that the tax might be a useful protection for still-fragile banking systems in emerging economies. When it comes to protecting the banking system as well as raising income, the tax may well not be uniform. It may be levied with different rates depending on the term of the transaction, including a possible surcharge on the shortest term transactions considered as speculative attacks (Spahn, 1996).

What is suggested here is a Coubertobin tax with four purposes: (1) covering part of the education and training costs in the home country of players transferred abroad; (2) providing a stronger disincentive to transfer an athlete or a player from a developing country, based on player age at the time of transfer; (3) slowing the muscle drain transfer from developing countries to professional player markets in developed countries; and (4) accruing revenues to a fund for sports development in the home country, which would first finance sports-facility building and maintenance, thus facilitating practice for all in the sport. Second, the fund would finance physical education programs in schools, a sporting education reimbursement for the home countries of migrant athletes.

The idea is to levy the tax at a 1% rate on all transfer fees and initial wages agreed on in each labor contract signed by players from developing countries with foreign partners (usually foreign professional clubs and/or player agents). By its very existence, the Coubertobin tax should slow the muscle drain. A windfall benefit might be to slightly reduce the strong incentive for players to leave their home country by lowering the labor cost differential (including the tax) in home developing countries and host developed countries. Although not the only muscle drain, a specifically crucial issue is the international transfer of teenage athletes (mainly soccer players) from Africa and Latin America. The following suggests a graduated tax, including a surcharge on the transfer fee and initial wage of teenage and very young players, as follows. Let:

FR stand for the revenues raised through the taxation that are to be placed in a fund for sports development in the home developing country;

Pi stand for the international transfer price (fee) augmented with the first annual wage of the transferred player or athlete (in order to prevent a switch from the fee to the wage offered, or the other way around);

Vl stand for the player's value on the local market in the player's home country;

r stand for the exchange rate between the domestic currency in the home country and the hard currency of the importing host country;

T stand for a Coubertobin tax at a uniform rate of 1% for all transferred players, including those over 18 years old;

s stand for a tax surcharge for players under 18;

a be the player's age at the date of transfer;

a_1 be a first age threshold below which a tax surcharge is to be paid;

a_2 be a second age threshold below which the tax surcharge should be as much deterrent as possible;

a_3 be a third age threshold below which the tax is so heavy that it must have a prohibitive effect on transfers of extremely young players.

For instance, if a_1 = 18 years, a_2 = 14 years, and a_3 = 10 years, we can envisage a tax surcharge such as:

if $a_1 < a < a_2$, the tax surcharge s_1 will be 2% more for each month under the age of 18 at the date of transfer (thus transfering a player of 16 will cost a 48% surcharge),

if $a_2 < a < a_3$, the surcharge s_2 will be 10% more for each month below the age of 14 at the date of transfer (thus transfering a player of 12 will cost a 240% surcharge),

if $a < a_3$, the surcharge s_3 will be a 1000% lump sum tax (for instance a_3 = 10).

Thus the full formula of the Coubertin tax will be, under previous assumptions:

$$FR = (Pi - r.Vl) . T, \text{ if } a > a_1 \tag{1}$$

$$FR = (Pi - r.Vl) . [T + s_1 (a - a_1)], \text{ if } a_1 < a < a_2 \tag{2}$$

$$FR = (Pi - r.Vl) . [T + s_2 (a - a_2)], \text{ if } a_2 < a < a_3 \tag{3}$$

$$FR = (Pi - r.Vl) . (T + s_3), \text{ if } a < a_3 \tag{4}$$

Needless to say, and as with all tax schemes, tax and surcharge rates and age thresholds can be adjusted and revised to reach the four goals. The question naturally arises, "Who will pay the Courbertobin tax and possible surcharge?" It must be the affiliated professional club or the player agent responsible for the transfer that pays the bill for the transfer fee and the first year wage. If both are involved, both will help pay. Of course, in order to avoid double taxation, the tax should only be collected in the developing country. Furthermore, since there is a risk of bargaining and corruption surrounding the tax collection in developing countries, the collection of the Coubertobin tax should be monitored and supervised by an international organization. There are likely existing candidates, like the UN Development Programme or the World Bank, or an ad hoc international organization could be created (a sort of world agency for the Coubertobin tax, for instance, under the joint auspices of the UN and International Olympic Committee [IOC]). This international organization would govern the whole process of tax calculation, collection, and allocation and would have to solve any emerging conflict between a player's home country or nursery club and the recruiting professional club or player agent.

FEASIBILITY OF THE TAX AND POSSIBLE HINDRANCES

It is fair to expect that the new tax would meet with both hindrance and resistance. First, the Coubertobin tax will not be easy to implement and enforce insofar as it has to be accepted on a worldwide basis. But if it isn't, some free-riding developed countries (professional clubs) will still transfer teenage players without paying the tax, and this would both concentrate the most talented Third World migrant athletes and deprive some developing countries of the money that is intended to accrue to their sports development funds. Just like the Tobin tax (Bourguinat, 1987), the Coubertobin tax must be generalized if it is to to be efficient. There will be some (transaction) costs in levying the tax, borne by the home country, and a cost of supervision borne by the above-mentioned international organization, which will receive some determined percentage of the tax revenues. In any case, a cooperation is required between host and home countries, between Ministries for Sports, national Olympic committees, and sports federations. Since tax evasion would probably be higher than zero, as is the case for the Tobin tax (Baker, 2001), a specific fine should apply if tax evasion were discovered.

It is clear that the Coubertobin tax cannot be introduced without some sort of general agreement by all countries involved in athlete transfers (as with the general agreement on trades and tariffs, or GATT, one could call this a general agreement on tax and trade of athletes, or GATTA). Black market athlete transfers from countries that had not joined the agreement should be forbidden, those that do occur should be nullified and the responsible countries fined. It should be expected that professional leagues and clubs all over the world would attempt to resist the new taxation. The joint efforts of the UN, IOC, and international associations or federations (like FIFA in soccer), as well as political will in home and host countries, would be necessary to overcome the resistance. The international organization in charge of the tax administration should monitor that tax revenues are actually spent on sports development in home countries, including training the most talented players until they are eighteen in order to raise their international market value. Nevertheless, the suggested Coubertobin tax seems no less desirable and feasible than the Tobin tax (Palley, 2001) insofar as transfers of teenage or younger players is assessed as a harmful practice, specifically for developing countries.

A BRIEF COMPARISON OF THE TAX AND NEW FIFA REGULATION

The 1995 Bosman case removed restrictions on the free mobility of foreign soccer players within the European Union and the European Economic Area. However, in 1998, the European Commission issued a statement objecting to FIFA international transfer rules regarding the payment of transfer fees and the prohibition of early contract termination. A new FIFA transfer regulation (FIFA, 2001) came into force on September 1, 2001, containing a number of clauses relating to the protection of minors, training compensation, and a solidarity mechanism.

The new transfer rules limit the international transfer of minors (those under eighteen). Transfers of minors are prohibited unless the player's family moves for nonsoccer-related reasons. Within the EU-EEA, players under eighteen can only move if teams provide both athletic and academic training. The new rules also establish that compensation for training costs incurred between the ages of twelve and twenty-one is payable when the player signs his first professional contract and on each subsequent move to another team, up to the age of twenty-three.[4] The first payment of training compensation is distributed on a pro rata basis among the teams contributing to the player's training. The calculation of the training compensation is based on a four-tier categorization of teams to be determined by individual national soccer associations (federations). Finally, the new rules include a solidarity mechanism whereby 5% of all compensation payments for transfers involving players over the age of twenty-three will be distributed to those teams involved in the training of the player between the ages of twelve and twenty-three. FIFA has introduced new rules basically for securing a training compensation to nursery clubs, and for preventing player movement under eighteen, unless it is for athletic or academic training. However, there is no sports development objective for home countries.

The new FIFA regulation is a step forward in the same direction as the Coubertobin tax (Gerrard, 2002). In the first analysis, since the FIFA regulation is already in place, it is enforceable, although there may be chances for host professional clubs, player agents, and teenage players (or their parents) to circumvent them. We could imagine a player being naturalized on purpose, soccer-related moves by the player's family hidden behind apparently nonsoccer-related reasons, and false declarations about the player's age (a very common practice in developing countries). Further, by its very nature, the new FIFA regulation is restricted to soccer, whereas the suggested Coubertobin tax is applicable to all professional sports, both team and individual. If only for this reason, the tax would have a higher return and a stronger impact on financing sports development in home developing countries. Take the example of the Dominican Republic, which exports no soccer players but over 1,300 North American baseball players. Under the new FIFA rules, Dominican baseball associations or clubs would have received no compensation. But under the Coubertobin tax, a significant inflow of dollars would have helped sports development in the Dominican Republic (Andreff, 2002b).

There are a few other comparisions between the FIFA regulation and the Coubertobin tax. Levying such a tax would certainly incur a bureaucratic process. Implementing the FIFA rules is no less bureaucratic; however, it would be more cumbersome to calculate the amount of the FIFA-regulated training compensation than to apply the Coubertobin tax rate to a declared value Pi of the international transfer fee and initial wage. The return of the FIFA rules is surely higher for the transfer of players over age twenty-three (5% for the solidarity mechanism against 1% for the Coubertobin tax) and even for all players over eighteen, since the FIFA regulation applies to all cross-border transfers of a player, whereas the Coubertobin tax is suggested to be levied only on the first transfer from the home developing country. In this respect, the Coubertobin tax mechanism may be improved or adjusted by increasing the basic tax rate T up to 5%. On the other hand, the amount of money accruing to the home developing country will not be higher with the FIFA regulation than with the Coubertobin tax, since all the subsequent transfers (after the first one) of an African or Latin American player usually occur within European and/or North American labor markets, and not back to any Third World country.

When it comes to teenage players under eighteen the Coubertobin tax definitely outperforms the new FIFA rules. With the FIFA regulation, all transfers of players under age eighteen are prohibited from non-EU-EEA areas, thus generating no money for the home developing country. On the other hand, the FIFA rules absolutely block any sort of market mechanism and reduce teenage player mobility to exactly nothing, negating the usual economic and social right to free labor mobility and, possibly, the basic right of human mobility. For example, a teenage player may wish to be educated and trained *and* have his family live with him, once national migration laws had been taken into account. Therefore, the new FIFA regulation is neither economically nor ethically desirable compared to the Coubertobin tax.

Although it is throwing sand into the wheels of the market, the tax works with the market mechanism up to the point where the tax rate becomes prohibitive (s_3). But, even at this point, a club that is eager to transfer a player under age ten can still pay 1000% of his value for the privilege. No economic right (to trade) and no human right (to move) is eliminated. Moreover, the return generated by the Coubertobin tax is higher than with the FIFA rules for players under eighteen, and, in this respect, the former is more likely to favor sport development in home developing countries than the latter. The younger the transferred player, the larger the gap between the taxation and what the FIFA regulation yields (zero under age eighteen).

SUPERVISION OF THE PLAYERS' AGENT BUSINESS

Players' agents are obviously at the core of the international transfer business. A number of them have obtained a FIFA permit in order to enter the business. These officially recognized agents consider the rest to be unfair competition earning their return through nontransparent transactions. Although FIFA has established an approval procedure for player agents, reinforced by law in some European countries (for instance, article 15-2 of the French law passed in 1984), illicit transfers develop for two reasons. First, European clubs keep on dealing with unrecognized agents, despite FIFA disapproval. Second, some approved agents start player management companies that hire and work with unapproved agents. This even occurs in France, despite a law forbidding it. Outlaw agents are more inclined to deal with African and Latin American nonaffiliated associations and directly with teenage players themselves (and their parents) insofar as they are crowded out by approved agents from the more profitable market of transactions transferring the most famous European and non-European professional players. We can expect outlaw agents to keep on circumventing the new FIFA regulation by falsifying the age of players under eighteen. The lack of tight FIFA supervision over all player agents is detrimental to the whole business. In France, for example, only forty-six of over 200 agents hold a FIFA permit; in Belgium, the ratio is twenty-six out of 200.

FIFA has not yet recognized the right of national associations (federations) and nation-states to sue outlaw players' agents involved in dubious transactions. FIFA has launched official recognition of players' agents without involving nation-states, but no uniform regulation is in place to outlaw confidence tricks. The fact that FIFA has favored the development of the players' agent business without fixing any sort of juridical penalty and economic sanction in case of illicit transactions is the crux of the matter. Anyone who intends to act as a players' agent must exhibit a clean police record, must not be an attorney in his or her home country, and has to submit himself or herself to an interview with his or her domestic national soccer federation (an interview which is in no way an examination). Players' agents are a source of revenue for FIFA since each of them is required to post 200,000 Swiss francs (roughly $125,000) in order to obtain the FIFA permit. Anyone who can post this amount can start up a business with no further supervision.

A Conference of the Ministers for Youth and Sports from all French-speaking countries was held in December 2000 in Bamako, Mali, where the issue of FIFA de facto protecting the players' agents business in spite of many misdeeds was raised. The upshot of the conference was that FIFA should relinquish the permit and transfer permit allocation to national soccer federations, after a simple FIFA approval. In Belgium, a new regulation was adopted thereafter compelling anyone willing to enter the business, with or without a FIFA permit, to obtain a permit from both Belgian political and sporting authorities. With the new FIFA rules of September 2001 (FIFA, 2001, article 6), a soccer player who wants to move abroad must obtain an international transfer certificate from the national soccer federation he intends to leave. National federations are forbidden to raise any emolument or to levy a tax in relation to their delivery of international transfer certificates (article 8). This certificate would not hinder illicit transfers and bribes unless FIFA were to incite national and continental federations (like the European Union des Associations Européennes de Football [UEFA]) to adopt restrictive rules forbidding their affiliated clubs to deal with outlaw player agents and to sanction them otherwise. FIFA should also make it compulsory for any club or association in developing countries to be affiliated with the national soccer federation and thus be supervised regarding international transfers of its players abroad. Tshimanga (2001) suggests the creation of an international professional association of players' agents based on the model of the Bar—the association of barristers (attorneys)—that would sanction those guilty of misdeeds in the business. Such a player agent association should define and supervise fees and honorariums earned on international transfers of soccer players. All legal, administrative, and sports authorities together should converge toward the enforcement of clear contracts linking players to their agent. This should be binding on agents in order to stay in the business.

CONCLUSION

The reader must be aware of the limited scope of the policy recommendations sketched in this chapter. No long-term solution to the muscle drain of talented teenage players can avoid an integrated policy for sports development in developing countries. The broader issue involves generating the required finances for sports development, a factor that cannot be divorced from progress toward self-sustained economic development and reducing wage gaps between developed and developing countries, including the gap between professional athletes. Unfortunately, the regulation of the international mobility of teenage players can only alleviate the most undesirable consequences of the muscle drain. The suggested Coubertobin tax can put a brake on international transfers of very young players,whereas the new FIFA regulation pretends to abolish them simply by forbidding them. Neither of these two regulations is likely to be 100% efficient. Neither will entirely phase out illicit transfers undertaken by outlaw player agents. We reach the point where economic tools must be complemented by administrative and legal measures that aim to control the players' agent business.

NOTES

1. Or even immediately, when a young player has been imported from a developing country—in particular through the underground market at a dumping price, one much lower than the player's actual value (see Chapter 5 of this volume). Thus, investing in a talented young player from the Third World is often an opportunity for a European club to gain some surplus value after a resale. (For information on player trade as a source of finance for European professional clubs, see Andreff and Staudohar, 2000). The dumping price most likely appears when it does not even cover the cost invested by the nursery club in the player's education and training, which is fairly typical for African and Latin American players transferred to Europe.

2. It may be argued that such "recruit and sell" transactions exhibit Rottenberg's (1956) invariance principle at work.

3. In some African countries, the executives of the national football federation utilize the international transfers of players from their country as a way to make illicit money, asking for bribes before delivering the exit letter required for the young player to leave the country. For example, the Ghanaian football federation seems to have been plagued with bribes and embezzlements for delivering exit letters in a number of illegal transfers, as it revealed in 2000 (Tshimanga, 2001).

4. The idea that backs this rule may be expressed as follows: The surplus value appearing in each player's transfer from a European club to another one must be redistributed, including to the nursery club located in a developing country. It should help soccer clubs of the Third World to muddle through their deep financial problems (Tshimanga, 2001).

Part III

Western Europe: Competitive Balance Issues

7

Economic Inequalities within and between Professional Soccer Leagues in Europe: Sporting Consequences and Policy Options

H. F. Moorhouse

INTRODUCTION

Professional soccer is Europe's major sport. Traditionally, with a few very minor exceptions, soccer has been organized through a series of national leagues under the control of national soccer associations. The top European soccer authority is the Union des Associations Européennes de Football (UEFA), a federation of national associations, which has ultimate control over all competitions—including in national leagues—within its region. Since the 1950s, international club tournaments have been organized under the control of UEFA, as another layer of competition. The main new competition, the European Cup, began as a straightforward, traditional knockout competition. Champions of national leagues within Europe qualified to join the competition in the next season. Teams were drawn "out of a hat" in pairs. The two teams played each other at home and away, and the overall winner went into the next round, where new pairings were drawn. Eventually, other competitions—notably the UEFA Cup—were devised to allow other teams from national leagues to meet in pan-European contests. In time, qualification for this international competition also came to depend on success in national leagues (i.e., clubs finishing in second place, third place, etc.) or, occasionally, in national cup competitions. In this way, success in domestic national leagues has become a means to a major additional source of prestige, extra games, and increased revenue through international competition. In the mid-1990s, UEFA bowed to the pressure of a threatened breakaway by some of the biggest clubs in Europe, and made various changes to the format of the European Cup. The competition was rebranded as the Champions League, but the new arrangement is not just for champions, nor is it entirely a league. The number of participants expanded to include not only the winners of national leagues, but those that finished second, third, and even fourth in the biggest countries (media markets). Moreover, the champions of various small nations (media markets) had to play through more qualifying rounds in order to enter the Champions League proper. Then the format moved away from a traditional cup competition to include one, and later two, league group stages on the way to qualifying for the last eight places, when a cup format took over again. In these and other ways, the entry of top clubs in the biggest countries to the most important and lucrative pan-European competition was facilitated, whereas the top clubs of small countries had to jump extra hurdles in order to participate. The distribution of revenues from the Champions League for the 2000–2001 season reveals that clubs from the "Big 5" leagues of Italy, Spain, England, Germany, and France gained over 75% of the money available in principle to clubs from all over Europe. In many cases, payments made in relation to the size of their national market were much greater than what clubs earned via sporting success, especially for the clubs from Germany and France (details found at www.UEFA.com, August 21, 2001).

Thus, a handful of the biggest European clubs is involved in a structure unforeseen in the conventional economic theory of sports leagues, usually based on American sports and American evidence. These clubs now operate simultaneously in two "league competitions"—at a national level and an international level. Contemporary pan-European club competitions are taking on something like the form (as well as the name) of leagues, and, so the biggest clubs argue, this requires that they generate and spend sums roughly equivalent to their Continental rivals. The issues about sporting and economic competition that tend to preoccupy these elite clubs relate to a European, rather than a narrowly national, context. However, the clubs regularly involved in European competition now earn much more money than other clubs, however "big" they are in the history of various nations, which cannot achieve such continuous participation. These clubs are coming to dominate their national leagues more firmly than in the past. However, many giants on a national scene become very small at the international level. Thus, the trend is for a double level of predictability within European soccer. National competitions are becoming more dominated than ever before by just a few clubs, most of which are inherent "also-rans"' at the Continental level of competition. But neither clubs nor soccer authorities nor European political institutions have given much indication that they are ready to discuss issues about "maintaining the league," and "uncertainty of outcome," and to address issues about effective revenue sharing at the national, let alone at the European, level. The crucial issues facing contemporary European soccer are (a) recognizing and understanding the effects of great income disparity between supposedly comparable sporting rivals; (b) figuring out how competitive balance is to be maintained; (c) maintaining and increasing spectator interest in soccer in all geographic regions (media markets); and (d) not allowing unregulated market forces to decide the competitive patterning of the sport. Yet such issues are little discussed in Europe and do not influence policy development (Moorhouse, 2002). Hence, one issue for comparative economic analysis is that European soccer is operating on a (mainly non-discussed) adherence to market forces that puts American sports to shame. And, as I will address later, a lot of recent academic analysis and consultancy reports explicitly or implicitly promote market forces as the desirable, or even the only, principle upon which the sport can be efficiently organized. The comparison with sports in the United States could scarcely be starker.

INEQUALITIES

In this chapter I focus on one aspect of the general issue. I will detail and discuss a growing imbalance between traditionally major clubs based in nations with large, and relatively affluent, populations and traditionally major clubs based in nations with small populations, however affluent they may be.

The *Deloitte & Touche Annual Review of Football Finance* (2002) contained, as a new feature, a review of the finances of clubs in the top divisions of the various national leagues across Europe. The accountants estimated the total income accruing to these top clubs in Europe as 6.6 billion euros; the share of this total for clubs based in different countries is shown in Table 1.

Table 1 certainly does not tell the entire story of income with regard to top European soccer teams. For example, in many countries rich benefactors, sometimes even the state, intervene with certain clubs to provide them with income or income-generating opportunities that do not show up in balance sheets in any transparent way. Still, with such a caveat made, Table 1 does reveal the broad outline of some of the important income inequalities operating in European soccer.

In European discussions it has become conventional to refer to the dominance of the Big 5. As Table 1 reveals, the top clubs in these leagues do take 78% of the income made by all the top clubs within UEFA. But, even within this dominance there are profound inequalities. The top eighteen clubs in France have well under half the income of the twenty supposedly equivalent clubs in England. And, as I will discuss later, such imbalances are all the more marked once we note that there are notable inequalities between clubs within various leagues. To give one example, the G14 group of clubs that acts as a lobbying group (by no means, as I note below, the fourteen richest clubs in Europe) takes about one-third of the total aggregate income for all of the top ninety-four clubs within the Big 5 leagues. TV payments are the largest

Table 1
Estimated Percentage of Total Income of All Top Clubs in UEFA Accruing to Clubs in Various Nations, Financial Year 2000–2001

Nation	%	Clubs Involved
England	24	20
Italy	17	18
Spain	14	20
Germany	13	18
France	10	18
Netherlands	4	18
Scotland	4	10
Portugal	2	18
Belgium	2	na
Greece	2	na
Austria	1	na
Switzerland	1	na
Denmark	1	12
Norway	1	14
Sweden	1	14
Other 36 countries in UEFA	3	na
	100% = euro 6.6 billion	

Source: Developed from Chart 1.10, Deloitte & Touche (2002, 16).

single contributor to club income, providing 2.4 billion euros, or 46%, of the 5.2 billion euros total income going to the Big 5 (Deloitte & Touche, 2002, 9–11).

Leagues and big clubs based in countries with smaller populations cannot match this kind of income. TV income provides no more than 23% of total income, and in Denmark and Norway it is only 4% of top league revenue. Two elite European clubs—Manchester United (England) and Real Madrid (Spain)—have incomes greater than all of the top clubs in Denmark, Norway, and Sweden combined (Deloitte & Touche, 2002, 11–12). Such comparisons make clear that even the top clubs in small nations simply cannot compete in economic terms with big clubs in bigger nations and that this is likely to have sporting effects. Deloitte & Touche refer to this: "Income for the 'big five' Leagues is growing faster then in small markets; hence clubs in the 'big five' Leagues are gaining a significant competitive advantage every year that goes by. Therefore, in order to stay competitive on the field, clubs located in smaller markets feel they need to payout the same absolute levels of wages, which consumes relatively more of their income, leading to their decline in operating profitability" (15).

And that same source provides its own explanation:

> Firstly, and most importantly, the maturing of the TV markets in the "big five" countries—and the consequent rapid increase in broadcasting income to clubs located there—has a consequential impact on clubs based in smaller markets. When, before that time, most clubs had a revenue split made up principally of gate income, then there was a much higher degree of financial balance between clubs across Europe—whether your club was in Rotterdam or Rome wouldn't make that much difference. However, now that TV income is the single largest income source in the larger markets—where you are located (and the demographics of your home market) really does matter to your income. Secondly, the Bosman ruling precipitated the full internationalisation of the market for players. This, in turn, has allowed the gravitation of players to where the money is. (15)

But, having raised the issue, the Deloitte & Touche volume avoids analyzing all the sporting and policy issues here, lapsing into only posing rhetorical questions: "Will this landscape of market share polarise yet further? Or will the smaller countries manage to turn the tide, through, for example, cross-border competitions?" (16). For in fact, Deloitte & Touche's focus, like many other analysts, is very concentrated on the biggest clubs in the biggest leagues, and, indeed, on promoting their interests as an inevitable aspect of the marvelous magic of market forces.

A COMPARISON OF THE FINANCIAL SITUATION OF DUTCH, PORTUGUESE, SCOTTISH, AND ENGLISH CLUBS

To illustrate some of the issues involved in this inequality, I have gathered information on four major leagues in Europe. The English Premier League is one of the Big 5 leagues, as previously discussed. Holland, Portugal, and Scotland represent cases of small countries that have traditionally big clubs within them—clubs good enough, on occasion, to win European club competitions.

Table 2 reiterates the pattern of inequalities revealed in the Deloitte & Touche summary. The top divisions in Holland and Scotland earned approximately the same in the 1998–1999 season (although the number of clubs involved was different). Portugal is well below this level, revealing disparities even within the grouping of small nations. But all of the small nations lag far behind the income of England's main clubs. Already, it should be clear that clubs based in these leagues are likely to face problems in sporting competition with clubs based in big countries.

Table 3 shows the patterns of income inequality within as well as between leagues. If anything, the patterns understate the levels of inequality because it is now the top three, or even two, clubs in most leagues that are the economically dominant grouping. Nevertheless, Table 3 does reveal significant

Table 2
Income of Premier League in Dutch Florins (Dfl.), 1998–1999

Holland:	Dfl. 400m	(18 clubs)
Portugal:	Dfl. 240m	(18 clubs)
Scotland:	Dfl. 369m (i.e. £107m)	(10 clubs)
England:	Dfl. 2,318m (i.e. £670m)	(20 clubs)

Source: Deloitte & Touche, 2000; Koninklijke Nederlandsche Voetbalbond, 2000; PricewaterhouseCoopers, 2000; Portuguese National Sports Ministry, 2002.

inequalities within the clubs based in the top division of their respective national leagues. In the smaller countries, the top four clubs take from 53% to 79% of all income accruing to the big clubs of their countries, whereas in England, the top four take only 39% of Premier League income. So, assuming the income distribution is reasonably similar for other years, these clubs have a big economic advantage in their national competitions, and they are indeed the clubs that, increasingly, dominate national leagues. But, to take the extremes, the biggest four clubs of Portugal have an average income of around 43 million Dutch Florin (Netherlands Guilder) each, whereas the average income for an English club in a similar structural position is over five times this sum at 228 million Dutch Florin. Remember, these are the big clubs in each national league that are likely to meet in pan-European sporting competition, yet the economic disparities are so great that it seems quite unlikely that the big clubs from small leagues will be able to compete effectively in sporting terms, and, empirically, increasingly they do not. Remember, too, that some clubs that finish lower down the leagues and are not in the top four clubs economically are likely to meet in other European-wide competitions. Here again, to take an example the bottom fourteen clubs in Holland have an average income of 14 million Dutch Florin, whereas the average income for an English club in a similar structural position is six times

Table 3
Income of Top Four Clubs in Premier League in Dutch Florins (Dfl.), 1998–1999

Holland:	Dfl. 210m	(i.e. 53% of league total)
Portugal:	Dfl. 172m	(i.e. 72% of league total)
Scotland:	Dfl. 292m	(i.e. 79% of league total)
England:	Dfl. 912m	(i.e. 39% of league total)

Source: See Table 2.

Table 4
Top Four Clubs' TV Income from Domestic League Games in Dutch Florins (Dfl.), 1998–1999

Holland:	Dfl. 10m
Portugal:	Dfl. 21m
Scotland:	not available but 2 top clubs got around Dfl. 9m (i.e. £2.6m) *each* from this source
England:	Dfl. 140m (i.e. £40.5)

Source: See Table 2.

this sum at 88 million Dutch Florin. Again, a major structural economic inequality seems likely to militate against the sporting achievement of clubs from small nations even in Europe's "secondary competition."

Similar patterns are revealed in Table 4, which shows how the top four clubs in each league fare from their national TV deals. The clubs in Portugal and Scotland get broadly comparable sums. The clubs in Holland get significantly less. But the clubs in England are far in advance of them all, and this relative advantage has increased tremendously since the 1998–1999 season. Traditional mechanisms to redistribute income within leagues have been marginal in Europe and have been truncated in recent years, and new vibrant streams of income have developed outside their limited scope (Moorhouse, 2000). Given the disparities of TV income, which is not much shared within leagues, let alone between leagues, it is clear that big clubs in small countries are facing a new and more or less insurmountable obstacle to effective sporting competition.

In addition, evidence on the cost structures of clubs in the various leagues reveal that wage costs for those in small countries form a much higher proportion of total costs than in the league in England. And this advantage for clubs located in bigger markets is maintained, even extended, when the wage costs of the elite clubs in each league are compared. Among other things, this means big clubs in small countries have less money available to create other income streams and to develop local talent. In the current structuring of European soccer, all advantages lie with clubs located in big markets. Clubs, however traditionally big, located in small markets seem to have two main options: They can gamble, spending money they do not have in order to compete and hope that success in European competition will produce the extra income to bridge the gap, or they can rein in their ambitions and cease trying to compete at the highest level of European club competition.

In this section I have tried to supply more detail about the size and ramifications of current inequalities between supposedly comparable sports teams in Europe's key sport. Given the likely sporting consequences of what I have shown, what policy options are currently being proposed to deal with this situation? What solutions are being offered for the plight of traditionally big clubs located in small countries?

POLICY OPTIONS: RELIANCE UPON UEFA?

UEFA, as the official governing body for European soccer, tends to deny the issue as I have presented it, starting rather from the Bosman case of 1995. It argues that the European Court's intervention disrupted an otherwise automatically equilibrating system based on labor market restrictions, and, particularly, on the workings of the traditional transfer system.

In 2001, under pressure from the European Commission, UEFA had to defend the post-Bosman transfer system. In the document it prepared for the Commission UEFA constantly refers to the transfer system as "the most effective wealth redistribution mechanism" and claims that

> the transfer system is a market-based system which helps to hold the game to-gether, redistributing wealth from the rich to the poor, enabling investment in youth systems and ensuring the integrity and competitiveness of football across a wide geographical area . . . the current system has a positive stabilising and wealth redistributing effect. (UEFA, 2000, 1)

It asserts:

> Transfer fees provide the crucial element of solidarity in a world of football that is increasingly polarised between large and small, rich and poor. It is a natural—workable and working—mechanism for the redistribution of wealth between large and small countries, leagues and clubs, which ensures that European foot-ball remains the diverse family that has made it so successful. (UEFA, 2000, 2)

UEFA provides evidence that supposedly supports these claims, which I reproduce in Table 5. Via this table—which excludes international transfers to and from countries outside the European area—UEFA tries to show that "certain European countries—England, Spain, and Italy for example—are net transfer spenders redistributing their relative wealth to other European leagues. The majority of countries are net receivers of transfer fees" (UEFA, 2000, 2).

There are various problems with UEFA's line of analysis. To begin with, UEFA claims to draw this information from a survey of its national associa-tions. But although national associations are concerned with the bureaucratic transfer of player registrations between clubs (and hence nations), it is not at all clear that they will have knowledge of the financial details of transfers, which are commercial transactions between clubs constituted as legal enti-ties. And, in countries such as England where transfer details show up on

Table 5
Net Transfer Spending for Sample of UEFA
Member Countries (Transfer to/from Other
European Union/European Economic Area
Countries)—Aggregate 1997–1998 to 1999–
2000 (Euro Millions)

England	−263
Spain	−147.6
Italy	−104.4
Scotland	−87.4
France	−28.8
Germany	−6.5
Wales	0
Luxembourg	0
N. Ireland	+0.3
Hungary	+1.3
Slovenia	+1.4
Iceland	+1.9
Finland	+3.8
Poland	+5.8
Slovakia	+6.6
Denmark	+7.5
Belgium	+13.1
Sweden	+16.2
Netherlands	+44.1
Hungary	+49.6
Norway	+57.2

Source: UEFA (2000, Figure 1).

company balance sheets (although not in any standardized way), they would not be disaggregated as between internal transfers, external between members of the European region, and external to the rest of the world. So UEFA's figures must be estimated in some undisclosed way, and I suggest that these figures are probably much less accurate than UEFA might want its readers to believe.

That said, we can also see that there are various oddities in Table 5 that UEFA does not mention. First, Table 5 contains information for twenty-one soccer countries out of UEFA's total of fifty-one or so at the time of this writing. The total outflow from the six countries that are net spenders is 637.7 million euros, of which about 40% comes from one country, England. The total inflow to the thirteen countries shown as net receivers is only 208.5 million euros, less than a third of the supposed outflow. Some of the missing money may flow to the many members of UEFA not included in Table 5. However, it would be odd politics on UEFA's part not to mention the lack of inclusion if that were the case, for those not listed include many small countries that, so UEFA claims, benefit from the redistribution effects of the transfer mechanism. But, as UEFA claims the information in Table 5 does not concern international transfers outside Europe—to Africa, Latin America, and so forth—which can have little do with any "solidarity" system between big and small, rich and poor, within Europe, where the missing 400 million plus euros actually went is something of a puzzle.

Second, the sums involved here need to be put in perspective. Table 5 shows an apparent redistribution of 208.5 million euros over three seasons, an average of around 70 million euros per season, shared among thirteen countries. Table 1 above shows that Deloitte & Touche (2002) put the total income for only the top clubs across Europe in the season immediately following those summarized in Table 5 at 6.6 billion euros. It follows from the disparity between these figures that any redistribution between rich and poor within Europe affected through any "automatic," "natural" workings of the transfer system is minuscule in relation to total income, especially the income of the big leagues and the biggest clubs within those leagues. Moreover, we can see that any redistribution is highly concentrated. Of the 208.5 million euros over three years, nearly three-quarters, 150.9 million euros, flows to just three countries—the Netherlands, Hungary, and Norway. So, as is always the case, any financial redistribution from the transfer system flows to just a few beneficiaries (Moorhouse, 1999). Last, and of great interest, we find that UEFA does not comment on the fact that Germany—one of the rich Big 5— redistributes very little revenue via the transfer system, whereas one of the biggest net spenders—Scotland—is a soccer country with clubs in exactly the same structural position as those in the Netherlands and Norway (see Table 1 above). These two examples alone suggest that the transfer system does not operate in any automatic way, trickling money down a hierarchy from rich to poor. In fact, the position of Scotland in Table 5, reflecting the attempt of the two biggest clubs there to match the spending of the biggest clubs in Europe, actually reveals the dangers that threaten all big clubs based in small countries. Both these Scots clubs now carry massive debts, have had to renounce the expansive transfer and wage policies that placed them in this position, and are downsizing their sporting ambitions.

UEFA insists that "football's transfer system . . . is a working system redistributing wealth generally, and particularly from 'big clubs' and 'big leagues' to 'smaller clubs' and 'smaller leagues'" (UEFA, 2000, 2).

Yet its own figures simply do not support this assertion. It can only make this kind of claim by not subjecting its evidence to the kind of critical analysis I have sketched out here. In addition, we should note that UEFA seems to be quite content, indeed even seems to advocate, that small countries, and the traditionally big clubs in them, *should* exist financially by selling their best talent to bigger leagues and clubs in those leagues. Here, and quite characteristic of European analysis, American theoretical and practical concern with maintaining competitive balance in sports tends to slip into an argument about some natural route to securing the economic viability of the existing structure. This way of framing "the crucial question" facing European soccer virtually ensures that big clubs based in small markets will have no chance of competing at the Continental level, but can only hope to exist as developers of talent for clubs in bigger markets.

I have tried to show that UEFA is obsessed with labor market restrictions as the route to maintaining financial viability of the current soccer structure in Europe and tends to conflate this objective with that of maintaining competitive balance. UEFA seems to regard small countries and clubs within those countries as inevitably subservient to big countries and clubs within those countries, and it avoids the whole issue of revenue sharing. Crucially, it has been very successful in passing its version of the "problem" of European soccer on to the European political authorities. But following UEFA's policy prescriptions will not address the problems of competitive balance within European soccer, which is steadily becoming more critical.

POLICY OPTIONS: RELIANCE UPON THE G14 CLUBS?

As mentioned, G14 is a grouping of clubs and acts as a lobbying group with UEFA and the European political authorities. The original fourteen clubs were made up of three from Italy; two each from Spain, Germany, England, France, and Holland; and one from Portugal. The conventional shorthand description of them as "Europe's richest clubs" is far from true—the clubs from France, Holland, and Portugal certainly do not belong in that category—and disguises the complexities inherent in European soccer. The grouping was originally formed by a handful of economically dominant clubs, but, as a gesture to sporting inclusion, a few historically successful teams were added. The result is something of a mishmash. Indeed, we have the anomalous situation that the three clubs within the G14 from Holland and Portugal are among those that, in recent years, have tried at least twice to establish a new transnational Euro League so they could have a chance of staying in economic touch with their fellow G14 members (Moorhouse, 2002).

The G14 countries want to persuade UEFA and national associations to allow clubs a bigger part in decision making; to have more discussion about who should be able to exploit the rights to competitions in which clubs are playing; and to control the explosion of costs in soccer. And there are some major differences in views. Whereas UEFA wants to cut the number of matches played in the Champions League competition, the secretary general of the G14 argues for more games, on the grounds that if you make it a little bit bigger, the interest will be stronger. . . . There are various possibilities. Either you restrict access to the Champions League, or you increase the number of teams which come from stronger footballing nations. . . . G14 as a general principle wants fewer weak teams in the Champions League. . . . You could increase the number of teams from the biggest countries. (*The Observer* [UK], 2002)

In brief, what the G14 grouping (expanded by another four clubs in 2002, one new club each from England, Germany, France, and Spain) really wants to achieve is the creation of a permanent elite of rich clubs based in bigger nations of Europe and exercising more overall control of soccer. This already much advantaged group would then have an even more privileged access to pan-European club competitions, and the income that they generate, than it does now. And it would in effect restrict the ability of other clubs, including those based in small countries, to ever compete with this elite. The G14 group rarely mentions revenue sharing or issues of competitive balance, and offers very little hope to big clubs based in small countries, many of which have applied, unsuccessfully, to become members of the group.

POLICY OPTIONS: NORTH AMERICAN–TYPE SALARY CAPS?

One policy option being much promoted in European soccer at the present time is the introduction of salary caps. In mid-2002, *The Financial Times* hailed a series of "groundbreaking measures" agreed to by the G14 countries aimed at curbing spiraling costs and introducing self-regulation:

The proposals mark the first time leading football clubs have unilaterally committed themselves to avoiding overspending. . . . The group aims to stop this from happening by introducing self-regulation, which, it hopes, will eventually be adopted by all the other professional clubs in Europe. . . . [T]he first aim was to reduce the competition between G14 clubs in the transfer market. (*The Financial Times* [UK], 2002)

The principles fell short of a full salary cap, which might have alarmed the competition authorities of the European Union, so *The Financial Times* claimed that the culture commissioner of the European Union had helped the G14 group draft its measures. UEFA expressed support for the G14 proposals and linked the initiative to its own plan to license clubs financially before they would be allowed to enter its pan-European competitions. However, UEFA stated that it could not legislate for a general salary cap throughout European soccer, as this might fall foul of European law.

Later in 2002 the chief executive of the English Football Association promoted his "fight to rationalise the wild economics of English football" announcing the setting up of an American-style clearing house to monitor and supervise all transfer deals. It will also monitor the role of players' agents, who have over recent years been driving up the wages of individual players while often flouting the terms and spirit of existing contracts. There will be discussions . . . on the pressing need to cap salaries and general budgets, which is a concept long accepted in the multimillion-dollar professional sports industry in the United States. (*The Independent* [UK], 2002)

The British Society for Sport and Law arranged a discussion on salary caps in May 2002 (*Sport and the Law Journal*, 2002), which was notable because it contained a contribution by the head of the Deloitte & Touche soccer analysis team—the company the G14 group had announced would monitor the operation of its new gentlemanly cap. The analyst argued that soccer had to stop the rise in players' wages. It was impossible to get a flat cap, but one calculated as a percentage of turnover would be achievable. And other policies could be put in place to bolster the success of a cap: (a) players' pay should be more related to performance, (b) there should be agreed limits on the size of clubs' playing squads, (c) clubs should come to gentlemanly agreements to limit the size of transfer fees, and (d) there should be more benchmarking and information exchange between clubs because currently players' agents were often much better informed. The representative from Deloitte & Touche, who had acted as a consultant to both UEFA and the G14, did not mention competitive balance and did not express much interest in the problems of small European leagues and big clubs in those leagues.

Recent European discussion on salary caps suffers from a number of flaws. If, as the G14 countries have stated, their unofficial cap is not intended to discriminate against the very richest clubs, then it is not going to be a meaningful intervention in terms of competitive balance. Their proposal for a salary cap is intended to help out some of the biggest European clubs currently suffering financial embarrassment, but not to actually inconvenience any of them. Proponents have certainly not gotten down to the hard issues of how any cap would be positioned so as to promote competitive balance. But then the initiative is not really about balance. Much of the recent promotion of salary caps as a necessary innovation reveals the characteristic tendency of European analysis to pluck policy elements from the United States without any concern, even as lip service, for issues of competitive balance, but rather as a means through which to mount arguments for the extension of labor market restrictions. Via salary caps an old policy is being justified through a "modern" U.S.-legitimated rhetoric, but is one that is unlikely to withstand legal challenge. And, if implemented and if successful (both highly unlikely), it would again freeze the current dominant position of some clubs. The real danger is that the idea of salary caps as the solution to the problems of European soccer could prove very attractive to the European Commission. It would serve their political ends in appearing to "do something" about the state of European soccer and check "greedy players," without any comprehensive and well-documented discussion of what the critical problems of the sport actually are and how best they might be solved.

POLICY OPTIONS: ACADEMIC ANALYSES

The concentration of big clubs and big money has not gone unnoticed by academics, but the issues I have tried to raise here are not subject to any deep analysis in most of a recent deluge of books purporting to uncover the crucial features of "the new soccer business" (Morrow, 1999; Hamil et al., 1999; Hamil, Michie, and Oughton, 2000; Garland, Malcom, and Rowe, 2000). Hoehn and Szymanski (1999) certainly do directly confront some of the issues I have been emphasizing, but they argue against revenue sharing on the grounds that, theoretically, it has perverse effects, although they are moved to note:

> Given the theoretical prediction that revenue sharing will adversely affect competitive balance and investment opportunities, it is perhaps surprising that the National Football League in the USA manages to maintain both a relatively balanced competition and a high level of playing investment. One explanation might have to do with the objectives of owners. (Hoehn and Szymanski, 1999, 221)

Which is to say that controllers of European soccer clubs might actually be utility maximizers, which would profoundly disturb Hoehn and Szymanski's basic theoretical assumption.

Hoehn and Szymanski advocate a closed U.S.-style franchise system as the way forward for European soccer. Their article focuses on revenue sharing only to dismiss it as an irrelevant mechanism for Europe. They move on to concentrate on a few possible labor market restrictions, but there are many difficulties in their analysis, both in their outline of the problems of European soccer and in the solutions they supply. Among the most crucial are that they do not follow the full logic of American systems of sports organization, but pick and choose the elements they want; and they accept current economic imbalances between clubs as given and do not see that they may need curbing if clubs from all parts of Europe are to have the chance to participate meaningfully in elite competition.

In brief, what Hoehn and Szymanski offer, based on some doubtful theoretical assumptions, is a mainly unregulated future for European soccer in which market forces will decide patterns of sporting competition. They seem to assume that this scenario will somehow allow more than a tiny handful of European clubs to compete meaningfully for the major prizes and that all Europe does not need (or deserve) to be drawn together via its paramount sport. In this cold appraisal, small markets must expect to have less fun.

One other recent academic text appears to make more of an effort than most to get at the issue of competitive balance, declaring it the most fundamental issue in the economics of team sports (Dobson and Goddard, 2001, 16). Dobson and Goddard stress the analytical difficulties that arise in applying theory derived from American sports to the European context:

> Two important premises of the US literature seem questionable in respect of European football: first, the assumption of profit maximising behaviour on the part of clubs; and, second, the assumption that the available stock of playing talent is fixed. (2001, 125)

They suggest that most European clubs seek a more modest goal than profit maximization and argue that the European model for the organization and regulation of team sports varies from U.S. model in many crucial ways: (a) the greater number of clubs, (b) the system of promotion and relegation of clubs, (c) the absence of profit maximizing behaviors, (d) the extensive transfer system, and (e) the lack of development of revenue sharing systems. Still, they tend to equivocate on exactly what this means in policy terms:

> North American assumption of closed player labour markets and profit maximising behaviour do not necessarily transfer directly across the Atlantic. Nevertheless the theoretical literature does suggest strongly that caution needs to be exercised before advocating simplistic remedies for perceived trends towards excessive championship domination by a handful of big-market teams, both in England and elsewhere in Europe. (Dobson and Goddard, 2001, 187)

When they directly address the current situation in Europe, Dobson and Goddard try to indicate what has caused new problems of competitive balance but then go on:

> Having identified rising competitive imbalance as perhaps the most fundamental problem currently facing professional football, and having pin-pointed growth in the market for televised football as its ultimate cause, it is now possible to move on to examine a number of specific policy issues currently facing decision makers, including the sport's governing bodies, clubs owners, broadcasters, sponsors and legislators. The discussion will be organised into three subsections, which consider current proposals for European leagues; the issue of players' wage inflation; and issues of ownership, control and media interest in football. (2001, 425)

Theirs is a very disappointing culmination, because, having raised the fundamental policy problem of competitive balance, these authors avoid addressing it directly, choosing rather to discuss issues peripheral to the main one. There is a real failure of analytical drive to confront directly the crucial problems of competitive balance as they are showing themselves in European soccer (see Szymanski, 2003, for a somewhat similar judgment).

CONCLUSION

I have outlined some of the major economic inequalities in European soccer and pointed to the likely sporting consequences. Basically, big clubs based in small countries can no longer compete effectively, as they once could, in pan-European tournaments, and this is only one aspect of a much wider problem. But there is no willingness to face up to this problem in European discussion. As I have indicated, analysis is often truncated, theories based on American experience and evidence are something of a straitjacket on discussion, and the governing bodies—and the consultants they hire— tend to confuse issues so as to align predetermined "solutions" with a backward-looking and empirically suspect agenda. National and European political authorities will likely continue to accept these "authoritative" pronouncements of "the problem" and "the solutions" unless and until issues reach the courts, if they ever do.

In such a situation, academic discussion becomes one of the few potential sources of more dispassionate and rational analysis. Academics need to engage more closely with the fundamental issues and offer more critical evaluations of the arguments and evidence of the soccer world authorities. They need to make realistic assumptions about the aims and objectives of the owners and controllers of European clubs, and they need to be prepared to branch out when necessary from American theory and American evidence. At the very least, they need to state clearly and then debate the advantages and disadvantages of comprehensive systems of revenue sharing in European soccer, at both the national and Continental levels of competition. And they need to ensure that their discussions reach national sports ministries and the European Commission officials concerned with sports. For some years, European soccer, at its highest levels, appeared to be thriving. But the apparent health likely contained and covered deeper flaws and trends that, in not too long a time frame, poisoned the whole structure. Now is the time for sports economists to create a truly comprehensive discussion of the causes, and likely consequences, of the range of economic inequalities that have become embedded in the organization of European soccer.

8

Buying Success: Team Performance and Wage Bills in U.S. and European Sports Leagues

Robert Simmons and David Forrest

INTRODUCTION

The question posed in this chapter is: To what extent, if any, does expenditure on playing talent, as measured by team wage bills, translate effectively and reliably into playing success? The bulk of the theoretical literature on sports economics, from El Hodiri and Quirk (1971) on, assumes the relationship to be robust. Large market teams will dominate small market teams because they hire more talent, and they hire more talent because high win percent is more valuable to them. The chain of reasoning depends entirely on the assumption that greater spending on talent will indeed translate to higher win percent. Yet, puzzlingly, some North American literature reviewed below and relating mainly to baseball in the 1980s, posited no empirical link between wage expenditure and playing success. The puzzle is potentially resolvable with two possible explanations. First, there may be potential for mistakes in assessing talent prior to the signing of long-term contracts so that, for example, a winner's curse might operate, undermining any clear relationship between wage expenditure and playing success. Second, institutional restrictions on player mobility, brought about by mechanisms such as the college draft in North American sports, could create a monopsonistic players' labor market and break the relationship between wages and success in team sports.

Such explanations may not be needed. Baseball in the 1980s may be an aberration, and in this chapter we show that a statistically significant relationship between team salaries and team performance measures can, in fact, be derived across a wide variety of sports leagues, which vary greatly in degrees of league regulation of the players' labor market as well as in physical game characteristics and in the structure of the tournament played. These leagues are the English Premiership (previously First Division) soccer, Italian Serie A soccer, German first division soccer (Bundesliga 1), Major League Baseball (MLB), National Basketball Association (NBA), National Football League (NFL), and National Hockey League (NHL). Each of the seven leagues analyzed delivers a significant team salary-performance relationship when points ratio or win percent are used as measures of team performance.

First, team performance is measured by win percent ratios for North American leagues and by points achieved divided by maximum possible for European soccer. Second, team performance is analyzed using probability of qualification for playoff competition in the North American sports and probability of obtaining a top six position in European soccer leagues. As far as possible, we construct our panels for the various leagues over a fairly uniform time period, the 1980s and 1990s. Although measures of team salaries will inevitably differ in scope across the leagues, it is still worthwhile to attempt a comparative analysis of pay-performance relationships across different sports leagues.

The structure of the chapter is as follows. We begin by reviewing previous literature and setting out our empirical models. We then report the data to be used and address some measurement issues. Next, we assess results from estimates of win percent (or points ratios) for different leagues and also report results from probit estimation of probability of achievement of a playoff berth in North American sports and top six league position in European soccer leagues. A final section offers concluding remarks.

LITERATURE REVIEW AND MODELS

A number of writers have suggested that there is at best a loose association between team salaries and performance in North American sports (Buchanan and Slottje, 1996, 144; Quirk and Fort, 1999, 83–87; Sanderson and Siegfried, 1997, 10; Scully, 1995, 94; Zimbalist, 1992, 96). Such statements are not always supported by empirical evidence and are strongly influenced by observation of baseball. Zimbalist found for MLB that between 1984 and 1989 average team salary explained less than 10% of the variance in team win percent. This lack of correlation between average team salary and team performance was attributed by Zimbalist to a failure of team owners to sign top performing free agents and also a failure to pay players according to their output. Conversely, a strong correlation would be indicative of a close relationship between player salary levels and their contributions to revenues. Scully argues that increased expenditure on playing, coaching, and managerial talent is a necessary, but not sufficient, condition for improving a team's win percent ratio, and this would again reduce the strength of any correlation.

Two papers in a recent symposium revisited the relationship between team salaries and team performance in North American sports. Hall, Szymanski, and Zimbalist (2002) replicate Zimbalist's earlier (1992) result of lack of correlation between team payrolls and win percent values in regular season MLB play in the 1980s. Using single season regressions rather than pooled data, which would improve efficiency of estimation, a robust, statistically significant annual correlation between wage bill and win percent emerges only after 1994. Probing further with the use of Granger causality tests, the authors find evidence of two-way causation between payroll and performance after 1994. Reverse causation from performance to payroll is argued to be due to restrictions of trade in top players and to the occurrence of long-term employment contracts. If success is correlated across seasons, then free agents and players one year away from free agency can earn large pay increases when the team is doing well. Owners will still be reluctant to trade players close to free agent status if a surplus over marginal revenue product remains.

A simpler reason why team salaries may be determined by team performance is that salary data may be compiled toward the end of the season when performance closely approximates final league standings. Zimbalist (2002) shows that, in the NHL, midseason payrolls are more closely correlated with win percent than beginning-of-season payrolls. This again suggests two-way causation between payroll and performance. Teams doing well midseason will likely spend more acquiring better players to enhance their prospects of play-off appearance. Moreover, use of performance-related bonuses may obscure any underlying relationship between salary bill and performance.

Szymanski and Kuypers (1999) investigated pay-performance relationships for English soccer in the post-war period, building on work in Szymanski and Smith (1997). Their dependent variable was average log odds of league position, defined as the average value for each club of log (position/93-position) over a given sample period. There were ninety-two clubs in the league structure over the periods considered. The independent variable was log of club average wage expenditure for a sample period relative to the average of the sample. Their analysis was hampered by lack of availability of financial data for all clubs, restricting the sample to forty over the 1978–1997 period and twenty-eight over 1950–1960. Nevertheless, significant regressions were obtained for each period, with a higher goodness of fit (0.78 compared to 0.50) found for 1978–1997. The authors interpreted their results as support for the notion of greater efficiency of the labor market for soccer players following a reduction of league regulation and considerable movement toward "freedom of contract" for players after 1978.

Following the work of Szymanski and his colleagues, we expect to find a stronger relationship between team payrolls and team performance in European soccer leagues, as indicated by goodness of fit and size and significance of regression coefficients. But we shall show that this relationship can be generalized to North American sports as well. This generalization is achieved despite the greater extent of player market regulation in North American sports leagues.

The context for North American interventionist measures is a restricted global market for player talent. Given that credible rival leagues to the North American majors do not exist, players tend to be drawn from domestic sources, and imported talent is rare.

With profit maximization in North American sports, players with the highest marginal revenue product gravitate to the teams best suited for their talents. The efficient matching of teams and players is hindered by player market intervention measures, but some correlation between individual pay and productivity should remain. Aggregating across team squads, we predict some correlation between total payroll and team performance in North American leagues.

The model to be estimated for North American leagues is:

$$WIN\ PERCENT = \alpha_0 + \alpha_1 RELATIVE\ WAGE\ BILL \qquad (1)$$
$$+\ \alpha_2 RELATIVE\ WAGE\ BILL\ SQUARED$$
$$+\ \alpha_3 RELOCATION + \alpha_4 EXPANSION + \text{team effects}$$
$$+\ \text{error}$$

Relative wage is defined as team i's wage bill divided by the league average in a given season. This, rather than total wage bill or average wage, is used as the primary independent variable. This is so that dependent and independent variables each have comparable scales, thereby reducing the scope for heteroscedasticity in the residuals. Also, the use of relative wage automatically controls for salary inflation, which, in all leagues surveyed, was far in excess of economywide wage inflation over the sample periods.

We include some league-specific control variables. Franchise expansion in North American sports leagues is modeled by means of a dummy variable, *EXPANSION*, which has the value of one for the first two seasons of a new franchise. Examples of new franchises are the Colorado Rockies (MLB, 1993) and the Jacksonville Jaguars (NFL, 1997). For the NFL, we distinguish between expansion franchises and franchise relocation. The latter case is captured by another dummy variable, *RELOCATION*. An example is the move of the Los Angeles Rams to St. Louis, Missouri, in 1995. We hypothesize that relocation teams will have lower win percents than established teams for given relative wage since they must pay higher salaries to their players to compensate for the costs and disruption of moving in midcareer. A relocation team may have to pay more in total salary than an established team to maintain the same win percent and may also suffer reduced home advantage for a time (Pollard, 2002).

The case of expansion teams is less clear cut. In the NFL, expansion teams receive favorable treatment in two ways. One is the "expansion draft," under which new teams can pick up to three players per team from a designated list of rivals' players. Second, expansion teams receive favorable treatment in signing free agents under salary cap rules. New teams generally build their squads as a combination of expansion draftees and free agents. League rules may permit the formation of a more talented squad, for a given wage bill, than is possible for existing teams. However, it is possible that NFL players who are drafted from existing franchises would expect to be compensated in salary for their perhaps involuntary move. Then expansion teams might have to pay more than established teams for players of given talent.

All of the European leagues had some restrictions on free agency for part of the sample period. In European soccer, prior to the 1995 Bosman ruling, a player could not move between different national associations without the consent of the club holding the player's registration. Also, European leagues restricted the number of foreign players on each domestic team. For example, only three foreign players could appear in an Italian league team. These restrictions were ruled in the Bosman case to be contrary to the principle of free movement of labor as embodied in the Treaty of Rome (Simmons, 1997). A consequence has been the internationalization of European soccer teams through opening up trade in player talent and resulting in movement of players worldwide. The proportion of domestic players in English, German, and Italian clubs has fallen considerably.

For European soccer, therefore, we predict a relationship between club relative wage bill and club performance, measured as the ratio of points achieved to the maximum possible. For these leagues our model is:

$$POINTS\ RATIO = \beta_0 + \beta_1 RELATIVE\ WAGE\ BILL \qquad (2)$$
$$+\ \beta_2 RELATIVE\ WAGE\ BILL\ SQUARED$$
$$+\ \beta_3 PROMOTION + \beta_4 THREE\ POINTS$$
$$+\ \text{team effects} + \text{error}$$

The dummy variable *PROMOTION* has the value of 1 for clubs promoted at the end of the previous season. In England, three clubs are promoted and relegated to and from the twenty-member Premier League clubs each season. In Italy, four of eighteen clubs are relegated from Serie A, to be replaced by promoted clubs. As noted above, the value of points per win has been increased in European soccer leagues; we denote the new regime by the dummy variable *THREE POINTS*.

The choice of functional forms in equations (1) and (2) is based on goodness of fit together with Ramsey RESET tests. A variety of functional forms (linear, log-linear, and linear-log) failed to improve on the quadratic specification. The quadratic form suggests diminishing returns to relative payroll in the performance function. Successive increments to team payroll relative to competitors deliver smaller gains to win percent or points ratio.

In assessing team performance, the emphasis on winning percent or points ratio may well be misplaced. A team in a league competition is probably less concerned with win percent or points ratio than with its relative standing. In all leagues surveyed here, there is the opportunity to go forward into a higher level of competition. All major North American leagues have play-offs, leading to a grand championship such as the World Series, the Super Bowl, or the Stanley Cup. With varying playoff structures, the probability of playoff qualification, and not just win percent, is a plausible target for North American franchises, and this suggests that we can usefully model team performance using a probit specification with probability of playoff qualification (*PLAYOFF*) as the dependent variable. Independent variables are as specified earlier, and we retain the quadratic form in relative wage where this is supported by the data. Where retaining the quadratic form is not possible, we simply report results with relative wage as the independent variable. Since the probit model is nonlinear, we report marginal effects at varying magnitudes of relative wage. The probit model contains the same variables as for the win percent and points ratio models supplemented by dummy variables for particular seasons when the number of playoff qualifiers was greater than normal. This kind of probit model has not, to our knowledge, been estimated previously in the sports economics literature.

European soccer teams can also qualify for a higher level of competition than the top division of their leagues. Good performance this season is rewarded by qualification for a Europe-wide competition the following season, which is played concurrently with the domestic leagues. The two competitions currently offered are the European Champions League and the less prestigious Union des Associations Européennes de Football (UEFA) Cup. For European soccer, our dependent variable in a probit model is the probability of appearance in the top six places in the domestic league (*TOP 6*). For many teams, however, a more realistic objective than entry into European competition is simply survival in the top division, especially as demotion to the division below typically entails large losses of revenue from sales of broadcasting rights, sponsorship, and gate receipts. Hence, we use another probit model for probability of relegation from the top division, which is predicted to be negatively related to relative wage. For this probit model, the quadratic form of relative wage was clearly rejected.

DATA

The use of win percent ratios for evaluation of team performance is standard in North American sports. Ties do not occur in MLB or the NBA and are comparatively rare in the NFL. The only North American league to feature ties prominently is the NHL, which has, since 1999–2000, the additional feature of allowing each team in a match one point if regulation time ends in a tie, and an extra point if a team wins the match in overtime. For the NHL, we measure total points scored divided by 164, which represents eighty-two games at two points per game.[1]

In the computation of the point ratios for European soccer, we divide points achieved by maximum possible points. The European norm is currently three points for a win and one for a draw. Exceptions in our data are for England in seasons 1977–1978 to 1980–1981, Germany in seasons 1981–1982 to 1994–1995, and Italy in seasons 1987–1988 to 1993–1994, when a win was awarded two points. A dummy variable captures the later regime of three points for a win.

Wage bills were compiled from various sources, noted in the Data Sources section at the end of this chapter. North American data were taken from Web sites, selected as those offering greatest consistency in measurement over several seasons. For the NHL, we had access to individual salaries as well as team wage bills, and aggregating wage bills across player rosters gave similar totals to those reported as aggregate wage bills on other Web sites. Where narrow and broad definitions of pay were offered, as in the NFL where signing bonuses were reported, we took the narrower figure. The selected wage variable for the NFL is the narrowest available, containing "base salary" only and excluding signing bonuses. Base salaries are paid only to players who are on the active roster. Frick, Dilger, and Prinz (2002) offer empirical evidence from the NFL to show that signing bonuses have adverse impacts on player effort and team performance because payment is essentially made to depend on expected performance, resulting in a "hold-up" problem. Thus, inclusion of signing bonuses in the wage variable would probably lower the size of the coefficient on relative wage in the NFL regression.

Our aim was to obtain salary data across the 1990s, and we succeeded for all main North American sports except from the NHL, where consistent data begin in 1995. It should be stressed that the North American wage bills represent total salaries, usually at beginning of season, of players only and do not include payments to coaching or administrative staff or other personnel.

In contrast, the European figures for wage bills represent wages and salaries paid to all staff, not just players, and are taken from clubs' accounts. In German soccer, the measure of wage bill is the "budget," which is planned expenditure on labor costs for the following season, used as a proxy for the actual wage bill. Hence, salaries of coaching staff are included in the European data. Unavoidably, the wage bills of North American and European sports are not directly comparable.[2]

Descriptive statistics of win percent, points ratio, and relative wage bill are shown in Table 1. In European soccer, the award of three points for a win reduces the mean points ratio below 0.5. In Germany, the sample excludes some relegated clubs, and this raises the mean points ratio above 0.5. In North America, win percents must have a mean of 0.5 by construction,

Table 1
Descriptive Statistics of Win Percent, Points Ratio, and Relative Wage

	Points ratio or win percent				Relative wage		
	Mean	**Min**	**Max**	**S.D.**	**Min**	**Max**	**S.D.**
English Soccer (n=364)	0.473	0.190	0.810	0.120	0.226	2.325	0.377
German Soccer (n=246)	0.520	0.206	0.779	0.111	0.281	2.828	0.425
Italian Soccer (n=214)	0.480	0.118	0.853	0.134	0.266	3.101	0.628
MLB (n=441)	0.500	0.327	0.716	0.067	0.202	1.836	0.332
NBA (n=429)	0.500	0.134	0.878	0.161	0.499	2.043	0.220
NFL (n=574)	0.500	0.056	0.938	0.186	0.586	1.532	0.149
NHL (n=263)	0.510	0.238	0.794	0.099	0.460	1.879	0.275

with the exception of the NHL and its recently instituted "extra point for overtime" rule.

Only MLB comes close to the European soccer leagues in standard deviation of relative wage, with a value of 0.332, somewhat below 0.377 for English soccer. The impression from the descriptive statistics is of fairly compressed distribution of total wage bills in North American leagues, in contrast to wider distributions of payrolls across European leagues. In part, this difference reflects the franchise method of team allocation in North America in which each team must be capable of commanding a suitably large market size in order to maintain its franchise status. In European soccer, admission to the top division is by promotion rather than by submission of a financial case by a franchisee. In Europe, any small market team can in principle soar to the top division, regardless of its balance sheet and the number of competing teams in its locality, whereas North American leagues tend to implement a high degree of geographical separation between teams. To this can be added the deliberate design of pay compression across teams in North American leagues, by reverse order draft, salary caps, and restrictions on free agency.

EMPIRICAL RESULTS

Win Percent and Points Ratio Models

Results from fixed effects estimation of equations (1) and (2) are shown in Tables 2A and 2B.

Fixed effects are significant for all leagues. For North America, the expansion and relocation dummies are not significant, except that NBA expansion teams do worse than established teams in terms of win percent. In English soccer, but not German or Italian, we find that promoted clubs have higher points ratio for given relative wage than established clubs. This difference may be due partly to sluggish adjustment of player contracts, with some still being paid relatively low salaries based on contracts negotiated when the club had lower status. As contracts are renegotiated to reflect top division status, players' salaries will tend to rise. There may also be a momentum effect associated with promotion.

The best fitting model is for Italian soccer, with an R-squared value of 0.60. With fixed effects included, the adjusted R-squared is much higher for European soccer leagues than for the North American leagues. This is consistent with the argument of Szymanski and Kuypers (1999) that relaxation of labor market regulation should induce an improved fit of the aggregate pay-performance relationship. However, we must caution that when the contribution of unknown fixed effects is stripped out, the within R-squared shows similarly low values across all leagues, Italy excepted. The possibility of omitted variable bias remains serious.

The weakest equation is for the NFL, where both the within and total R-squared values are very small (0.03), unsurprising given the very regulated nature of this league. The NFL has a reverse order player draft, restrictions on free agency, and a "hard" salary cap to regulate the player market. Both the range and standard deviation of relative wage values are much smaller than for the other leagues. Also, the NFL has a fixture schedule such that teams with high performance levels play more difficult games against opponents from outside their divisions than do teams with weaker records. This arrangement, along with ticket revenue sharing, reinforces

Table 2A

OLS Pay-Performance Regressions with Fixed Effects, European Soccer, Top Division (Dependent Variable Is Points Ratio)

Variable	England	Germany	Italy
RELATIVE WAGE	0.380	0.107	0.308
	(4.12)	(4.78)	(5.13)
RELATIVE WAGE SQUARED	-0.087		-0.056
	(2.55)		(2.86)
PROMOTION	0.042	-0.018	0.012
	(2.38)	(0.84)	(0.72)
THREE POINTS	-0.053	-0.020	-0.056
	(3.69)	(0.86)	(4.57)
CONSTANT	0.233	0.417	0.271
	(3.96)	(17.85)	(7.08)
Seasons	1977/8-2000/1	1981/2-1995/6	1987/8-1998/9
N	364	246	214
R-squared (within)	0.17	0.11	0.32
R-squared	0.42	0.38	0.61
Turning point on *RELATIVE WAGE*	2.18		2.75
Number of observations beyond turning point	1		5
Impact of 0.1 increase in rel. wage, points ratio=			
0.5	0.029	0.011	0.025
1	0.021	0.011	0.020
1.5	0.012	0.011	0.014
2	0.003	0.011	0.008
2.5	-0.006	0.011	0.003

Note: In all tables, figures in parentheses are *t*-statistics.

the process of deliberate equalization of team strength. With such an array of tough intervention measures it is perhaps surprising that any correlation between team payrolls and team win percents can be discerned. A further reason for a poorly fitting equation for the NFL is that noise dominates the pay-performance relationship when the fixture list is so short (six-

Table 2B
OLS Pay-Performance Regressions with Fixed Effects, North American Leagues:
MLB, NBA, NFL, and NHL (Dependent Variable Is Win Percent)

Variable	MLB	NBA	NFL	NHL
RELATIVE WAGE	0.093	0.719	1.136	0.487
	(8.37)	(3.88)	(2.73)	(3.10)
RELATIVE WAGE SQUARED		-0.217	-0.476	-0.179
		(2.80)	(1.92)	(2.62)
RELOCATION			-0.054	-0.090
			(0.99)	(1.36)
EXPANSION	0.010	-0.111	-0.052	0.073
	(0.46)	(2.64)	(0.50)	(1.34)
CONSTANT	0.406	0.013	-0.147	0.213
	(35.18)	(0.12)	(0.57)	(2.44)
Seasons	1985-2001	1985-2001	1981-2000	1989,1995-2001
N	441	429	574	263
R-squared (within)	0.15	0.14	0.03	0.06
R-squared	0.18	0.19	0.03	0.19
Turning point on *RELATIVE WAGE*		1.66	1.19	1.36
Number of observations beyond turning point		8	58	26
Impact of 0.1 increase in rel. wage, points ratio=				
0.5	0.009	0.050	0.066	0.031
1	**0.009**	**0.029**	**0.018**	**0.013**
1.5	0.009	0.007	-0.030	-0.005

teen games). Expenditure on playing talent is inherently risky when luck can play a large part in the standings.

Our central finding from Tables 2A and 2B is that a higher relative wage raises performance in all seven leagues, despite institutional heterogeneity. Also, the squared term in relative wage is significant in all leagues except German soccer and MLB. This supports our notion of diminishing returns in wage bill: teams enhancing their performance measures by increasing spending on wages relative to their competitors but at a decreasing rate.

In Tables 2A and 2B, we report turning points and marginal effects of relative wage. For all five leagues where the quadratic form is supported, the turning point is inside the sample range; an increase in relative wage beyond the turning point appears actually to harm team performance. The number of cases in the range in which negative returns to relative wage is encountered is very small in English and Italian soccer, but quite substantial in the NFL and NHL. With a compressed salary distribution across teams, as is apparent in the NFL and NHL, it is also not surprising that several teams stray into the territory of negative returns to relative wage. Such an outcome may simply be due to inaccuracy in gauging the appropriate team wage bill when total wage bills are so equal.

What is striking about the results in Tables 2A and 2B is their similarity despite considerable variation in league structures and labor markets. The quadratic form in relative wage is supported in all but two leagues, and the marginal effects of relative wage at the mean are not hugely dissimilar, except perhaps for the NBA. The within R-squared values, picking up the extent of variation accounted for by the explanatory variables, are similar for some U.S. and European leagues. Notable exceptions are Italian soccer and the NFL; we would argue that the latter is an extreme case within North American sports. The strongest differences are to be found in the turning points of relative wage in the leagues in which the quadratic form is supported. The relative wage at which further increases appear actually to harm team performance is rather low in the NFL and NHL, at below 1.4, partly reflecting the narrow dispersion of wage bills in these leagues. In contrast, teams in English and Italian soccer can push total spending on wages and salaries to well beyond double the league average without damaging prospects for league standings. Diminishing returns to relative wage set in much earlier for North American leagues than for European soccer.

Probit Models of Probability of Top-Six Place or Playoff Qualification

Results from probit estimation of probability of reaching a top-six place in European soccer leagues are reported in Table 3A, and Table 3B shows probit estimates of probability of relegation. Table 3C shows results from probit estimation of playoff qualification for North American leagues. Conditional fixed effects estimation of a probit model is not possible since the fixed effects cannot be conditioned out of the likelihood function. Imposition of team-specific dummy variables (unconditional fixed effects) would result in biased estimates. Experimentation with a random effects specification failed to improve on the reported estimates. For ease of interpretation, the tables report marginal effects rather than coefficients.

Table 3A
Probit Estimates of Probability of Achieving Top-Six Place in European Soccer
Leagues, Marginal Effects

Variable	England	Germany	Italy
RELATIVE WAGE	1.968	1.174	1.886
	(3.85)	(3.71)	(5.42)
RELATIVE WAGE	-0.432	-0.203	-0.425
SQUARED	(2.17)	(1.65)	(4.16)
PROMOTION	0.173	-0.140	0.083
	(1.67)	(0.10)	(0.54)
Seasons	1977/8-2000/1	1981/2-1995/6	1987/8-1998/9
N	364	246	214
Pseudo R squared	0.32	0.24	0.45
Turning point on *RELATIVE WAGE*	2.28	2.89	2.22
Marginal effect of 0.1 increase in relative wage from:			
0.5	0.010	0.025	0.016
1	**0.111**	**0.077**	**0.104**
1.5	0.058	0.053	0.081
2	0.010	0.020	0.008

Note: In Tables 3A to 3C, all marginal effects are computed using robust standard errors.

The squared term on relative wage is significant (at 10%) in five out of seven leagues; the exceptions are MLB and the NFL. In the case of German soccer, the value of relative wage that maximizes probability of a top-six place is higher than the sample maximum. In English soccer, there is just one observation of a team that has a relative wage in the range beyond the turning point such that an increase in relative wage actually reduces probability of a top-six appearance. Even in Italian soccer, there are only eleven observations beyond the turning point. Hence, the role of the squared term in relative wage is to raise the degree of nonlinearity in what is already a nonlinear model.

The reported marginal effects capture nonlinearity in the relative wage term. These show some interesting differences, both across levels of relative wage for a given league and across leagues. In all three European soccer leagues, raising the relative wage from a value of 0.5 has little impact on probability of a top-six place. For these teams, such an achievement is simply

Table 3B
Probit Estimates of Relegation in European Soccer Leagues, Marginal Effects

Variable	England	Germany	Italy
RELATIVE WAGE	-0.246	-0.150	-0.209
	(4.04)	(2.32)	(5.60)
PROMOTION	0.091	0.052	-0.019
	(2.35)	(1.03)	(1.61)
Seasons	1977/8-2000/1	1981/2-1995/6	1987/8-1998/9
N	364	246	214
Pseudo R squared	0.20	0.14	0.34
Marginal effect, 0.1 increase in rel. wage from 0.5	-0.073	-0.041	-0.149

Note: In Tables 3A to 3C, all marginal effects are computed using robust standard errors.

not realistic, and their objective will simply be to retain top division status by avoiding relegation. At a relative wage of 1, marginal effects of a 0.1 increase in relative wage become much greater for English and Italian soccer. At a relative wage of 1.5, diminishing returns of top-six probability to relative wage set in sharply. A relative wage of 1.5 should be sufficient to ensure a high chance of a top-six place and further increases in relative wage bill will not add substantially to the prospects of a place in next season's European competitions.[3]

In the case of European soccer leagues, promoted teams do not have any different probability of a top-six place in Germany and Italy, for given relative wage. There is slight evidence (at 10% significance) that promoted teams to the English top division enjoy greater probability of a top-six place, possibly through a momentum effect, but results for probability of relegation also reveal a higher probability.

From the probit model of relegation in Table 3B, we observe substantial marginal effects of relative wage at a relative wage of 0.5; around this value, teams that are at high risk from relegation and extra spending on salaries will be highly likely to pay off in terms of safety. At a relative wage of 1, teams that are very likely to have spent enough to avoid demotion and further increases in wage bill have much less additional payoff than at lower relative wage values. Hence, spending one's way out of relegation trouble is a plausible strategy in European soccer leagues. There is the caveat, however, in England: Promoted clubs have a higher risk of relegation at given relative wage and so must spend even more than comparable teams to ensure safety.

In the cases of North American leagues, we experimented with a set of year dummies to control for the various strikes and lockouts that may have

Table 3C
Probit Estimates of Playoff Appearance in North American Leagues, Marginal Effects

Variable	MLB	NBA	NFL	NHL
RELATIVE WAGE	0.498	2.345	0.380	2.516
	(6.97)	(3.81)	(2.75)	(4.48)
RELATIVE WAGE SQUARED		-0.656		-0.967
		(2.55)		(3.75)
EXPANSION	-0.088	-0.291	-0.036	-0.134
	(0.69)	(1.64)	(0.18)	(1.00)
RELOCATION			-0.260	
			(2.83)	
1982 STRIKE			0.177	
			(1.82)	
Seasons	1985-2001	1985-2001	1981-2000	1989, 1995-2001
N	441	429	574	263
Pseudo R squared	0.11	0.11	0.02	0.09
Turning point on **RELATIVE WAGE**		1.85		1.31
Marginal effect, 0.1 increase in rel. wage from:				
0.5	0.023	0.064	0.029	0.101
1	**0.050**	**0.103**	**0.038**	**0.059**
1.5	0.060	0.019	0.038	-0.034
2	0.041	-0.007	0.030	

Note: In Tables 3A to 3C, all marginal effects are computed using robust standard errors.

led to a revision of the number of teams eligible for playoffs. The only significant dummy variable (at 10%) for any league was for the 1982–1983 NFL season (*1982 STRIKE*). In that season, the strike by players shortened the regular season, and sixteen teams rather than ten qualified for playoffs. Hence, 1982–1983 NFL teams had a greater chance of playoff qualification given relative wage.

Also in the NFL, we find that relocation teams have a lower probability of playoff qualification, given relative wage, than established franchises. Alongside the need for relocation teams to pay higher wages to compensate players for the disutility of moving, we may add the difficulties faced by in-coming franchises in gaining fan support and in establishing team and sta-dium infrastructure. In contrast, expansion teams do not suffer any reduced probability of playoff appearance, given relative wage, in any league (at 10% significance).

For North America, it should be borne in mind that the NBA and NHL have a greater number of playoff places relative to league size, sixteen out of twenty-nine, compared to MLB and the NFL. Arithmetically, then, play-off qualification is easier in the NBA and NHL. The NBA and especially the NHL stand out as the two cases for which a low spending team (relative wage of 0.5) can substantially enhance its playoff prospects. In contrast, starting from a relative wage of 0.5, MLB and NFL teams add little to their playoff prospects by increasing their relative spending on salaries. At a relative wage of 1, the marginal effect of an increase in relative wage for NBA teams is on a par with that of European soccer teams for appearance in the top six in their leagues. Moving to the top end of aggregate salary distribution, with a relative wage of 1.5, MLB teams still have substantial increases in playoff prospects, whereas diminishing returns set in for NBA and NHL teams, very severely in the latter case.

The flatness of marginal effects across relative wage levels in the NFL stands in sharp contrast to the nonlinearity observed in other North American leagues. The marginal effects of a 0.1 increase in relative wage are less than 0.04 at all relative wage levels in the NFL. This highlights the extraordinar-ily interventionist product and labor market arrangements in this league, as suggested earlier. What emerges from our probit estimates is that the mar-ginal effect on playoff appearance for an NFL team is virtually the same re-gardless of how much is spent on salaries relative to the league average. This suggests that playoff qualification in the NFL is largely a lottery. The NFL playoff lottery is due to league regulation, as noted above, exacerbated by a short regular season of sixteen games in which luck plays a greater part in playoff allocations than it would in a bigger schedule. A team that has two or three bad results due to bad luck, including injuries and refereeing deci-sions, may find itself out of playoff contention despite investing substantially in its playing squad.

Faced with our empirical results, a prospective bidder for a major league franchise would be ill-advised to invest in the NFL. The return to invest-ment is simply too risky. Instead, the potential investor ought perhaps to look closely at the NBA, for it is there that more secure returns can be found. Starting at a wage bill close to the league average, the new owner can gain a more substantial increase in playoff probability than would occur in our other leagues from an investment in playing talent. The potential investor would similarly do well by pursuing this strategy with a top division English or Italian soccer club.

CONCLUSIONS

We have estimated team salary-performance relationships for seven sports leagues, four from North America and three from European soccer. Our main findings are:

- Higher relative spending on team salaries will generate higher win percent or higher points ratio in any league, regardless of league design or specific measures to regulate the player labor market. This finding holds even for the "egalitarian" NFL, albeit with low R-squared.
- Overall R-squared values are lower for regressions in North American leagues than for regressions in European soccer. This reflects the greater extent of regulation of player labor markets in North American sports compared to European soccer.
- For most leagues, spending on wages and salaries that outstrips rivals' spending is subject to diminishing returns. In some cases, such as the NFL and NHL, negative returns to relative wage arise at just over the average wage bill.
- In European soccer leagues, a higher relative wage is associated with increased probability of a top-six place in the division. This normally implies qualification for higher level European competition in the following season. Further, at the lower end of the wage bill distribution, an increase in relative wage lowers the probability of demotion, an outcome that would have severe adverse impacts on team revenues.
- In North American sports, a higher relative wage is associated with increased probability of playoff qualification. The marginal effects of relative wage from probit regressions of playoff probability show considerably different patterns across the four major sports leagues. The NBA has a highly nonlinear profile across relative wage values, with large marginal effects at low relative wage values, whereas the NFL has a flat profile. Playoff qualification for the NFL appears to be a "lottery."

NOTES

1. Use of total points rather than win percent for the NHL made little difference in our results.

2. Unfortunately, there is a further problem in that, up to the 1993–1994 season, not all English top division clubs filed accounts, and so for seasons prior to 1993–1994 we have missing information on salaries. Similarly, for Germany, we also have missing records of the budget, mainly for relegated teams. Financial data for Italian soccer are complete. See Noll (2002) for a full discussion of criticisms of the use of balance sheet data for analysis of English soccer.

3. The number of observations where relative wage exceeds 2 is four in England, seven in Germany, and eighteen in Italy. This suggests that most teams plan their budgets so that negative marginal returns to wage bill are avoided.

DATA SOURCES

English soccer: Wage bills up to 1992–1993 from Szymanski and Kuypers (1999); thereafter from various editions of Deloitte & Touche, *The Annual Review of Football Finance*; performance measures from various editions of *Rothmans Football Yearbook*.

German soccer: data provided by Erik Lehmann.

Italian soccer: data provided by Umberto Lago.

MLB: Player salaries from http://baseball1.com/bb-dta, compiled by Doug Pappas. League standings from StatsCentral, http://statsc.freeservers.com/mlb/mlb_90st.html, and http://sportsillustrated.cnn.com/baseball/mlb/standings.

NBA: Player salaries from www.dfw.net/~patricia, compiled by Patricia Bender. League standings from StatsCentral (see MLB).

NFL: Team wage bills from Rod Fort's Web site, http://users.pullman.com/rodfort/SportsBusiness/BizFrame.htm, collated by *USA Today* from NFL Players Association reports. League standings from http://www.geocities.com.

NHL: Player salaries from http://www.lchockey.com and http://www.nhlpa.com, reported by NHL Players' Association. League standings from http://www.geocities.com.

9

Revenue-Sharing Arrangements and the Survival of Promoted Teams: Empirical Evidence from the Major European Soccer Leagues

Bernd Frick and Joachim Prinz

Fans get to see the best in the places where it pays the most and the rest
of the fans get to enjoy the level of play that they are willing to support,
financially.

—R. Fort (2000, 439)

INTRODUCTION

Since the publication of Rottenberg's (1956) and El Hodiri and Quirk's
(1971) seminal papers, the question of whether market forces can (or ought)
to be restricted in order to maintain or foster competitive balance has been
a constant topic in discussions among sports economists. Whereas some argue that such interference is necessary to produce an attractive and commercially viable product, others maintain that any such interference is to the
detriment of sports fans, and possibly also the players. This discussion has
for a long time precluded the theoretical and empirical analysis of alternative organizational structures, some of which may be more incentive compatible than others without threatening the long-term legitimacy and
integrity of the sport (Franck, 1995). We intend to fill this gap in the literature by providing a "comparative institutional analysis," à la Williamson—
an analysis that looks at a specific outcome of a specific organizational feature
of almost all major team sports leagues in Europe. At the end of each season the weakest performers in the top division are relegated to the second

division in the league hierarchy, and the best performing clubs from the second league are promoted to the top division.[1] One of the most interesting questions arising in this context is whether certain institutions or changes in the institutional framework substantially affect the survival probabilities of promoted teams.

To the best of our knowledge, a comparative study of the relative performance of promoted teams does not exist yet. This chapter attempts to fill that gap by looking at the performance of newcomers (which very often are not really new because many of them are "yo yo-teams" that get promoted and relegated fairly often) in twelve of the most important European soccer leagues. Since we are especially interested in the question of whether the survival probability depends upon the degree of revenue sharing (especially from the collective sale of national TV rights),[2] we not only study the sporting success of new teams in Western European leagues (where we can observe relatively high degrees of professionalization and commercialization), but also look at some (formerly) Eastern European leagues, where the financial well-being of the clubs depended exclusively on ticket sales and—in some cases—close relationships with the political elite (be it the Communist Party, the secret service, or the army).

Since newcomers are usually financially weak compared to the average competitor (ticket prices are significantly lower in the second divisions, attendance is smaller, and TV revenues are lower), their survival probabilities should be significantly lower than the respective probability of the more established teams. However, the observationally rather poor survival probabilities may be significantly improved by redistributing financial means from the established to the new members of a given league.

In some of the European soccer leagues, revenues from the sale of broadcasting rights are evenly distributed/redistributed among the teams playing in that league. In other leagues, every team sells the broadcasting rights for its home matches itself (and keeps the money). And in still other leagues the broadcasting rights are again sold collectively, but the teams are awarded different amounts of money depending on their league position either after every single match day or at the end of the season.

Using a large data set from twelve major European soccer leagues and covering a period of twenty-five years (1976–2000), we find that a more or less equal redistribution of the means earned through the collective sale of broadcasting rights (which may account for up to 50% of the teams' budgets) leaves the survival probabilities of recently promoted teams totally unaffected. Moreover, since 1996, a player whose contract has elapsed may join another team without the obligation for the new team to pay a transfer fee to the player's former employer, a recent change in the institutional environment that may be thought to benefit newcomers and yet proves to be detrimental for the promoted teams in many of the leagues under consideration.

LITERATURE REVIEW AND HYPOTHESES

Compared to the situation in the United States, where a new team can become a member of an established league only through a super-majority vote of the established franchises, and where one team cannot enter the home territory of another without the incumbent's explicit approval, the possibility of promotion from lower leagues in Europe provides a certain competitive threat to the successful teams with a lucrative local monopoly (Noll, 1999).

Compared to a closed-shop league, a promotion-and-relegation system not only tends to raise consumer welfare by increasing competition among the teams in a league, it also increases the incentives of teams to invest in team quality, either to avoid relegation or to win championships, thereby considerably reducing the economic rents accruing to the clubs (Szymanski and Ross, 2000). Thus, free-rider behavior or even incentives to lose strategically—both of which threaten the integrity of the sport—are highly unlikely to occur in an environment where a poor performance on the field is immediately punished by demotion from that league at the end of the season.

Accepting for a moment the hypothesis that fans prefer a balanced competition to an unbalanced one—we will, however, challenge this assumption by presenting empirical evidence not compatible with it—it is usually argued that the differences in the drawing potential of large and small market teams can only be reduced by redistributing parts or all of the revenues generated by the individual members of a league (thereby avoiding a boring season with the champion being known to everybody in advance). One major problem, however, is that revenue sharing is nothing but a tax on team quality, because part of the incremental increase in revenues arising from greater team quality goes to other clubs. If such a tax dampens the incentives of teams to overpay players, it should at the same time foster the survival of newcomers by reducing entry costs.

If teams are trying to maximize wins subject to a zero profit constraint,[3] any form of revenue sharing will enable inferior clubs to spend more money without going into the red each year (Ross, 1999).[4] Win-maximizing behavior is even more likely to occur if redistribution is not only accompanied by the threat of relegation, but also if the amounts to be earned from redistribution differ significantly between the teams' first and second best alternative (in the second division, German soccer clubs receive only about 25% of the TV money available for each team in the first division).[5] The larger the difference to be earned, the more effort small market teams will expend to remain in the upper echelon of the league hierarchy.

Revenue sharing is usually seen as an easy to implement instrument to maintain or to foster competitive balance that, in turn, helps to explain its widespread use. However, in the case of European team sports leagues in general and soccer in particular, the use of competitive balance to justify restraints on competition among teams is highly questionable. First, it is not at all clear whether a close competition is indeed more entertaining than an unequal one—to present this as an axiom is to impose preferences upon consumers (Szymanski, 1999, 157). Second, recent empirical analyses seem to contradict this critical assumption. Using longitudinal data from the German Bundesliga, Frick (1999) shows that various measures of competitive balance do have a significant impact on ticket sales. However, this influence only proves to be statistically significant. From an economic point of view this effect is more or less irrelevant; that is, overall ticket sales drop only slightly upon a decrease in competitive balance.[6] Reinforcing these findings is another study (Frick, 2003) showing that teams with a high number of star players (such as Bayern Munich or Borussia Dortmund) have a significantly higher drawing potential while on the road than average teams—although the home team in these cases is not very likely to win the match.

The "redistribution hypothesis"—as put forward by many writers emphasizing the "peculiar economics" of professional team sports leagues (Neale, 1964)—suggests that in order to maintain competitive balance, teams with a weak drawing potential should be subsidized by the more wealthy clubs. The teams that have recently been promoted from the second to the first division are most likely to be unable to assemble a squad of high quality players because of their poor drawing potential in the second division. In Germany, admission prices differ significantly between the two leagues (by about 20%), and the number of tickets sold per game by the three teams that have been promoted from the second to the first division for example in 1999 and 2000 increased from 12,400 to 18,600 (+50%), whereas the respective figures for the three relegated teams dropped from 22,300 to 12,800 (–57%).[7] Thus, apart from an increase in the number of tickets sold, the teams that have been recently promoted should be the main beneficiaries of any arrangement that redistributes financial resources from a joint marketing of the broadcasting rights. The more equal the sharing rule, the higher the survival probabilities of the new members of the first division, ceteris paribus.

H_1: If the redistribution of TV money leads to a more balanced—and thus more attractive—league, we would expect the survival probabilities of "newcomers" to be higher in leagues with a high degree of revenue sharing as opposed to leagues in which TV money is either not shared at all or in which the teams that dominate on the field benefit more from TV money than the less successful clubs.

Another institutional feature that deserves to be mentioned in this context results from a highly controversial decision of the European Court of Justice. Prior to the 1995–1996 season most European soccer leagues operated transfer markets based on two principles: First, a transfer fee would be payable even if a player wanted to change clubs after his previous contract had expired. Second, virtually all leagues restricted the number of foreign-born players who could appear in a particular match (usually three players).[8] In 1995, these principles were challenged by the Belgian soccer player Jean-Marc Bosman, whose contract with RFC Liège—a first division club in Belgium—had expired and who wanted to move to a French second division team, the FC Dunkerque, because his old team offered him a new contract at inferior terms to the previous one. After RFC Liège refused permission for Bosman to join FC Dunkerque, the player sued his old club, citing restraint of trade. In December 1995, the European Court of Justice ruled that the provision, whereby out-of-contract players could only move between two teams in different European Union (EU) countries if a transfer (fee) was agreed upon between the clubs, was incompatible with article 48 of the Treaty of Rome, which guarantees freedom of movement of labor within the EU. Contrary to the view expressed in the literature (that the abolition of the old tranfer fee system would be detrimental to small market teams, which usually developed and then sold young players to top teams across Europe), we expect that the new system should be especially advantageous for small market and recently promoted teams.

H_2: If the Bosman ruling of the European Court of Justice in December 1995 improved the chances of newcomers to sign more high quality players (because their old contracts had elapsed and no transfer fees could be claimed by the last team for which the player was active), we would expect that the survival probabilities of promoted teams increased significantly after the 1995–1996 season.

DATA AND METHODS

Our empirical analysis is based on data from twelve different European soccer leagues with a high degree of variation in the implemented revenue-sharing arrangements and covering a period of twenty-five consecutive seasons (1976–2000). We estimate fixed effects and semiparametric regression models to analyze performance on the field and the survival probabilities of those teams that have recently been promoted to the respective first division.[9]

The following countries from Western Europe have been included in the sample: Belgium, England, France, Germany, Holland, Italy, Portugal, and Spain. Moreover, from the former socialist countries, the German Democratic Republic (GDR), Czechoslovakia, Yugoslavia, and the Soviet Union have also been included. The choice of the countries under consideration was motivated first by the fact that, according to the annual Union des Associations Européennes de Football (UEFA) rankings, these soccer leagues have been the most successful in Europe (measured by the performance of the teams representing their national league in the European cup competitions). Second, the fact that the sample also includes leagues from formerly socialist countries (where the commercialization of soccer—as opposed to the professionalization—was always less pronounced than in Western Europe)

Table 1
Composition of Major European Soccer Leagues, 1976–2000[1]

Country	Team-Year Observations[2]	#Different Teams	#Promotions		#Relegations	
	n	n	n	%[3]	n	%[3]
Germany	452	40	69	15.3	67	14.8
Netherlands	450	36	57	12.7	58	12.9
England	533	46	74	13.9	76	14.3
Italy	424	40	87	20.5	86	20.3
Portugal	432	54	85	19.7	87	20.1
France	494	44	68	13.8	70	14.2
Spain	480	42	74	15.4	75	15.6
GDR[4]	224	23	32	14.3	36	16.1
Yugoslavia[5]	347	46	63	18.2	53	15.3
Czechoslovakia[6]	392	49	52	13.3	47	12.0
Soviet Union[7]	421	50	76	18.1	71	16.9
Belgium	451	38	50	11.1	47	10.4
Total	5,100	508	787	15.4	773	15.2

[1]The choice of the national leagues is mainly based on the different countries' UEFA ranking in 1976. Moreover, we wanted to include a reasonable number of (formerly) socialist countries. Although it belonged to the top twelve in 1976, we excluded the Hungarian league (ranked twelfth in 1976, but only twenty-third in 2000), because the country never really belonged to the Eastern bloc (we chose Czechoslovakia instead). Further, we excluded Scotland (ranked thirteenth in 1976 and fifteenth in 2000) and chose Portugal instead (due to its better average position: fourteenth in 1976 and tenth in 2000). The ranking itself is based on a league's success in previous European cup competitions (five-year moving average) and is adjusted on an annual basis. Of the twelve leagues in our sample, nine still belonged to the top twelve in 1999–2000 (the GDR ceased to exist, Belgium dropped from third to seventeenth, and Yugoslavia from ninth to twenty-eighth. Yugoslavia, however, would still belong to the top twelve if it still existed in its 1990 political borders. Slovenian and Croatian teams have recently been more successful in international cup competitions than teams from the now remaining "core" of Yugoslavia).

[2]Taking the German Bundesliga as an example, we calculated the team-year observations as follows: The league played for all but one of the twenty-five seasons with eighteen teams. In 1991–1992 when teams from the former GDR joined the Bundesliga, the number was increased to twenty (after that season four teams were relegated and only two were promoted for the following season). Thus, the number of team-year observations is ([24 * 18] + [1 * 20]) = 452. In some of the other leagues, the number of teams admitted changed more often and, sometimes, to a much higher degree than in Germany (for example in Yugoslavia the number of teams increased by eight in 1999–2000 and was reduced by six the following season).

enables us to compare leagues for which the financial means have in most cases been distributed more or less equally with leagues for which the different drawing potentials always resulted in a highly unequal distribution of the available resources. (This is even more applicable if one takes into consideration that the top teams in the former socialist countries—such as ZSKA Moskau, Partizan Belgrad, or Dynamo Berlin—always had strong ties either with the Communist Party, the secret service, or the army and were therefore much better equipped with financial resources than the remaining teams. The rest of the teams from the former Soviet socialist countries, in turn, were more or less equally poor—independent of the duration of their membership in the first division.)

Table 1 shows that the size of the leagues under consideration varies considerably: Whereas the average number of teams playing in the British Premier League was about twenty-one, the Oberliga in the former GDR always consisted of fourteen member teams only. On average, about 15% of the first division clubs are relegated each year and replaced by the strongest teams from the respective second division. Since the average annual number of clubs per league is seventeen, this implies that two to three teams are exchanged every season. There are, however, some notable deviations from the overall

---

[3]Promoted (relegated) teams as a percentage of all teams.

[4]The East German Oberliga was abandoned after the season 1990–1991 (therefore our research period covers only sixteen years). Two teams (out of fourteen) joined the first and sixth teams of the second division of the German Bundesliga for the 1991–1992 season.

[5]Data not available for the 1975–1976 to 1978–1979 seasons (therefore our research period covers only twenty-one seasons). Since 1994, the league has admitted only teams from the "core" of the former Republic of Yugoslavia (including Serbia-Montenegro); Bosnia-Herzegovina, Croatia, Macedonia, and Slovenia started to form their own separate first divisions. Only a third of the teams playing in the first division in 1976 still belonged to that league in 1999–2000. The majority of the remaining teams are now playing in the first divisions of Slovenia and Bosnia-Herzegovina (eight out of eighteen).

[6]Since 1993, the year of the first Czech division. In that year, Slovakia formed its own first division. In the 1999–2000 season, half of the teams that played in the first Czechoslovakian division in 1976 were still playing in what is now the Czech League, and four were playing in the first Slovakian league. The remaining four teams had been relegated to one of the two second divisions.

[7]Since 1992, the year of the first Russian division. Most of the former Soviet republics and now independent states (Armenia, Azerbaijan, Belarus, Estonia, Georgia, Latvia, Lithuania, Moldova, Ukraine) have formed their own major soccer league. Due to its top team, Dynamo Kiev, the Ukrainian league has in the meantime already reached the top twelve in Europe. The now independent republics of Kazakhstan, Kyrgyzstan, Tajikistan, Turkmenistan, and Uzbekistan have not yet formed their own soccer leagues. Out of the sixteen teams that played in the first Soviet division in 1976, only six are still playing there. Another six are playing in the first Ukrainian league, one is playing in Armenia, and one in Belarus. Two teams (one from Kyrgyzstan and one from Uzbekistan) do not participate in league soccer any longer because no such league exists in their countries.

picture. In Belgium, the Netherlands, and the now Czech Republic, annual team turnover is rather low, whereas in Italy and Portugal it is especially high.

Using this cross-section time-series data, we first estimate a fixed effects model with the number of points scored (PS) as the dependent variable (measuring the performance on the field during the season)[10] and a promotion dummy (UP) plus an interaction term (UP * BOS) as our major independent variables. The equation is of the following general form:

$$PS = \alpha_0 + \alpha_1 \, UP + \alpha_2 \, SD + \alpha_3 \, TPR + \alpha_4 \, BOS + \alpha_5 \, UP * TPR \quad (1)$$
$$+ \, \alpha_6 \, UP * BOS + \alpha_7 \, TT + \varepsilon$$

Control variables are the duration of the respective spell (SD), the introduction of the three point rule (TPR; dummy with 0 = no; 1 = yes), a dummy separating the period before the decision of the European Court of Justice from the period afterwards (BOS; dummy with 0 = no; 1 = yes), a second interaction term (UP * TPR) plus a linear time trend (TT).

Second, we estimate a fixed effects logit model with a dummy as the dependent variable (indicating whether a team was relegated or not [REL; 0 = no; 1 = yes]):

$$REL = \alpha_0 + \alpha_1 \, UP + \alpha_2 \, PS + \alpha_3 \, SD + \alpha_4 \, TPR + \alpha_5 \, BOS + \alpha_6 \, UP*BOS \quad (2)$$
$$+ \, \alpha_7 \, GINI + \alpha_8 \, TT + \varepsilon$$

The additional explanatory variable (GINI) serves as a measure for the degree of competitive balance/imbalance on winning percents in the leagues under consideration (we expect that a higher degree of competitive imbalance is due to a higher number of promotions and relegations).[11]

Finally, the third equation to be estimated is a Cox proportional hazard model with spell duration as the independent variable. The equation is of the following general form:

$$SD = \alpha_0 + \alpha_1 \, UP + \alpha_2 \, TPR + \alpha_3 \, BOS + \alpha_4 \, UP*BOS + \alpha_5 \, GINI + \alpha_6 \, PS + \varepsilon \quad (3)$$

Before turning to the findings of our econometric investigation, we will first present some descriptive evidence that proves to be compatible with our two main hypotheses. We start with a description of the relative performance of promoted teams as compared to the more established clubs followed by a first descriptive analysis of the survival of the teams that have recently been promoted.

EMPIRICAL FINDINGS

Table 2 shows that in general the performance of the promoted team is relatively poor. On average, a team that has been promoted recently wins

Table 2
Relative Performance of Promoted and Established Teams in Major European
Soccer Leagues, 1976–2000

Country	Promoted Teams[1]	Established Teams[2]	Points PT/ET[3]	T-Test
Germany	30.3	37.7	80.4	33.7
Netherlands	27.7	37.9	73.1	35.7
England	46.5	52.6	88.4	12.3
Italy	28.8	36.8	78.3	34.2
Portugal	28.0	37.2	75.3	38.5
France	35.8	42.1	85.0	21.1
Spain	32.2	41.1	78.4	34.1
GDR	17.3	27.5	62.9	59.7
Yugoslavia	29.8	36.1	82.6	13.9
Czechoslovakia	27.7	33.6	82.4	16.6
Soviet Union	29.2	34.7	84.2	13.8
Belgium	29.2	37.6	77.7	24.0
Total	38.8	31.0	79.9	247.21

[1]Average number of points scored by recently promoted teams (i.e., clubs playing their first season in the respective league).
[2]Average number of points scored by established teams (i.e., teams that played at least their second season in the respective league).
[3]Points scored by promoted teams relative to points scored by established teams (in %).
All entries here are significant at $p < .01$.

only about 80% of the points scored by an already established competitor. In England, France, and in the former Soviet Union, first-year newcomers seem to be especially successful, as they score between 84% and 88% of the points realized by the rest of the teams in these leagues. On the other hand, over the last twenty-five years, the poorest performance by far has been by newcomers in the East German Oberliga, followed by Dutch and Portuguese newcomers.

This picture, however, changes dramatically when the persistence of the promoted teams is compared across the different European soccer leagues (see Table 3). It now appears that, apart from the already mentioned East

Table 3

Persistence of Promoted Teams in Major European Soccer Leagues[1]

Country	Number of Promoted Teams Surviving ... Years								Total
	1		2		3		4+		
	n	%	n	%	n	%	n	%	N
Germany	30	43.5	13	18.8	7	10.1	19	27.5	69
Netherlands	18	31.6	11	19.3	5	8.8	23	40.4	57
England	23	31.1	8	10.8	6	8.1	37	50.0	74
Italy	35	40.2	19	21.8	8	9.2	25	28.7	87
Portugal	33	38.8	19	22.4	11	12.9	22	25.9	85
France	26	38.2	7	10.3	7	10.3	28	41.2	68
Spain	31	41.9	13	17.6	10	13.5	20	27.0	74
GDR	18	56.3	4	12.5	2	6.3	8	25.0	32
Yugoslavia	24	38.1	11	17.5	5	7.9	23	36.5	63
Czechoslovakia	19	36.5	7	13.5	4	7.7	22	42.3	52
Soviet Union	24	32.0	17	22.0	6	8.0	29	38.0	76
Belgium	12	24.4	8	15.6	3	6.7	27	53.3	50
Total	293	37.2	137	17.4	74	9.4	283	36.0	787

[1]The plotted values of Kaplan-Meier estimates are available from the authors upon request.

German Oberliga, teams from the Bundesliga (former West and now unified Germany), the Serie A (Italy), and the Primera Division (Spain) have the lowest probability of surviving their first season. In any of these latter three leagues about 60% of the newcomers are relegated again after only one season. On the other hand, in England and in Belgium about half of the promoted teams are able to survive four or more consecutive seasons in the first division.

Thus, it appears that the relative number of points scored during a season on the one hand and the one- and four-year survival rates on the other hand turn out to be quite different dimensions of a professional soccer team's performance. In the context of our chapter this implies that in some leagues from time to time a promoted team is able to climb up to the top ranks in its first season, whereas in other leagues such an event is highly unlikely to occur. In other words, in some leagues there seems to be a fairly high degree of heterogeneity among the promoted teams, whereas in others the promoted teams are much more homogenous with regard to their first-year

Table 4
Determinants of Points Scored and Relegation

Variable	Dependent Variable: PS (Model (1)) – Fixed Effects			Dependent Variable: REL (Model (2)) – Fixed Effects Logit		
	B	T	p	B	Z	P
UP	-1.00	1.19	+	0.28	1.98	**
SD	0.00	0.05	+	-0.06	3.91	***
PS	-	-	-	-0.31	18.00	***
TPR	+10.64	22.43	***	2.42	6.05	***
BOS	1.70	3.26	***	0.23	0.63	+
UP*TPR	0.33	0.36	+	-	-	-
UP*BOS	-3.76	3.06	***	0.31	0.82	+
GINI	-	-	-	-23.60	11.23	***
TT	0.06	1.93	*	0.05	4.75	***
CONST	45.84	70.25	***	13.75	14.74	***
N of Cases	5,080			5,080		
N of Teams	508			508		
$R^2 * 100$	26.0			-		

+ = not significantly different from zero. $*p < .10$. $**p < .05$. $***p < .01$.

performance. These differences, which are neither related to league size, the number of qualification slots for supranational cup competitions, and/or the annual number of promotions and relegations, are likely to explain the different findings in Tables 2 and 3 that might at first seem incompatible.

Turning now to the results of our econometric analyses, it first appears that our two hypotheses are by and large supported by the data (see Table 4). On the one hand, the interaction term (*UP*BOS*) in model (1) has a significantly negative influence on the number of points scored, suggesting that in the post-Bosman era the relative performance of newcomers has deteriorated even further. This shift means that the recent changes in the institutional environment—induced by a verdict of the European Court of Justice—are detrimental to teams entering the market and may thus be interpreted as a new (and obviously unintended) entry barrier. A plausible interpretation is that under the new system promoted teams do not save any money when signing out-of-contract players: First, the money that has hitherto been paid to the player's old team in the form of a transfer fee now goes to the player himself in the form of a signing bonus. Second, risk averse players who are presumably well informed about the liability of newness,[12] the above average risk of immediate relegation of the newcomers, will most likely command a risk premium when signing a contract with a new team that has just been promoted to the first division.

Moreover, it also appears from Table 4 that, other things being equal, teams that have been promoted recently face a higher risk of immediate relegation than otherwise similar teams that have been playing in that respective league for a number of years[13] (i.e., the longer the duration of a particular spell, the lower the risk of relegation), with the negative effect of a recent promotion being especially pronounced.[14]

In order to complete our empirical analysis, we now turn to the results of our semiparametric regression estimates. As before, we are interested in the impact of newcomer status and the Bosman verdict's influence on newcomers' risk of being cut from the league.

Contrary to our analyses so far, we now split our database into twelve different subsamples in order to be able to compare the influence of the liability of newness on team performance in different institutional environments.

Although we do not have reliable information on the concrete sharing rules according to which TV money is distributed among the first division teams in the different national leagues (even less so on how the rules developed over time), it appears from Table 5 that in all eleven leagues for which we were able to estimate our model recently promoted teams have a below average probability of survival; that is, irrespective of the specific institutional environment, the additional revenues do not enable the newcomers to field a really competitive team. This observation does not, of course, suggest that TV money is unimportant for the teams; it simply implies that its distribution does not affect the teams' sporting performance. In leagues where TV money plays a negligible role (Yugoslavia, Czech Republic, and Russia), the survival probabilities of newcomers are as low as in leagues where all teams benefit roughly to the same extent (such as Germany, England, France, and Italy),[15] or in leagues where some of the teams sell their broadcasting rights individually (thereby raising much more money, such as FC Barcelona and Real Madrid in Spain).

A final result that deserves to be mentioned in this context is that the Bosman verdict has led to a further deterioration of newcomers' survival probabilities in five of the eleven leagues for which we were able to estimate the respective model (England, Portugal, France, Italy, and Spain). With the exception of Portugal, established teams that have recently signed particularly large numbers of foreign-born players dominate these leagues—something that newcomers are only able to do under exceptional circumstances. On the contrary, especially in Yugoslavia (and to a lesser extent

Table 5
Survival of Promoted Teams in Major European Soccer Leagues, 1976–2000[1]

Country	Independent Variable	Dependent Variable: Spell Duration[2] (Model (3))		
		B	SE B	Wald
Germany	UP	1.63	0.37	17.56***
	UP*BOS	1.38	0.84	2.59+
Netherlands	UP	2.61	0.76	11.64***
	UP*BOS	1.17	0.91	1.67+
England	UP	3.27	0.64	26.04***
	UP*BOS	1.16	0.68	2.94*
Italy	UP	3.05	0.74	16.89***
	UP*BOS	1.44	0.66	4.72**
Portugal	UP	2.55	0.54	22.18***
	UP*BOS	1.17	0.69	2.87*
France	UP	3.18	0.75	17.92***
	UP*BOS	1.28	0.68	3.57*
Spain	UP	2.99	0.75	15.95***
	UP*BOS	2.73	0.77	12.64***
GDR[3]	UP	-	-	-
	UP*BOS	-	-	-
Yugoslavia	UP	2.59	0.43	35.99***
	UP*BOS	-2.63	0.77	11.69***
Czechoslovakia	UP	1.68	0.45	13.99***
	UP*BOS	-1.33	0.88	2.25+
Soviet Union	UP	2.89	0.47	38.04***
	UP*BOS	-0.11	0.88	0.01+
Belgium	UP	2.21	0.70	9.83***
	UP*BOS	-10.20	152.79	0.00+

[1]Coefficients are point estimates from Cox proportional hazard models. Additional controls: three point rule (dummy; 0 = no; 1 = yes), post-Bosman era (dummy; 0 = no; 1 = yes), inequality of competition (*GINI* coefficient of distribution of points), and points scored. For ease of presentation, we do not document the coefficients of the control variables and the usual information on the overall fit of the estimates. However, all this is available from the authors upon request.

[2]Spell duration is number of years in the first division since last promotion.

[3]Coefficients did not converge; the information matrix became singular after eight iterations.

+ = not significantly different from zero. *$p < .10$. **$p < .05$. ***$p < .01$.

in Czechoslovakia, Russia, and Belgium), the survival probabilities of newcomers have increased in the post-Bosman era. This probably surprising finding can be explained by the fact that in these leagues the dominant teams have lost many of their star players to foreign clubs. This change, in turn, has not only led to an increase in competitive balance in Yugoslavia, Czechoslovakia, Russia, and Belgium, but has also increased the survival probabilities of newcomers. Thus, in these countries newcomers benefit from the Bosman ruling indirectly insofar as their more established competitors have been weakened through an "exodus" of their best players, who can earn much more in some of the Western European leagues than in their respective home countries.

SUMMARY

Using a large cross-section time-series database from twelve European countries covering a period of twenty-five consecutive seasons (1976–2000) and controlling for a number of changes in the institutional environments in the soccer leagues under consideration, we show that the extent of revenue sharing does not at all affect the survival probabilities of recently promoted teams. On the one hand, this conclusion is certainly at odds with the assumption that an equalization of the financial situation of the teams within a league is a necessary condition for balanced competition. On the other hand, our findings are highly compatible with the notion that as long as teams are located in cities of widely varying revenue potentials, cross-subsidization of weak-drawing teams neither provides profit incentives for team owners nor does it promote the survival of weak-drawing clubs. In summary, these findings seem to support the invariance principle as proposed by Rottenberg (1956) and the theoretical model as developed by El Hodiri and Quirk (1971).

Whether our findings are convincing, especially to league organizers—who typically favor redistribution schemes for reasons not always made explicit—certainly depends on the outcomes of our future research. If they complement those presented in this chapter, the findings would be much more difficult to reject. Therefore, the next steps to be taken are, first, identification of the concrete reasons for success and failure in professional team sports. Our prior belief is that the quality of the incumbent management in particular is of paramount importance. Second, a comparative analysis of the correlation of sporting success over time is urgently required. If—as we expect—the correlation between last year's performance and this year's sporting success is not only relatively stable over time (controlling for changes in the institutional environment) but also similar among the countries we have studied in this chapter, we would have another piece of evidence challenging the redistribution hypothesis.

ACKNOWLEDGMENTS

We wish to thank Martin Modzelewski and Frank Tolsdorf for their excellent assistance in compiling the data set used in this study.

NOTES

1. The number of promotions and relegations not only varies among countries, but also over time within a given country. In years when a league expands, the number of promotions either exceeds the number of relegations or—as happens occasionally—a number of clubs are promoted and no team is relegated. In years of contraction, the number of relegated teams is higher than the number of promoted clubs, but there is always at least one promotion.

2. Contrary to the situation in the United States, local TV revenues are virtually unknown in professional team sports leagues in Europe.

3. This has been suggested over and over again in the United States as well as the European sports economics literature (see, for example, Canes, 1974; Sloane, 1976; Daly 1992; Késenne 1999).

4. Under profit maximization, revenue sharing is unlikely to lead the management of small market teams to significantly increase their payroll. Here the profit-maximizing strategy is to pocket the subsidy and to maintain sporting mediocrity (Fort and Quirk, 1995; Vrooman 1995). Such behavior is even more likely to occur if there is no threat of relocation.

5. This is in line with an argument presented by Szymanski and Ross (2000, 18), who suggest that the larger the difference in the revenue-generating potential, the more the threat of relegation works. Ross (1999, 102–103) discusses several alternatives to revenue sharing that may overcome the free-rider problem in a closed-shop league.

6. If the decrease in number of tickets sold is concentrated in cities with rather poor performing clubs while the top teams sell out regularly, the net effect of a smaller number of aggregate ticket sales may even be positive, because the latter teams usually charge higher entry fees.

7. A similar picture emerges for the 2000–2001 and 2001–2002 seasons. Whereas the three promoted teams increased their average attendance by 40% (from 18,900 to 26,400), the three relegated teams lost about 50% of their spectators (average attendance figures dropped from 17,400 to 8,800). The figures presented by Noll (2002, 192–196) for the English Premier League are very similar.

8. For a detailed economic analysis of the European Court of Justice's decision (issued in December 1995) in the case of *Jean-Marc Bosman v. Union Royale Belge des Sociétés de Football Association* see Antonioni and Cubbin (2000) and Simmons (1997).

9. Although we use state-of-the-art econometric tools we prefer to put more emphasis on the intuition of our argument and the economic consequences of our findings. Readers interested in the econometric details are kindly invited to contact the authors for details on the methodology and the stability of our findings.

10. Estimating this as well as the following models with the final rank instead of the points scored leaves the findings virtually unchanged.

11. Estimating the model with others measures of competitive balance—such as the standard deviation of the winning percentage—leaves the findings virtually unchanged (see Utt and Fort, 2002).

12. This expression is borrowed from the organizational ecology literature. It suggests that, other things being equal, recently founded enterprises face a significantly higher risk of failure throughout the first years of their existence than more established firms; see, for example, Carroll (1984).

13. Unfortunately, we are not able to control for other potential determinants of sporting success. Although the team fixed effects certainly capture most of the unobserved heterogeneity, we would like to know more about the factors that are included in the fixed effects.

14. We admit, however, that the point estimates of our dummy variable (*UP*) in model (1) as well as the interaction term (*UP * BOS*) in model (2) are not significantly different from zero at conventional levels (we note in parentheses that both coefficients have the expected sign).

15. We are, of course, aware of the fact that the sharing rules differ substantially between the leagues: In England, for example, a much higher share of the money to be distributed depends upon a team's sporting performance (TV appearances and final standing) than, for example, in Germany.

Part IV

Western Europe: League Evolution, Broadcasting, and the Stock Market

10

Common Origins, Common Future? A Comparative Analysis of Association Football and Rugby League Football in the UK

Paul Downward and Ian Jackson

INTRODUCTION

This chapter provides a comparative economic analysis of the two oldest professional team sports in the UK: Rugby Football League (RL) and Association Football (soccer). Despite sharing common origins, the games have evolved substantially, with soccer rising to preeminence as a spectator sport.

In the next section the historically common origins of the two games are briefly outlined together with a description of the key developments in the sports up until the modern era. Subsequent sections use economic theory to explain these developments as well as to assess the likely future developments of the sports. Explaining Historical League Evolution describes the developments of sporting leagues with reference to competing models of sports league evolution. From Decline to the Modern Era deepens the analysis by referring to the emergent economic literature since the 1970s. It focuses upon the demand for each sport and discusses key findings from the literature on sporting labor markets and the market for broadcast sports. Arguing that a cartel-based model of sports evolution is more apposite, it draws together a discussion of the commercial pressures that have led to recent changes in each league structures and offers some empirical analysis of competitive balance. It concludes the analysis by offering predictions for future developments in the sports. It is argued that although characterized by different forms of commercial development, similar economic forces have emerged producing financial fragility among smaller clubs in both games and that competitive balance appears to be the outcome and not the source of league developments.

COMMON ORIGINS AND COMPETING LEAGUES: THE DEVELOPMENT OF FOOTBALL VARIANTS

As Moorhouse (1995) notes, the history of football in Britain—prior to the formalized codes that we now observe—probably has its roots in the Roman game of *harpastum*. Yet the first official documentary evidence of such a game occurs historically in 1175 when men met in local fields to play ball on Shrove Tuesday. "Shrove Tuesday Football," or *ffotebale*, spread throughout the British Isles, although there were wide variations in "rules" captured by the historical remnants still celebrated today in Ashbourne and Cumbria.

Formalities increased with the involvement of the six main public schools of England: Charterhouse, Eton, Harrow, Shrewsbury, Westminster, Winchester, and Rugby.[1] Although the characteristics of the games differed, with the exception of the latter school, a uniform game emerged with the formation of Association Football in 1863. Prime movers were former school pupils now at Cambridge University. In contrast, Rugby School developed its own distinctive set of rules (Moorhouse, 1995, 17). There is no doubt that there was concern over the development of the Cambridge rules, so by 1862, a code of Rugby rules was established to allow "old Rugbeians" to introduce an alternative to those interested in football. Elements of the modern game of rugby were in place by the mid-nineteenth century. Thus, there was competition between the codes at their inception. There was, however, also a growing concern about managing the increased popularity of both games, in large part prompted by the inauguration of cup competitions (Williams, 1994, 44). And yet alternative strategies evolved to cope with the expansion, particularly at the elite level.

By 1888 and the formation of the English Football League (EFL), the top soccer clubs embraced professionalism and began to incorporate themselves as limited companies. The rapidly growing potential for earning money meant that enclosed stadia were built, entrance fees for spectators extracted, and players paid and bought and sold. The need to pay to attract the best players existed even before the formation of the EFL, with evidence that paid professionals existed in 1876 (Vamplew, 1988).

As Dobson and Goddard (2001) note, the original twelve teams expanded to sixteen in the top division in 1893. A further twelve clubs facilitated the creation of a second division before World War I. Movement between the divisions was based on merit. After the war, further expansion included a segmented third division constituted on geographical lines for the north and south of England. Creation of this league was achieved by incorporating elements of a previous Southern League, which included some clubs from South Wales. By 1951, ninety-two league teams existed in the four divisions, and in 1959 the geographical basis of the division three segmentation was replaced by a division three and four, based on merit. During the 1970s and 1980s, various changes took place. The most important of these included increasing the numbers of teams relegated and promoted, and the introduction of a playoff system to determine one of the promotion places. In 1993, the Premier League was formed by a break away of the division one sides.

Over the same period, the Rugby code was characterized by a schism that was based on alternative approaches to rejecting professionalism. The divide occurred along broadly geographical as well as class lines. Many rugby clubs were restricted to the professional classes, particularly in the south of England but also in Liverpool, Sale, and Manchester in the north. In contrast, in the north of England and South Wales the game was opened up to working men and artisans. Because of the length of the working week, which included Saturday mornings until 1 P.M., it was common for Northern Rugby Union clubs to offer "broken-time" payments to compensate for loss of earnings. However, the Rugby Football Union in London was vehemently against this development. Following a vote in 1893 against allowing this practice to continue, in 1895, twenty-one clubs of the Northern Rugby Union, based in Yorkshire and Lancashire, broke away to form their own league—the Northern Rugby Football League. Professional players were allowed providing they were employed full-time, and players could transfer between clubs if allowed by the Northern Union (Moorhouse, 1995, 61). By 1922, the group was relabeled as the Rugby Football League (RL) to distinguish it from the Rugby Football Union (RFU) that managed the amateur game for the remaining teams.

Convoluted changes to both the structure of competition and rules followed the RL's break from the RFU.[2] Regarding the former, traditionally structured county championships were contested for five years following the first season. By 1902, two divisions were introduced with eighteen sides each and promotion and relegation based on merit. By 1905, the second division had contracted and the two divisions were scrapped again. A unique system was then adopted within which approximately thirty-one teams competed for a single championship decided upon based on percentage of wins rather than the total number of points. Beginning in 1907, the top four contested the championship by playoff. The next major change came in 1962 when eastern and western divisions were installed, but that change was scrapped in 1964. In the new single division a playoff of the top sixteen clubs decided the championship. This structure lasted until 1974 when two divisions were reinstated along with playoff finals. The next major change was the creation of three divisions in 1995, making way for the creation of the Super League in 1996 for the top sides. Since 1998, both the Super League and the first division championships have been decided in playoffs.

In the case of rule changes, attempts were made to speed up the game and encourage further handling of the ball. Team sizes were reduced in number and the "play-of-the-ball" rule was introduced, which removed the need for a scrum following a tackle.

EXPLAINING HISTORICAL LEAGUE EVOLUTION

Although historical accounts of the above developments have been extensive, there has been no attempt to explain them in economic terms. To begin this process it is instructive to outline the economic approaches that have thus far been offered to explain league evolution.

To begin with, it is clear that in general once cup competitions established the potential economic viability of sporting contests, leagues became inevitable as forms of organizing repeat transactions. Regularity of attendance and gate money was necessary to meet emergent wage bills, which required organizing encounters through a fixture list. Likewise, enclosed stadia were necessary to extract spectators' payment.[3] Teams also needed to buy and sell players to compete effectively. In short, the presence of money through professionalism set in motion standard economic forces.[4]

As well as the standard economic pressures, it is possible that other unique forces were set in motion, such as the need for uncertainty of outcome. Uncertainty of outcome, first noted by Rottenberg (1956) in the context of baseball, has been presented as an organizing principle in the economics of sports since Neale's (1964) seminal commentary on sports in general and league evolution in particular. Neale argued that sports competitions would evolve into a natural monopoly because of the greater value being placed upon higher level competition that monopoly can supply. The limit of the market would be governed by the feasibility of economic or sporting bases for competition.

The above discussion in the development of rugby football suggests that Neale's perspective has some relevance. Yet, by failing to capture the dynamics at play, it can also be seen as too benign. In contrast, Sloane (1971) argues that sporting leagues and organizations are best represented by cartels that have to manage the mutual independence of teams based on uncertainty of outcome. Indeed, there is tacit legal representation of leagues according to this definition. Sloane's arguments thus point toward the potential instability and evolution of cartels and have more explanatory power.

To begin with, soccer and RL were from the outset in direct competition for fans and playing talent. Occasionally, teams such as Preston North End flirted with playing both codes. In general, as part of a well-organized league with strongly professional aspirations, soccer teams flourished, which was evidenced by the growth in scale of the EFL as opposed to the RL (Williams, 1994, 82). Part of this expansion was at the expense of RL teams such as Radcliffe and Walkden in Lancashire, which became unsustainable in the face of competition for fans provided by the Bolton Wanderers and Bury FC, which were successful teams. Others, the most notable being Manningham, which had won the inaugural Northern Union championship, converted to soccer in 1903 and reemerged as Bradford City FC, which today competes in division one of the EFL. Players also switched between codes. Part of the expansion, however, was to monopolize the "vacant" midlands lying between the disputed geographical territories of rugby football.

It was in direct response to the threat from soccer that RL struggled to adjust its form of competition and the rules of the game—to establish barriers to entry. It was important that the Yorkshire and Lancashire clubs play one another because the initial competition with soccer was in the latter rather than the former county (Williams, 1994). Indeed, the consolidation of talent in the former ensured that Yorkshire teams were dominant in the early years of RL. Beginning in 1889, they won the county championship against their rivals in seven of the first eight seasons, and hence it was by no accident that they were the most vocal elements in the breakaway.

Of course, although the breakaway is indicative of Sloane's (1971) cartel thesis, it is not clear that uncertainty of outcome provided the motivation. The breakaway was more complex than simply a set of northern rugby clubs challenging those in the south. In fact, it was economic power that drove the agenda. Prior to the breakaway, coalitions were already forming. It was the ten largest Yorkshire clubs and the nine largest Lancashire clubs that forced the county unions—the traditional organizing body of the game in the north—to accept and organize competition at a county level on the terms of the senior teams rather than those of clubs in the north per se (*Yorkshire Post* [UK], September 9, 1895). One can also explain the rule and team-size changes in RL as following primarily from the need to offer a sporting alternative to soccer rather than from intrinsic desire.

That said, it is plausible that economic barriers to entry also played a role in developing each code. In the former case, the concept of travel costs that led to the argued need for broken-time payments constrained full integration of the Lancashire and Yorkshire teams into one Northern Rugby League. These costs were not trivial. Even in the more widely played and commercially powerful code of soccer, as noted above, it was not until the 1950s that a geographical basis of competition was removed for the weakest EFL teams. Thus, to a degree, geographical barriers to entry helped maintain the wedge between soccer and rugby codes in the midlands.

It is interesting to note from the discussion in the previous section that, by the 1970s, soccer also introduced innovations in league competitions by implementing playoffs for promotion and relegation. Contrary to the widespread use of such devices in RL, the reasons in soccer were caused by more worrying developments. By the 1970s, attendance at professional sports events generally were falling radically from their all-time high in the immediate post–World War II era, and there was a clear need to revitalize the sport.

Explaining the evolution of soccer and RL in this period thus requires more detailed attention of the revenues and costs facing teams and, as will be shown, will also draw upon Sloane's (1971) definition of sports leagues. Yet again, however, economic power rather than uncertainty of outcome seems to have played a central role in defining leagues.

FROM DECLINE TO THE MODERN ERA

The Cyclical Pattern of Demand

As Dobson and Goddard (2001), Szymanski and Kuypers (1999), and Simmons (1996) note, soccer attendance has been cyclical. In the first season of the EFL, attendance was 612,000, rising rapidly to an all-time high in 1948 of 41,271,141 spectators. Soccer was the domain of the working class "shilling supporter" (Fishwick, 1989). Subsequently, steady decline occurred. By 1988, the figure had more than halved, to 18,464,000. The falls were about three times greater in divisions three and four as than in division one. There was therefore a redistribution of demand as well as a fall in totals (Szymanski and Kuypers, 1999, 43–48). Similar patterns applied to RL, but, of course, the totals were always less than in soccer. So, in 1948, the peak reached 6.86 million spectators, falling to approximately half that figure by 1958 and reaching an extremely low point in 1974, when only 800,000 spectators watched live RL (Moorhouse, 1995).

It is almost certain that during the 1950s and 1960s some fundamental shifts in consumer tastes coupled with the provision of leisure alternatives took place, which would explain these findings, as discussed later. In contrast, recession coupled with the fear of hooliganism that had emerged in the 1970s in soccer, as outlined in the Home Office Chester Report in 1983 (Chester, 1983), are held as responsible in the later period. The decline in the sports was particularly severe in RL, in which historically celebrated stadia were lost—indicating over capacity—including Huddersfield's Fartown, Swinton's Station Road, and Hull Kingston Rovers' Craven Park. Part of the problem was the inability to pay for ground improvements and insurance policies in stadia that had not been invested in during the post–World War II era and that led to disasters in soccer with a fatal fire in one of Bradford City's wooden stands.[5] The impact of the Chester Report on ground safety was thus far-reaching.

Yet by the mid-1980s, attendance was once again on the increase, as indicated by Figures 1 and 2. The upturn was, however, prompted by a much more commercial edge to the sports, driven by larger clubs, and in large part this reflected a recognized shift of emphasis to promote demand. This shift was particularly the case in soccer. Indeed, to an extent, the pattern of development in RL can be seen as an attempt to echo the success of soccer. Justification for these arguments follows from a review of the emergent economic research into the demand and supply factors of the modern era.

Figure 1
Rugby Attendance, 1970–2000

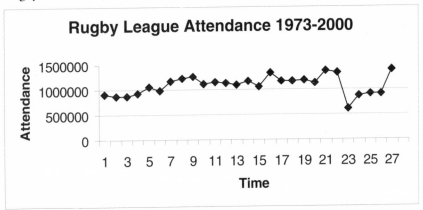

Figure 2
Soccer League Attendance, 1973–2000

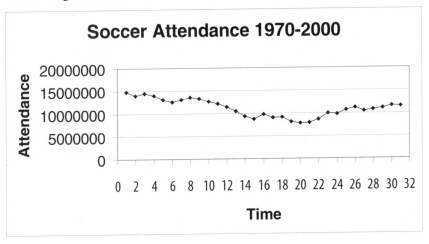

The Demand for Soccer and Rugby Leagues

Economic research into sports has a relatively recent pedigree in the UK and Europe generally, as distinct from the United States (Downward and Dawson, 2000). There is also a bias in terms of research toward popular sports with available data. This is the case with the demand for professional team sports generally where, as Cairns (1990) and Downward and Dawson show, more studies are devoted to baseball in the United States and soccer in Europe than to other sports. Naturally, the latter finding is echoed in terms of UK sports. Thus, there are six studies of the demand for rugby league in existence to date compared to a large selection of papers and a number of books devoted to soccer (Szymanski and Kuypers, 1999; Hamil et al., 1999; Dobson and Goddard, 2001).

Downward and Dawson (2000) survey a large number of studies in detail, and the general results are echoed in both RL and soccer, for example, the studies of RL by Baimbridge, Cameron, and Dawson (1995); Carmichael, Millington, and Simmons (1999); and Jones, Schofield, and Giles (2000); and the more numerous studies in soccer by, for example, Hart, Hutton, and Sharot (1975); Jennett (1984); Walker (1986); Peel and Thomas (1988); Cairns (1988); Baimbridge, Cameron, and Dawson (1996); and Kuypers (1996).

This suggests that typically attendance at soccer and RL games is positively enhanced by the catchment areas—a factor that clearly contributes to the historical existence of dominant clubs, in both RL and soccer, in the major metropolitan areas. The effects of price and income are, however, less robust. One can argue that a more robust impact of (economic) price is revealed when distances between competing clubs are included in regression studies. A negative sign is typically observed, which broadly supports the concept of travel costs, for example, discussed in previous sections. The effects of price are probably understated for other reasons too. Dobson and Goddard (1995) and Simmons (1996) produce long-run disaggregated club-level studies of soccer attendance and produce more theoretically consistent impacts of price. Often, a lagged dependent term is included in regression analyses with the intention of measuring habit persistence or loyalty. However, as Dawson and Downward (2000) note, this loyalty interpretation is misleading. Such effects probably capture sluggish adjustment to price changes more than habit persistence.

There is also emergent evidence that live TV is not a substitute for watching soccer or RL at traditional weekend times. Finally, a particularly interesting finding is that the reported effects of uncertainty of outcome appear countertheoretical. In most studies, teams' successes rather than the uncertainty of their results are strongly associated with attendance, as are the contributing factors of player and team quality. The importance of success also seems to be the case across divisions. For example, Burkitt and Cameron (1992) show that although the introduction of two divisions in 1972 boosted RL attendance overall, the increases were confined to the first division, with reductions in the second division. This same result might help to explain why attendance at lower divisions in soccer have also lagged behind those of the first division, as detailed, for example, in Szymanski and Kuypers (1999) and Dobson and Goddard (1995, 2001).[6]

However, it should be emphasized that most of the studies may not be particularly relevant in this regard because the literature estimates demand for particular teams over short time periods, and Dobson and Goddard (1995) and Simmons (1996) do not address the uncertainty of outcome

Table 1
ADF Tests of Stationarity

Variable	Soccer 1970-2000 Test Statistic	ADF Statistic	RL 1975-2000 Test Statistic	ADF Statistic
ATT	-1.4755	-2.9665	-3.4548	-2.985
CB	-4.2295	-2.9665	-4.6655	-2.9798
DATT	-4.2155	-2.9706	N/A	N/A
DCB	N/A	N/A	N/A	N/A

Note: In all cases, information criteria suggested that the basic ADF test was appropriate. Tests are all at the 5% level of significance.

hypothesis. To investigate this issue Tables 1, 2, and 3 present some time-series econometric results for both soccer and RL from the 1970s to 2000. Table 1 reports the results of Augmented Dickey Fuller (ADF) tests for the stationarity of the variables. In each case, the variable *ATT* measures total attendance in the top divisions of each sport and *CB* refers to competitive balance in each league. Competitive balance is measured by the standard deviation of points in each league.[7] *PL* and *SL* are dummy variables measuring the introduction of the Premier League and the Super League respectively, and *POINTS* is a dummy variable to capture the effects of three points instead of two points being awarded for a win in soccer. All variables are measured in natural logs. A letter *D* before a variable indicates a first difference.

The results suggest that attendance and competitive balance are stationary in RL. Attendance is nonstationary in soccer, although its first difference is, whereas competitive balance is stationary. This result suggests that there is a possibility of a long-run equilibrium between the two variables in RL but not in soccer. To further investigate the relationships, regressions between the variables in both directions—in the manner of causality tests—were conducted. In all cases, asterisks indicate significant statistics at the 5% level, and each regression is supported by an appropriate set of diagnostics.

Table 2 presents the results from valid regressions between stationary measures of competitive balance and attendance. It is clear that in soccer, competitive balance does not affect changes in attendance and vice versa.

Table 3 presents the results for RL. In the attendance function, persistent first-order serial correlation was removed by a Cochrane-Orcutt transformation.[8] In contrast to soccer, the RL regressions reveal a two-directional relationship between competitive balance and attendance. An increase in the

Table 2
Regression Results for Soccer, 1970–2000

Independent Variable	Dependent Variable: DATT	
	Coefficient	T-Ratio
Constant	0.00573	0.0276
PL	0.0359	1.156
POINTS	-0.0011	-0.038
CB	-0.0088	-0.1118
R-Squared	0.056278	
F[3,26]	0.5168	
Serial Correlation	0.154	
Functional Form	0.354	
Normality	2.215	
Independent Variable	Dependent Variable CB	
	Coefficient	T-Ratio
Constant	2.5962	45.3815
PL	0.0287	0.3666
POINTS	-0.0221	-0.301
DATT	-0.054	-0.1118
R-Squared	0.00636	
F[3, 26]	0.0555	
Serial Correlation	1.3432	
Functional Form	0.4137	
Normality	1.0315	

Note: POINTS is included in the attendance function because the incentive effects might promote a more attacking game.

Table 3
Regression Results for RL, 1973–2000

	Dependent Variable: DATT	
Independent Variable	**Coefficient**	**T-Ratio**
Constant	12.7169*	29.68
SL	-0.0126	-0.071
CB	0.5018*	2.75
R-Squared	0.33806	
F[3, 22]	3.74	
Serial Correlation	5.0636*	
Functional Form	0.029	
Normality	1.8477	
	Dependent Variable CB	
Independent Variable	Coefficient	T-Ratio
Constant	-2.611	-1.1617
SL	0.1266	1.5493
ATT	0.35641*	2.2037
R-Squared	0.208	
F[2,24]	3.1674	
Serial Correlation	0.22423	
Functional Form	0.0664	
Normality	1.7334	

value of one of these variables is associated with an increase in the value of the other. An important feature of these results is that, because competitive balance is measured by the standard deviation of points, a *decrease* in the standard deviation is associated with an *increase* in competitive balance. The results tend to suggest that increases in success promote greater attendance, which then promotes further success—because of resource availability. There does not appear to be a self-correcting evolution managed by uncertainty of outcome. It also doesn't appear evident that changes to the Premier League or Super League have structurally changed these relationships.

Further support for these findings is in studies by Davies, Downward, and Jackson (1995) and Dobson and Goddard (1998) of RL and soccer respectively. These earlier authors detect a reversal of causality between attendance or revenue and success, which indicates both that simultaneous equation bias may be evident in demand studies and reinforces the view that resources of clubs may well be instrumental in determining league development and then uncertainty of outcome. Thus, coupled with the results found in this chapter, there is some evidence that uncertainty of outcome emerges, rather like a residual out of the evolving basis of sporting competition, and doesn't operate "independently" to correct league resource allocation. In contrast, there is evidence that resources and fan interest are increasingly likely to focus around successful clubs. If this is the case, then the financial survival of less successful teams is open to question.

The upshot of this general discussion is that since the 1970s, at least, the longer-term trend variations in attendance in both sports are unlikely to be explained by simple variation in economic variables and sporting competition between the codes.[9] This is contrary to Neale's (1964) explanation, and to an extent, that implied by Sloane (1971). Deeper structural changes in tastes seem to be the reason for differences in attendance levels. To the extent that other variables affect attendance patterns—and hence revenue—historical market size of the dominant metropolitan clubs and the success of these clubs seem to matter most. There is evidence too of a "positive" feedback such that changes in supply conditions—because of resource availability—affect the levels of sporting competition, and thus league development, through promoting success and the acquisition of quality players. This thesis seems to concur with the historical role played by dominant clubs, say, in RL in promoting key changes to the sport. The final section outlines how recent changes in supply conditions in both codes are at work to potentially reinforce this developmental pattern. The implications are also discussed.

Recent Supply Changes in RL and Soccer

Both soccer and RL have experienced similar changes in the supply side of sports markets. The key changes have been to the labor market and cross-subsidization policies in each sport and to the broadcasting of each. As Szymanski and Kuypers (1999), Downward and Dawson (2000), and Dobson and Goddard (2001) note, gate revenue-sharing arrangements have effectively disappeared between the larger and smaller clubs; for example, between the Premier League and the English Football League, and between the Super League and other RL clubs. The well-documented implications of the Bosman ruling, and subsequent further scrutiny by the European Union, have revealed that the labor market for athletes is also now freer. Indeed, the progressive relaxation of these restrictions, which fueled salary increases, coupled with the decline in attendance noted earlier, contributed to the financial crisis in soccer, which merited a government inquiry (Chester,

1968). Similar problems were, of course, endemic to RL, although player salaries and transfers were far less than in soccer.

With rising player costs and following the upturn in attendance, the successful soccer teams have capitalized by increasing prices and exploiting merchandising and sponsorship markets. Consistent with the idea of price inelasticity, Dobson and Goddard (2001) show that admission prices have increased threefold and revenues fourfold between 1976 and 1999, with the vast majority of the increase being associated with division one/Premier League. Sponsorship and merchandising deals have also increased rapidly. As Szymanski and Kuypers (1999) note, by 1994 top clubs such as Arsenal received only about 40% of their total revenue from gate revenues. In contrast, in RL, stationary attendances meant that clubs have been reluctant to increase prices in a pronounced way. Gate revenues are also still the largest source of revenue for clubs, which indicates that the sponsorship, merchandising, and TV deals have been far less significant than for soccer (MINTEL Report, 1997). The financial fragility of clubs also meant that a salary cap was installed with the creation of the Super League.

Yet the single biggest increase in revenue is associated with the growth of TV rights for broadcasting each sport. Historically, the rights to show live and highlighted major sports in the UK were enshrined in law, reflecting public service and initially monopoly supply by the BBC. Even when independent TV began, this regulation remained in force through the 1981 and 1984 Broadcasting Acts, and a "cartel" arrangement emerged that kept fees for televising matches down. In turn, clubs received equal and modest sums in return. Initially, the TV cartel received implicit support from the courts. In the case of soccer, London Weekend Television in 1978—an ITV company—attempted to secure the exclusive rights to televise and distribute Association Football around the network. Although the Office of Fair Trading ruled against this arrangement, a qualitative shift in the relationship between sports and TV occurred in the UK. This increased "commercial edge" to contract negotiations continued to gather speed. Ten live league fixtures were televised for the first time in 1983 and again in 1984. This two-year contract between the BBC and ITV involved a notable increase in revenues. Competition from the satellite broadcasters BSB and SKY prompted ITV to break free of the existing pattern of negotiations and effectively outbid the BBC for exclusive live coverage of Association Football matches. A four-year deal worth £11 million per annum was agreed upon. Significantly, the larger, more successful clubs received most of the funds. Thus, £8.25 million of the £11 million funds went to division one of the soccer league. In addition, £3.5 million of it went to Arsenal, Everton, Liverpool, Manchester United, and Tottenham Hotspur (Dobson and Goddard, 1998). Once again, there is evidence in keeping with Sloane's (1971) cartel-based explanation of sports league development, yet again, not particularly associated with uncertainty of outcome. Of course, the bargaining power of larger clubs ultimately led division one to break away from the soccer league to form the Premier League for the 1992–1993 season. Since this period, the merged satellite broadcaster, BSkyB, has won the collective rights to broadcast soccer, paying a recent record of over £1 billion for three years. In addtion to generally providing many of the resources to fuel wage increases in a freer labor market, BSkyB's TV revenue allocation formula also consistently skews financial rewards toward successful clubs in keeping with their demands.

The arrival of satellite TV revenues, and the Premier League discussed earlier, has also heralded changes in European Association Football competitions. Previously, European competitions between clubs involved various knockout cup competitions. There is now access to a Champions League for the top clubs in the Premier League. Currently broadcast by On Digital and ITV, this Champions League involves an initial "league" stage involving groups of teams. The winners and best runners-up then move forward into a knockout stage. This structure has prompted much speculation that the top teams will eventually evolve into a full-blown European Super League.

Despite the novel buoyancy of the market for top soccer clubs, the Premier League has provided a model for both RL and the remaining three divisions of the EFL to attempt to overcome their own financial problems. In both cases, further outside options such as European competition are lacking.[10] In RL, as Thomas (1997) notes, in key policy documents issued by the Rugby Football League in the early 1990s, the opinion was aired that, like soccer, the traditional sources of finance in the sport were lacking and that facilities needed upgrading. In addition, it was felt that the game needed more widespread promotion. By 1995, BSkyB had tabled an offer for the exclusive rights to show matches for £87 million over five years. Yet currently, the relatively weak standing of RL saw the deal revised to about £45 million over five years, beginning in 1999. Key aspects of the original deal, which were accepted, were that the game should switch to the summer and that a super league similar to the Premier League should be established. A salary cap, as noted earlier, was, based on their turnover, also introduced in RL, to help promote financial stability. The proposed merger of clubs has not taken place, although traditional names have been changed. Moreover, attempts to expand the support to London, the northeast, and even Paris have met with mixed success.

Although the EFL has not been subject to further fragmentation yet, it too has attempted to emulate the Premier League by looking toward TV as a source of revenue in light of relatively static gate revenues, and yet with salary increases needed to compete for talent in soccer. A three-year contract for £315 million was recently signed with ITV Digital to screen live matches. The collapse of this company in the face of, what one could argue was an inevitable weak demand, and the subsequent withdrawal of funds has led to ongoing legal action. Large numbers of smaller clubs face formal bankruptcy, and players have been laid off because of clubs' inability to meet wage bills (*Soccer Investor*, 2002). With the EFL, financial security would thus appear to rest with gate-drawing power and the downward revision of the affordability of players that might generate success and potential access to the Premier League.

SUMMARY AND CONCLUSION

This chapter has analyzed the common origins and development of the two oldest professional team sports in the UK. In second and third sections, an outline and economic analysis of the leagues' historical evolution was presented, showing that barriers to entry of both a sporting and economic character have evolved to produce distinct games, as implied by Neale's (1964) natural monopoly thesis. However, it was also argued that a cartel-based explanation of development, drawing upon Sloane (1971), and emphasizing the power of particular clubs, seems to have played a key part in these developments. This interpretation received support in the fourth section, which analyzes the economics of the sports in the modern era by drawing upon the growing economic literature and some new empirical results. The latter show that competitive balance seems to be the outcome rather than the source of league development in both sports, because resources are funneled toward success. In this regard, uncertainty of outcome does not appear to play a major role in regulating the growth or success of the sports. With this in mind, the recent growth of TV revenues appears to have accelerated this tendency, producing the Premier League and Super League. In general, it seems that the current economic reality of these oldest of professional team sports lies with smaller numbers of teams than either sport has supported historically. RL appears to have stabilized at what appear to be historically sustainable numbers of professional clubs captured in the Super League. For the larger soccer clubs, European competition seems to be a very clear prospect. It seems, therefore, that the Premier League will remain buoyant and possibly further evolve, whereas the EFL will contract around larger gate-drawing clubs able to withstand the financial pressures. In both cases, economic barriers to entry to the Premier League or Super League will be consolidated.

NOTES

1. *Public* is used in the sense that the schools were not owned by the headmaster, but which pupils—typically sons of aristocrats—paid to attend. Poor scholars were also accepted according to benefactors.

2. See any *Rothmans Rugby League Yearbook* for a summary of key historical developments.

3. Before this, and often during cup competitions, payment was often made by collection; for example, at Wigan. In contrast, Rochdale played in an enclosed field (Moorhouse, 1995, 29).

4. To illustrate this point, note that in rugby union, which adhered strongly to its amateur ethos until recently, many clubs remained in existence through ties to schools, "old boys," and indeed traditional fixtures.

5. Cited in Moorhouse (1995, 42).

6. Somewhat ironically, thus, the lack of investment of one of the founders of RL who switched code led to the demise of other traditional RL grounds.

7. Points rather than win-percents are used because of the high number of draws in soccer. For further discussion of measures of competitive balance see Downward and Dawson (2000).

8. Points rather than win-percents are used because of the high number of draws in soccer. For further discussion of measures of competitive balance see Downward and Dawson (2000).

9. An autoregressive form was also tried but this induced problems of normality.

10. Dobson and Goddard (1995) do identify differences in patterns of attendance between Southern and Northern clubs in soccer, with the former having greater attendances. Primarily this was an attempt to assess the impact of soccer's geographically divided division three. However, it could be linked to the presence of RL teams in the north.

11

Sports and Broadcasting: Comparisons between the United States and Europe

Chris Gratton and Harry Arne Solberg

INTRODUCTION

The most significant change in the sports industry over the last twenty years has been the increasing importance of broadcast demand, leading to massive escalation in the prices of broadcasting rights for professional team sports and major sports events. At the beginning of the twenty-first century, for the major professional team sports in both the United States and Europe, income from the sale of broadcasting rights has become more important than the amount of income generated by selling tickets to spectators at the stadia. This development first emerged in the United States in the 1980s, but Europe started to catch up in the 1990s. Although there are close similarities between the price escalation for broadcasting rights for professional team sports in both the United States and Europe, there are important differences in terms of the way these rights are distributed over different categories of television channels. This chapter will look at the history of broadcasting and sports in both the United States and Europe and then go on to analyze how the essentially same economic forces in the relationship between sports and broadcasting have led to substantially different outcomes on the two continents, drawing on several analyses that have focused on various aspects related to the economics of sports and broadcasting (Solberg, 2002a, 2002b; Cave and Crandall, 2000; Gaustad, 2000; Solberg and Gratton, 2000; Szymanski, 2000; Boardman and Hargreaves-Heap, 1999; Quirk and Fort,

1997, 1999; Cowie and Williams, 1997). First, however, we look at the landscape of TV channels on the two continents.

THE LANDSCAPE OF TV CHANNELS

The essential difference between the United States and Europe in the availability of different categories of television channels is the historical importance of public service broadcasting (PSB) channels in Europe. Although the U.S. market also has public television channels, these have not been involved in sports broadcasting. In 1980, only three countries in Europe—the UK, Italy, and Luxembourg—had commercial television stations. In the rest, television was a state monopoly. Since the mid-1980s, however, European broadcasting has been liberalized. Since then, a large number of commercial channels have emerged, and the market conditions have altered as a result.

Despite this, PSB channels still have a strong position in European broadcasting, even though their market position is considerably weaker than twenty years ago. The European PSB concept covers noncommercial channels that receive their entire income from license fees or public grants and commercial PSB channels that are allowed to advertise. In addition, some channels combine these two sources of revenue. The majority of PSB channels achieve a penetration of close to 100% of the TV households in their respective countries.

Such channels have objectives other than the entertainment of viewers and maximizing profits. One objective has been to provide to the public with so-called "merit goods" programs, which are known as commodities that ought to be provided even if the members of society do not demand them (Musgrave, 1959). Charging for television programs introduces economic inefficiency. Potential viewers are deterred from watching the programs, even though the marginal resource cost of their viewing would be zero. Thus, PSB channels have not been allowed to charge viewers, except for the general license fee.

These obligations reduce the amount that PSB channels have available to spend on sports rights. The BBC in the UK, for example, has the objective that 80% of their programs should be produced in-house. However, since the production of TV programs is characterized by high "first copy" costs, this is generally more expensive than purchasing programs from other channels (Brown and Cave, 1992).

The regulations that influence the program menu also reduce the income potential for commercial PSB channels. Although the reception of TV programs is regarded as a public good, this does not apply to the resources being used in the programs' production. These resources are regarded as private goods, which means that channels cannot use them on more than one task simultaneously. Thus, when a PSB channel is obliged to broadcast programs targeting minority groups, it is also restricted from using the same resources simultaneously to broadcast for a mass audience, which would have given the channel higher advertising revenues. Hence, the revenues forgone represent alternative costs for commercial channels.

Advertising channels deliver programs that are free to watch. The only price the viewer pays is the time spent on watching commercials. Advertisers seek to shift the demand curve for their product, and/or make it more inelastic, and will continue to supply advertising up to the point where the marginal cost of advertising equals the marginal revenue from advertising (Kaldor, 1950). Advertisers want to maximize the number of potential customers. Thus, the amount of revenue received from the advertiser is broadly proportional to audience size.

Advertising channels have traditionally been the dominating force in U.S. broadcasting, and the number of channels has increased considerably over the years. Nowadays the supply side includes the major broadcasting networks, ABC, NBC, CBS, and Fox, but also cable networks as well as hundreds of local stations. It is the major broadcasting networks that have the highest penetration. To achieve this penetration, the broadcasting networks are connected to several hundred local affiliates. These affiliates receive cash compensation to carry the scheduled national programming that is provided free by the networks (Dunnett, 1990). Despite the deregulation process in the 1980s, advertising on TV in general is still considerably more regulated in Europe than in the United States, where no federal law of regulation limits the amount of commercial matter that may be broadcast at any given time. The exception is television programs aimed at children twelve years and under, for which advertising may not exceed ten and one-half minutes an hour on weekends and twelve minutes an hour on weekdays. In the UK, however, the BBC is not allowed to take any advertising, Channels 4, 5, and ITV are limited to seven and one-half minutes per hour, while BSkyB is limited to nine minutes per hour. Similarly, in Germany, PSB channels are limited to twenty minutes per day, and private channels are limited to twelve minutes of advertising per hour. In addition, Europe also has other regulations on advertising. Several countries ban advertising for alcohol and tobacco. In the Scandinavian countries, advertising connected to all children's TV programs is banned.

The third category of television channels, pay service channels, take account of the intensity of viewers' preferences expressed in financial terms, which is different from advertiser-supported broadcasting. It is the consumer surplus that the viewers would have obtained if the programs were broadcast on free channels that represents the potential income. Thus, programs that do not attract large audiences can still be profitable, assuming a sufficient number of viewers have a high willingness to pay for watching them. Pay service channels also sell advertising, but these revenues account for a considerably smaller proportion of the total revenues than for pure advertising channels. Since viewers have to pay extra charges, these channels have a considerably lower penetration than free air channels. Pay channels have expanded in both the United States and Europe in the past decade, but within that time they have had a much more significant effect on sports broadcasting in Europe than in the United States.

THE HISTORY OF SPORTS AND BROADCASTING: UNITED STATES

Quirk and Fort (1997) chronicle the early years of televised professional team sports in the United States, which focused on the trade-off between new income from television and lost revenues from reduced attendance. In 1950, the Los Angeles Rams signed a contract to televise six home games to viewers in the Los Angeles area. The contract specified that the sponsor would make up any loss resulting from lower attendance due to the live coverage. The two home games that were not televised generated an average revenue of $77,000. The six televised games averaged only $42,000 per game, resulting in the sponsor having to pay $198,000 in compensation. The contract was not renewed in 1951. In these early years of televised professional team sports in the United States, the perceived negative impact on attendance was a major constraint on the development of more television coverage.

In the 1960s, however, increased competition among the three major networks, CBS, NBC, and ABC, led to more television coverage of the four major team sports: American football, baseball, basketball, and ice hockey. Downward and Dawson (2000) and Cashmore (1994) argue that ABC in particular led the way with an aggressive attempt to broaden the interest in televised sports beyond the normal male audience, introducing technical innovations such as slow motion replays, close-ups, and split screens. Increasing advertising revenues generated through televised sports drove the networks to extend their coverage.

By 1970, the National Football League (NFL) earned $49 million a year from the sale of broadcasting rights, and this had increased to $167 million by 1980 (Quirk and Fort, 1997). It was in the 1980s, however, that growth in the size of deals for sports broadcasting rights accelerated dramatically. Quirk and Fort (1997) estimated that in 1991, broadcast revenue accounted for 25% of National Hockey League (NHL) revenues, 30% of National Basketball Association (NBA) revenues, 50% of Major League Baseball (MLB) revenues, and 60% of NFL revenues.

The escalation in the price of broadcasting rights continued during the 1990s. In early 1998, American broadcasters agreed to pay $17.6 billion for the NFL rights for eight years. In America, the major funding for these television deals has come from free channels. Sports attract massive audiences, and American football is definitely the number one sport. Nine of the all-time top ten programs are Super Bowl finals, which generally attract a domestic TV audience of more than 130 million. Such figures are equivalent to almost 50% of the U.S. TV households. In recent years, MLB and the NBA have competed for the number two status, and the NHL has ranked number four among the professional leagues. This picture is confirmed in Table 1, which shows the TV rights for the four major professional leagues. The table shows strong price increases, although one also finds periods with slower growth, for example in the early 1990s. Table 1 confirms the NFL's dominating position also in monetary terms. However, as the table only includes deals between national channels and the leagues, it does not convey the complete story. Over the years, MLB, the NBA, and the NHL have received considerable amounts of money from selling TV rights to local stations.

The motive of the television companies in bidding for sports broadcast rights is the ability to sell advertising time at hugely inflated prices during the games, which last two or three times longer than the equivalent in Europe, and are broken more frequently by commercials than is the case in Europe. During the 1990s, it seemed that no major network could afford to be without some football coverage. CBS plunged from first to third in the television rankings after it lost out to Fox, which is owned by Rupert Murdoch's News Corporation (News Corp), in the auction of broadcast rights for football in 1993. With its coverage of sports, Fox moved up the ratings and the big three became the big four. In 1998, when the rights came up for renewal, CBS paid $4 billion (twice the old price) for its package of games, Fox paid $4.4 billion for its share of games, and ABC and ESPN (both owned by Disney) paid a further $9.2 billion. The NFL, which earned $500 million a year from TV rights in 1990, earned $2.2 billion a year under the 1998 deal.

This scenario illustrates that the benefits of televising football go beyond the advertising revenues generated during the games. In fact, in most cases, the price of broadcasting rights exceeds considerably the amount of money generated in advertising. Quirk and Fort (1999) estimated that NBC's four-year NFL contract between 1990 and 1994 lost the network $200 million, with CBS losing almost twice as much on the deal. Nevertheless, both networks bid for the next contract, although CBS lost out to Fox.

THE HISTORY OF SPORTS AND BROADCASTING: EUROPE

In contrast to the United States, there was little or no competition in the European television market in the early postwar years. Here, we use a case study of the UK to indicate the different position of Europe as compared to the United States in the history of sports broadcasting.

Table 1
North American Sports Rights—Central Deals Only

Period	Annual fees ($ 1000)
NFL	
1998 – 2005	2 200 000
1994 – 1997	1 097 000
1990 – 1993	900 000
1987 – 1989	468 000
1982 – 1986	378 000
NBA	
1998 – 2002	660 000
1994 – 1998	276 000
1990 – 1994	219 000
1986 – 1900	63 000
1983 – 1986	22 000
MLB	
2001 – 2006	570 000
1996 – 2000	340 000
1990 – 1993	352 000
NHL	
1999 – 2005	120 000
1994 – 1999	43 000

Source: SportsBusinessNews.com. (Originally, August 16, 2002.)

In the UK, until 1955 there was only one television channel, the BBC, a noncommercial public service broadcaster. Over this period, the BBC developed extensive televised sports coverage in Britain, televising all the major national sports spectacles and establishing the annual cycle of major sports events, beginning in January with the Five Nations Rugby Union tournament, then the Boat Race, Grand National, Rugby League Challenge Cup final, Football Association (FA) Cup final, Derby, cricket test matches, Wimbledon, and Open Golf Championship. Over this period, however, there was no live television coverage of the matches in the main professional team sports because of fears within these sports that live television coverage would reduce attendance at matches.

Whannel (1992) suggests that there were good economic reasons for the BBC to put so much emphasis on sports. Until ITV was established in 1955, the BBC was the only buyer for televised sports in a market where there were many suppliers. This lack of competition allowed the BBC to keep rights fees very low and televised sports were cheap broadcasting.

However, as the 1950s progressed, it became increasingly evident that such a policy could not be sustained. The arrival in 1955 of ITV, a commercial public service broadcaster, destroyed the BBC's monopoly on the buying side of the market and increased the level of fees. However, the BBC continued to dominate the sports broadcasting.

Whannel gives three reasons why ITV did not in the 1950s and 1960s provide stronger competition for the BBC. First, the BBC had a head start. It had developed a substantial competitive advantage with its outside broadcasting expertise. It had also tied up many sports with long-term exclusive contracts. Second, the regional structure of ITV meant that no single company had a big enough audience to justify substantial investment in outside broadcasting facilities or to make large enough bids for exclusive contracts. Third, in the 1950s it was not clearly established that sports were an obvious audience winner.

ITV was dealt a further competitive blow by the introduction of BBC2 in 1964, which gave the BBC a tremendous advantage for those events that took place over a long period of time: cricket test matches, Wimbledon, golf, and major snooker championships. Barnett (1990) indicates how the introduction of BBC2 further enhanced the BBC's competitive advantage by allowing coverage to be switched to BBC2, allowing BBC1 to maintain its regular programs. Whereas no single channel could allow six or seven hours of continuous golf, tennis, or cricket, it was possible for a broadcaster with two channels at its disposal.

During the 1960s and 1970s, ITV did attempt to match the BBC in one sport, soccer. In 1964, "the BBC initiated what was to become the hallmark of British football coverage and the centrepiece of Saturday night programming—recorded highlights on *Match of the Day*" (Barnett, 1990).

The Big Match on Sunday afternoons was ITV's answer to *Match of the Day* and was introduced in the 1968–1969 season. Both the BBC and ITV showed the FA Cup final over this period but the BBC's audience was twice that of ITV.

Throughout the 1970s, soccer coverage was handled by negotiation between the BBC and ITV and the Football League and the Football Association, in what Whannel (1992) describes as "the old cosy BBC/ITV sharing of football."

It was late in the 1980s that ITV became a serious threat to the BBC in football coverage. In the 1988 to 1992 period, it pushed up the price of broadcasting rights by 250% and outbid the BBC to obtain exclusive rights.

It was not, however, until BSkyB entered the scene, most notably with its bid for soccer's Premiership matches for the 1992 to 1997 period that the landscape of sports broadcasting in Britain changed dramatically. BSkyB, with its owner Rupert Murdoch's News Corp (also owner of Fox), accustomed to the much stronger competition for sports broadcasting rights in the United States, simply raised the price for the rights from its artificially depressed level. BSkyB acquired the rights for English Premier League live matches for the period from 1992 to 1997 at a price that was three times the value of the previous deal, which was held by ITV. However, whereas the former deal included only eighteen live matches annually, BSkyB increased this number to sixty. Hence the price per match hardly increased in 1992. The large increases for annual Premier League rights came when they were renewed in 1997 and again in 2001. The annual Premier League fees quadrupled in 1997 and tripled again in 2001. On these occasions, the price per match also increased substantially. BSkyB has held the rights for live matches since 1992 and has financed the lion's share of the total Premier League value. The deal for the 2001 to 2004 period pays the twenty clubs in the league more than $750 million annually. This is the most lucrative deal in Europe.

For BSkyB, however, sports became much more important economically than they ever were for the BBC. The BBC received its revenue from the license fee and had a responsibility to provide a breadth of programs to satisfy "the national interest," which included prominence for sports because of their historically important role in British culture. However, the BBC could never dedicate the share of its income (nearly 50%) that BSkyB dedicates to sports, as this would be regarded as unbalanced for a public service provider. BSkyB is not bound by such considerations. Sports have proved to be the difference between high levels of profit and bankruptcy for BSkyB. Most financial analysts see BSkyB's share value as crucially dependent on its ownership of sports broadcasting rights.

A similar tendency characterizes developments in other European countries. In the 1987–1988 season, the German premier league (Bundesliga) brought in $10.8 million in annual TV right fees, whereas in the 2001–2002 season, the fee had increased to $341 million. In the 1999–2000 season, the Italian premier league (Serie A) clubs earned an annual income of $451 million from their sale of TV rights (Solberg, 2002b).

Soccer has become the dominant TV sport in Europe, both in terms of rating figures and rights fees. In 1998, a soccer match topped the television program popularity ranking lists in 75% of fifty European countries. In Germany and France, eighty-six and seventy-three respectively of the top 100 programs were soccer related. In 1998, six of the top ten TV programs in the UK were soccer matches from the World Cup finals (Solberg, 2002b).

In the rest of Europe, as in the UK, the price escalation took off during the 1990s. This increase, however, did not correspond with the rest of the economy, as Table 2 reveals. In each of the "Big 5" soccer nations, the UK, Spain, Italy, Germany, and France, the value of sports rights increased considerably more than the gross domestic product. For example, the Italian soccer rights increased by 152% in a period during which the activity in the overall economy decreased by 4% (see Table 2). In Italy, soccer absorbed 64% of the total amount spent on sports rights in 2000. This proportion was 51% in the UK and Spain, 41% in Germany, and 39% in France (Kagan World Media Ltd., 2002).

With regard to sports broadcasting over the postwar period, we can therefore see major differences between the European situation and that in the United States. In Europe, professional team sports programs were mainly broadcast on PSB channels until late in the 1980s, but in recent years this pattern has changed. Pay service channels have acquired a large slice of the most attractive soccer rights, whereas PSB channels and other channels with maximum penetration have been restricted to highlights programs. Live matches from the domestic premier leagues in the Big 5 European soccer nations (England, France, Germany, Italy, and Spain) are almost entirely screened on pay service channels.

In the U.S. market, advertising channels have dominated the sports rights markets during the last five decades. Major broadcasting networks, as well as some of the national cable networks, have spent enormous amounts of money on sports rights. In addition, there are plenty of attractive sports on local stations. Although pay channels have also acquired popular sports rights in the United States, these deals have not contained the same degree of

Table 2
Percentage Increases: European Sports Rights, 1992–1997

	UK	Germany	Italy	France	Spain
Soccer	97	137	152	78	132
Other sport	74	92	28	56	83
GDP	41	9	-4	10	2

Source: Kagan World Media, Ltd. (2000).

exclusiveness as the European soccer deals (Cave and Crandall, 2000). U.S. TV viewers would probably find it difficult to imagine the most attractive NFL games being screened exclusively on a pay channel, with only some delayed highlights on a national network. In the United States, it is fair to regard pay service channels as a supplement to advertising channels, rather than as a competitor.

DISCUSSION

The figures presented in the previous section show that, until the 1990s, European prices were significantly cheaper than American prices for sports broadcasting rights. The main reason for this difference was a lack of competition in Europe, combined with the strict regulation of broadcasting, that made it impossible for the channels to spend the same amount on sports rights as the U.S. networks. This pattern changed late in the 1980s as a consequence of the liberalization of European broadcasting. Over the years, a large number of profit-maximizing TV channels entered the scene and acquired sports rights in order to strengthen their market position. Advertising channels have given priority to programs that are able to achieve high ratings figures. Pay channels have concentrated on acquiring sports rights that attract a sufficient number of viewers willing to pay to watch. The latter channels have especially been successful in acquiring the rights to live matches from the domestic soccer leagues.

However, even if European broadcasting has been liberalized in recent years, it has not been completely deregulated. The regulations particularly influence the channels with the highest penetration, such as the PSB channels that still are used as tools to achieve the noncommercial objectives discussed earlier. In addition, there is general regulation of TV advertising. A consequence of this regulation policy is that European free channels face worse market conditions than their colleagues on the other side of the Atlantic. Thus, sports rights are still considerably cheaper in Europe than in the United States if the seller prefers channels with maximum penetration. As an example, the European Summer Olympics TV rights for the period 1996 to 2008 cost 50% of the U.S. prices—whereas for the Winter Olympics the proportion is only 20% (Solberg, 2002a).

Although the owners of European sports rights have learned to benefit from auctioning the rights, the regulation of European broadcasting can also influence the outcome of auctions. To illustrate this point, let us imagine an open auction in which there are two bidders, one noncommercial PSB channel and one profit-maximizing commercial channel. Most likely, the latter channel will have the better cards in this competition due to the regulations that restrict the PSB channel. However, the commercial channel is not interested in paying more than necessary. In the case of open auctions, the optimal policy will be to submit bids that are slightly above the PSB channel. The final price may still be considerably lower than what the commercial channel would have been willing to bid if several other commercial channels were bidding (Johnsen, 2000). The consequences will be quite similar in the case of a sealed auction, even though the bidders lack information about the competitors' bids. The dilemma is to avoid bidding more than what is necessary to win the contract, but at the same time to avoid losing it by bidding lower than the competitor. However, if the only competitor is a noncommercial PSB channel, the commercial channel should have fairly good information to predict the maximum that the competitor is able to bid.

The prices on sports rights do not only depend on the regulation policy of TV channels, but also on the market behavior of the sellers. Although the sellers of sports rights in Europe have become more experienced during the last decade, they still have some lessons to learn from their colleagues on the other side of the Atlantic. As an example, it is not uncommon for networks to submit joint bids. Such collusion reduces the number of bidders, and hence also the rights fees.

The U.S. broadcasting networks started to bid for sports rights in the 1960s. Since then, the number of commercial channels has increased and hence also the competition. This increase includes cable networks as well as a large number of local stations. However, it is the major broadcasting networks that have the highest penetration. Due to more liberal regulations than their European colleagues, U.S. networks are able to submit higher bids, although as we have seen, these high profile deals for sports broadcasting rights often do not yield clear profits. Consequently, the U.S. market does not have any trade-off between maximizing the exposure and maximizing the TV rights. Since the main income comes from advertising, the broadcasters' objective has been to increase—or to uphold—the ratings figures. U.S. broadcasting is characterized by a permanent struggle to maximize the number of viewers, and the networks are always willing to take the necessary steps to improve unacceptable ratings figures. Sports broadcasts are no exception. When the ratings figures have declined, both channels and leagues have been willing to make adjustments according to contract clauses.

It is extremely important for the broadcasting networks to offer a popular menu of programs, not only to maximize the ratings figures, and thereby the advertising revenues, but also to uphold (or increase) the number of affiliates they are connected to. The higher the penetration is, the higher the price of advertising time. Hence, the acquisition of attractive sports rights also generates indirect revenues for the networks. A well-known example was Fox's first acquisition of NFL rights in 1993, which gave them status as the fourth broadcasting network. In contrast, in Europe, collusion has been banned unless the channels belong to the same parent company.

Pay service channels have found it difficult to attract enough subscribers in markets where the viewers can choose among a large number of free channels. This has been the case in the United States and also in Germany, which has the largest domestic TV market in Europe, with more than thirty free channels. Thus, Premiere, the German pay service channel owned by KirchMedia, has not achieved the same success as its colleagues in other European countries; for example, BSkyB and Canal Plus.

Occasionally, the success of some channels has attracted too many new entrants, which in the end has resulted in an abundance of TV sports. Sports enthusiasts, as anybody else, have a limited amount of time and financial resources. Thus, on some occasions, TV deals that originally looked to be profitable have resulted in financial losses for the channels. The most notable example was the collapse of ITV Digital in England in 2002, after it paid too much for the rights to nationwide soccer matches. After the collapse, BSkyB acquired the rights for less than a quarter of what ITV Digital had paid.

On some occasions, the winner of an auction has overestimated the popularity of sports programs, a phenomenon known as the winner's curse syndrome (Rasmussen, 2001). Similar impacts have occurred in cases when a recession in the economy has reduced the demand for advertising in general. In the United States, it has been claimed that the so-called "September 11 effect" has caused the largest decline in advertising since World War II.

One way of solving such problems is by implementing clauses in the contracts that tie rights fees to ratings figures, hence sharing the risk between the sellers and buyers. Since late in the 1990s, however, the tough competition among TV channels has made it a "seller's market." Therefore the sellers have been unwilling to share the risk with the TV channels. However, this pattern could change if the current signs of a halt in the escalation of rights fees continue.

Pay service channels have not obtained the same commercial success with the acquisition of other sports rights, such as skiing (Nordic games), handball, and rugby, as they have with soccer. These sports are considerably less popular than soccer and have not been able to recruit the same number of subscribers. In addition, sports federations are also running a high risk by selling all the rights exclusively to pay channels. It is not uncommon that channels that cannot afford to acquire the broadcasting rights boycott these sports, which in the long rung can reduce the the sports' recruiting power as well as the revenues from sponsors. Thus, second-rated sports and advertising channels have a mutual goal of maximizing the number of viewers.

CONCLUSION

The price of broadcasting rights for Europe's number one professional team sport, soccer, is (at the time of this writing) on a comparable level with the price paid for NFL games in the United States (after adjusting for differences in population). However, whereas we have seen a similar price escalation in the broadcasting rights for the second, third, and fourth professional team sports (basketball, baseball, and ice hockey) in the United States, the acceleration in the growth of the price of broadcasting sports in Europe has pushed soccer way ahead of the rest. The main reason for the price escalation in Europe was the deregulation of the broadcasting market in the 1980s, creating much greater competition for sports broadcasting rights and turning a buyer's market into a seller's market.

However, the long history of regulation, with the dominance of public service broadcasting, meant that when deregulation arrived the nature of competition for broadcasting rights in Europe that emerged was substantially different from that in the United States. The end result is that whereas in the United States the main broadcasts of professional team sports are on free channels received by virtually the whole population, in Europe supporters of the most popular professional team sports must pay an expensive additional subscription to a pay service provider, broadcasting to a minority of the population, to see live broadcasts of matches. It is ironic that Europe, with its long tradition of market intervention in television to ensure it provides for all the interests of the population, has emerged with an outcome that excludes so much of its population from sports television programs with the consequent loss of consumer surplus. The unregulated competition in the United States, in contrast, has managed to provide attractive TV sports without such deadweight losses.

12

Ownership and Finance of Professional Soccer in England and Europe

Stephen Dobson and John Goddard

INTRODUCTION

Major changes in the ownership and financial structure of professional clubs in European (association) soccer have been underway in recent years. To date, more than twenty English clubs have obtained stock market listings, mostly since the mid-1990s. More recently, the flotation trend has spread throughout Europe, providing opportunities for clubs to raise new money from previously inaccessible sources and creating pressure for the modernization of many of soccer's traditional management practices. Meanwhile, the secondary market in soccer clubs' stock has proven to be highly volatile, with recent large price falls driven partly by concerns over wage inflation and over the future value of television rights.

This chapter explores trends in the ownership and financing of professional soccer in England and draws some Europe-wide comparisons. The chapter also includes an empirical section, in the form of an event study that identifies the impact of specific events, both on and off the playing field, on the share prices of quoted English soccer clubs, both individually and collectively.

THE OWNERSHIP AND FINANCIAL STRUCTURE OF ENGLISH SOCCER

Until the final two decades of the twentieth century, the commercial and financial management of professional soccer in England had seemed impervious to modernization pressures. Remarkably little had changed since the dawn of professionalism in the late-Victorian era. Typically, chairmen, directors, and major shareholders of soccer clubs were local businessmen, for whom success elsewhere in trade or commerce had provided the means to intervene in the running of the local soccer club. Ownership and control were often handed down through the generations, from father to son. Although some working-class supporters had a stake in clubs, typically these shareholdings were too small to confer much influence over running the club. The share certificates were prized mainly for their sentimental or antique value, or as a token of loyalty.

The financial structure of the typical English soccer club during this era is outlined by Morrow (1999). Most were small, privately owned companies, which tended to be undercapitalized with little money raised either from issues of new equity (because owners were often unwilling to dilute their personal control) or from retained profit (because usually there was no profit). In many cases, however, club owners or directors provided additional long-term financing through personal loans, which for practical purposes were similar to equity finance. Bank loans and overdrafts were the other principal source of (mainly short-term) financing.

English soccer's nonprofit ethos was underpinned by Football Association (FA) regulations limiting the amounts that could be received by shareholders and directors in the form of dividends or salaries; requiring existing chairmen to approve any major transfer of shares, eliminating the possibility of hostile takeover; and stipulating that a club's assets would revert to the FA in the event that it ceased playing soccer, hence preventing any club from being taken over and closed in order to realize a quick profit by selling its stadium (Conn, 1998; Horrie, 2002). Eventually, however, these restrictions proved insufficiently watertight to prevent the succession of a new generation of hard-headed, commercially minded chairmen at many of the leading clubs.

Having become a director of Manchester United in the late 1950s, Louis Edwards, owner of a family butcher business in Salford, began a surreptitious campaign to buy out the club's minor shareholders, many of whom were delighted to be offered sums of £15 per share for certificates they had inherited and assumed to be of no cash value. For a total investment of perhaps £40,000, Edwards accumulated a 54% shareholding and took control in January 1964. A rights issue in 1979 massively increased the number of shares without diluting the Edwards family's control and conveniently circumvented the FA's limitation on dividend payments, expressed as a percentage of the face value of each share. In many ways, the passing of the Manchester United chairmanship from Louis Edwards to his son, Martin, in 1980 typifies the broader trend toward the replacement of old-style chairmen by the new entrepreneurial breed that would call most of the shots in the future.

At the beginning of the 1980s, north London property developer Irving Scholar initiated a similar low-key campaign to buy out small Tottenham Hotspur shareholders. Legend has it that Scholar marked his assumption of control by turning up at a directors' meeting to announce himself as the new chairman, much to the astonishment of other board members. He set about refinancing the debt-ridden club by floating a new holding company, Tottenham Hotspur PLC, on the London Stock Exchange. The holding company would circumvent FA regulations on dividend payments by owning the soccer club as a subsidiary, together with a number of other leisure, clothing, and catering businesses. The flotation in October 1983 raised £3.3 million—a sum considerably larger at the time than it may seem by present-day standards and sufficient to eliminate the debts inherited from the previous ownership. Indifferent results in several of the other diversified businesses, however, meant that in the long term the flotation was less than an unqualified success.

Perhaps because the holding company's financial performance did not offer strong encouragement to others, for several years Tottenham remained the only English club with a stock market listing. Nevertheless, others did eventually follow suit. The flotations of Millwall (October 1989) and Manchester United (June 1991) raised £4.8 million and £6.7 million, respectively. Again, the early experiences of the quoted companies were discouraging. Following relegation from the old first division soon after flotation, Millwall shares collapsed in value and trading was suspended. Manchester United shares were less than 50% subscribed at flotation. Meanwhile, other clubs were experimenting with alternative methods of raising external financing, such as bond schemes guaranteeing the right to purchase a season ticket for a specific seat in perpetuity. Such schemes were not overwhelmingly popular with fans, however, and were soon dropped.

Despite the indifferent results of these early attempts to expand and diversify English soccer's capital base, by the early 1990s events and sentiment were starting to move in a direction more favorable to the sport's commercial development. Decisive action on the part of soccer's governing bodies, clubs, and the government over issues such as safety and hooliganism had raised hopes that the stadium disasters and other problems of the 1980s could finally be lain to rest. Meanwhile, the formation of the Premier League in 1992 freed the twenty-two top division clubs from the obligation to share both revenues and voting rights with the seventy lower division clubs. The sale of the Premier League's television rights to the satellite broadcaster BSkyB for £191.5 million over five years from 1992 produced a sudden and unprecedented cash windfall. As the Premier League got under way, a surge of optimistic sentiment concerning future prospects led to massive appreciation in the share prices of the two clubs that had already floated. Between 1994 and 1996, Tottenham Hotspur and Manchester United shares both increased in value by more than 300%.

The circumstances were therefore favorable for the spate of fifteen further flotations on the London Stock Exchange Official List and Alternative Investment Market that took place between September 1995 and October 1997.[1] By far the largest flotation, worth over £50 million, was that of Newcastle United in April 1997. Including clubs listed on OFEX, an unregulated market for small unquoted companies, twenty-three of the ninety-two Premier League and Football League clubs had experimented with some form of stock market listing by the summer of 2002, and nineteen were still listed. According to Deloitte & Touche (2002), English clubs had raised around £175 million of new money from the stock exchange. As of June 2002, the combined capitalization of the nineteen listed English clubs was £651 million. In addition, the four quoted Scottish clubs had a combined capitalization of £124 million. Table 1 summarizes trends in the share prices since the mid-1990s of a number of leading English clubs.

A shift of emphasis was already underway, however, by the time of the Newcastle flotation. For the large institutional investors, investment in the shares of soccer clubs was never more than a minor sideline, accounting for only a minuscule proportion of their total investment portfolios. Further, since 1997 the institutions appear to have taken a pessimistic view of the soccer sector's prospects, and consequently have scaled back their involvement. Media companies, on the other hand, may have specific strategic motives for seeking representation in the ownership and involvement in running soccer. Accordingly, the late 1990s witnessed significant expansion in direct media investment in English soccer clubs.

The issue of vertical integration between media companies and soccer clubs first attracted headline attention in Britain in September 1998, with the announcement that the Manchester United board was accepting a 100% takeover bid valued at £623 million from BSkyB. Following a storm of protest from soccer fans and those parts of the British media not owned by Rupert Murdoch's News Corporation (News Corp), the government subsequently referred the bid to the Monopolies and Mergers Commission (MMC). In March 1999, the MMC ruled that the merger would damage competition between broadcasters and would be detrimental to the wider interests of soccer, and in April 1999, the government blocked the takeover. The MMC ruling also torpedoed an agreement for the cable operator NTL to take a controlling interest in Newcastle United if the Manchester United takeover went ahead.

Although direct ownership of major English clubs by media companies has been ruled out, companies can still acquire minority stakes in more than one club, subject to an FA regulation restricting parties with multiple interests to a maximum 10% shareholding in each club. Accordingly, BSkyB, Granada Media, and NTL have each acquired minority shareholdings in a number of clubs. In addition, several leading clubs signed deals with media companies to develop Internet broadcasting and e-commerce services. Overall, Deloitte

Table 1
Share Price Index Values for English Soccer Clubs (December 1997 = 100)

	Aston Villa	Bolton Wdrs	Charlt'n Athletic	Chelsea	Leeds United	Leic'ter City	Man United	Newc'st United	Preston NE	Sheff United	South-ampton	Sunder-land	Tott'ham Hotspur	BSkyB	FTSE 100
12/95							31.0		89.9				59.3	89.1	71.8
06/96				59.1			68.7		121.3				129.5	96.5	72.3
12/96				100.0	193.7		105.6		132.6			217.4	165.3	114.5	80.2
06/97	116.7	160.4	106.8	96.1	107.4		96.0	144.4	122.5	87.1	127.0	107.2	132.5	96.5	89.7
12/97	100.0	100.0	100.0	100.0	100.0	100.0	100.0	100.0	100.0	100.0	100.0	100.0	100.0	100.0	100.0
06/98	67.6	60.4	118.4	62.2	65.3	70.2	100.3	78.8	96.6	54.5	90.1	128.7	88.1	95.0	113.6
12/98	95.8	66.0	94.2	70.9	72.6	66.9	141.5	102.6	76.4	45.5	53.9	182.6	96.7	100.1	114.5
06/99	61.3	60.4	71.8	57.8	67.4	70.2	125.9	86.2	64.0	35.6	53.3	127.5	84.8	129.1	123.0
12/99	52.3	54.7	83.5	51.7	86.3	73.6	129.7	73.0	60.1	32.7	55.3	181.2	85.4	218.5	134.9
06/00	59.6	35.8	100.0	47.4	93.7	80.2	221.2	57.1	53.9	28.7	55.6	121.7	94.7	283.3	122.9
12/00	38.7	32.1	82.5	39.1	52.6	90.9	141.8	48.7	53.9	26.7	53.3	115.9	68.9	245.8	121.2
06/01	23.3	32.1	65.0	28.3	41.1	82.6	94.6	39.2	50.0	18.3	60.5	126.1	67.5	150.0	109.9
12/01	22.1	17.0	41.7	22.6	44.2	44.6	91.8	27.5	39.9	12.4	50.7	105.1	58.3	165.8	101.6
06/02	16.8	13.2	27.2	16.1	24.2	23.1	77.2	21.7	27.0	9.9	44.7	73.2	38.4	137.9	90.7

Note: All data are end-of-month values.
Source: Subscription data service, Thomson Datastream.

& Touche (2002) estimate that strategic media investment in English soccer has amounted to at least £240 million.

To what extent have the developments described in this section transformed the ownership and financial structure of English soccer? According to data compiled by Deloitte & Touche (2002), the Football League remains more reliant than the Premier League on traditional sources of financing such as short-term bank borrowing and long-term loans from directors or other benefactors. Share capital and retained profit accounted for 62% of the total financing of Premier League clubs in 2000 and 2001, but just 10% for the Football League. In recent seasons, the Blackburn Rovers, Fulham, Reading, Wigan Athletic, and the Wolverhampton Wanderers have all received large loans from benefactors. Meanwhile, several Premier League clubs have experimented with new mechanisms for raising nonequity finance from institutional investors. These include player finance contracts, involving the sale and leaseback of players' registrations; and securitization, involving the capitalization of future anticipated flows of ticket or other commercial income. Although these types of arrangements have generated less media excitement than stock market flotation and high profile multimillion pound media company investments, the sums raised are significant. Deloitte & Touche estimate that by the summer of 2002, £120 million had been raised through player finance techniques, and £223 million through securitization.

ENGLISH SOCCER'S RECENT STOCK MARKET DECLINE

Table 1 shows that the downturn in soccer clubs' share prices that began during 1997 has continued with little respite for about five years. For the second half of this period, the trend in the market as a whole has also been downward. Nevertheless, it is clear that the financial markets' view of the soccer sector has been especially gloomy. Why? Naturally there has been abundant commentary in the financial and mainstream press and elsewhere. Much of this discussion centers on two key issues: first, inflation in players' wages and salaries, and second, the recent decline in the market for television rights.

Wage Inflation

Table 2 shows that wage inflation at all levels of English soccer over the four-year period ending with the 2000–2001 season outstripped revenue growth. By the end of this period the average ratio of wages and salaries to revenue was approaching the 70% benchmark suggested by Deloitte & Touche as the maximum likely to be sustainable for any individual club over the long term. Indeed, for the Football League the average was significantly above this benchmark for most of the period.

Table 2
Average Revenue and Wage Expenditure, English Soccer Clubs

	Premier League	Division One	Division Two	Division Three	All
Average revenue (£'000)					
1996-7	21638	6744	2595	1115	7855
2000-1	45794	9894	3465	1983	16115
Average wages and salaries (£'000)					
1996-7	10357	4180	1845	951	4279
2000-1	28403	7978	3344	1598	10904
Wages and salaries as % revenue					
1996-7	47.9	62.0	71.1	85.3	54.5
2000-1	62.0	80.6	96.5	80.6	67.7

Source: Deloitte & Touche (2002).

Against this background the need for some form of collective restraint has been widely debated. Given the openness of the post-Bosman soccer players' labor market, however, it is likely that a North American–style salary cap would have to operate Europe-wide or not at all. However, the practical and legal obstacles may well prove insurmountable. Meanwhile, European soccer's governing body, Union des Associations Européennes de Football (UEFA), plans to introduce a licensing scheme, imposing conditions on the financial management of clubs, at the start of the 2004–2005 season. In the recent and current absence of any such form of restraint, however, one interpretation of the soccer sector's five-year stock market decline is that it reflects a realization on the part of the markets that soccer's loss-making propensities are systemic and perhaps in the final analysis cannot be eradicated.

The Market for Television Rights

The escalating value of English soccer's television rights since live transmissions began in the early 1980s has been documented extensively elsewhere

(Cave and Crandall, 2001). It seems likely that the most recent auction, concluded in June 2000 and placing a combined value of more than £2.4 billion on the rights for the 2001–2002 to 2003–2004 seasons, signifies a peak in this market. A subscriber list of around 5 million, each being charged between £30 and £40 per month, provided a secure basis for BSkyB to pay £1.1 billion to retain the rights to screen sixty-six live Premier League matches in each of the three seasons. As soon as the June 2000 sale was concluded, however, speculation was rife that some other parts of the package were overpriced—a judgment soon confirmed by NTL's withdrawal from its £328 million contract to screen a further forty live matches on a pay-per-view basis. The pay-per-view package was subsequently licensed to all four UK pay-TV platforms for a combined payment of around half the original price.

Meanwhile, ITV originally scheduled its Premier League highlights package for prime time, early Saturday evening viewing on its national free network. But after several weeks of critical reviews and low ratings, it was switched to a more traditional late evening slot. Only a fraction of the £183 million fee would ever be recouped through advertising revenues. Even worse for ITV, the lure of live Football League coverage failed to attract more than about 200,000 subscribers to its fledgling terrestrial pay-TV service, ITV Digital. Although a market for live lower division soccer does exist in England, most of it was already committed to BSkyB and was unwilling to acquire the additional decoder and subscription needed to receive ITV Digital. BSkyB had its own obvious strategic reasons for stalling over a deal to permit transmission of ITV Digital channels via its satellite platform, which if concluded could have brought the service within reach of its niche audience. Reportedly, some of ITV Digital's live coverage, acquired at an approximate cost of £1 million per match, attracted audiences of only around 1,000. In the summer of 2002, ITV Digital folded, with £178.5 million of the original £315 million purchase price unpaid.[2] None of the debt was recovered, and the Football League's live rights for the next four seasons were sold off to BSkyB for £95 million. Significantly, this valued the rights slightly below the £125 million BSkyB had paid previously for the five-year period from 1996 to 2001.

Amid predictably exaggerated claims that many were on the verge of collapse, Football League clubs immediately set about the task of scaling down their wage expenditure in line with their diminished projected future revenue streams. Competition among broadcasters clearly contributed to some of the stratospheric sums achieved in the 2000 television rights sale, but with ITV Digital in liquidation and the loss-making cable operators NTL and Telewest heavily indebted, BSkyB's domination of the British pay-TV market appears unchallenged for the foreseeable future. Moreover, thanks to technological constraint and consumer indifference, the commercial potential of Internet broadcasting now looks significantly less than it may have appeared two or three years ago. Accordingly, gloom concerning the possible value of the next sale of television and other broadcasting rights (due to be concluded in 2003) has been widespread, fueling the continuing falls in soccer clubs' share prices and stock market capitalizations described above.

EUROPEAN COMPARISONS

Elsewhere in Europe, several alternatives to the British model of soccer ownership and finance operate. A number of major European soccer clubs were established or are owned by large manufacturing or service sector companies. The French club Sochaux, established by Peugeot in the 1930s, was an early prototype. Despite the reluctance of the British competition authorities to sanction vertical integration between soccer clubs and broadcasters, a handful of prominent European clubs are owned by media companies, most notably Paris Saint Germain (PSG) owned by Canal Plus (discussed below), and AC Milan owned by Mediaset. In France, there has also been a strong tradition of municipal participation in the financing and administration of soccer, including local authority ownership of many major stadia. Because this violates European competition law, however, municipal financing of French soccer is currently being scaled down.

Spanish soccer operates under even more radical democratic structures. Clubs are set up as nonprofit institutions, with ordinary fans as members who vote in elections to determine posts such as club president. Financing comes mainly in the form of long-term bank lending. There is little incentive for club presidents, commonly held accountable by the membership for failings on the playing field, to cut back on borrowing, with the result that many leading clubs have been or still are saddled with huge debts. Foreclosure is never a likely option for the banks, however, in view of the sport's political influence and popularity (McGill, 2001).

A number of the developments affecting British soccer's relationship with the media during the 1990s were anticipated by earlier events involving the French cable TV company Canal Plus. Formed in 1984, Canal Plus developed the first viable European model for pay TV. The company rapidly discovered that soccer, rather than movies, was the key ingredient required to convert new subscribers and established a business model that would be imitated with similar success by BSkyB in Britain and other pay-TV companies throughout Europe. Similarly prescient was Canal Plus's acquisition of a 40% controlling interest in the ailing PSG in 1991. Although Canal Plus's motivation may have been primarily strategic, their financial and organizational acumen helped revive PSG's competitive and commercial fortunes (Eastham, 1999).

In recent years, the British model of stock exchange flotation has been copied by a number of other European clubs. At the end of June 2002, three major Italian clubs, Roma, Juventus, and Lazio, were quoted with a combined capitalization of £268 million. Other major quoted clubs were Borussia

Dortmund (Germany, £38 million) and Ajax (Netherlands, £49 million). At the smaller end of the scale, Porto and Sporting Lisbon (Portugal, £19 million combined capitalization), Besiktas and Galatasaray (Turkey, £11 million), and six Danish clubs (£49 million) were also quoted. These clubs have not been immune to the pressures that have driven down share prices in England. For example, during the twelve months ending June 2002, Roma's share price fell by 56%, Borussia Dortmund's by 43%, and Ajax's by 25%.

Compiled from data on the top division clubs in England, France, Germany, and Italy, Table 3 suggests that the English tendency for wage inflation to outstrip revenue growth was fairly typical of the major European leagues (estimates for Spain, for which complete data were unavailable, suggest a similar pattern). The problem was especially severe in Italy, with all eighteen Serie A clubs returning an operating loss in the 2000–2001 season. One exception, perhaps attributable to the relatively strict licensing regulations for soccer clubs in Germany, was the Bundesliga 1 clubs, which appear to have exercised some restraint in their wage expenditure.

Table 3 also highlights the relative importance of television income in the major Continental leagues. For the top Continental clubs, television's percentage share in total revenue significantly exceeds that of their English counterparts, but there are variations in the way in which television rights are bundled and sold. In England and Germany, rights are sold collectively (by the leagues, not the clubs) and exclusively (to a single broadcaster). In France, rights are also sold collectively, but there is no exclusivity. As of 2002, the two digital broadcasters, Canal Plus and TPS, shared the rights. In Italy and Spain, clubs sell their rights individually. Under all of these systems, uncertainties increased significantly during 2002.

Current German rights holders KirchMedia declared insolvency in April 2002, with two years of a £960 million contract covering the period 2000 to 2004 still to run. In the subsequent bidding round, KirchMedia regained the rights for a fee that was reduced by around 20%. KirchMedia subsequently entered negotiations to sell the rights to Deutsche Telekom. In Spain, the massive disparities between the sums realizable from the sale of rights by the big two, Real Madrid and Barcelona, and the rest appear at times to threaten the cohesion of the league. Current contracts expire at the end of the 2002–2003 season, but Real Madrid and Barcelona have already signed new deals for the period to the end of 2008, worth £249 million and £234 million with the digital platforms Canal Satellite Digital and Via Digital, respectively.

At the time of this writing (summer 2002), however, it was in Italy that the atmosphere of crisis was most intense. The start of the 2002–2003 season was eventually postponed, with the league having failed to agree to a fee for its weekly highlights package with state broadcaster RAI. RAI was offering £28 million, around half the amount paid for the 2001–2002 season.

Table 3
Total Revenue and Wages in Top Divisions of Four European Leagues

	England	France	Germany	Italy
Total revenue (£ million)				
1996-7	771	293	444	551
2000-1	1556	644	1151	1151
% change	*102*	*120*	*159*	*109*
Wages and salaries (£ million)				
1996-7	363	178	206	317
2000-1	933	414	440	868
% change	*157*	*133*	*114*	*174*
Components of 2000-1 revenue (% shares)				
Matchday	*31*	*16*	*18*	*16*
Television	*39*	*51*	*45*	*54*
Other	*30*	*33*	*36*	*30*

Source: Deloitte & Touche (2002).

Moreover, eight of the smaller Serie A clubs had failed to strike deals for the sale of pay-TV rights with either of the two digital platforms, Stream or Telepiu. The clubs were holding out for deals of around £6 million each; the companies were offering half this sum. Both digital broadcasters were heavily indebted. A suggested merger having already been blocked by the regulatory authorities, negotiations commenced for parent company Vivendi Universal to sell Telepiu to Murdoch's News Corp, already a co-owner of Stream. As in Britain, after a phase of rapid audience growth and escalating rights fees driven partly by competition between broadcasters, the "natural monopoly" characteristics of the pay-TV sector (decreasing average costs and marginal costs close to zero as audience size increases) appeared to be re-asserting themselves with a vengeance.

DETERMINANTS OF SHORT-TERM MOVEMENTS IN SOCCER CLUBS' SHARE PRICES

This section reports an updated version of an event study investigating major determinants of short-term movements in the share prices of English soccer clubs floated on the stock exchange. Dobson and Goddard (2001) report an earlier version of this study based on data for the period July 1997 to July 1999. The present version is based on a larger, more recent data set covering the period July 1998 to July 2002.

If information about an event is impounded rapidly into the company's share price, the effect on the share price or the company's valuation can be deduced from movements in the share price immediately after the event occurs. Event study methodology provides a simple means of disentangling the effect of general stock market movements on a company's valuation from the effect of the event of interest. In the present study, the relevant events are regular league match results, end-of-season outcomes of promotion or relegation campaigns, elimination from domestic cup or European competition, and one extraneous event known to have had a major short-term effect on soccer clubs' share prices: the announcement and subsequent abandonment of the 1998 BSkyB takeover bid for Manchester United.

The data set comprises the daily closing prices of the shares of the thirteen quoted English soccer clubs identified in Table 1. Two other clubs that were quoted throughout the period from 1998 to 2002, Birmingham City and West Bromwich Albion, are excluded because there was usually little daily variation in their share prices. Several other clubs that were quoted for only part of the period are also excluded. Table 4 reports the results of ordinary least squares estimation of a regression model for the determinants of share price returns, using data pooled across all thirteen clubs. The dependent variable is the daily logarithmic return in each club's share price, $r_{i,t} = 100\{\log_e(P_{i,t}) - \log_e(P_{i,t-1})\}$, where $P_{i,t}$ is club i's share price on trading day t. The estimation results for each set of independent variables are in the following section.

Constant and Market Index

The negative estimated constant term of -0.11 (*alpha* in textbook finance terminology) reflects the general downward trend in soccer clubs' share prices from 1998 to 2002. The daily logarithmic return on the FTSE-100 index, $r_{m,t} = 100\{\log_e(P_{m,t}) - \log_e(P_{m,t-1})\}$ where $P_{m,t}$ is the index value on day t, is used to proxy for general market movements. An estimated coefficient on $r_{m,t}$ of 0.17 (the textbook *beta*) suggests a relatively weak link between market movements and movements in the soccer sector. Other things being equal, a 1% rise in the market index translates into an average rise of 0.17% in soccer club share prices on the same day.

Table 4
Estimation Results for Determinants of Share Price Returns, Pooled Model

Market returns & league match results		FA Cup/Europe		BSkyB bid: Man Utd		BSkyB bid: other clubs	
Constant	-0.11*** (0.02)	$F_{i,1,t}$	-0.70** (0.35)	$B_{1,1,t}$	25.65*** (2.38)	$B_{1,1,t}$	6.28*** (0.69)
$r_{m,t}$	0.17*** (0.02)	$F_{i,2,t}$	-0.16 (0.35)	$B_{1,2,t}$	-3.08 (2.38)	$B_{1,2,t}$	1.40** (0.69)
$Y_{i,t}$	1.28*** (0.13)	$F_{i,3,t}$	0.18 (0.34)	$B_{1,3,t}$	7.68*** (2.38)	$B_{1,3,t}$	2.25*** (0.69)
Promotion/relegation		$F_{i,4,t}$	-0.12 (0.34)	$B_{1,4,t}$	3.34 (2.38)	$B_{1,4,t}$	3.67*** (0.69)
$U_{i,1,t}$	2.73** (1.07)	$F_{i,5,t}$	0.58* (0.34)	$B_{1,5,t}$	-0.05 (2.38)	$B_{1,5,t}$	5.27*** (0.69)
$U_{i,2,t}$	-1.15 (1.07)	$E_{i,1,t}$	-2.49*** (0.62)	$B_{2,1,t}$	-8.87*** (2.38)	$B_{2,1,t}$	-2.78*** (0.69)
$U_{i,3,t}$	-0.09 (1.06)	$E_{i,2,t}$	-0.23 (0.62)	$B_{2,2,t}$	0.64 (2.38)	$B_{2,2,t}$	0.89 (0.69)
$U_{i,4,t}$	-0.36 (1.07)	$E_{i,3,t}$	0.17 (0.62)	$B_{2,3,t}$	1.33 (2.38)	$B_{2,3,t}$	-0.09 (0.69)
$U_{i,5,t}$	-0.88 (1.06)	$E_{i,4,t}$	-0.69 (0.62)	$B_{2,4,t}$	-0.09 (2.38)	$B_{2,4,t}$	1.18* (0.69)
$D_{i,1,t}$	-14.78*** (0.97)	$E_{i,5,t}$	0.24 (0.62)	$B_{2,5,t}$	0.37 (2.38)	$B_{2,5,t}$	0.78 (0.69)
$D_{i,2,t}$	1.76* (0.97)			$B_{3,1,t}$	-16.09*** (2.38)	$B_{3,1,t}$	-3.23*** (0.69)

(continued)

Table 4 (*continued*)

$D_{i,3,t}$	0.05			$B_{3,2,t}$	-0.07	$B_{3,2,t}$	-0.29
	(0.97)				(2.38)		(0.69)
$D_{i,4,t}$	0.61			$B_{3,3,t}$	0.45	$B_{3,3,t}$	-0.52
	(0.97)				(2.38)		(0.69)
$D_{i,5,t}$	-1.08			$B_{3,4,t}$	2.81	$B_{3,4,t}$	-2.08***
	(0.97)				(2.38)		(0.69)
				$B_{3,5,t}$	6.01**	$B_{3,5,t}$	0.19
$n = 13,065$ S.E. of regression $= 2.38$ $R^2 = 0.07$					(2.38)		(0.69)

Note: Standard errors of estimated coefficients are shown in parentheses. Dependent variable is $r_{i,t}$ (daily return on club share prices).

*** = significantly different from zero, 1% level; ** = 5% level; * = 10% level.

League Match Results

The result of the league match between home team i and away team j is coded $W_{i,j} = 1$ if team i won, 0.5 if team i drew, and 0 if team i lost. Using prior probabilities for each possible match result imputed from the fixed odds quoted by the high street bookmaker William Hill, it is also possible to define the expected result, $\hat{W} = \phi_{i,j}^{H} + 0.5\phi_{i,j}^{D}$, where $\phi_{i,j}^{H}$ is the imputed bookmaker's probability that home team i wins, and $\phi_{i,j}^{D}$ is the imputed bookmaker's probability of a draw.[3] The actual and expected results are used to define an "expectations-adjusted league match result" variable:

$Y_{i,t} = W_{i,j} - \hat{W}_{i,j}$ if team i played team j at home between trading day t – 1 and trading day t,

$Y_{i,t} = W_{j,i} - \hat{W}_{i,j}$ if team i played team j away between trading day t – 1 and trading day t,

$Y_{i,t} = 0$ if team i did not play a match between trading day t – 1 and trading day t.

For a fully unanticipated win (expected result = 0), $Y_{i,t}$ takes a value of 1. For a fully anticipated win (expected result = 1) $Y_{i,t}$ takes a value of 0. Similarly, $Y_{i,t}$ takes values of 0 and –1 for defeats that were fully anticipated and unanticipated, respectively. $Y_{i,t} > 0$ therefore indicates good news (better-than-anticipated performance), and $Y_{i,t} < 0$ indicates bad news (worse-than-anticipated performance).

An estimated coefficient on $Y_{i,t}$ of 1.28, significant at the 1% level, quantifies the link between the unanticipated component of league match results and the share price movement on the next trading day. If a quoted team wins a match it was expected to lose (with win/draw/lose probabilities of 0.1/ 0.3/0.6, say, producing an expected result of $\hat{W}_{i,j} = 0.25$), the model's expected share price movement is $1.28 \times (1 - 0.25)$, or just under +1%. If the team wins a match it was expected to win (with probabilities of 0.6/0.3/ 0.1 producing $\hat{W}_{i,j} = 0.75$) the expected price movement is $1.28 \times (1 - 0.75)$, or just over +0.3%.

Promotion and Relegation

It is expected that events such as promotion or relegation, or (equally important) narrowly missing promotion or avoiding relegation, will affect investors' assessment of the club's future profitability much more than would normally be expected from the result of the individual match that finally determines the team's fate.[4] For clubs involved in end-of-season promotion and relegation issues, the following dummies are defined:

$U_{i,k,t} = 1$ on trading day t if team i gained promotion or avoided relegation as a result of a match played between trading days $t-k$ and $t-k+1$, for $k = 1 \ldots 5$, and 0 elsewhere;

$D_{i,k,t} = 1$ on trading day t if team i was relegated or failed to win promotion as a result of a match played between trading days $t-k$ and $t-k+1$, for $k = 1 \ldots 5$, and 0 elsewhere.

For these and the other events described below, dummy variables are included for up to five days after each event, to allow for the possibility that full reappraisal of a club's future profit potential takes several days.

Although the estimated coefficients on $U_{i,k,t}$ and $D_{i,k,t}$ reported in Table 4 are both significant, their magnitudes differ. Promotion or avoidance of relegation produced an average logarithmic return of +2.7% on the next trading day, whereas relegation or failure to achieve promotion produced a return of −14.8%. This asymmetry may reflect a realistic if slightly unromantic assessment on the part of the markets of the financial realities associated with divisional change. Membership in a lower division is clearly bad for profitability due to loss of television and other revenue. But membership in a higher division is not necessarily good news either, because it brings immediate pressure to ratchet up spending on wages and transfers in an effort to avoid demotion the next time around. Based on a set of individual estimations of the share price model for each of the thirteen clubs, Table 5 reports the estimated logarithmic return on the day after the decisive match on each occasion any of the clubs was involved in end-of-season promotion or relegation issues.

Table 5
Estimated Returns for Clubs with Promotion/Relegation Issues, Individual Models

Team	Event	Date	Estimated next-day share price reaction (%)
Bolton Wanderers	missed promotion to PL	31/5/99	-28.8***
	missed promotion to PL	17/5/00	-40.7***
	promoted to PL	28/5/01	0.3
Charlton Athletic	relegated to FLD1	16/5/99	-8.7***
	promoted to PL	22/4/00	4.3***
Leicester City	relegated to FLD1	6/4/02	0.5
Preston North End	missed promotion to FLD1	19/5/99	-8.1***
	promoted to FLD1	24/4/00	0.2
	missed promotion to PL	28/5/01	-3.2***
Southampton	avoided relegation to FLD1	16/5/99	14.8***
Sunderland	promoted to PL	13/4/99	-8.1***

Note: PL = Premier League; FLD1 = Football League Division One.
*** = significantly different from zero, 1% level; ** = 5% level; * = 10% level.

FA Cup and European Elimination

For matches played in the FA Cup or in European competition, the following event dummies are included to capture the share price reaction following elimination from these tournaments:

$F_{i,k,t}$ = 1 on trading day t if team i was eliminated from the FA Cup between trading days t–k and t–k + 1, for k = 1 . . . 5, and 0 elsewhere;

$E_{i,k,t}$ = 1 on trading day t if team i was eliminated from European competition between trading days t–k and t–k + 1, for k = 1 . . . 5, and 0 elsewhere.

The estimated coefficients on $F_{i,k,t}$ and $E_{i,k,t}$ indicate that European elimination is viewed by the markets as the more serious setback, reducing a club's market value by about 2.5% on average. The corresponding reduction following elimination from the FA Cup is 0.7%.

The BSkyB Bid for Manchester United

Dobson and Goddard (2001) show that when it was announced on September 7, 1998, BSkyB's takeover bid for Manchester United had an immediate effect on the club's share price and on the share prices of other quoted clubs. Press reports that the MMC was recommending prevention of the takeover appeared on March 17, 1999, and this decision was confirmed by the UK government on April 4, 1999. The relevant event dummies are as follows:

$B_{1,k,t} = 1$ on the $k-1$'th trading day after September 7, 1998, for $k = 1 \ldots 5$, and 0 elsewhere;

$B_{2,k,t} = 1$ on the $k-1$'th trading day after March 17, 1999, for $k = 1 \ldots 5$, and 0 elsewhere;

$B_{3,k,t} = 1$ on the $k-1$'th trading day after April 4, 1999, for $k = 1 \ldots 5$, and 0 elsewhere.

Since the effect of the news on Manchester United's share price should differ from its effect on other clubs' share prices, one set of coefficients on $B_{j,k,t}$ is estimated specifically for Manchester United, and a second set is estimated for all other clubs. Table 4 shows that United's shares jumped in value by 25.7% on the day of the announcement, and by a further 7.7% later in the same week, when the final bid was submitted and accepted. Overall, other clubs' share prices were marked up by 6.3% on average on the day of the initial announcement, and 18.9% over the course of the first week. Adverse share price reactions when the MMC recommended rejection of the bid, and when the government accepted this recommendation, are also reflected in the coefficients reported in Table 4.

CONCLUSION

Recent years have witnessed fantastic growth on both the revenue and the cost side of soccer clubs' activities throughout Europe's major domestic leagues. Significant changes affecting the ownership and financing of the soccer sector described in this chapter have been part cause and part consequence of the growth in cash flow fueled by soccer's popular renaissance. Following such a spell, which has naturally engendered much optimistic sentiment about the commercial future of the soccer sector, it was perhaps inevitable that at some point the pendulum would swing in the reverse direction, and a phase of retrenchment would set in.

Judging from the tenor of most of the recent media coverage of the business and financial aspects of soccer, in 2002 retrenchment was emphatically the order of the day. Pessimism concerning the effect of wage inflation on soccer clubs' profitability and the possible decline in the value of television rights fueled continuing falls in share prices and market capitalizations. Throughout Europe, the 2002 summer transfer market was notably inactive, with many clubs that would not have blinked two years earlier hesitating to commit to new player contracts perhaps not due to expire before 2006 or 2007.

Amid all the gloom, however, it is worth noting that soccer's appeal to both live spectators and television audiences remains undimmed. The sector's core product, in other words, is still as popular as ever. In view of this, recent traumas may perhaps come to be seen more realistically as a necessary correction to past excesses than as another dot.com or telecommunications bubble. Although both the market for television rights and the stock market's infatuation with the soccer sector have now progressed beyond (way beyond in the case of the market) their rapid growth phases of the mid- or late 1990s, the long-term future may yet turn out to be more secure than recent trends and current pessimism might suggest.

NOTES

1. Morrow (1999) and Dobson and Goddard (2001) provide full details.

2. Remarkably, two years earlier the Football League had failed to acquire the signatures of ITV Digital's parent companies Carlton and Granada on the contract guaranteeing the commitments entered into by their subsidiary.

3. Instead of bookmakers' probabilities, Dobson and Goddard (2001) use prior probabilities obtained from a match results forecasting model. In the present context, the difference between the two sets of probabilities is minimal.

4. Prior to the decisive match, the share price should be a probability-weighted average of the prices that would apply if the team ends up either in the higher or in the lower division. Following the decisive match, the price should adjust accordingly. This means the magnitudes of the estimated adjustments reported here are "contaminated" by the market's prior probabilities concerning the outcome of the decisive match.

Part V

Canadian Professional Football

13

The Professional Football Industry in Canada: Economic and Policy Issues

Neil Longley

INTRODUCTION

The major professional sports industry in Canada spans four sports—hockey, baseball, basketball, and (North American) football. In the former three, there are no independent Canadian leagues. As of 2002, all Canadian-based franchises in these sports were simply members of the major U.S.-based leagues. Canada has two Major League Baseball (MLB) franchises, one National Basketball Association (NBA) franchise, and six National Hockey League (NHL) franchises. In football, however, the situation is different in that the U.S.-based National Football League (NFL) has never had a franchise in Canada. Instead, the independent Canadian Football League (CFL) has long operated. Although the CFL has a history that goes back over 100 years, the league has often been overshadowed on the North American sports landscape by the more powerful U.S.-based leagues.

One result of this overshadowing is that the sports economics literature contains almost no analysis of the CFL.[1] This absence of research is unfortunate, since the economics of the CFL are somewhat peculiar and can provide numerous insights for sports economists. In this regard, the present chapter attempts to highlight two particular issues that differentiate the CFL from the broader North American professional sports industry. First, the chapter explores the reasons for the CFL's economic decline over the past two decades—a decline that occurred during a time period when other North American professional sports leagues experienced unprecedented booms. The chapter argues that the relative decline of the CFL can be traced to its gradual loss of monopoly power in the sports market. Second, the chapter examines the unique (at least in North American sports) quota system that the CFL employs in its labor market. This system ensures that Canadian players are guaranteed a minimum number of spots on each team's roster. The chapter argues that the quota system has impacts not only on player salaries and team payrolls, but may also act as a de facto quota on the number of black players in the league.

A BRIEF BACKGROUND ON THE CFL'S ECONOMICS

The game of Canadian football can be traced back to the late nineteenth century. The game evolved from English rugby, and gradually transformed itself into a distinct game. By the 1930s, professionalism in the sport was becoming more common, and teams began importing professional players from the United States. Two professional leagues emerged—one in eastern Canada and another in western Canada. These two leagues were separate entities and relatively independent of one another, but they were both members of the Canadian Rugby Union (CRU), the predecessor of the CFL. In 1958, the two leagues agreed to formally integrate, forming the CFL, with four teams in the Eastern Conference and five teams in the Western Conference.

From 1954 to 1986, the CFL (and its predecessor, the CRU) operated with the same nine franchises. This was a period of remarkable franchise stability in the CFL—there were no expansions, no franchise failures, nor any franchise relocations. During the 1980s, however, the CFL began a gradual decline. In 1987, the Montreal franchise folded. In 1993, the CFL, desperate for a cash injection to survive, began a three-year experiment of granting expansion franchises to U.S. cities. By 1995, the CFL operated as a thirteen-team league, with eight franchises in Canada and five in the United States. At the end of the 1995 season, four of the five U.S. franchises folded, and the only remaining U.S. franchise—in Baltimore—was transferred to Montreal, making the CFL again an exclusively Canadian league. In 1997, the Ottawa franchise folded, but Ottawa was readmitted to the league in 2002 as an expansion franchise. Thus, by 2002, the CFL had come full circle in that it was again a nine-team league, with the nine franchises located in exactly the same cities as they had been in 1954.

This franchise instability over the past two decades is a reflection of the general decline in the economic fortunes of the league. This decline can be measured along numerous dimensions. For example, Table 1 illustrates the long-term decline in attendance. Even though attendance rose significantly from 1967 to 1977, these gains were almost completely dissipated over the subsequent twenty years. Between 1977 and 1997, average per-game atten-

Table 1
Change in Average Per-Game Attendance

1967	1972	1977	1982	1987	1992	1997	2001
20,082	23,300	31,307	29,377	25,990	25,367	21,295	24,971

Source: Derived from Canadian Football League, *Facts, Figures & Records* (various editions).

dance in the CFL decreased 32%. The decrease in fan interest in Vancouver and Toronto—two of Canada's three largest cities—has been a particular problem for the league. In 1968, these two franchises were flagships of the league—average per-game attendance in Vancouver was 134% of the CFL average, and in Toronto, average per-game attendance was 128% of the CFL average. Contrast this with 2001, when Vancouver and Toronto's attendance had fallen to only 82% and 65%, respectively, of the league average.[2] This long-term decrease in fan support in Vancouver and Toronto has had impacts beyond just these franchises, since the value of national TV contracts is heavily dependent upon viewership in these major population areas.

The CFL's revenue problems have correspondingly put strong downward pressure on player salaries, as illustrated in Table 2. Over the past two decades, real CFL salaries have decreased substantially, both in absolute terms and relative to NFL salaries. During the 1970s, the relative salary parity between the CFL and the NFL even allowed the CFL to occasionally sign high profile American players. For example, in 1972, Heisman Trophy winner Johnny Rodgers joined Montreal for $100,000 per season. In 1979, the first overall selection in the NFL draft—Tom Cousineau from Ohio State—spurned an offer by the NFL's Buffalo Bills to sign with Montreal. Also during that era, Montreal signed Vince Ferragamo—a star NFL quarterback who had just led the Los Angeles Rams to a 1980 Super Bowl appearance—for $400,000 per season. However, as the salary disparities between the CFL and NFL became greater, such high profile signings became increasingly rare.

Over the past twenty years, most individual CFL franchises have faced precarious financial situations. Although only two (Canadian-based)

Table 2
Estimated Average Player Salaries

	1975	1985	1995
CFL Salaries (000, 1995 Cdn dollars)	73	86	50
CFL Salaries (000, 1995 US dollars)	72	63	36
CFL Salaries (US dollars) as Approximate % of NFL Salaries	67 %	29 %	5 %

franchises actually folded, most of the other privately owned teams saw rapid turnover in ownership, with their survival depending on the existence of a constant stream of investors willing to intervene to rescue the team, hoping that it would be the one to turn the team around. The community-owned franchises have also faced financial hardships and have often had to rally community support to avoid the prospect of bankruptcy.

During the late 1990s, the CFL did begin to regain some measure of financial stability. The league benefited from the franchise fees extracted from the American expansion teams. Also, the NFL provided the CFL with a $4 million loan in 1997, further lessening the immediate financial crisis the league was facing.[3] Perhaps most important, fan interest increased, with both attendance and TV ratings showing significant improvements. This upward trend has continued into the early part of the twenty-first century, but it is still too early to determine whether it signals a fundamental shift in the long-term fortunes of the league or is simply a cyclical phenomenon that cannot be sustained.

ANALYZING THE CFL'S DECLINE

The decline of the CFL over the past two decades, a time when the professional sports industry in North America was booming, may seem to be a paradox. In essence, however, the CFL's decline may have been *caused* by the boom in the rest of the industry. Prior to the 1980s, the CFL was relatively sheltered from competition and thus possessed significant monopoly power. It is the assertion of this section that the decline of the CFL can be traced directly to the erosion of this monopoly power. Three factors are hypothesized to have been particularly important: (1) increased competition in the output market, (2) increased competition in the input market, and (3) a loss of political influence for the league.

Competition in the Output Market

Part of the CFL's decline can be traced to an increase in the availability of substitute products in the professional sports market. In 1970, for example, only two of the nine CFL franchises faced competition from an NHL franchise in the same city. By 1980, six CFL franchises faced such direct competition from the NHL. Baseball also began to present increased direct competition for the CFL, with Montreal entering the Major Leagues in 1969 and Toronto entering in 1977. In addition, other CFL cities such as Vancouver, Calgary, and Edmonton all received AAA baseball franchises during that era.[4]

The widespread installation of cable TV in Canadian homes during the 1970s also presented a competitive threat to the CFL. Cable TV allowed

Canadians to access the major U.S. networks, providing viewers with a wide range of professional and college sports to which they previously did not have access. In essence, cable TV resulted in the CFL losing its captive market. For some Canadians, increased access to American sports, particularly the NFL, diminished their interest in the CFL.

Exacerbating the problem was that the NFL was beginning to emerge as the dominant league in all of North American team sports. Its enormous growth in popularity further widened the gaps between the CFL and the NFL. In some ways, the CFL became unfashionable. There was the growing perception among some Canadians that the CFL was simply a "minor" league whose extinction was near. Thus, in a sense, the NFL began to emerge as a competitor for the CFL. Even though the NFL had no franchises in Canada, it was beginning to actively compete with the CFL for the interests of Canadian fans.

Competition in the Input Market

Throughout its history, the CFL has always relied heavily on recruiting American players. In general, however, it has not attempted to compete directly with the NFL for such players. Instead, the CFL found a niche in the market, and focused on recruiting those Americans who were unable to earn NFL positions. For many American players, one of the attractions of the CFL, despite its relatively low salaries, has always been that it allows them to continue their playing careers, with the ultimate hope of rejoining the NFL.[5]

For the CFL, it has been U.S. start-up leagues that have posed the most serious threats in input markets. These leagues have included the American Football League of the early 1960s, the World Football League (WFL) of the mid-1970s, the United States Football League (USFL) of the mid-1980s, and the World League of American Football (WLAF) of the early 1990s. These leagues have tended to employ the same type of second-tier (i.e., non-NFL) players that the CFL employs. Thus, the presence of these leagues not only increases CFL salaries, but also lowers the league's overall talent pool.

Particularly damaging to the CFL was the emergence of the USFL in 1983. Not only did the USFL emerge at a time when the CFL was facing competitive threats in the output market (as discussed earlier), the USFL was particularly successful in luring many of the CFL's top players, coaches, and managerial personnel to the new league. In fact, if one examines CFL attendance and TV revenue figures around the time of the USFL's formation, the influence is clear. The CFL experienced a 13% drop in attendance between 1983—the first year of the USFL's existence—and 1985, the USFL's last year.[6] This seemed to be the beginning of a trend, as attendance continued to fall throughout the remainder of the 1980s. Similarly, TV revenues per team fell from over $1.2 million in 1983 to only about $325,000 by 1987 (Barnes, 1996).

Loss of Political Influence

Throughout the 1960s and 1970s, the CFL became increasingly concerned about a U.S.-based league (either the NFL or a start-up league) establishing a franchise in Canada. During this era, the CFL actively lobbied the federal government for protection to ensure no rival leagues entered Canada. The CFL presented the issue as one of "national unity." The CFL was the only exclusively Canadian professional sports league in Canada. Its championship, the Grey Cup game, pitted the winners of the Western and Eastern Conferences and captured the competitive rivalries between the two different parts of the country. In addition, the CFL's quota system guaranteed a certain number of roster spots for players of Canadian origin. These arguments by the CFL were consistent with a political strategy that had long been effective in Canada—justifying protection by playing to fears of U.S. domination of Canada.

The issue came to a dramatic head in 1974, when the fledgling U.S.-based WFL proposed to locate a franchise in Toronto. CFL officials viewed such a development as not only a threat to the viability of the Toronto Argonauts, but also (because of revenue sharing) a threat to the entire league. The federal government of the day, led by Prime Minister Pierre Trudeau of the Liberal Party, had a strong nationalistic orientation and believed that Canadian business and culture were being increasingly dominated by American interests. Thus, in April 1974, just months before the WFL was to begin its first season, the government introduced a bill into the House of Commons that would have prohibited any foreign football league from operating in Canada. The bill's preamble stated that the CFL had "developed for itself a unique national institution contributing to the strengthening of the bonds of nationhood" (see Barnes, 1983). Shortly after the bill was introduced, a federal election was called, and the bill never officially became law. The matter became moot when the owner of the WFL's Toronto franchise announced that he was moving his franchise to Memphis.

During the 1980s, Canada's political climate changed considerably. The Progressive Conservative Party—led by Prime Minister Brian Mulroney—came to power in 1983 and subsequently negotiated a free trade agreement with the United States. Since the Mulroney government's political agenda was to remove trade and investment barriers with the United States, the CFL's protectionist desires no longer met with much sympathy. As Barnes (1996) notes, perhaps indicative of the CFL's decline in importance, both to governments and fans, was that no legislative bill similar to that of 1974 was put forward when the WLAF granted a franchise to Montreal in 1990.

THE CFL'S LABOR MARKET QUOTAS

The Basics of the Quota

Perhaps the feature that most differentiates the CFL from the other major North American sports leagues is that the CFL employs a quota system in its labor market.[7] This quota ensures that a minimum number of roster spots must go to Canadian-born players. Without the quota system, it is presumed that few, if any, Canadian players would be employed by CFL teams. Relative to Canada, the United States produces a large number of talented football players, hence there has long been a desire by CFL teams to recruit Americans. To counter these natural market forces, the CFL has for many years maintained the quota system. The first use of the quota was in 1936, when it limited teams to employing a maximum of five Americans (Barnes, 1996). Since that time, there have been successive increases to this limit, and, beginning in 1996, teams have been allowed to employ seventeen Americans (excluding three quarterbacks, which can be either American or Canadian) on their thirty-nine-man roster; the remaining nineteen players must be Canadians.[8] Given that each team has twenty-four starting players (twelve on offence, twelve on defense), and given that one of the Americans must be a special teams player, this ensures that at least seven Canadians are starters.

The remainder of this section analyzes the economic rationales for the quota and examines some of its impacts.

Modeling the Quota Decision

Officially, the CFL justifies the quota system on the grounds that it ensures a "Canadian-presence" in the game.[9] However, this quota system is presumably a profit-maximizing choice by the league. The quota is essentially a cartel-like attempt to limit competition among the CFL's member teams. Since Americans are generally superior players to Canadians, and hence are paid more,[10] a quota that limits the number of American players on a team should serve to reduce team payrolls. In the absence of the quota, individual teams acting alone may have a profit incentive to increase the number of Americans on their team, perhaps to the point where all players on the team were Americans. Since all teams would face the same basic incentive structure, no team would gain any real competitive advantage over any other, but all teams would see their payrolls rise. Thus, the CFL's quota system may be acting to maximize collective profits by ensuring that teams do not "excessively" compete on the basis of player quality.

However, the quota may also have negative effects on CFL teams, in that it artificially lowers the absolute quality of play in the league. To the extent that absolute quality of play is important for fan interest, the quota will reduce overall league revenues.[11] Thus, from the CFL's collective perspective, the optimal level of the quota is found by balancing two opposing factors, payroll increases and revenue increases: increasing the quota increases team payrolls, but, to the extent it increases fan interest due to an increase in the absolute quality of play, it may also increase team revenues.

Team-Level Choices

Given the existence of league-imposed quotas, individual teams will allocate their American players to their most profitable uses. For example, Americans will presumably always be used in starting positions, and never as backups. Teams, however, will always have to employ some Canadians in starting positions, since the number of Americans allowed is less than the number of starting positions on a team. Thus, teams are faced with an allocation decision: How should the American players be distributed across positions to maximize team profits?[12] Alternatively, the question can be framed this way: Given that Canadians must fill seven starting positions, at which positions should these Canadians be used? It is hypothesized that the decision can be modeled as follows:

$$A = f(D, I) \tag{1}$$

where:

A = the probability of using an American, as opposed to a Canadian, in a given position

D = the average difference in talent at the position between American and Canadian players

I = the impact that the position has on overall team success/revenues.

The variable D reflects the fact that the average talent difference between Americans and Canadians will vary from position to position. In general, one could hypothesize that the talent difference is greater at the so-called "skill" positions—positions such as quarterback, running back, receiver, and defensive back. Thus, all else being equal, one would expect Americans to fill a disproportionate number of these positions. Conversely, positions that rely more on strength and technique, rather than on pure athletic ability— positions such as offensive lineman—are positions for which talent differences between Canadians and Americans should be less.

For the variable I, it is hypothesized that Americans will tend to fill those positions that have greater impacts on team success/revenues. As with the variable D, this would seem to indicate that it is the skill positions that are the most likely to be filled by Americans.[13] Not only are these, arguably, the most crucial to team success, they are the highest profile, and the most identifiable by the fans and media.

Table 3
Percentage of Games Started by Americans, by Position, 1995

Quarterbacks	100 %
Running Backs	58 %
Receivers	67 %
Offensive Line	2 %
Defensive Line/Linebackers	73 %
Defensive Backs	89 %
Kickers	0 %

Source: Derived from Canadian Football League, *Facts, Figures & Records* (various editions).

Table 3 examines the distribution, by position, of Americans on Canadian-based teams during the 1995 season.

The data in Table 3 support the hypothesis in that Americans disproportionately occupy certain positions. At one extreme, there is complete domination by Americans in the quarterback position. Americans also dominate the defensive line/linebacker positions and the defensive back positions. At the other extreme, offensive linemen are almost exclusively Canadian.

Salary Effects

The quota system creates an artificial demand for Canadians, not only to fill all backup positions, but also to fill seven starting positions. However, the supply conditions for Canadian players are very different from those for American players. Given the large number of quality football players in the United States, CFL teams face a highly elastic supply of U.S. players. Most American players (excluding the star players) are relatively easily replaced,[14] since there are always a large number of other American players, of almost equal talent, simply waiting for their opportunity.

Conversely, the talent pool of Canadian players is much smaller. For any given level of talent, not only are there fewer Canadians than Americans, but the talent gap between any particular Canadian player and the next best Canadian player is often much greater than is the corresponding gap for American players. In other words, it is much more difficult (in terms of a talent drop-off) for a team to replace any given Canadian player with another Canadian player than it is for the team to replace any given American player (of equal talent to the Canadian) with another American player.

These market conditions should result, for a given level of talent, in Canadian players receiving a salary premium over their American counterparts.[15] Analyzing the 1995[16] salaries of veteran[17] CFL receivers (on Canadian-based teams) tests this hypothesis. The receiving position is chosen because there is good mix of Canadian and Americans at that position and because performance is relatively easily measured at that position. The model's specification and the regression results are summarized below.

$$\ln(S) = 10.10 + .001954(GP) + .16033(RPG) + .010757(YPC) + .22438(C)$$
$$\quad\quad\quad\quad (3.22)\quad\quad\quad\quad (7.65)\quad\quad\quad\quad (1.24)\quad\quad\quad\quad (3.61)\quad (2)$$

N = 35 (23 Canadians, and 12 Americans)
R^2 = .83

where:

S = the player's 1995 salary
GP = the player's career games played in the CFL
RPG = the player's career receptions per game in the CFL
YPC = the player's average career yards per catch in the CFL
C = 1 if the player is Canadian, and 0 if the player is American.

The variable GP is a measure of the player's CFL experience, and both RPG and YPC are intended to capture productivity.

The results support the hypothesis, in that Canadian receivers do appear to receive a premium.[18] For a given level of experience and productivity, Canadian players earned 22% more than their American counterparts. The artificial demand that the quota creates for Canadian players, combined with the relatively inelastic supply of Canadian players, would seem to force teams to pay a premium for these players. One must still use caution in interpreting the results, since the sample size is, by necessity, small. However, some confidence is gained by the R^2 being relatively high. In addition, the control variables are all of the expected sign, with two of the three control variables having statistically significant coefficients.

Racial Effects

The CFL's quota on Americans dates back to the 1930s. At that time, all American players entering the league were white. Gradually, however, as African Americans were given more opportunities to participate in high level sports in the United States, the number of African Americans entering the CFL began to increase.

With this increase in predominance of African American athletes in the United States, and with blacks comprising a much smaller proportion of the population in Canada than in the United States, the CFL's quota on Americans has become a de facto quota on the number of black players in the league. Table 4 provides an analysis of the racial composition of American versus Canadian players for the 1993 season.

Table 4
Racial Composition of Canadian and
American Players, 1993

Americans (N = 201)		Canadians (N = 204)	
Black	White	Black	White
86 %	14 %	20%	80%

Source: Derived from Canadian Football League, *Facts, Figures & Records* (various editions).

Although it is not necessarily the intent of the quota rule to act as a racial barrier, it is clear from Table 4 that the effect of the rule has been to limit the number of black players in the league.

SUMMARY

Because the economics of the CFL are somewhat different from those of other North American sports leagues, the league provides sports economists with some unique research opportunities. This chapter has attempted to highlight two aspects of the CFL that differentiate it from the broader North American professional sports industry. The chapter examines the CFL's economic decline over the past two decades—a decline that occurred during a time period when other North American professional sports leagues experienced unprecedented booms—and argues that the decline can be traced to the CFL's gradual loss of monopoly power in the sports market. The chapter also examines the quota system that the CFL employs in its labor market and finds that this system has impacts on a wide variety of areas—on player salaries, on positional segregation, and on the racial composition of teams.

ACKNOWLEDGMENT

I thank Torben Andersen for helpful comments on an earlier draft of this chapter. Any errors are mine.

NOTES

1. Most Canadian sports economists have focused on the sport of hockey. A particularly popular research question has been whether French Canadians suffer from discrimination in the National Hockey League (see, for example, Lavoie, Grenier, and Coulombe, 1987; Longley, 1995).

2. Data from the 2001 season indicate that, for the league as a whole, the correlation coefficient between attendance and city size is strongly negative, at –0.56.

3. The agreement between the NFL and the CFL allows NFL teams to sign CFL players who are entering their option years. In exchange for this signing privilege, the NFL provided the CFL with a $4 million loan to help the league survive its financial distress. From the NFL's perspective, the reasons for this agreement would seem to be twofold. First, it allows the NFL earlier access to some of the best CFL players. Second, it is hypothesized that the NFL has an interest in seeing the CFL survive, since the existence of the CFL may lessen the likelihood of a rival (to the NFL) U.S.-based league forming. Such a rival league would have to compete not only with the NFL for players, but would have to compete with the CFL. The CFL presents no real competition for the NFL, but it does employ a group of second-tier players who would otherwise be attractive to a start-up league.

4. More recently, the CFL has faced direct competition from the NBA, with both Toronto and Vancouver receiving expansion franchises in 1996 (Vancouver's franchise has since moved to Memphis, Tennessee).

5. For example, star NFL quarterbacks such as Joe Kapp, Joe Theismann, Warren Moon, and, more recently, Jeff Garcia all began their professional careers in the CFL. Each year NFL teams also sign many lesser-known CFL players.

6. As a further example of the effects of the USFL, between 1981 and 1985, CFL players' salaries, as a percentage of gross gate revenues, increased from 58% to 75% (Cosentino, 1995).

7. It should be noted that many professional sports leagues outside of North America do employ quotas. For example, many European soccer leagues restrict the number of non–European Union players per team.

8. The CFL does not actually use the terms "Americans" and "Canadians." Instead, to avoid any notion of discriminating based on national origin, the terms "imports" and "non-imports" are used. Non-imports are defined as any player who has never received football training outside of Canada or who was physically resident in Canada for an aggregate period of five years prior to attaining the age of fifteen years.

9. During the 1980s, a complaint was filed with the Canadian Human Rights Commission on behalf of American players released from CFL rosters. The complaint alleged that the CFL's quota rule was discriminatory. The commission rejected the complaint on the grounds that the quota was necessary to help Canadian football players overcome "disadvantages in preparation and opportunity" (Barnes, 1983).

10. For example, in 1995, rookie (i.e., no previous CFL experience) Canadian receivers were paid an average of $31,000 per season, whereas rookie American receivers were paid an average of $51,000 per season.

11. These revenue-decreasing effects of the quota will be mitigated somewhat if Canadian fans, all else being equal, prefer to watch "homegrown" players.

12. Ball (1976) uses a sociological model to investigate positional "stacking" of Americans in the CFL.

13. It is assumed here that the marginal revenue from using Americans in skill positions rather than other positions is greater than the corresponding increases in payroll. Many American skill position players have limited bargaining power, given both the highly elastic supply of such players, and given the CFL's tight salary cap policies.

14. In fact, it is not unusual in the CFL for an American player to be a starter one week and to be released and off the roster the following week.

15. The market in the CFL for veteran players is relatively competitive. Since 1983, all CFL players playing out their options have been unrestricted free agents and can sign with any CFL team. The CFL was the first North American sports league to have unrestricted (i.e., without compensation) free agency.

16. The 1995 season was used out of conservatis; 1995 was the third and final year of the CFL's American expansion. U.S.-based CFL teams, that were not bound by the quota, employed only American players and signed many American free agents away from Canadian-based CFL teams. Thus, one would expect that the salaries of American players (on Canadian-based teams) would be higher than normal during this season.

17. For the purposes of the analysis, veterans are defined as those players who had played at least eighteen CFL games (the equivalent of one season) prior to the 1995 season.

18. Because most (but not all) Canadian receivers are white and most (but not all) American receivers are black, it is conceivable that the variable C is picking up the player's race, rather than his national origin. To test for this possibility, the variable C was replaced with the variable W, where W is a dummy variable equaling one if the player is white, and zero if the player is black. The regression was rerun, and the variable W was found not to be statistically significant.

Part VI

Southern Hemisphere
Rugby Union

14

Professionalization and Competitive Balance in New Zealand Rugby Union

P. Dorian Owen and Clayton R. Weatherston

> Rugby football . . . the best of all our pleasures: . . . religion and desire and fulfilment all in one.
>
> —J. Mulgan (1947, 7)

> The need for balance, of playing the game and running the business, of respecting our traditions and shaping the future . . . achieving local touch in New Zealand while achieving global reach with the game.
>
> —M. McCaw, Chairman,
> New Zealand Rugby Football Union (2001)

INTRODUCTION

After over a century as an amateur sport, the International Rugby Board (IRB), the world governing body for rugby union, declared in 1995 that players could be paid for playing rugby union. The transformation from an amateur to a professional sport has led to significant changes in the structure of rugby union in the Southern Hemisphere. This has had particular implications for New Zealand, where rugby is more than just the national sport; as reflected in the quote by Mulgan, it borders on the status of a de facto religion and is an important part of the nation's sense of identity (Fougere, 1989).

The change to "pay for play" (in contrast to what was labeled "shamateurism," the under-the-table rewards indirectly afforded players prior to professionalism) has brought to rugby a much greater business orientation. This shift has changed the relationships among the players, the teams, and the administration in New Zealand rugby, although traditions from the amateur era remain strong. As broadcasting rights and sponsorship have become the dominant sources of revenue, New Zealand rugby administrators have not underestimated the importance of winning in order to preserve the elite-brand status of the All Blacks, the national team, and to retain the interest of broadcasters, sponsors, and the public.

The main focus of this chapter is competitive balance in the different competitions in New Zealand under the current post-professionalization organizational structures. First, we discuss the forces that led to professionalization after more than a century of amateurism. We outline the nature of the different rugby competitions in which New Zealand teams are involved and the roles of the national and cross-national organizing bodies, including provincial unions, the New Zealand Rugby Football Union (NZRFU), and SANZAR (made up of the three national organizing bodies: the Australian Rugby Union [ARU], the NZRFU, and the South African Rugby Football Union [SARFU]). We also consider aspects of the centralized contracting system in the market for players in New Zealand and the emphasis placed on the performance of the national team, which both appear to be unique compared to other professional sports. Finally, we examine the degree of competitive balance in the main rugby competitions in New Zealand under the current organizational structure and discuss some current issues of concern.

THE EVOLUTION TOWARD PROFESSIONALIZATION

Rugby union has a long tradition as an amateur game in New Zealand, dating from the 1870s. Matches involving a New Zealand team against overseas opposition were an early feature of rugby's development.[1] In addition to the early success of the national team, a key element in establishing rugby union as the dominant spectator sport in New Zealand was the development of domestic interprovincial competitions, with teams selected from the best players in the provinces' local clubs. Given the residency qualifications imposed, this created a strong sense of local/regional identity and loyalty, which still underpins the current competitive structures. Initially, these interprovincial matches were predominantly "friendlies," played at irregular intervals outside a league/cup framework, or "challenge" matches, such as for the Ranfurly Shield (Obel, 2001, 83–85).

A significant step on the path to a professional-style league was the introduction in 1976 of a domestic interprovincial competition, the National Provincial Championship (NPC). Teams were based on provincial units but were affiliated with a centrally organized league structure. Spectator interest in the NPC increased, especially after 1992 with the move to a centrally organized schedule of matches and the introduction of playoffs in each division, whereby the top four teams after the round-robin matches play semifinals (first versus fourth and second versus third), and the winners of these play the final. This change enhanced uncertainty of outcome of the overall competition winner and increased spectator interest for teams still in contention for the top four positions in the later stages of the round robin. The NPC is popularly credited with having maintained the high standard of rugby in New Zealand.[2] The current format has a first division of ten teams, a second division of eight teams, and a third division of nine teams. Promotion to and relegation from the first division is based on a playoff between the bottom-placed team in the first division and the champions of the second division (NZRFU, 2002a).

Concurrent with developments in the NPC, rugby union had begun to develop its appeal in the wider global context. The inaugural Rugby World Cup (RWC), held in 1987, was the first time international teams were able to gauge their relative standing in a single competition. More important, however, it provided a vehicle to sell rugby to a wider global television audience (see Table 1). Indeed, the IRB now promotes the RWC as "one of the world's top three sporting competitions."[3]

Despite the increasing revenue raised from television rights, sponsorships, and advertising, the IRB attempted to maintain its cherished principles of amateurism. However, by the mid-1990s, the pressure to allow players to be paid openly for playing became too intense. The impetus for change came particularly from the Southern Hemisphere national unions as a result of a combination of factors, including competition between rugby union and professional rugby league for players, the deregulation of broadcasting in both Australia and New Zealand, and a struggle for television rights in both union and league.

Deregulation of broadcasting brought an increased demand for the rights to broadcast popular sports, including league and union. Prior to 1989, the public broadcaster, Television New Zealand (TVNZ), had a monopoly on television sports coverage in New Zealand. However, the situation changed

Table 1
Rugby World Cup Statistics

1967	1972	1977	1982	1987	1992	1997	2001
20,082	23,300	31,307	29,377	25,990	25,367	21,295	24,971

Source: http://www.RugbyWorldCupWeb.com (reprinted in New Zealand Institute of Economic Research, *Update*, 2002).

with the establishment of TV3 (a privately owned terrestrial channel) in 1989 and, even more significantly, Sky Television (a pay-TV satellite provider) in 1990. In 1992, the NZRFU sold the broadcasting rights of the All Blacks' tour of South Africa to Sky Television, a deal that provided the NZRFU with significant additional revenue, boosted significantly the number of Sky Television subscribers, and ended TVNZ's monopoly on televising rugby union matches (Obel, 2001).

In Australia, deregulation of broadcasting in 1995 intensified competition for television rights, especially for rugby league, leading to a split into two rival professional competitions: the Australian Rugby League backed by Kerry Packer's Optus Vision and Super League backed by Rupert Murdoch's News Corporation (News Corp). This put upward pressure on salaries of league players and increased the attraction of defection to league from still-amateur union players in Australia and New Zealand. In response to a potentially damaging drain of players to league, and the market opportunity that existed for union competitions that would meet the increased demand for televised rugby union, the national organizing bodies, the NZRFU, the ARU, and the SARFU combined to form SANZAR, agreeing to a contract with News Corp worth $550 million over ten years. This combination provided SANZAR a dominant position with commercial control over the most exciting and valuable competitions in Southern Hemisphere rugby. It was thus able to exert sufficient pressure on the IRB to renounce the amateur eligibility rules and hence legalize the Southern Hemisphere professional contracts.

The Super 12 competition is an annual transnational competition involving twelve regional teams (three from Australia, four from South Africa, and five from New Zealand) organized through the award of franchises by SANZAR. A franchise effectively guarantees a team a regional monopoly, similar to the territorial monopoly granted to team owners of franchises in North American baseball. Compared to the NPC, there is a much greater degree of centralization in the construction of the Super 12 teams. In New Zealand, provinces close together were brought together under regional banners with home games spread among different centers, but with a majority of matches at the main population center. Each New Zealand franchise has associated with it a "brand": the Blues, the Chiefs, the Crusaders, the Hurricanes, and the Highlanders. Initially, the four South African sides were provincial, but by 1998 they also became regionally based (the Bulls, the Cats, the Sharks, and the Stormers). The three Australian teams are state teams: the Brumbies (Australian Capital Territory), the Reds (Queensland), and the Waratahs (New South Wales). Each team plays every other team once (home or away) in a round robin, with the top four qualifying for the semifinals. The Super 12 format builds upon intense traditional rivalries both within New Zealand among the main urban-center provinces, which are the core of each of the five New Zealand franchises, and, at the international level, among the three Southern Hemisphere countries that have among

Figure 1
The Financial Impact of Professionalism

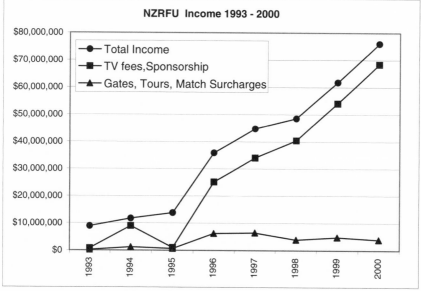

Source: NZRFU *Annual Reports*, 1996–2001.

them won the four RWC competitions. Both SANZAR and News Corp are also involved in the annual Tri-Nations competition, which features the three countries' national teams: the All Blacks, the Springboks (South Africa), and the Wallabies (Australia). Every season, each team plays home and away matches against its opponents.

The television rights deal signed with News Corp, plus commercial sponsorship of the All Blacks and the various competitions, represented a major structural shift in the NZRFU's revenue streams. As Figure 1 clearly demonstrates, the NZRFU gained control over substantial media-generated sponsorship income, which quickly came to dwarf its revenue from admission fees.

Although a highly dominant team can still maintain spectator interest from partisan traditional and core supporters, such an arrangement is less likely to be attractive to a wider television audience interested in attractive competitive matches and close overall competitions. The huge growth in the importance of broadcast revenue for New Zealand rugby has the potential to have significant effects on the structure of competitions involving New Zealand rugby teams, and competitive balance may matter more in future media-led developments. Hence, a natural focus is the level of and changes in the degree of outcome uncertainty and competitive balance of the various competitions, which are considered in the following section.

ORGANIZATIONAL STRUCTURES AND COMPETITIVE BALANCE

The conventional view in the literature on the economics of professional sports is that "sports leagues are in the business of selling competition on the playing field" (Fort and Quirk, 1995, 1265). The uncertainty of outcome hypothesis (Rottenberg, 1956) postulates that a positive relationship exists between spectator interest (and hence admission fees, television audiences, and other revenue sources) and the uncertainty of outcome of individual matches and of the overall competition. Competitive balance matters because it ensures a degree of uncertainty of outcome. If teams end up with greater financial resources (due to larger or more committed fan bases, more lucrative sponsorship deals, etc.), then, in a free market, they have the ability to hire better players, improve team performance, and increase their dominance, which, in turn, undermines competitive balance and uncertainty of outcome. Restraints on trade and other policy interventions (including revenue redistribution, through sharing of gate and television revenue, and labor market policies, such as the implementation of reserve option clauses, player drafts, salary caps/maximum wage) have often been justified as means to cross-subsidize teams on the grounds that unfettered competition will not produce competitive balance.[4]

However, the theoretical implications of free agency and specific policy restrictions for competitive balance depend on the assumptions made about, inter alia, the objectives of the teams and whether the league is "closed"; that is, whether the total stock of player talent is fixed, so that one team's gain when attracting a star player is another's loss. Under profit maximization in a closed league, a key result is the invariance of competitive balance regardless of different institutional arrangements in the labor market for players; interventions such as a maximum wage, a reserve clause, and sharing gate revenue do not affect competitive balance relative to a free market outcome, although they are likely to affect the distribution of revenues (Fort and Quirk, 1995).[5] Revenue sharing can, however, offset revenue imbalances due to the different sizes of local markets, and it can ensure the viability of teams in markets that generate less revenue, although it reduces players' salaries (Fort, 2000; Dobson and Goddard, 2001).

However, if teams aim to maximize win ratios rather than profits, then revenue sharing does affect competitive balance (Késenne, 2000). Also, analyses of European soccer (e.g., Dobson and Goddard, 2001, Chapter 3) favor the use of an open model, in which player talent can be traded with teams from outside the domestic league. For comparable objectives of teams, competition should be more balanced in open leagues than in closed leagues. Win-ratio maximizing teams make for less balanced competition than profit-maximizing teams because of the latter's reluctance to overspend on players (Dobson and Goddard, 2001, 140–146).

In terms of the supply of player talent and the closed or open characterization, New Zealand rugby lies somewhere between the two extremes, but closer to the closed version. Player eligibility restrictions currently allow an NPC team to include only two players who are ineligible to play for New Zealand national teams (NZRFU, 2002b). However, the model is much more open in the other direction; New Zealand rugby players can switch to rugby league or play union in other countries.[6] The current eligibility requirements might, therefore, be interpretable in terms of a partially closed model in that, particularly in terms of elite players, teams are effectively competing for players from the domestic pool. However, the zero-sum characteristic, arising from reallocation of a fixed stock of player talent, of the closed model is an important driver of its predictions. An aspect of the New Zealand rugby scene (and other sports) that could possibly alter conclusions from such a model is the extent of the flow of new talent that comes through the network of school and club rugby and/or lower divisions. The allocation of this flow is unlikely to be independent of the existing distribution of financial resources, as provinces with franchise bases in the Super 12 are attractive to the best new talent.

In addition, for the NPC, the Super 12, and for New Zealand rugby overall, the assumption that teams aim to maximize their win ratios subject to a financial constraint is likely to be more appropriate, at least at this stage in the development of professionalization, than the profit-maximizing assumption. However, if Fort's (2000) argument that profit-maximizing national structures dominate win-ratio-maximizing structures is correct, then it will be of interest to monitor SANZAR's and the NZRFU's decisions over time as rugby continues to move into the professional era.

A distinctive feature of New Zealand rugby that is not represented in existing theoretical models in the literature on professional team sports is the importance of the international success of national teams (in this case, particularly, the All Blacks), noted by McMillan (1997, 98) as an important element of the justification for some degree of restriction on free market outcomes in the case of New Zealand rugby. Because of its importance to commercial and sporting interest in New Zealand rugby, this objective is emphasized in two of the four "key focus areas" identified by the NZRFU (2001): "Ensuring the All Blacks are the best in the world" and "Taking a managed approach to the game nationally to build the basis of strong international teams." In team sports, there is a well-known externality whereby competition in leagues will not necessarily be forthcoming on the basis of incentives facing individual teams. In New Zealand rugby, there is also what could be described as the "All Blacks externality": If maximizing the performance of the national team is an important objective, then provinces maximizing their own objective functions in a free market will not necessarily achieve this.

The emphasis on the All Blacks' success has led to a player labor market with some unique features. Effectively, the NZRFU has monopsony power in terms of the market for professional rugby union players in New Zealand and has implemented payment structures, as well as regulations on mobility and eligibility, that, it would argue, are designed to strengthen the All Blacks team. A distinctive aspect of the NZRFU's approach is a centralized contracting system in which Super 12 players and franchise coaches hold contracts with the NZRFU, not the franchises or the provincial unions. These contracts require a player to play (if selected) for up to five different teams, including Super 12, NPC, All Blacks, and other national representative teams (Obel, 2001, 169).

Initially, Super 12 coaches select players from the provincial teams from their franchises. Players not selected for the Super 12 squad from their home franchise are placed into a pool of "draft" players, and Super 12 coaches can call on this pool to fill any "deficient" positions in their squad. In some cases, however, the NZRFU exerts some control over the composition of the Super 12 squads or the playing positions of particular players, sometimes even against the wishes of the Super 12 coaches, in order to develop a wider set of players than would otherwise have occurred. Obel (2001, 168) interprets this as the NZRFU aiming "not to create balance in the competitive strength of the teams . . . but rather to strengthen the pool of players from which to select the All Blacks team *and* to ensure New Zealand success in the Super 12 competition."

In addition to the potentially high degree of central control the NZRFU has to allocate players with Super 12 contracts to a particular franchise, a domestic transfer system was established with the aim of preventing richer unions from bidding away all the top players from smaller unions in the NPC. This system limits the number of players a provincial union can "buy in" in any year and specifies maximum transfer fees (McMillan, 1997, 102–103; Obel, 2001, 221–224), but the system does not appear to have been a major barrier to the recruitment of top players by the unions with Super 12 bases (Obel, 2001, 223).

In terms of revenue sharing, the NZRFU initially took a hands-off approach, particularly in comparison with arrangements common in North American professional sports leagues. The allocation of gate revenue, whereby unions retain gate revenue from their home round-robin matches, favors the urban-based unions with larger population bases, further accentuated by their greater ability to attract major sponsorship, hence creating significant financial inequality. Since 1997, the five provincial unions that host Super 12 teams have been able to retain their home gate revenues and use their allocation of a Super 12 team to generate further income through sponsorship, which in turn enables them to strengthen their NPC teams. Also, in addition to superior financial resources, these unions have the advantage in attracting top emerging players to their union because of better prospects of obtaining Super 12 contracts and the opportunities to reap rewards (in terms of attracting the attention of the All Blacks selectors) from the synergies of playing with other top players on winning teams.

Fort (2000, 447) emphasizes that "both competitive imbalance and spending imbalance follow revenue imbalance." The small size of New Zealand's population (approximately 3.8 million people) and its distribution (approximately 54% of the population in the five main urban centers with Super 12 franchises—Auckland, Christchurch, Dunedin, Hamilton, and Wellington) underlies the importance of ensuring the viability of teams from smaller population centers, so some degree of revenue sharing as a cross-subsidy is desirable. As noted earlier, predictions about whether this affects competitive balance depend on the structure of the labor market and the objectives of teams and of the NZRFU. The growing financial inequality has been partly addressed by an increasing degree of subsidy to the smaller unions from the NZRFU's media and sponsorship contracts (see Owen and Weatherston, 2002b for details). However, in comparison with schemes used elsewhere, there is scope for further general revenue sharing if issues of competitive and financial balance are considered to be a problem that can be addressed by this approach.

MEASUREMENT OF COMPETITIVE BALANCE IN NEW ZEALAND RUGBY UNION

In this section, we examine the degree of competitive balance in the NPC and Super 12 competitions in the professional era, post-1995, using a range of different measures. Competitive balance in a given season is conventionally measured by comparing the actual standard deviation of win ratios across the teams with the expected standard deviation in the case of teams of equal playing strength (Fort and Quirk, 1995; Downward and Dawson, 2000, Appendix 4.1), and the variation in this ex post measure can be tracked over time.[7] We follow this approach, but also consider the variation in competition points. There are potentially five competition points to be gained from each game (four for a win plus a bonus point for scoring four or more tries); a bonus point is also available to a team for losing by seven points or less. We do not attempt to standardize the variation because different allocations of points are consistent with even games, depending on whether they are high or low scoring in terms of the number of tries.

The ratios of the actual to "ideal" standard deviations of winning percentages and the coefficients of variation of competition points in Table 2 reveal a higher degree of competitive imbalance in the domestic NPC competition compared to the Super 12, except for 2002, when both measures increased markedly for the latter. The coefficients of variation suggest there is relatively little evidence of the imbalance changing over this time period. However, these do not adjust for the effect on the standard deviations of the different

Table 2
Measures of Competitive Balance in the NPC and Super 12 Competitions

	1975	*1985*	*1995*
CFL Salaries (000, 1995 Cdn dollars)	73	86	50
CFL Salaries (000, 1995 US dollars)	72	63	36
CFL Salaries (US dollars) as Approximate % of NFL Salaries	67 %	29 %	5 %

Sources: Odds from the New Zealand TAB; competition points and winning percentages calculated from *Rugby Almanack of New Zealand* (various editions).

numbers of games played. The ratios of actual to "idealized" standard deviations imply there was an increase in competitive imbalance in the NPC in 2000 and 2001, but a slight decrease in 2002. A three-year moving average of this ratio (results not reported) shows increases every year for the NPC from 1998 to 2002.

An alternative way to evaluate competitive balance is to look at the frequency of championships across the different teams, with balanced competition more likely to be associated with different winners. In the first seven years of the professional era, four different unions won the first division championship: Auckland in 1996, 1999, and 2002; Canterbury in 1997 and 2001; Otago in 1998; and Wellington in 2000. In contrast, although the variation in win ratios and points totals suggests that the Super 12 is usually a more balanced competition than the NPC, only three different teams have won the Super 12: the Crusaders four times (1998, 1999, 2000, 2002), the Blues twice (1996, 1997), and the Brumbies once (2001). Focusing solely on championship winning frequencies, however, ignores other useful information. For example, over the duration of the Super 12, eleven teams have qualified for the semifinals. Over the corresponding period, eight provinces out of a possible twelve have been represented in the NPC semifinals. The four non-semifinalists essentially fill the bottom places each year. In the NPC, the five Super 12 franchise-based unions achieved win ratios, aggregated over the professional era, between 54% and 73%, whereas the four historically relatively poorest-performing teams had ratios between 0% and 31%. Comparable data for the Super 12 shows historically a relatively narrower spread of win ratios, between 44% and 63% for all but the two poorest-performing teams (Owen and Weatherston, 2002b).

The notion of outcome uncertainty, which has traditionally been viewed as a key concept in analyzing attendance demand (Neale, 1964; El Hodiri and Quirk, 1971), is an ex ante concept. The use of ex post win ratios or competition points is therefore not entirely consistent with the idea that it is the public's *expectation* of match uncertainty or *perception* of competitive balance that is important. With this motivation, various studies of attendance determinants at sporting events (Peel and Thomas, 1988, 1992; Knowles, Sherony, and Haupert, 1992; Czarnitzki and Stadtmann, 2002; Owen and Weatherston, 2002a) measure uncertainty of individual match outcomes by the probability of a home-team win, based on (some transformation of) betting odds published prior to each game. These measures are regarded as superior to "entirely backward-looking" measures (such as prematch league standings or points differences) as ex ante proxies for individual match uncertainty (Downward and Dawson, 2000, 134) because they take into account a wider set of information than such partial measures. In Table 2, we therefore also report coefficients of variation, across matches in a season, of the individual-match uncertainty measured by the probability of a home-team win obtained, when available, from the opening odds of the New Zealand Totalisator Agency Board (TAB).[8] These show greater variation across individual match probabilities for the domestic NPC competition (first division) relative to the Super 12, consistent with relatively greater perceived competitive imbalance in the NPC.

On all the measures considered (other than championship frequencies) there is generally a higher degree of competitive imbalance in the NPC compared to the Super 12, and, until 2002, this appeared to be worsening over the professional era, although it must be emphasized that this is a relatively short period. Some commentators have expressed the view that "the professional game is pulling talent away from the provinces into the metropolitan unions that act as hosts to the Super 12 franchises" and that this trend will continue unless there is more drastic regulatory intervention (such as a cap on the number of professional players in any NPC squad).[9] The NZRFU itself has also expressed concern over the degree of competitive balance in the NPC (NZRFU, 2001). The additional NZRFU cross-subsidization of financially weaker unions is a partial response to the perception that lack of financial equality has led to lack of competitive balance, as is the announcement of a major review of the NPC. However, in terms of championships, the domination of the main-center unions is not a recent phenomenon attributable solely to the professional era. In twenty-seven years of the NPC, there have been only three championship winners from outside the "big five" unions (Auckland, Canterbury, Otago, Waikato, and Wellington).[10] Despite this dominance, even in recent years, unions outside the big five have made the semifinals of the NPC (Taranaki in 1998 and 2000, and North Harbour in 1999 and 2001).

The optimal degree of competitive balance in the case of New Zealand rugby union is unclear on a priori grounds. Differences in willingness to pay when there are large-revenue-market and small-revenue-market teams make equal competitive balance outcomes inefficient (Fort, 2000). Successful teams with large fan bases yield greater total utility than successful teams with smaller fan bases, so that an equally balanced competition is unlikely to be socially optimal (Szymanski, 2001). For the higher objective of All Blacks' success, it is not obvious that more competition (in terms of a higher degree of competitive balance in the NPC) is necessarily better competition (in terms of developing a successful All Blacks' squad). It has been argued that the current format and structure of the NPC works well as a "breeding ground" for Super 12 and international players, and that, for example, forced amalgamation or other attempts to reduce the number of teams in the first division and/or divisions in the NPC would narrow the base of players from which international players are developed.[11] Any enhancement of competitive balance that reduces the playing strength of the top teams could have adverse effects on the quality of play in the league as a whole, which is likely to compromise the objective of maximizing the All Blacks' win ratio.[12] The mechanisms usually considered are not necessarily well suited to improve competitive balance and, simultaneously, maintain or improve the overall quality of play. For example, given the partially open/partially closed nature of the player market in New Zealand, a local salary cap, even if it were to improve competitive balance (which is disputed), is likely to increase the flow of players going overseas and reduce the available pool of players and overall quality to some degree.

Recent performance figures for the All Blacks in the professional era show no significant deviation from historical averages, with only the win ratio against the Wallabies showing a notable drop in the post-1996 era to 2001 (Owen and Weatherston, 2002b). However, the All Blacks have won the Tri-Nations competition four times in the seven years between 1996 and 2002 (compared to twice for the Wallabies and only once for the Springboks). Also, there does not appear to be a simple contemporaneous within-season relationship between the performance of New Zealand teams in the Super 12 and the performance of the All Blacks, which is perhaps not surprising when comparing the results of a handful of games involving relatively evenly matched teams. For example, in 1998 New Zealand teams filled three of the four semifinals positions in the Super 12, yet the All Blacks lost all five of their test matches against Australia and South Africa. Whether strong performances in the Super 12 translate into a winning All Blacks team is better investigated on a long-term basis, when longer runs of data become available. A test of the link between the performances of New Zealand teams in the Super 12 and the performance of the All Blacks could occur in 2003, as players from the Crusaders, the outstanding Super 12 team in recent years, dominated team selections for the All Blacks in 2002. It will be interesting to see if the All Blacks' performance in the 2003 Rugby World Cup will be a repeat of the 1980s when a very strong Auckland provincial team translated into a strongly performing All Blacks team. If such a strategy is successful, it will raise further questions about whether attempting to maximize competitive balance in the NPC and between New Zealand teams in the Super 12 is optimal in terms of the NZRFU's aspirations for the All Blacks.

While there is an extensive literature on modeling the effects of competitive balance on attendance and, to a lesser extent, television audiences in other sports (see Downward and Dawson, 2000, Chapters 5–6; Dobson and Goddard, 2001, Chapter 7), there is very little published work on rugby union. Owen and Weatherston (2002a) investigate the attendance determinants at New Zealand matches in the Super 12 competition in the 1999 to 2001 seasons, with emphasis placed on testing the effects of within-season and match-specific uncertainty of outcome on demand. Their results suggest that the factors with a statistically significant effect on attendance mainly reflect habit and tradition, such as lagged attendance, traditional rivalries, and antipathy toward non–New Zealand teams, or are beyond the control of administrators, such as rainfall and team finishes. There is very little evidence that individual match uncertainty, measured by probabilities of a home-team win based on TAB odds, is a statistically significant factor in determining match attendances. Apart from the stage of the season itself, other, sharper proxies for seasonal uncertainty also appear to have little relevance. Moreover, there is currently no published evidence on the effects of uncertainty of outcome and competitive balance measures on television ratings for rugby union. Given the increasing importance of media and sponsorship income in funding New Zealand rugby, this is clearly an area where further work is required. If major changes are to be made to the structure of competitions, the extent of cross-subsidization, and regulations on the market for players with the aim of improving competitive balance in the NPC, then it is essential to have a clearer idea of the effects of differing degrees of competitive balance. Currently, there is very little hard evidence on the implications for any of the key variables of interest: attendance, television ratings of televised matches, sponsorship interest, flow-on effects to the Super 12 competition, and the performance of the All Blacks.

CONCLUDING COMMENTS

As a result of the 1995 move from amateurism to professionalism, rugby union in New Zealand has experienced major changes in the structure of its competitions, including new transnational ventures (Super 12 and Tri-Nations), and in the relationships among players, local provincial unions, and the NZRFU. During the twentieth century, the emphasis had shifted from a "player-centered" form of pure amateurism to a more "spectator-oriented" focus (Obel, 2001, 99). Since professionalization, rugby has become "media-centered" due to the increasingly important role of television and sponsorship revenue relative to gate revenue. Tensions have emerged in fitting both the new and the more traditional competitions, such as the NPC, into the lengthening rugby season. The media influence is pervasive and extends, for example, to the scheduling of more evening matches, even when, due to less comfortable weather conditions, these can have adverse effects on playing standards and match attendance.

The NZRFU is aware that "global sporting trends present both an opportunity for and a threat to New Zealand rugby" (NZRFU, 2000, 5). With the increasing global interest in rugby union, especially from television audiences, and the need to maintain the flow of media income into New Zealand rugby, the success of its international teams, particularly the All Blacks, is an important objective for the NZRFU, supplementing the traditional motivation of national pride. The primacy of this objective has been used as a justification for the high degree of central control over the market for professional rugby players in New Zealand, which exhibits some unique contracting features that limit players' payments, eligibility, and movement. It also underpins the emphasis placed on maintaining the breadth and depth of (still largely amateur) club and provincial rugby, and, in particular, the NPC as a conduit for the development of players for the Super 12 and national teams.

The current state of Southern Hemisphere rugby is not necessarily stable. The future structure of the Super 12 and Tri-Nations is due for renegotiation in 2005, and future changes will be an important litmus test of the strength of different objectives (e.g., on-field performance and competitive balance versus market coverage and revenue or profit maximization) as well as the distribution of bargaining power within SANZAR, and between SANZAR and News Corp.[13] From New Zealand's perspective, similar trade-offs will be relevant if, for example, it is forced to drop one of its franchises. The alternative of Super 12 expansion would involve issues relating to player burnout and conflicts with NPC scheduling. A two-tier competition involving franchises from other Pacific nations and promotion/relegation may, however, be a viable compromise.

There is clear evidence of a persistent lack of competitive balance in the first division of New Zealand's domestic provincial competition, relative to the Super 12, and there is some empirical support for the view that the provincial unions that host the five Super 12 franchises are becoming more dominant, both financially and in terms of playing strength. However, a degree of competitive imbalance in the NPC is not a phenomenon that is new to professionalization, and the pattern of imbalance largely reflects the distribution of the population, which is relatively highly concentrated in a small number of urban centers. Under such circumstances, perfect competitive balance is unlikely to be efficient or welfare maximizing. The optimal degree of competitive balance for New Zealand rugby, taking into account the objective of maximizing the All Blacks' success, is also not clear on a priori grounds. Whether New Zealand and Southern Hemisphere rugby will converge with North American models of professional sports leagues, and, if so, at what speed, is an open question. However, in the current state of the game's development, more work is required to establish, for example, the importance of competitive balance for match attendance, television-viewing patterns (both domestically and for an international audience), and the linkages, if any, to the success of the All Blacks. If it is decided that a higher degree of competitive balance in domestic competitions is desirable, then a careful analysis of the costs, benefits, and distributional implications of any further interventions is required. Given the partially open structure of rugby in New Zealand and other Southern Hemisphere countries, restrictions such as salary caps or player quotas are likely to have more adverse side effects than revenue sharing as instruments to enhance competitive balance. Also, Super 12 franchise bases are always likely to maintain some of their historical advantages for top players (as a route to the All Blacks and as environments offering complementary educational and other opportunities).

At a time when the standard of rugby union in other countries is generally rising in response to the effects of professionalism on improving players, coaches, and managers, and with greater flows of resources into the game in larger countries, New Zealand's dominant position in the new global game is not necessarily guaranteed. Rugby union in New Zealand is at a crucial stage of its development, with major changes having taken place in a relatively short period of time, but still with strong links to the traditions and values of the amateur era. Difficult decisions on competition structure, on competitive balance policies, and on how best to renegotiate future media contracts are imminent. However, we are acutely aware of the lack of analytical and empirical work in the area of sports economics that is specific to rugby union and that could provide a framework for such decisions.

ACKNOWLEDGMENTS

We are grateful to Steve Dobson, John Howells, Stephen Knowles, Martin Richardson, and Niven Winchester for helpful comments, and to Helen Quirke (TAB) and Amanda Temperton (NZRFU) for providing data. More detailed discussions of many of the issues considered here are available in a longer working paper version (Owen and Weatherston, 2002b). The views expressed in this chapter are those of the authors and do not necessarily reflect the views of the New Zealand Treasury.

NOTES

1. In the 1905–1906 season, the "original" All Blacks toured Britain, Ireland, France, and North America and won thirty-four of the thirty-five games played.

2. For example, see Alastair McMurran, "NPC Credited with Keeping New Zealand Rugby Strong," *Otago* (New Zealand) *Daily Times*, August 8, 2002.

3. Source: IRB Web site at http://www.irb.com/events/worldcup.cfm.

4. Fort and Quirk (1995), McMillan (1997), Downward and Dawson (2000), and Dobson and Goddard (2001) provide useful discussions of the different methods used to attempt to restore balance.

5. Szymanski (1998) and Hoehn and Szymanski (1999) question this conclusion and argue that, in a model with profit-maximizing teams but diminishing marginal increases in win ratios in response to increases in talent, gate-revenue sharing makes competition less balanced, whereas sharing of television revenues can enhance competitive balance. Fort and Quirk (1995) argue that a salary cap can improve competitive balance, but Vrooman (2000) argues that it can worsen it. Either way, enforcement is a major problem.

6. In 2002, there were over 650 registered New Zealanders playing rugby professionally overseas (Paul Verdon, "Is Our National Game Truly Losing Ground?" *National Business Review* (New Zealand), September 20, 2002). An erosion in the depth of experienced quality players could affect the development of new players and coaches along with competitive balance, particularly in the NPC (Laurie Mains, "Keeping Players in New Zealand Has to Become a Priority," *Otago Daily Times* (New Zealand), October 4, 2002).

7. In the benchmark case, the probability of winning each match is usually taken to be 0.5 (ignoring draws, which are relatively rare in rugby union, and assuming that there is no home advantage). The standard deviation of winning percentages in this case is $0.5/(n^{1/2})$, where n is the number of games played by each team in a season. Comparison with this benchmark allows for the implication that the dispersion of win ratios will be smaller the more games that are played (even if all teams are of equal strength). The greater the value of the ratio (> 1), the greater is the degree of competitive imbalance.

8. The probabilities of each team winning, estimated from the opening odds, are calculated as $100/(HTH(1+p))$, where *HTH* are the opening head-to-head TAB odds and p is an 8% profit margin.

9. The quote and suggested intervention is from former All Black Chris Laidlaw's "A Dirty Word May Be the Key to the Future Health of the NPC," *Otago Daily Times* (New Zealand), August 16, 2002 (the "dirty word" being *regulation*). It is important to note that, despite professionalization, many of the players in the first division are not fully professional; e.g., Southland and Bay of Plenty had only two and three players, respectively, with Super 12 contracts in their squads in 2002.

10. Indeed, Downward and Dawson (2000) argue that long-term dominance is the "natural order" in sports leagues, although television revenues can cause changes in the structures of leagues, and hence competitive balance, to occur more rapidly, which, somewhat paradoxically, may increase the importance of competitive balance.

11. This is a view expressed by Laurie Mains (ex–All Blacks coach), "'If It Ain't Broke, Don't Fix It'—Does the NPC Need Changing?" *Otago Daily Times* (New Zealand), September 13, 2002.

12. As Vrooman (2000, 374–375) observes, "A blind pursuit of competitive balance *per se* may result in an inferior league product of equally bad teams beating one another."

13. Owen and Weatherston (2002b) examine the debate, at times acrimonious, among the SANZAR partners about possible options for the future configuration of the Super 12.

Part VII

Brazilian Soccer

15

Recent History of Brazilian Soccer

Antônio Carlos Kfouri Aidar, Clarissa Bueno de Ameida, and Renato Giosa Miralla

INTRODUCTION

Brazilian soccer is experiencing dramatic organizational change. In a way, Brazil is now like England was in the late 1980s. At that time, English soccer was going downhill until the Lord Taylor Report (Taylor, 1990) led English soccer down a new course following the Hillsborough disaster in 1989. Today, English soccer is much better organized and has become a strong business. Brazil has faced problems similar to those in England. Leagues have been in disarray, and the economic viability of soccer in Brazil was in jeopardy.

As minister of sports, Pelé strove to modernize the organization of Brazilian soccer by proposing the Pelé Law (1998). However, Congress eventually passed the much less ambitious Maguito Law (1998), named after the primary opponent of the Pelé Law, Senator Maguito Villela. But in late December 2000, Brazil had its own Hillsborough, fortunately without the same number of casualties. Vasco da Gama and São Caetano were playing the final match of the Brazilian Football Tournament when fences collapsed as a result of the overcrowded terrace. The federal government, which had just a few years prior watered down the Pelé Law, exerted pressure for change. This pressure led to an alliance between Pelé—by this time already out of the government—and some of the traditional soccer leadership to revamp the sport. The result was the PM Law (Provisional Measure 2193/2001). At the same time, both houses of Congress stepped up an ongoing investigation into corruption in soccer.

In our opinion, the ongoing reform process is far from perfect but headed in a promising direction. However, state federations and the Brazilian Confederation of Football (CBF) are striving to undermine this modernization process. Some of its managers were fingered by the congressional investigations and are now under accusation of corruption. It is very important that the new Football Law obtains the approval of Congress without modification (other than to minor mistakes made in the original text) and that the leagues be consolidated. Recently, moves in that direction have occurred. In June 2002, PM 39/02 was put forward but was rejected by Congress. Finally, in November 2002, PM 79/02 was published and was approved by Congress to last until April 2003. PM 79/02 is an extension that improves upon the text of the original Pelé Law.

This chapter covers the recent history of Brazilian soccer and addresses its basic transformation. The numbers given are educated guesses; reliable numbers are available only from 2002 on, after the new legislation came into effect, requiring figures to be audited and made available to the public. The basic structure of Brazilian soccer is presented, including its new calendar. Past problems in Brazilian soccer are documented. The details and impacts of the new legislation, primarily concerning transparency, rules for investors, and rules for transfers, leads naturally into a discussion of the current state of Brazilian soccer and comparisons with Europe.

BRAZILIAN SOCCER: STRUCTURE AND COMPARISONS

The general structure of Brazilian soccer competition is shown in Figure 1. In this section, the details of each component are spelled out and the new soccer calendar is discussed. Some interim observations on the current structure of Brazilian soccer round out the section.

State Tournaments

Champions of each state tournament qualify for the Brazil Cup. First, they must play a qualifying round to secure a position in their respective regional tournaments. Because many states take part in all the regional tournaments (bear in mind that Brazil is a large country), state champions do not automatically qualify for the regional tournament; they have to compete for it. One exception is the Rio de Janero–São Paulo regional tournament, in which only the teams from these two states participate. In this case, each state champion is entitled to take part in the regional tournament without having to play a qualifying round. Teams ranking last are relegated to the second division of their respective state cup, whereas the top teams of second divisions are promoted. Clubs that play in regional tournaments do not play for state cups.

Figure 1
Soccer Competition Linkages in Brazil

Regional Tournaments

Regional tournaments are now organized by the respective regional leagues (this represents progress in terms of independence from the CBF). There are five regional tournaments—Rio de Janeiro–São Paulo (region one, sixteen clubs), South-Minas Gerais (region two, sixteen clubs), Northeast (region three, sixteen clubs), North (region four, eight clubs), and Mid-West (region five, eight clubs).

Teams that rank last in their respective regional tournaments are relegated to playing in state tournaments. The number of teams relegated depends on the rules for each regional tournament: in the North and in the Mid-West regional tournaments, only the teams ranking last are relegated, whereas in the Northeast and South-Minas regionals, the teams ranking last and next to last are relegated. In the Rio–São Paulo tournament, one club from São Paulo and one from Rio de Janeiro ranking last in the regional are compulsorily relegated. Regional tournaments are played for the Champions Cup. A preset number of clubs qualifies for the Champions Cup, as explained in the following section.

Champions Cup

The Champions Cup is organized by the CBF and sixteen teams compete, including the previous year's Champions Cup winner, the champions of the North and Mid-West regional tournaments, the top three teams in the Northeast regional tournament, the top four teams in the South-Minas regional rournament, and the top six teams in the Rio–São Paulo regional tournament.

In the first round, the sixteen teams are divided into four groups of four teams each for round-robin play (each team plays all three of the other teams in their group). The top two teams from each group qualify for the quarter-finals, in which the "knockout system" is used (single elimination). Winners move on to the semifinals, which are also played in a single match. The final is played in two games. If a match ends in a draw, the criteria for determining the winner are goal difference and penalty kicks, after the second match. The winner of the Champions Cup qualifies for the Libertadores da America Cup.

Brazil Cup

The Brazil Cup is organized by the CBF, and sixty-four teams compete, including twenty-seven state champions from the previous year, teams that will compete in the first division of the Brazilian Tournament that year, and teams invited by the CBF. As we will see, when the new calendar was presented, the Brazilian Tournament introduced a four-year calendar with twenty-eight teams but is expected to close the fourth year with twenty-four teams. The number of teams taking part in the Brazil Cup has been set at sixty-four. To reach this number, CBF can invite teams to the cup.

The Brazil Cup is played in six rounds. In the first two rounds, teams are divided into groups of two and hold playoffs on a home and away basis. CBF forms the groups and lays down the laws of the game. If the visiting team wins the first match with more than one goal, it will qualify for the following round without having to play the second game. As of round of sixteen, the two games (one home and one away) are mandatory. Playoffs are held up until the final. If the two teams have won the same number of points after the two matches have been played, the criteria to determine the winner are goal difference, higher number of goals scored away from home, and taking penalty kicks. The Brazil Cup winner, like the winner of the Champions Cup, qualifies for the Libertadores da America Cup.

Brazilian Tournament, Series A

The Brazilian Tournament is organized by the CBF. Following the formation in 2002 of the National League, the competition to determine its organizer in 2003 is sure to be fierce. As of 2003, twenty-four clubs will participate in the Brazilian Tournament. Since the four-year calendar was introduced with twenty-eight clubs, to arrive at twenty-four, four clubs were relegated in 2001 and another four will be relegated in 2002, and only two were promoted in 2001 and another two in 2002. As of 2003, two clubs will be promoted (the winner and the runner-up of series B), and two clubs will be relegated at each Brazilian Tournament. The Brazilian Tournament has three series: A, B, and C.

In the first round, round-robin play sends the top eight teams to the second round. In the second round, the playoff series begin (the top team plays the eighth ranking team, the second ranking team plays the seventh ranking, and so forth, both at home and away from home). The two best teams qualify for the final. In case of a draw, the winner is determined according to number of wins, goal difference, goals scored, direct confrontation, and drafting. The winner and the runner-up are entitled to take part in the Libertadores da America Cup. The teams ranking last and next to last are relegated to series B of the Brazilian Tournament.

Libertadores da America Cup

Overall, thirty-two teams participate in the international Libertadores Cup, divided into eight groups of four teams each. The four Brazilian teams that participate in the Libertadores da America Cup (Libertadores Cup) are the winner of the Brazil Cup, the winner of the Champions Cup, and the winner and runner-up of the Brazilian Tournament, series A. In the event the winner of the Libertadores Cup of the previous year was a Brazilian team, then five Brazilian teams take part in the competition.

In the first round, teams play matches against the other teams in the group at home and away from home. If teams are equal in ranking, the winner is determined according to goal difference, greater number of scored goals, direct confrontation, and drafting. After six rounds, the two top ranking teams in each group qualify for the round of sixteen. These sixteen teams are divided into eight groups of two teams each, which hold playoffs at home and away from home. Quarterfinals, semifinals, and finals are held the same way. In these rounds, if the teams are on equal standing in terms of number of points and goal difference, they qualify for the following round by taking penalty kicks.

The New Four-Year Calendar

Up until 2001, Brazil had no calendar, and every year would see a change, new rules, and so forth. Planning was impossible. And how could season tickets be sold under these conditions? Moreover, some tournaments were held for the sole purpose of satisfying vested interests and did not link up with each other. Therefore, they drew no public attention. Top Brazilian teams would play some ninety matches a year. In certain cases, this number would exceed 100 games. Some traditional matches with rivalry equal to a Celtic-Rangers soccer game in Scotland, for example, would have an empty house. Then, in 2001, the four-year calendar was introduced as a result of Pelé's action. Although some of the 2002 dates have been changed because of the World Cup, the calendar is essentially as depicted in Figure 2.

Showing that struggles over the organization of Brazilian Football continue, as of this writing the CBF had revealed its displeasure with the National League and the regional leagues by proposing a new calendar for 2003. The

Figure 2
Brazilian Soccer Calendar, 2002–2005

	Jan		Fev		Mar		Abr		Mai		Jun		Jul		Ago		Set		Out		Nov		Dez	
	1	2	1	2	1	2	1	2	1	2	1	2	1	2	1	2	1	2	1	2	1	2	1	2
Campeonatos Estaduais		x	x	x	x	x	x	x	x															
Campeonatos Regionais		x	x	x	x	x	x	x	x															
Copa do Brasil				x	x	x	x	x	x	x														
Copa Libertadores		x	x	x	x	x	x	x	x			x	x											
Copa dos Campeões											x	x	x											
Campeonato Brasileiro															x	x	x	x	x	x	x	x	x	

new calendar proposal, shown in Figure 2A, eliminates the regional tournaments and the Champions Cup. In fact, this calendar would eliminate the regional leagues, a central focus in the struggle between the old CBF and the newly formed professional leagues. In the proposed calendar, state federations would organize the state tournaments, and CBF would organize the Brazilian Tournament and the Brazil Cup. This arrangement would obviously weaken the newly formed National League. As the calendar shows, CBF would lure teams first with a longer Brazilian Tournament, played as a round-robin formula with two legs, home and away. As in Europe, the champion would be the club with the highest number of points. Second, together with Conmebol (The South America Federation), CBF organizes the Pan American Cup, comprising South and Central American clubs. The proposed calendar solidifies CBF's hold over post-season play.

Figure 2A
Brazilian Soccer Calendar: CBF's 2003 Proposal

	Jan		Fev		Mar		Abr		Mai		Jun		Jul		Ago		Set		Out		Nov		Dez	
	1	2	1	2	1	2	1	2	1	2	1	2	1	2	1	2	1	2	1	2	1	2	1	2
Campeonatos Estaduais		x	x	x	x																			
Copa do Brasil				x	x	x	x	x	x	x	x	x	x											
Copa Libertadores				x	x	x	x	x	x	x	x	x	x											
Copa Pan Americana															x	x	x	x	x	x	x	x	x	
Campeonato Brasileiro						x	x	x	x	x	x	x	x	x	x	x	x	x	x	x	x	x	x	X

Figure 2B
Soccer Competition Linkages in Brazil under CBF's 2003 Proposal

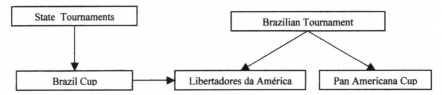

If the new calendar is implemented, the linkages in Figure 1 would change to those in Figure 2B. As today, the champion and runner-up of the Brazilian Tournament would go to the Libertadores, but so too would the champion and runner-up of the Brazil Cup. Hence, the runner-up of the Brazil Cup replaces the champion of the Champions Cup at the Libertadores, sending the third through eighth finishes in the Brazilian Tournament to the Pan American Cup. Theoretically, this change means more money for the big clubs (a longer Brazilian Tournament) and a calendar more or less like Europe's; Libertadores mirrors the Champions League and Pan Americana mirrors the Union des Associations Européennes de Football (UEFA) Cup.

In our opinion, after the lawyers wrestle over the calendar dispute for 2003, Brazilian soccer will emerge something like in Figure 2C, a victory for the leagues. The state tournaments are not economically attractive for the big clubs, and there would be no calendar space for the Champions Cup. The link would be in between the state tournaments and the regional tournaments and between the regional tournaments and the Brazil Cup. On the other hand, the round-robin Brazilian Tournament and the Pan American Cup are very welcome in this scheme.

Comparisons: Brazil, the United States, and Europe

It is worth mentioning that because Brazil is a continental country, it has some peculiarities. Brazil has 170 million soccer lovers, and over 500

Figure 2C
Predicted Soccer Competition Linkages in Brazil

registered professional teams. In Europe, some countries (the Netherlands, Belgium, Scotland, Norway, Portugal, Sweden, and Denmark) are so small in terms of population and soccer that they are seriously thinking of making tournaments regional instead of national. Even countries of tournament scale, such as England and Italy, can easily accommodate a national league and a national tournament (playoffs).

In Brazil, in addition to the national tournament (playoffs) and the National League (three series), there are also state and regional tournaments. It is very difficult to pair up local competition with economic feasibility. The Getúlio Vargas Foundation (2001) conducted a study regarding this problem and came to the conclusion that it would be hard to solve. We are currently doing more research in this respect. It is our opinion, however, that many small teams will merge or die.

This kind of process is well known in other industries and is part of capitalist development. For the sake of economic feasibility, as said above, we feel that Brazil will eventually have a calendar similar to Europe's, with National League round-robin play at home and away from home, the champion holding the most points, and the national cup champion winning the playoffs. In order for Brazil to get to this point, it must first solve two problems: how to maintain the greatest number of small clubs (perhaps through community support) and how to introduce a UEFA Cup–type competition in the Americas—in addition to the Libertadores Cup—to promote greater interest in the National League, should one or two of the National League clubs be much farther ahead in the bracket and the others having no chance of winning the competition. In this case of great disparity in terms of winning the competition, the Pan American Cup is one path toward a solution.

When discussing this topic, the pro sports leagues in the United States automatically come to mind. For example, there is no relegation system in the National Basketball Association, and the arenas are often full. Of course, the quality of the games and the show business characteristics are fundamental to its success. We wonder if it would be possible to have full stadiums in soccer just for the sake of game quality instead of competition. We feel this would be impossible for soccer fans to fathom, which serves to emphasize that we must have something in the Americas like the UEFA Cup for Brazil to make it to the final calendar.

The economic data on Brazilian soccer primarily cover television revenue. Up until 1988, the soccer state federations and the CBF were responsible for the deals made with television. The Club of the 13 (Clube dos 13), similar to Europe's G14, was founded in 1987 by the top Brazilian teams, in a strategy to gain independence from CBF and to try to obtain better TV deals. After fifteen years, the Club of the 13 degenerated, losing the power of representation, and has now been replaced by the leagues, mainly the National League.

Income sharing has always been a problem in Brazil, but leagues appear to be doing a better job of it than their federation predecessors. The share of smaller teams has increased and the share of top teams has decreased. Basically, only the top teams from the state of São Paulo have lost income share. The main reason is that, unlike other state tournaments, the former State of São Paulo Tournament had economies of scale. As soon as the new regional tournaments came into being and were negotiated with television, the total pie remained the same but, as mentioned earlier, income shares have changed.

The total payment made by television is expected to increase as soon as soccer organization improves, creating a better product. As an outcome of all the changes mentioned earlier, we believe that this process is promisingly underway. Moreover, the monopoly of TV network Rede Globo (the only TV soccer buyer) is in serious danger of ending. Congress recently legalized a 30% foreign capital share in the media business.

With the new law promoting accounting transparency (discussed in the next section), league development, and a better calendar, the show will improve and have greater value. Table 1 shows the huge difference between European and Brazilian soccer. Even considering per capita income differences, the figures are absurd.

Currently, Rede Globo has broken its existing contract. Payments for National League TV coverage have been reduced to US$50 million for the 2002 coverage and US$60 million for the 2003 coverage, a 37% reduction. The reason indicated by Rede Globo was the enormous change in the

Table 1
Top League Attendance, TV Revenues, and Total Revenues, 1999–2000 Season

	Average Attendance	TV Revenues (US$,000)	Total Club Revenues (US$,000)
Germany	31,882	158,000	540,000
England	30,707	300,000	795,000
Italy	29,887	390,000	645,000
Spain	26,984	285,000	570,000
France	21,861	315,000	345,000
Brazil*	15,000	80,000	200,000

*Sources for the Brazilian tournament, estimates by Antonio Carlos Aidar. All other data from Dobson and Goddard (2001).

exchange rate since the four-year contract was signed. Within that period, the dollar more than doubled against the real.

More data exist for three general levels of estimated revenues for major clubs in Brazil (not including player transfers). We must remember that official numbers for 2002 will be available only in 2003. Nevertheless, the numbers given in Table 2 closely reflect the actual figures. As shown in Table 2, TV has by far the greatest shares of the total amounts and attendance has decreased over time, due to poor quality shows and violence both inside and outside the stadiums. A new criminal code also promises to be very helpful in not only improving the show but also increasing attendance.

The results in Table 2 suggest an enormous gap in revenue between Brazilian and European teams. This point was already hinted at when differences in TV payment were mentioned. Even accounting for income differences among countries, the differences in club revenues at the top end of Brazilian and European soccer are quite pronounced. European clubs such as Barcelona, Manchester United, Real Madrid, and AC Milan all typically have revenues exceeding US$100 million. This is especially striking given that Flamengo has about 25 million declared fans, far greater than any European team. Our firm opinion is that Brazilian revenues are comparatively small due to past problems with the organization of Brazilian soccer. We also believe that the new friendly environment that has been created (detailed in subsequent sections) will enhance the value of Brazilian soccer in the years to come.

On a final comparative note, wage data for two teams São Paulo and Corinthians suggest problems in Brazilian soccer. Revenues for the two clubs were US$14.5 million, and wages were US$12 million, hence 83% of revenues went to pay players. The result was an operating deficit for the two clubs of US$4.5 million.

The problem of wages is as serious in Brazilian soccer as it is for teams around the world. In Brazil, it is very common to see wages running at more than 100% of revenues. But, as we write, all Brazilian teams are cutting wages. Partly, this is an expected outcome now that the 2002 World Cup is over.

Table 2
Club Revenues, Three Different Levels (U.S. Dollars)

Clubs	Turnover
Flamengo, Corinthians, São Paulo, Palmeiras, Vasco	12.5-14.5 million
Santos, Fluminense, Botafogo	9-10.5 million
Internacional, Grêmio, Atlético MG, Cruzeiro, Bahia, Vitória	4-7 million

Declining pay is also occurring in Europe, especially in the Italian clubs. To what extent this means decreasing quality in Brazilian soccer depends on the movements in Europe that set wage parameters for the best Brazilian players. We suspect that wages will increase in Brazilian soccer only after the impacts of the new friendly environment (law, calendar, etc.) have occurred, spurring revenue increases.

OLD PROBLEMS, NEW LEGISLATION

The Pelé Law introduced free agency and, in the eyes of the policy makers, the problems associated with it. Without transfer fees, as in Europe, and longer contract lengths, it was feared that lower level clubs would not invest in the development of young talent. The returns would simply not be there. In addition, league structures, including league management of TV rights sales, did not facilitate balanced competition. Finally, professional private-sector initiative was lacking in club management because the types of legal club organizations reduced payoffs on investment.

Perceptions of corrupt management practices also were important in the development of modern Brazilian soccer. Accounting standards that encouraged transparency in management were lacking. In addition, no source of national policy advice or conflict mediation existed. Further, in the eyes of the fans, the governance of leagues by state federations and the Brazilian Football Confederation led to abuses by unscrupulous officials. National oversight was partly the result of these problematic practices.

The evolution of government intervention to solve Brazil's soccer problems is straightforward. It could be said that the Zico Law (Law 8672, July 6, 1993) paved the way for the introduction of a number of concepts that the Pelé Law eventually came to include. The Zico Law made it possible for clubs and federal associations to have for-profit companies manage their activities, introduced the concept of national and regional leagues, wrote sports rights into the context of sports legislation, and regulated the sports law.

The Pelé Law was passed on March 24, 1998, revoking the Zico Law. It provided for "implementing moralising measures" designed to steer Brazilian soccer in the future, to raise the level of professionalism in Brazilian soccer relations, and to introduce private sector initiative to develop it. Among these measures, two in particular stand out: the free agency system and the institutionalization of the club enterprise.

As explained in the introduction, the Pelé Law was cannibalized by the Maguito Law and partially redeemed by the PM Law (Provisional Measure 2193/2001). We turn now to the major points of the PM Law currently in effect, organized around the two problem areas identified in the last section. But it is worth noting that an extension of the Pelé Law, PM 79/02, now pending in Congress, practically forces clubs to turn into enterprises. The proposed extension grants continuity to the original Pelé Law.

The PM Law and Players

The PM Law addresses labor issues primarily in its specific treatment of initial contract length and transfer fees under the free agency system included in the Pelé Law. According to the PM Law, the club that initially trains young players is entitled to sign them up when they reach the age of sixteen. The term of this first professional contract cannot exceed five years. Before this PM was introduced, the term was two years. The extension was designed to encourage clubs to go on investing in training youths after the introduction of the free agency system.

The PM Law set forth two types of fees payable by the new employer to the training club. Both are calculated according to the wages defined in the soccer player's first professional contract. Educational compensation is the fee paid to the training club when another club signs up the player during the term of the first professional contract. This compensation must be less than 200 times the annual wages of the athlete. Promotional compensation is payable to the training club when the soccer player is hired by another club within six months following the expiration of the player's first professional contract. This compensation cannot exceed 150 times the athlete's annual wages. To be eligible for the compensation, the training club must prove it paid the player's monthly wages from the expiration date of the contract to the new hiring date (within that six-month period).

The PM Law also provides for the unusual situation in which players may remain bound to clubs after the expiration of their contracts. In this case, the training club can still charge a transfer fee in the six-month period following the expiration of the initial professional contract. This provision is designed to protect athletes after their contracts expire. They could otherwise find themselves in a situation where they would earn nothing for six months, should they not sign up with another club. Despite this particular protection, the text of the PM contains points that are not clear, and it does not address many of the situations that players could experience in those six months. Should the training club continue to pay wages, it is not clear whether the soccer player must play for the club, even if he has no contract. The PM does not define which contract provisions, if any, survive the expiration of the contract during this six-month period. After the contract has expired, it is difficult to justify payment of the player's wages, since such payment characterizes an effective employment relationship.

Strong exception may be taken to promotional compensation since this type of transfer fee hinders player movement. In practice, no club should be willing to hire during the six-month period during which the promotional compensation is due and payable. This may, in fact, hurt the career of many players since careers are short, and a six-month layoff could produce irreparable career harm.

In any event, extended initial contract length and the two types of compensation have already borne some practical results. Some clubs have negotiated contract extensions and higher wages in the first professional contracts of "budding talent." The rationale is that the higher the wage, the higher the compensation, in the event a player signs up with another club.

PM 79/02 also protects the training clubs. Under the PM, even before the first professional contract, if a player goes to another team, the club may get payments to cover training investments. The amount depends on the values that the training club is able to prove it invested in the player. Further, it must be proved that the player has been in school and that the club has provided all normal social benefits to the player. It makes sense to protect the roots of the game, and in that sense the PM 79/02 goes in the right direction.

The PM Law and Investment Incentives

Incentives to invest in teams were restored under the PM Law by revoking harmful wording in the cannibalized Pelé Law. The other feature of the PM Law aimed at soccer economic survival was its specific reworking of the payoffs to investment in clubs. The anti-investment culprits in the prior Pelé Law were Sections 3 and 4 of article 27:

§ 3: In any of the cases provided for in the heading of this Article, the sports club shall hold at least 51% of the voting stock and shall have managing authority over the new organisation; it will otherwise be barred from participating in professional sports competitions.

§ 4: Only officers with an effective commission from the sports clubs may execute agreements or commitments.

In addition to quite possibly violating the federal Constitution, these paragraphs led to the absurd conclusion that, unlike practically all private sector organizations, sports clubs could not even assign a power of attorney. As long as these paragraphs were in effect, a sizable number of investors shied away from the soccer business. Thus, revoking these provisions could encourage new investments in Brazilian clubs, and new business opportunities could open up in the areas of media, licensing, and merchandising.

Not only does PM 79/02 allow the clubs to be transformed into companies, there are penalties for clubs failing to do so. There are two main incentives. Unless they are companies, clubs do not get compensation payments for players prior to their turning professional, and club managers' personal assets are on the line to settle clubs' debts. It is expected that all the clubs will be transformed into companies if the PM 79/02 is approved.

The PM Law and Management Practices

Prior to the PM Law, management practices were the other problem area for Brazilian soccer. Corrections were in the areas of transparent accounting practices, the positions of leagues over federations, and the implementation of the National Sports Council.

We turn first to transparent accounting. Although making clubs business oriented may lead them to adopt transparent corporate management practices, strict adherence is better guaranteed by tax and social security incentives as has happened in other countries. Brazilian tax, labor, social security, and exchange laws provide just such incentives as well.

The PM Law retained provisions in the text of the Pelé Law that require sports practice organizations (clubs) and sports administration organizations (federations and confederations) to "prepare and publish financial statements and balance sheets every year, duly audited by independent auditors." Under the PM Law, directors and chairs of clubs and federations are personally liable for noncompliance with these provisions, and the provision clearly sets forth applicable punishments, in addition to those provided for elsewhere under Brazilian law. This change is precisely what has been demanded both by investors willing to put money in soccer and by Brazilian society, which has been regularly surprised by the abuses perpetrated by some Brazilian sports leaders.

The second element of the PM Law relevant to management practices concerns the establishment of national and regional professional soccer leagues under decree 3944 (September 28, 2001), which regulates article 20 of Law 9615. The role of the leagues was to develop a stable group that could inspire trust in the buyers of their products and increase the reliability of the organizations that administer soccer. Doing so entailed elimination of the vices committed by the state federations and by the CBF. Hence, the leagues are tools that can be plied to moralize soccer.

The worst problems faced by Brazilian soccer stem from acts of unscrupulous leaders. Ethical leaders will lay down clear rules and promote greater stability, thus enabling the development of soccer as an economic activity. Therefore, they will add value to soccer as a product. The leagues have implemented institutional controls that are clearer and more effective than those adopted by federations and confederations. They bring to the boardrooms the parties that are actually interested and that hold real political power. Because the league institutional controls are new, they attract media attention to their sporting activities. They have the potential as well as the basic legal tools to become major instruments in raising the reliability of Brazilian soccer. This is indeed the great merit of the leagues.

The actual operating structure of the two major Brazilian professional soccer leagues—the Rio de Janeiro–São Paulo Football League and South-Minas Professional Football League—do vary. The major difference is that the Rio–São Paulo League was incorporated as a commercial company, whereas the South-Minas League was incorporated as a professional corporation. That is to say, the Rio–São Paulo League places more emphasis on the business aspects of soccer. The two leagues also have different approaches to other issues, such as subordination to the prevailing system, negotiation of image rights, and management and decision-making authority over league members (clubs).

In addition, the ability of the league system to see to the economic welfare of teams should not be forgotten. Their most important goal was to increase the revenues of top soccer teams. Selling match broadcast rights accounts for the largest share of their revenues, which is detailed in the next section of this chapter. The regional tournaments on the new soccer calendar (presented earlier) provide an important business opportunity for these newly enabled leagues.

The final change promoted by the PM Law, relevant to management practices and corruption, was the establishment of the National Sports Council (CNE) to act as an advisory board, conflict mediator, decision facilitator, and crises appeaser for the Brazilian sports arena in general, including professional soccer. The CNE is a well-funded organization that is agile enough to act effectively on practical issues. Its formation sends the message that the government was concerned about broadening its scope of influence to sports-related issues.

Proposed Extensions to the PM Law

As we write, the federal government has come out with a new piece of legislation that will bring soccer organization to forefront of the professional age. This law is currently being discussed in Congress (Provisional Measure 79/2002, published June 14, 2002), with great pressure being put on it by the "old soccer boys" to block it. The chief items of the PM under consideration concern transfer rules and the institutional framework for investors. It consolidates the rules designed to improve management quality in Brazilian soccer, with three important provisions:

1. The Fiscal Accountability Law becomes applicable to clubs; therefore, they must publish financial statements audited by independent auditors.
2. Clubs are practically forced to become enterprises; clubs that refuse to do so will pay much higher taxes.
3. The role of independent auditors is emphasized; clubs that do not have their financial statement audited can be severely punished.

The proposed PM recognizes that Brazilian soccer is a cultural asset. Consequently, it makes it easier to investigate the organization of soccer, including CBF. Certainly, these provisions close in on the inefficiency and on the corruption of Brazilian soccer, bringing it closer to the point where the level of management is the same as the level of soccer shown by Brazilian players.

CONCLUSION

After years of struggling, it seems that Brazilian soccer will finally emerge from the Dark Ages. The new environment that has been shaped will allow leagues to exist and clubs to operate more like enterprises, with transparent and professional management. Only under these circumstances will it be possible to have a rational calendar and to combine competition and economic feasibility, without federations and the CBF being used to further personal and political ends. Hopefully, justice will deal effectively with the cases of past mismanagement. The clash between CBF and the leagues over the 2003 calendar makes clear that the battle over soccer is a fierce contest between old and new. We strongly believe that the leagues will win in the medium run, helped by the new legislation described in this chapter.

Clubs will in fact be obliged to convert into companies. Audited finances and transparency requirements will facilitate professional management and reduce corruption. CBF and the state federations will no longer have the support of shady club managers in exchange for favors. And the leagues will grow stronger.

Clubs that are converted into companies run by professionals will have the chance to adapt costs to revenues, separating passion from rational behavior. Without passion on the field, soccer would lose its appeal. But passion and corruption in management almost killed Brazilian soccer. Management needs rationalism and transparency, and the first steps have been taken in that direction. Costs—wages, in this case—are being reduced, and revenues will increase only within the new framework that is being put forward, producing a very good product and turning soccer fans into customers.

But a mess does still remain, especially for club managers trying to implement revenue enhancement strategies. It is impossible to raise revenues and to plan, if in January nobody knows with certainty the 2003 calendar. Rational management of season ticket sales and budgets is hindered. New legislation combined with strong professional leagues will make possible the rational, competitive, long-term calendar essential to the game. From that point, and with clubs converted into companies, it will be possible to bring the fans back to the stadiums assuring safe and entertaining spectacles. Then it will be possible for professional management to plan, bringing revenue figures closer to those enjoyed in Europe.

ACKNOWLEDGMENTS

Several people have contributed to this chapter. However, we would like to thank particularly Carlo Drago—EAESP FGV; Celso Grellet—Pelé Pró;

José Francisco C. Manssur—Pinheiro Neto Advogados; Luiz Roberto Castro—managing director of IBDD; Maurício Andrade—South-Minas League; and Luciana Franco Piva, who revised the English version of the paper.

Part VIII
Japanese and Korean Baseball

16

Baseball in Japan and the United States: Same Game, Same Rules, Same Results?

Akihiko Kawaura and Sumner J. La Croix

INTRODUCTION

Japanese and North American professional baseball players play the same game. The rules are virtually identical. Rule changes initiated by North American professional baseball leagues have been quickly adopted by Japan's professional baseball league. This parallel structure of rules and rule changes raises the possibility of comparing behavioral responses across the two baseball regimes to determine whether there is much cross-cultural variation in the response to rule changes. Understanding such effects has an importance beyond understanding the power of incentives in sports, as it is frequently alleged that different cultural environments condition responses to changes in incentives.

In this chapter, we investigate how two rule changes that occurred in both Japanese and North American baseball changed player and team behavior; and we compare the processes by which foreign players in the case of Japan and African American players in the case of North America were gradually employed by baseball teams. First, we investigate how a change in the rules for signing new players affected competitive balance in each of the two Japanese and two North American baseball leagues. In the 1965–1966 season, both Japanese and North American baseball moved from a bidding to a draft system for allocating new players. Our empirical findings indicate similar responses in competitive balance in both Japan and North America to the rule change. Second, in the 1970s, one league in Japan and one league in North America adopted the designated hitter rule, which allows another player to bat for the pitcher. Using Japanese data, we investigate the hypothesis that the designated hitter rule changed incentives for pitchers to hit batters. Our results reveal in both countries initial increases in hit batters in leagues allowing designated hitters. The increases were eventually reversed in both countries, albeit with differences in timing. We explain this reversal in Japan by appealing to endogenous rule changes that the increases in hit batsmen prompted. Finally, we compare the process of integration of African American players into North American baseball with the process of foreign player integration into Japanese baseball. In North American baseball, teams with the best records integrated more quickly than teams with poor records. By contrast, in Japanese baseball, teams with poor records integrated more foreign players into their rosters.

COMPETITIVE BALANCE AND TWO REGIMES FOR ALLOCATING ROOKIES

Rottenberg's (1956) classic analysis of baseball's reserve clause, which was formalized by Mohamed El Hodiri and James Quirk (1971), showed that the rules governing player allocation among Major League Baseball (MLB) teams do not affect their final allocation if transaction costs of exchanging player contracts are zero. Thus, it should not matter whether promising young players are allocated among teams via a player draft or by open bidding. Teams will exchange players to ensure that they are allocated to the teams for which they generate the highest marginal revenue product. If, however, it is costly for teams to exchange players, the initial allocation is more likely to persist over time. Costly contracting implies that competitive balance should improve both within a given season and over time under a draft regime in which player talent is initially allocated more evenly across teams.[1]

We investigate whether their analysis holds for professional baseball in Japan. We cannot expect team performances to be equalized even in a player draft regime with restrictions on player transfers due to the presence of foreign players on team rosters. The Nippon Professional Baseball (NPB) limits the number of foreign players on each team's roster and has adjusted the cap periodically (see Table 1). There is open bidding for new foreign players, and the player is bound by the NPB reserve clause after signing. The open market for foreign players implies that the highest quality foreign talent will sign with the teams that most value winning, and those teams will have a competitive edge. Thus, we focus on whether the draft regime generates *more* competitive balance than the open-bidding regime.

Table 1
Regulations on Number of Foreign Players in NPB

	Team Roster[a]	Registration for a Game
1952-1965	3	3
1966-1980	2	2
1981-1993	3	2
1994-1995	3	3[b]
1996-1997	No Restrictions	3[b]
1998-2000	No Restrictions	4[c]

[a]Team roster includes both major and minor league players.
[b]The three-player limit can only be reached by a combination of fielders and pitchers; that is, teams are not allowed to register three fielders or three pitchers for a game.
[c]The four-player limit can only be reached by a combination of two fielders and two pitchers; that is, teams are not allowed to register three fielders or three pitchers for a game.

Draft Recruit and Competitive Balance in Japanese Baseball

Until 1951, individual teams in Japan were free to compete for both veteran and rookie players. In June 1951, the NPB issued a rule granting to each team the exclusive right to negotiate future contracts with players already under contract. In effect, this rule established the reserve clause of North American MLB in Japan. NPB teams are allowed to exchange players through trades, and cash sales of players are allowed, although they rarely involve highly productive players. Open bidding for rookies continued until the introduction of the draft recruit system in 1965. Teams were granted exclusive rights to negotiate with the draftee for one year from the date of the draft conference and were not allowed to exchange draft rights for players or cash. The system of player allocation was fundamentally changed after the 1993 season, when free agency for veteran players was introduced.

La Croix and Kawaura (1999) provide some evidence from Japanese baseball that changes in the rules for assigning property rights to new baseball players changed the allocation of players among teams and affected competition within the two leagues. Our empirical results support the proposition that competitive balance over time increased in both leagues (Central and

Pacific Leagues) of the NPB under the player draft regime. Empirical results for competitive balance within a given season are less conclusive, as competitive balance increased substantially in the Pacific League but exhibited no statistically significant change in the Central League. The NPB results are virtually identical to Fort and Quirk's (1995) MLB results. They found that the concentration of league pennants among one or a few teams fell after MLB introduced the rookie draft in 1965. They also found a statistically significant decrease in the variation of winning percentage in the American League during the draft period but failed to find a statistically significant change in the National League data. The parallel empirical results for the NPB and MLB are particularly interesting because in the predraft period the New York Yankees dominated the American League in the United States, and the Yomiuri Giants the Central League in Japan (see Table 2). The decline of both teams in the draft era was the driving force behind improvement in competitive balance in both the National and Central Leagues.

INCENTIVES AND THE DESIGNATED HITTER RULE

In the sport of baseball, pitchers, due to their specialization in pitching rather than batting skills, have typically been an "easy out" when they bat. To improve team offensive production, the MLB's American League adopted a designated hitter (DH) rule in 1973.[2] The designated hitter's sole role is to bat and run the bases in place of the pitcher; he does not play in the field. An initial study (Goff, Shughart, and Tollison, 1997) of the DH rule argued that the rule increased the incentives of pitchers either to hit batsmen with pitches or to aim pitches very close to batsmen because offending pitchers would no longer personally face retaliation at the plate from opposing pitchers. Their regression results supported this moral hazard theory of pitcher behavior, but subsequent studies (Trandel, White, and Klein, 1998) found little support for the theory. Goff, Shughart, and Tollison (1998) replied that the contradictory results were due to improper regression specifications and to expansion in the number of teams in MLB's National League during the mid-1990s.

Kawaura and La Croix (2002) investigate whether the DH rule affected pitcher behavior in Japanese professional baseball. In 1975, the Pacific League adopted the DH rule, whereas the Central League did not. The parallel institutional structure in Japanese baseball—the same as that observed in MLB—allows for a comparative empirical test of the effects of the DH rule on pitcher behavior.

Summary Statistics in Japan

Figure 1 shows hit batsmen (HB) rates (HB/10,000 plate appearances) for the Pacific and Central Leagues since 1958. When the sample period is divided into two subperiods marked by the Pacific League's adoption of the

Table 2
Pennant Winners and League Attendance, 1958–1993

	Central League			Pacific League	
Year	Team	Attendance		Team	Attendance
1958	Giants	5,299,100		Lions*	3,585,100
1959	Giants	4,769,065		Hawks*	3,729,916
1960	Whales*	5,304,159		Orions	2,800,302
1961	Giants*	5,241,800		Hawks	3,476,790
1962	Tigers	5,706,009		Fighters*	3,894,277
1963	Giants*	5,883,375		Lions	3,847,918
1964	Tigers	6,270,820		Hawks*	3,418,935
1965	Giants*	6,251,500		Hawks	2,501,361
1966	Giants*	6,108,850		Hawks	2,709,571
1967	Giants*	5,610,150		Braves	2,744,593
1968	Giants*	6,069,900		Braves	2,847,350
1969	Giants*	6,578,400		Braves	3,018,472
1970	Giants*	6,542,750		Orions	3,069,300
1971	Giants*	6,021,200		Braves	2,584,500
1972	Giants*	6,195,500		Braves	2,536,100
1973	Giants*	7,650,800		Hawks	4,060,200
1974	Dragons	7,595,200		Orions*	3,501,300
1975	Carp	9,479,500		Braves*	3,201,900
1976	Giants	9,070,000		Braves*	3,344,600
1977	Giants	9,114,000		Braves*	4,114,000
1978	Swallows*	9,988,000		Braves	4,114,500
1979	Carp*	10,752,000		Buffaloes	5,220,000
1980	Carp*	10,322,000		Buffaloes	5,797,500
1981	Giants*	10,110,000		Fighters	5,546,300

(*continued*)

Table 2   (*continued*)

1982	Dragons	10,928,500	Lions*	4,817,200
1983	Giants	10,477,000	Lions*	4,991,000
1984	Carp*	11,010,000	Braves	5,162,300
1985	Tigers*	11,413,500	Lions	4,727,500
1986	Carp	11,367,000	Lions*	6,323,700
1987	Giants	12,061,500	Lions*	6,947,000
1988	Dragons	12,239,000	Lions*	8,271,500
1989	Giants*	12,048,500	Buffaloes	8,768,000
1990	Giants	12,020,000	Lions*	8,609,000
1991	Carp	12,391,000	Lions*	9,474,000
1992	Swallows	13,841,000	Lions*	9,522,000
1993	Swallows*	13,440,000	Lions	9,291,000

*Indicates the winner of the Japan Series.

DH rule in 1975, average HB rates are greater in the post-DH period in both leagues. In the Pacific League, the mean HB rate increased from 73.3 in the pre-DH period to 78.8 in the post-DH period, and in the Central League from 68.4 to 71.8. This change implies that the mean HB rate difference across the two leagues increased from 4.9 (with a standard deviation of 10.0) in the pre-DH period to 7.0 in the post-DH period (with standard deviation of 13.7). The null hypothesis that average HB rates for the post-DH period are equal across leagues is rejected by a t-test at the 5% significance level, whereas pre-DH data fail to reject the same hypothesis.

During the DH period, there was another rule change that could have affected the number of hit batsmen in the 1980s. In 1982, the acting chairman of the Pacific League issued a memorandum to the league umpires, stating that "dangerous balls" should not be tolerated. More specific action was taken in 1989 by both leagues when they revised the official rulebook to add a clause prohibiting "dangerous balls" by the pitcher. An umpire was given the authority, when he judged that a pitcher had intentionally thrown the ball at a batter, to either remove the pitcher or both the pitcher and his manager from the game. In the same year, the Pacific League adopted its own guidelines to umpires on the treatment of "dangerous balls." We note that the timing of the new rule is consistent with the declining HB rate gap during the DH period. In the 1989 season, the HB rate of the Pacific League

Figure 1
Pacific League and Central League Hit Batsmen

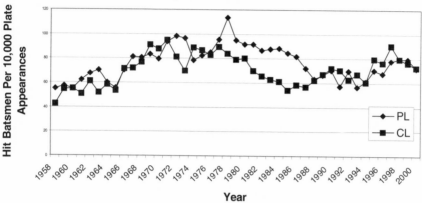

was lower (albeit only slightly) than the one for the Central League for the first time since 1975, the year the DH was adopted. Following Goff, Shughart, and Tollison (1997), we hypothesize that the DH rule increased incentives for pitchers in the Pacific League to throw at batters. As the HB rate gap widened after adoption of the DH rule, the Pacific League responded by adopting its "dangerous balls" rules. These rules—endogenous responses to the unforeseen consequences of the DH rules—effectively nullified the DH rule's additional incentives for pitchers to throw at hitters.

Econometric Analysis of Japanese Data

Our empirical analysis uses three regression equations. First, we replicate Goff, Shughart, and Tollison's (1997) original regression specification for the sample period 1958 to 2000, regressing differences in hit batsmen (HB_t) in the Pacific and Central Leagues on the differences in plate appearances (PA_t) and a dummy variable that equals 1 from the beginning of the DH rule in 1975:

$$HB_{Pt} - HB_{Ct} = \beta_0 + \beta_1 DH + \beta_2 (PA_{Pt} - PA_{Ct}) + \varepsilon_t \tag{1}$$

Second, we rerun the original Goff, Shughart, and Tollison (1997) specification and include a second dummy variable that represents changes in the rules governing penalties for hitting a batter:

$$HB_{Pt} - HB_{Ct} = \beta_0 + \beta_1 DH + \beta_2 DH_2 + \beta_3 (PA_{Pt} - PA_{Ct}) + \varepsilon_t \tag{2}$$

where DH_1 is a dummy variable to cover the 1975 to 1988 DH period with the prior hit batsmen rules; and DH_2 is a dummy variable to cover the DH period with the new hit batsmen rules. Third, we conduct the same analyses for Trandel, White, and Klein's (1998) revised regression specification:

$$NormHB_{Pt} - NormHB_{Ct} = \beta_0 + \beta_1 DH + \varepsilon_t, \tag{3}$$

$$NormHB_{Pt} - NormHB_{Ct} = \beta_0 + \beta_1 DH_1 + \beta_2 DH_2 + \varepsilon_t. \tag{4}$$

Trandel, White, and Klein (1998, 680–682) introduced the revised specification with normalized hit batsmen ($NormHB_t$), as there have been substantial changes over time in the ratios of hit batsmen to at bats in MLB.[3] Specifying a linear relationship between the two variables—as Goff, Shughart, and Tollison's equation does—could yield inconsistent coefficient estimates.

OLS regression results with the Goff, Shughart, and Tollison (1997) specification are presented in Table 3, columns 1 and 2, with column 2 results corrected for serial correlation. The estimated coefficients of the *DH* dummy are not statistically different from zero regardless of correction for serial correlation; this is inconsistent with the hypothesis that the DH rule would increase the number of hit batsmen in the Pacific League. Next, we report results using two *DH* dummies. Results uncorrected for serial correlation are reported in column 3. The estimated coefficient on DH_1 is positive and statistically significant, whereas the estimated coefficient on DH_2 is negative and statistically significant. Column 4 reports results corrected for serial correlation. The estimated coefficient on DH_1 is positive and statistically significant, whereas the estimated coefficient on DH_2 is negative and statistically insignificant. OLS regressions with the Trandel, White, and Klein (1998) specification are presented in Table 4, with results mirroring those in Table 3. All results are consistent with the hypothesis that the DH rule produced increased normalized hit batsmen rates until new hit batsmen rules changed incentives for pitchers and their managers.

INTEGRATING PLAYERS INTO JAPANESE BASEBALL

Goff, McCormick, and Tollison (2002) modeled the racial integration of African American players into MLB between 1947 and 1971 as an innovation in economic process. They investigated the characteristics of baseball teams that choose to integrate earlier than other teams. Their study yielded two main results: (1) the diffusion pattern of African American players among MLB teams followed a logistic distribution; and (2) MLB teams with better records were more likely to hire African American players than MLB teams with poorer records.

This section uses the same methodology to consider a similar yet different phenomenon in Japanese professional baseball: the integration and performance of foreign players into NPB teams between 1958 and 2000. The

Table 3
OLS Regressions: Pacific-Central League Hit Batsmen Difference

Independent Variables	(1)	(2)	(3)	(4)
DH Dummy (1975-2000=1)	10.66	12.41		
	(.80)	(.61)		
DH Dummy (1975-1988=1)			37.48	36.94
			(3.25)***	(2.64)***
DH Dummy (1988-2000=1)			-21.06	-18.10
			(1.76)*	(1.24)
PA_P-PA_C	.013	.01	.013	.013
	(1.54)	(1.49)	(1.93)*	(1.86)*
Constant	9.57	7.12	9.77	8.44
	(.86)	(.4)	(1.13)	(.80)
Rho		.57		.23
R^2-adj	.06	.01	.40	.29
D-W	.86	2.01	1.53	1.85
Number Observations	43	42	43	42

Note: *t*-statistics are in parentheses.
*Significantly different from zero at the 10% level.
***Significantly different from zero at the 1% level.

rosters of NPB teams were predominantly filled by Japanese players from the beginning of professional baseball in Japan through the 1940s. The number of foreign players began to expand in the 1950s, and both leagues began to limit the number of foreign players in 1952. After initially limiting each team to three foreign players, the leagues lowered the cap to two foreign players from 1966 through 1981.[4] During the 1970s and 1980s, many teams added the maximum number of players allowed. Since 1996, teams have been able to hire an unlimited number of foreign players for their full roster, but they could only register three players—and since 1998 four players—to play per game. Changes in NPB foreign player restriction over time are summarized in Table 1.

Table 4
OLS Regressions: Normalized Pacific-Central League Hit Batsmen Difference

Independent Variables	(1)	(2)	(3)	(4)
DH (Dummy 1975-2000=1)	.20	.37		
	(.52)	(.54)		
DH1 (Dummy 1975-1988=1)			1.12	1.11
			(3.21)***	(2.48)**
DH2 (Dummy 1988-2000=1)			-.87	-.75
			(2.39)**	(1.60)
Constant	.49	.32	.49	.44
	(1.64)	(.55)	(2.10)	(1.41)
Rho		.58		.25
R^2-adj	.01	.02	.41	.25
D-W	.83	2.04	1.50	1.88
Number Observations	43	42	43	42

Note: *t*-statistics are in parentheses.

**Significantly different from zero at the 5% level.
***Significantly different from zero at the 1% level.

Data and Econometric Model

Goff, McCormick, and Tollison (2002, 17) found that the pattern of integration of African American players into MLB teams generally took the form of a logistic function, with African American players initially added at an increasing rate and then at a decreasing rate. We examine the pattern of NPB integration of foreign players in the face of changes in the restrictions on the maximum number of players per team. Figure 2 provides data on the minimum, maximum, and average number of foreign players per NPB team from 1958 to 2000.[5] Teams added foreign players at an increasing rate through the mid-1960s, but the average number of foreign players per team declined in the late 1960s after the per-team cap on players was lowered. The average number of foreign players converged around the two-player cap in the 1970s, but the increase to a three-player cap in the 1980s was accom-

Figure 2
Foreign Players by Team in NPB

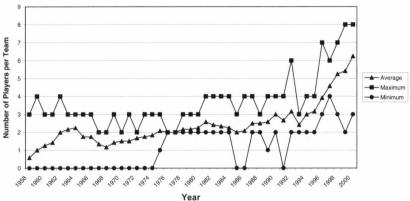

panied by five years of decreases in the average number of foreign players per team during the early 1980s. Since the early 1990s, the average number of foreign players has roughly doubled—from three to six players—in response to the removal of the cap on foreign players on team rosters.

Our econometric analysis of team choices to add foreign players to their rosters uses a variation of the Goff, McCormick, and Tollison (2002) fixed effect model to analyze the number of foreign players on each team i in year t:

$$FOREIGN_{it} = \alpha_t + \eta_i + \beta_1 GAMES_{it-1} + \beta_2 INCOME_{it} + \varepsilon_t \qquad (5)$$

The model includes a fixed effect time vector α_t to capture changes in social attitudes toward foreign players over time as well as changes in the maximum number of foreign players allowed on a team's roster. We also include a fixed effect team vector η_i to capture differences in team attitudes toward foreign players that are not captured by the independent variables. We incorporate two independent variables that are plausibly related to management's perception of the marginal revenue product from using additional foreign athletes—average per capita income in the team's prefecture (*INCOME*) and the number of games back of the league winner in the previous season (*GAMES*).[6] *GAMES* is included to test the proposition that relative team performance will affect the hiring of foreign players. Goff, McCormick, and Tollison (2002, 20) argue that *GAMES* is superior to other measures of relative team performance because a given winning percentage in one league may lead to higher relative performance than the same winning percentage in the other league.[7] *INCOME* is included because lower income individuals are more frequently associated with xenophobic attitudes than higher income individuals.[8]

Econometric Results and Interpretations

Table 5 reports estimated OLS coefficients for four variations of equation 5. Column 1 reports panel data results for all teams using *GAMES*. Column 2 reports panel data results for all teams using an alternative measure of relative performance, winning percentage (*WINPERCENT*). Columns 3 and 4 replicate the two previous specifications using a data set that drops the Giants baseball team. We drop the Giants since they are an outlier with respect to performance (very good) and use of foreign players (very low). The Giants had no foreign players on their roster between 1963 and 1974,

Table 5
OLS: Estimates of NPB Integration of Foreign Players

Independent Variables	W/Giants	W/Giants	w/o Giants	w/o Giants
	(1)	(2)	(3)	(4)
INCOME	.001	.001	.001	.001
	(5.32)***	(5.35)***	(3.66)***	(3.68)**
WINPERCENT		-1.14		-1.12
		(2.20)**		(2.08)**
GAMES	.009		.008	
	(2.23)**		(2.11)**	
Constant	-1.18	-.52	.97	1.62
	(2.07)**	(.85)	(2.20)**	(3.43)***
R^2-adj	.58	.58	.55	.55
Number Observations	492	492	451	451

Note: *t*-statistics are in parentheses.
**Significantly different from zero at the 5% level.
***Significantly different from zero at the 1% level.

yet won the Central League championship ten times during these twelve seasons (see Table 2). Dropping the Giants from the sample does not affect the regression results in any significant manner.

Our regressions display two consistent results. First, *INCOME* in all four specifications has a positive estimated coefficient and is statistically significant at the 1% level. This result provides some support to the common notion that higher income areas are less xenophobic, or that higher income areas have a higher demand for a winning team, regardless of the player composition. Second, the relative competition variable (whether *GAMES* or *WINPERCENT*) is statistically significant and has a sign consistent with poor performing teams adding foreign players.

These results are the opposite of those found for MLB, where high performing teams were more likely to add African American players than poor performing teams. We note, however, that NPB teams adding foreign players may be qualitatively different from MLB teams adding African American players. First, most foreign players on NPB teams had better opportunities in MLB than African Amerian players on MLB teams had. The only alternatives open to African American players were much lower paying black baseball leagues or occupations outside of baseball altogether. Second, life in Japan and on a Japanese baseball team proved difficult for many baseball players from the United States. There have been cases of players leaving Japan in midseason due to problems off the field, which is reflected in the midseason replacement of foreign players (see Note 5). Finally, the NPB leagues did not pay as well as MLB leagues, and this may have led to player selection problems. Were the players opting to play in Japan "lemons," or were they good talent overlooked by U.S. teams?

CONCLUSION

Economists have extensively studied North American MLB, partly due to an intrinsic interest in the sport and partly due to the massive array of team and player performance data that are publicly available for analysis. In contrast, economists have, to our knowledge, paid only limited attention to Japanese professional baseball. This is unfortunate, as the massive and comprehensive data compiled for Japanese baseball players and teams could provide economists with a significant opportunity to determine whether their findings using MLB data are robust. More generally, the NPB data allows us to examine whether the same "game" played within a different cultural setting generates the same behaviors.

Our empirical results for the two rule changes in Japan are remarkably similar with those from North America, leaving little variation for "culture" to explain. On the other hand, integration of foreign and African American players into team rosters proceeded along different lines in the NPB and MLB. Poorly performing teams in Japan were more likely to add foreign players to their rosters, whereas good teams in the United States were more likely to add African American players to their rosters. Whether culture can explain these differences or whether they are due to different constraints faced by teams in each country remains a question for future research.

ACKNOWLEDGMENTS

We thank the Baseball Hall of Fame and Museum in the Tokyo Dome for their assistance in locating information on foreign players and on the rules governing number of foreign players on team rosters and on the field, Akiko Sugimoto-Kawaura for assistance in preparing the data set, and Sang-Hyop Lee for insightful comments.

NOTES

1. In general, a league shows more competitive balance if teams are more closely clustered around the league performance mean (always .50) within a single season, individual teams exhibit more mobility in the standings over time, and league pennants and last place finishes are less concentrated among a few teams. Team performance is unlikely to be equalized in the short and medium runs even under a player draft regime that prohibits cash transfers of rookies and veteran players. Player injuries, management mistakes in evaluating rookie talent, variable player depreciation rates, and the limited supply of talent available to a team in each draft all lead to significant differences in team performance in the short and medium runs. Other nonplayer inputs, including the team general manager, field manager, coaches, conditioning trainers, team physicians, and scouts, are allocated in the open market; the highest quality talent will sign with the teams in cities that have a high demand for winning. See Kahn (1993) and the reference therein for discussions of the contribution of nonplayer inputs to team performance.

2. The second MLB league, the National League, only used the DH rule in World Series games in American League stadiums until interleague play began in 1997.

3. Goff, Shughart, and Tollison (1997) and Trandel, White, and Klein (1998) both use "at bats" as a basis to normalize hit batsmen statistics. We use "plate appearances" because hit batsmen occur as part of plate appearances. At bats exclude hit batsmen.

4. Although teams were permitted to have three foreign players starting in 1981, they could only register two of them for a game until 1993.

5. These are numbers of all foreign players that a team registered during the course of a season. When a player leaves a team in midseason and the team replaces him with another foreign player, both players are reflected in the number. This leads to cases where data in the Figure 2 exceed the foreign player limitation.

6. See Goff, McCormick, and Tollison (2002, 20).

7. Goff, McCormick, and Tollison (2002) find virtually identical results using winning percentage as a measure of relative performance rather than games back.

8. In their MLB study, Goff, McCormick, and Tollison (2002) also include the percentage of the population of a team's metropolitan area that is nonwhite. The comparable percentage in our study, that is, the percentage of the non-Japanese population in a team's metropolitan area, is extremely small and is unlikely to be associated with variation in the number of foreign players. Thus, we do not include this variable in our regressions.

17

Competitive Balance and Attendance in Japanese, Korean, and U.S. Professional Baseball Leagues

Young Hoon Lee

INTRODUCTION

Most studies of attendance at professional sports events, and the forces affecting attendance, have examined baseball. These studies can be categorized into two groups. The first group analyzes daily attendance at individual games, and the analyses are based on a single season or a few seasons (Hill, Madura, and Zuber, 1982; Marcum and Greenstein, 1985; Knowles, Sherony, and Haupert, 1992; Bruggink and Eaton, 1996). These studies provide insights into a number of factors that influence the demand for baseball games and identify strategies that team owners might use to rebuild attendance, in that fans make choices about attending individual games as opposed to making choices about seasons. The second group focuses on annual attendance, using time-series data for a longer period to examine longer-term secular trends, which are combined with season-to-season variations in attendance in order to determine baseball's popularity as a spectator sport (Demmert, 1973; Noll, 1974; Siegfried and Eisenberg, 1980; Scully, 1989; Coffin, 1996).

Most studies have focused on Major League Baseball (MLB) in America. However, this chapter intends to compare the competitive balance among MLB in America, the Japanese Professional Baseball League (JPBL), and the Korean Professional Baseball League (KPBL), as well as analyze attendance using panel data models. MLB has the longest history among the three leagues, established in 1901. The JPBL was established in 1936, and now has six teams in the Central League (CL) and six in the Pacific League (PL). Each team plays 126 regular season games. The KPBL is the youngest league, established in 1982. It has eight teams, each of which plays 132 games in a regular season.[1] Based on history and attendance, MLB and the JPBL can be regarded as developed baseball leagues, whereas the KPBL should be considered a developing baseball league.

This comparative study has a particular advantage over previous studies. The fact that income levels (and population) in Japan, Korea, and the United States are very different should provide clearer estimates of the relationship between income (and population) and attendance. The inconclusive empirical results of previous studies might have been caused by the relatively similar income data collected from cities within the same country.

One of the key factors in stimulating fans' interest in team sports is the excitement that is generated by the uncertainty of the outcome of league games (Rottenberg, 1956; El Hodiri and Quirk, 1971). The impact of uncertainty of outcome on attendance may differ with league maturity. Developed leagues may attract more "purist" fans than undeveloped leagues. These purist fans may simply enjoy watching outstanding athletes and may follow their favorite teams enthusiastically, regardless of the outcome. By contrast, the attendance of fans in developing leagues may be much more changeable and depend on the performance of their home team. Presumably, fans in developed baseball leagues have greater habit-persistence with respect to going to baseball stadiums than do those in developing leagues. If this assumption were true, then the season-to-season fluctuation in competitive balance would influence attendance at games in a developed league less than it would in a developing league. This comparative study aims to examine this postulate, as panel data models can analyze not only the effects of competitive balance on attendance but also differences in the magnitude of the effects between leagues.

ATTENDANCE AND COMPETITIVE BALANCE

Attendance

Figure 1 shows the attendance trends in MLB, the JPBL, and the KPBL beginning in the mid-1970s to present. As expected, MLB has the largest annual attendance, and the KPBL has the smallest. In 1982, the attendance for MLB, the JPBL, and the KPBL was 44.6, 15.7, and 1.4 million, respectively; MLB attendance was almost thirty times higher than that of the KPBL, and 2.8 times higher than that of the JPBL. In 1999, KPBL attendance was 3.2 million, the highest rate of increase with respect to the 1982 figure, whereas JPBL attendance was 22.4 million, the lowest rate of increase; MLB attendance was 70.1 million, twenty-one times and 3.1 times greater than attendance for the KPBL and JPBL, respectively. Overall, MLB attendance

Figure 1
Attendance (thousands)

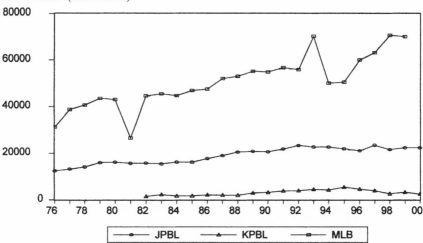

has increased, except during the strikes in 1981 and the 1994–1995 season. JPBL attendance increased until 1991 and has since remained constant, unlike the KPBL, for which attendance grew until 1995 and then declined.

As shown in Figure 2, the attendance per game in all three leagues shows trends similar to those for attendance over time. Unlike annual attendance, attendance per game in MLB and in the JPBL is very similar. The attendance per game in the JPBL and MLB was about 21,000 in 1982 and 28,000 in 1999, whereas the attendance per game in the KPBL was less than 10,000. Based on the attendance data, we define MLB and the JPBL as developed leagues and the KPBL as a developing league.

Competitive Balance

Rottenberg's (1956) "uncertainty of outcome" hypothesis argues that, all other things being equal, the closer the competition between teams, the greater the interest in the sport and, therefore, the greater the attendance. In the literature, uncertainty of outcome covers two elements. The first is game uncertainty (henceforth, GU). Fans may be more attracted to a game with a high probability of a close contest. The second is playoff uncertainty (henceforth, PU). Generally, attendance in September is lower than the average attendance, since division winners are already decided by then, and the home teams of most fans are already out of the pennant race. This trend implies that attendance in a league will increase if the pennant race winners are decided as late as possible. Fort and Rosenman (2001) not only present their empirical studies analyzing the relationship between attendance and GU

Figure 2
Attendance per Game

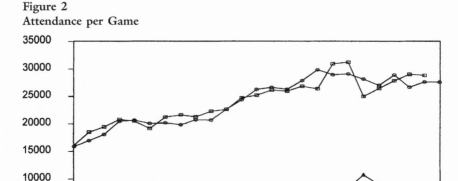

and/or PU, but also reviewed the previous studies (Hart, Hutton, and Sharot, 1975; Drever and McDonald, 1981; Schofield, 1983a, 1983b; Borland and Lye, 1992). According to their review, all of these works support PU, but they fail either to support or to address GU.

Various statistical measures relevant to competitive balance have been presented (Scully, 1989; Quirk and Fort, 1992; Depken, 1999; Eckard, 2001; Humphreys, 2002). The first measure of competitive balance is the ratio of actual to "idealized" standard deviation, henceforth referred to as the *RSD*. The second measure of competitive balance is "excess tail frequency" (Fort and Quirk, 1995), which measures the percentage share of teams with actual winning percentages outside a range of two or three standard deviations, under an assumption of the maximum degree of competitive balance. The measure considers the difference between the percentage of teams that actually lie in a certain tail of winning percentage distribution and the percentage of teams that would lie in a certain tail of winning percentage distribution if each team in a league had a 50% chance of winning or losing each game. If more than 5% of observations are beyond two standard deviations from the mean, the leagues are not competitively balanced at the maximum level. Excess tail frequency is appropriate for determining the long-term average of competitive balance in a league, but not for the season-to-season competitive balance in a league. Suppose that the range of two standard deviations in a six-team league, under an assumption of the maximum degree of competitive balance, is 0.42, 0.58. The winning percentages in seasons *t* and *s* are 0.60, 0.59, 0.55, 0.45, 0.41, 0.40 and 0.578,

0.575, 0.56, 0.44, 0.425, 0.422, respectively. In this example, the difference in the competitive balance between seasons t and s is narrow, but four teams are outside the range of two standard deviations in season t, whereas none is outside this range in season s. The measure of excess tail frequency is 66.7% in season t, but is 0% in season s. This problem is caused by the property of a measure that counts only the discrete number of teams outside two standard deviations and does not consider the winning percentages of the teams at the extremes of the two standard deviation range.

This chapter suggests a modified measure of excess tail frequency, which compensates for the weakness of the old statistic. Instead of considering a certain range of the standard deviation, it focuses on a certain percentage of the top and bottom teams in a league and where their actual winning percentages are located in the normal distribution under an assumption of the maximum degree of competitive balance. If a league becomes too unbalanced, with too much playing talent concentrated in a few top teams, then the winning percentages of those top teams will be extraordinarily high, and the likelihood that such high winning percentages will occur in the "idealized" normal distribution is very low.

Therefore, it is possible to define a measure of competitive balance as the sum of the densities of the winning percentages of a certain percentage of the top and bottom teams in a league with an "idealized" normal distribution.[2] We refer to this as the tail likelihood (TL).

$$TL = \Sigma_i f(Z_i), \tag{1}$$

where i is the index number of top and bottom teams as a certain percentage of the teams in the league, f is the standard normal probability density function, and $Z_i = (wp_i - 0.5)/s$, where wp_i is the winning percentage of team i and s is the "idealized" standard deviation. Here, i is not always an integer. For example, $i = 2.8$ for the top 20% of the teams in the American League (AL), since the AL consists of fourteen teams. In this case, we consider the weighted average of the second- and third-best winning percentages, to take into account the 0.8, in addition to the best and second-best winning percentages. The weights of the second- and third-best winning percentages are 0.8 and 0.2, respectively. A larger TL reflects a more competitive balance in a league.

The last measure of competitive balance is related to PU. A simple measure is the difference between the highest and second-highest winning percentages in a league in a season. Unlike the CL and PL in the JPBL and the KPBL,[3] the National League (NL) and AL in MLB consist of several divisions. Therefore, this measure in the NL or AL is the average of the difference between the highest and second-highest winning percentages in each division within a league. Since the 1994 season, it also takes into account the "wild card" team by considering the difference between the wild card team's winning percentage and the team in any division with the next best winning percentage when the average is calculated.

The data on teams' winning percentages and attendance were obtained from the *Korean Official Baseball Guide* (2001), *Japan Baseball Record Book* (2000), and *BaseballStats* (accessed January 6, 2001). Table 1 shows historical data from 1981 through 2000 for the average measures of competitive balance and the average attendance per game in the five different professional baseball leagues. Of the five leagues, the CL had the highest attendance per game. Although the CL and PL are both Japanese leagues, the CL is much more popular than the PL according to the attendance per game, although the gap between the two leagues is decreasing. This difference is somewhat peculiar when we consider the similarity of attendance per game in the NL and AL.

A perfect competitive balance in a league would have an *RSD* of 1. Based on the *RSD*, the AL has the most competitive balance, and the KPBL has the least. In the JPBL, the PL has a slightly more competitive balance than the CL. This is also somewhat surprising, since the average attendance per game is significantly greater in the CL than in the PL. The PL, with *RSD* = 1.134, almost attained the maximum competitive balance in the late 1990s. The *RSD* is more or less constant over time in the KPBL, whereas the competitive balance fluctuates most in the two leagues of the JPBL.

The greater the *TL*, the more competitive balance there is in a league. Much the same comments apply to *TL* data as to *RSD* data. The average PU is relevant to the competitive balance in a pennant race. The leagues with the most competitive balance in pennant races are the AL and NL, and the league with the least competitive balance is the KPBL; the PL and CL are intermediate. Unlike GU, the AL showed a decline in PU in the 1990s. In the 1990s, the NL was more balanced than the AL, based on PU. In summary, there is more uncertainty of outcome in developed baseball leagues than in developing leagues, according to the data for these sample leagues, since the measures of competitive balance among the AL, NL, CL, and PL are roughly equal, but are very different from the measures in the KPBL.

MODEL AND EMPIRICAL RESULTS

Model

The data used in this analysis are unbalanced panel data: KPBL (1982–2000) and the other leagues (1976–1999). The regression model is

$$\ln ATT_{it} = \beta_1 \ln POP_{it} + \beta_2 \ln GDP_{it} + \beta_3 GU_{it} + \beta_4 PU_{it} + \alpha_i + \varepsilon_{it} \qquad (2)$$

Annual attendance is not an appropriate dependent variable in the attendance equation, since the number of regular season games played in each

Table 1
Competitive Balance in the Five Professional Baseball Leagues

	1981-1985[*]	1986-1990	1991-1995	1996-2000[**]	Avg.
Average Attendance per Game					
NL	21,610	25,006	27,971	28,478	25,623
AL	20,631	24,914	28,240	27,624	25,233
CL	27,661	30,587	32,800	32,213	30,926
PL	12,946	19,859	23,945	22,978	20,059
KPBL	6,045	6,116	8,641	6,544	6,878
The Ratio of Actual to "Idealized" Standard Deviation (RSD)					
NL	1.6181	1.6540	1.7152	1.7903	1.6894
AL	1.6935	1.6130	1.5941	1.8331	1.6788
CL	1.8451	2.2167	1.5563	1.5812	1.7696
PL	1.8639	1.7831	2.2066	1.1339	1.7354
KPBL	2.1513	2.1572	2.1498	2.1471	2.1513
Tail Likelihood for 20% of top and bottom teams (TL): Modified Measure of Excess Tail Frequency					
NL	0.4210	0.3940	0.3677	0.3072	0.3759
AL	0.3681	0.4946	0.4458	0.3117	0.4100
CL	0.1633	0.0553	0.4944	0.2568	0.2633
PL	0.2787	0.2238	0.0900	0.5773	0.2964
KPBL	0.2767	0.1508	0.0941	0.1620	0.1654
The Measure of Playoff Uncertainty (PU)					
NL	0.0306	0.0499	0.0389	0.0392	0.0397
AL	0.0366	0.0299	0.0431	0.0513	0.0396
CL	0.0380	0.0808	0.0551	0.0507	0.0505
PL	0.0717	0.0397	0.0536	0.0342	0.0477
KPBL	0.0547	0.0483	0.0603	0.0558	0.0548

[*]KPBL is an average in 1982–1985.
[**]NL, AL, CL and PL are averages in 1996–1999.

league differs and changes over time. Therefore, we use the logarithm of annual attendance per game (ln ATT) as the dependent variable.

The explanatory variables can be divided into two groups: market factors and baseball factors. We used two market variables in this analysis.[4] The first is the logarithm of national population (ln POP) as a measure of market size. The second market variable is the logarithm of real per capita GDP (ln GDP), which is per capita GDP, divided by the consumer price index. The baseball factors include two measures of uncertainty: GU and PU. Here, the game uncertainty is measured using two variables (RSD and TL).

Here, α_i represents the ith league-specific effect that suggests differing relative performance of the ith league in attracting fans, given the market and baseball factors. Since it is assumed fixed, equation (2) is a fixed-effect panel data model. The league-specific effects can be interpreted as measuring fan loyalty, stadium capacity and quality, and league marketing. It is also possible to analyze whether the differences between the five leagues' success in attracting fans are statistically significant.

Equation (2) assumes that competitive balance has the same effect on attendance per game in all five baseball leagues. However, it is possible that differences among leagues will produce different intercept and slope coefficients. In order to analyze how much the effect in one league differs from those in other leagues, it is assumed that the response of the dependent variable to the explanatory variables of competitive balance differs for different leagues, while remaining constant over time for a given league. Then, equation (2) is modified as follows:

$$\ln ATT_{it} = \beta_1 \ln POP_{it} + \beta_2 \ln GDP_{it} + \beta_{3i} GU_{it} + \beta_{4i} PU_{it} + \alpha_i + \varepsilon_{it} \qquad (3)$$

In equation (3), we set $\beta_{3NL} = \beta_{3AL} = \beta_{3CL} = \beta_{3PL} = \beta_{3KPBL}$ to test whether a unit change in GU affects attendance per game by the same percentage in all five leagues. The effects of PU are also tested.[5]

Empirical Results

Equation (3) should test the hypothesis that the league coefficient vectors of competitive balance are all identical to the means. The test results are presented in Table 2. Column 2 shows the test results using regression equation (3) with RSD as the game uncertainty variable. The hypothesis that the coefficients of the RSD are equal for all leagues cannot be rejected at the 5% level of significance, since the F-value is 1.346 and the p-value is 0.259. The resulting test at the 1% level of significance indicates that the hypothesis "the coefficients of PU are constant from one league to another" can be rejected. League-specific effects are found to differ for all five leagues at the 1% level of significance. The test results using regression equation (3) with TL are shown in column 3. The results are the same as the test results using the model with RSD for the coefficients of PU and league-specific

Table 2
Hypotheses Test Results

Hypothesis	Model with RSD		Model with TL	
	F-value	p-value	F-value	p-value
Coefficients of RSD are equal for all five leagues	1.346	0.259		
Coefficients of TL are equal for all five leagues			3.481	0.010
Coefficients of PU are equal for all five leagues	3.966	0.005	3.663	0.008
League specific effects are equal for all five leagues	6.367	0.000	6.324	0.000

effects. However, the hypothesis that the coefficients of the game uncertainty are equal for all five leagues can be rejected at the 1% level of significance.

Based on the test results in Table 2, we specify the regression models: the panel data model including *RSD* with the coefficients of *PU* varying over cross-sectional units, and the panel data model including *TL* with the coefficients of *TL* and *PU* varying over cross-sectional units. We use Cochrane-Orcutt estimation to correct for autocorrelation detected in the original estimates. The estimation results are presented in columns 3 and 5 of Table 3. The estimates using equation (2), assuming that the coefficients of competitive balance are equal for all leagues, are shown in columns 2 and 4.

The effect of income on attendance is found to be positive, and the income elasticity is inelastic in the range 0.231 to 0.275. That is, a 1% increase in real per capita GDP causes attendance per game to increase by approximately 0.248. The effect of population on attendance was ambiguous in previous studies. For example, Coffin (1996) found that the effect was positive from 1976 to 1992, but negative from 1962 to 1975. In this study, the coefficient of population is estimated to be positive but insignificant.

Several empirical results concerning competitive balance can be drawn. The *GU* variable (*RSD* or *TL*) is not significant, while the *PU* is significant. Therefore, we may conclude that the relationship between attendance and PU is stronger than the relationship between attendance and GU. This result confirms previous empirical works such as Hart, Hutton, and Sharot (1975) and Fort and Rosenman (2001).

We turn our attention now to the league coefficients of competitive balance, to see how attendance in each league responds to a unit change in competitive balance. The league coefficients of *PU* vary over the five leagues. Those of the AL, PL, and KPBL are significantly negative, whereas those of the NL and CL are negative but insignificant in the models with either *RSD* or *TL*. It is somewhat peculiar that PU has different effects on attendance in the two leagues in MLB and in the JPBL: the AL coefficient of *PU* is

Table 3
Regression Results for Annual Attendance Model, 1976–2000

coefficient	Model with RSD				Model with TL			
	estimate	T	estimate	t	estimate	t	estimate	t
β_1	0.172	0.177	0.165	0.165	0.149	0.151	0.122	0.111
β_2	0.275**	3.202	0.263**	3.140	0.267**	3.100	0.231**	2.758
β_3	-0.017	-1.138	-0.022	-1.475	0.020	0.677		
β_4	-0.978**	-5.085			-0.977**	-4.986		
β_{3NL}							-0.005	-0.069
β_{3AL}							-0.074	-0.967
β_{3CL}							0.048	1.249
β_{3PL}							-0.082	-1.356
β_{3KPBL}							0.253**	3.208
β_{4NL}			-0.454	-0.625			-0.505	-0.734
β_{4AL}			-1.567**	-2.620			-1.577**	-2.781
β_{4CL}			-0.096	-0.292			-0.034	-0.107
β_{4PL}			-0.869*	-2.188			-1.274**	-3.198
β_{4KPBL}			-1.726**	-5.540			-1.541**	-5.175
α_{NL}	6.591		6.735		6.875		7.415	
α_{AL}	6.600		6.783		6.886		7.487	
α_{CL}	6.911		7.013		7.181		7.635	
α_{PL}	6.467		6.623		6.737		7.314	
α_{KPBL}	5.887		6.066		6.122		6.544	
AR(1)	0.767**	10.848	0.784**	11.485	0.770**	10.923	0.806**	12.494
D-W	2.154		2.137		2.165		1.993	
R^2	0.976		0.979		0.976		0.982	

*Significant at the 95% critical level.
**Significant at the 99% critical level.

significant, but the NL coefficient of *PU* is not, while the coefficient of *PU* is significant in the PL, but insignificant in the CL.

We found that annual attendance in the KPBL was the most sensitive to changes in PU, which represents competitive balance in pennant races. In the estimation of the model with *TL*, the KPBL also turned out to be the only league in which *TL* was significant. That is, GU and PU both influence attendance in the KPBL. Therefore, we conclude that the estimation results support both the GU hypothesis and the PU hypothesis for developing leagues, but support only PU for developed leagues. Moreover, the relationship between attendance and competitive balance in pennant races is much stronger in developing leagues than in developed leagues. This conclusion concurs with the assumption made in the introduction that fans in developed baseball leagues have greater habit-persistence to visit baseball stadiums than do fans in developing leagues.

The empirical evidence shows the same trend in league-specific effects. The league-specific effect is greatest in the CL and lowest in the KPBL. The high CL league-specific effect suggests that the CL is the most successful at attracting fans, given market and baseball factors. The league-specific effects of the two leagues in MLB are similar to each other and are greater than the effect in the PL. We can compare estimates of league-specific effects in developing versus developed leagues. The range of league-specific effects in the developed leagues is 6.62 to 7.18 or 7.31 to 7.64, whereas in the developing league the estimate is much lower, 6.07 or 6.54. This result is expected, since factors additional to market and competitive balance, such as stadium capacity and quality as well as league marketing, attract fans to the developed leagues.

CONCLUSION

Using panel data for five different professional baseball leagues from 1976 to 2000, this chapter examines the difference in the competitive balance among different leagues as well as the relationship between attendance and competitive balance. The five leagues were the KPBL, CL, PL, NL, and AL.

First, we compared the degree of competitive balance and concluded that there is more game and playoff uncertainty in developed leagues than in developing leagues, at least for this sample. Then we tested the hypothesis that the league coefficients of competitive balance variables are all identical to the means and showed that the coefficients of playoff uncertainty are not constant over leagues, whereas the results for a constant effect of game uncertainty across leagues were ambiguous. Third, we used a fixed-effects panel data model to analyze how attendance in each league responds to a unit change in competitive balance. The empirical evidence indicates that the relationship between attendance and playoff uncertainty is much stronger in developing leagues than in developed leagues. This conclusion conforms to the assumption that fans in developed baseball leagues have higher habit-persistence to visit baseball stadiums than do fans in developing leagues. In addition, playoff uncertainty was found to be a more important factor in attendance than game uncertainty.

The results suggest that more attention should be paid to competitive balance in developing leagues. Regulations for developing professional baseball leagues that enhance competitive balance are necessary to develop fan interest.

ACKNOWLEDGMENT

This research was financially supported by the Social Science Research Center, Hansung University, 2003.

NOTES

1. See Lee (2002) for more information about the Korean Professional Baseball League.

2. This new statistic is somewhat related to the works by Fama and Roll (1968, 1971) in terms of measuring "thick-tail." Fort and Quirk (1995) use the Studentized Range test suggested by Fama and Roll in order to test the invariance result that the change from a reserve option clause system to free agency system will have no effect on the distribution of winning percents in a league. However, the method of Fama and Roll is not appropriate for the season-to-season measure of competitive balance.

3. The KPBL temporarily consisted of two divisions in the 1999–2000 season. The Pacific League in JPBL adopted a split-season format from 1973 to 1982.

4. In this regression, a price variable could not be included. Neither ticket price nor gate revenue data are available in JPBL.

5. Equation (3) assumes that the coefficients of income and population are constant over different leagues. According to pilot studies, the hypothesis that income and population each has constant coefficient in all five different leagues cannot be rejected at the significance level of 5%.

Part IX
Australia

18

Professional Sports Competitions in Australia

Robert D. Macdonald and Jeff Borland

INTRODUCTION

On a per capita basis, Australia outperforms most nations at international sports events such as the Olympic Games and world championships.[1,2] Yet, whereas Australian gold medal–winning performances are lauded every four years, professional team sports, with their regular annual schedules of fixtures, are the sports of consistent and passionate interest to the vast majority of Australians. In this chapter, we review three sports selected from over fifteen Australian sports that have had a national league in the past decade (Cockerill, 1998). These sports, national leagues, and teams are outlined in Table 1. The chapter provides a brief historical profile and overview of the current corporate governance and competition structure in each sport; describes the regulatory framework of each league/sport, focusing upon labor market regulations and the role of collective bargaining agreements with players associations as well as product market regulations and fiscal redistribution systems; and compares each sport on the basis of the key performance indicators of market demand and the competitive balance.

THE HISTORY AND STRUCTURE OF AUSTRALIAN PROFESSIONAL TEAM SPORTS

Historians generally agree that sports were a part of the cultural "baggage" brought to Australia in the first century of British colonization, beginning

Table 1
Australian Professional Team Sports: Competition Structure

Sport	Australian Football		Basketball		Rugby League	
Controlling	Australian Football		NBL Management Ltd.		National Rugby League	
Organisation	League				Ltd.	
Competition	Australian Football		National Basketball		National Rugby League	
	League		League			
No. of Clubs (2002)	16 clubs		11 clubs		15 clubs	
Location of Clubs	Melbourne	9	Melbourne	2	Sydney	8.5
	Adelaide	2	Sydney	2	Auckland (NZ)	1
	Perth	2	Adelaide	1	Brisbane	1
	Brisbane	1	Brisbane	1	Canberra	1
	Geelong	1	Cairns	1	Melbourne	1
	Sydney	1	Canberra	1	Newcastle	1
			Perth	1	Townsville	1
			Townsville	1	Wollongong	0.5
			Wollongong	1		
Regular Season Length	22 games		28 games		26 games	
Clubs in Finals Series	8 clubs		6 clubs		8 clubs	
Timing of Season	March – September		October – April		February – October	
Competition Formed	1897 – as Victorian		1979 – as National		1908 – as New South	
	Football League		Invitational Basketball		Wales Rugby League	
			League			
Original League Size	8 clubs		10 clubs		9 clubs	
Average # of Clubs	11.56 clubs		13.00 clubs		10.82 clubs	
Historical Total #Clubs	19 clubs		27 clubs		32 clubs	

Note: Teams in all three leagues play in a single division, home and away league format.

in 1788 (e.g., Cashman, 1995). Organized sports emerged between 1820 and 1870, and influential sporting organizations such as the Melbourne Cricket Club and many of the football clubs that still compete in the Australian Football League (AFL) were formed during this era. Blainey (1995, 109) suggests that "Australia probably became the first country in the world to give a high emphasis to spectator sports," and professional sports quickly followed, with player payments a driving force behind the formation of both the Victorian Football League (VFL) in 1897 and the New South Wales Rugby League (NSWRL) in 1908.

Australian Football

League History

The first recorded game of Australian football was played in Melbourne in August 1858 at a location close to that of the current-day Melbourne Cricket Ground (MCG) in August.[3] The rules of Australian football, or "Victorian rules" as they were commonly known in the 1800s, were first codified in May 1859. Australian football is an indigenous sport that developed its own characteristics after borrowing critical elements of play from other football codes that were developing at the same time, including rugby, what was to become soccer, and possibly also an Aboriginal game known as Marn Grook.

The Victorian Football Association (VFA) was formed in 1877 by clubs from around Melbourne and Geelong. However, by 1896, the thirteen-club VFA competition was beset with problems similar to modern time; including the spectacle of the game itself and how it was played, player payments and professionalism, the relative strength of clubs and equity in the distribution of match gate-takings (Sandercock and Turner, 1981). These tensions, and dissatisfaction with the VFA administration, resulted in the leadership of several clubs conspiring to form their own "breakaway" league. These clubs, financially strong and among the most popular clubs of the time, formed the VFL in 1896 (Sandercock and Turner, 1981; Hess and Stewart, 1998; Pascoe, 1995).

Excluding the effects of World War II, the VFL enjoyed a long era of compositional stability from the mid-1920s through the mid-1980s. Stewart (1985) argues that the 1960s represented "a golden age" of high match attendance, financial stability, and on-field competitive balance. However, the combined impact of increasing player wages and player transfer fees along with declining match attendances in the 1980s increased the pressure on the VFL and the clubs to develop new revenue streams from the sale of corporate sponsorship and television broadcasting rights.

Serious financial and regulatory problems led the VFL to commission a strategic report, *Establishing the Basis for Future Success* (Victorian Football League, 1985), that recommended a fundamental restructuring of all key aspects of the VFL competition. The report recommended a rationalization of playing venues, which has ultimately seen the majority of VFL/AFL games played at major stadiums including the MCG, Waverley (or VFL) Park, Princes Park (Optus Oval) in Carlton, and the new Telstra Dome in the Melbourne Docklands precinct. Subsequent to the 1985 Task Force report, the VFL entered an era of growth and expansion with the League expanding from twelve to sixteen clubs in nine years, commencing in 1987 with the introduction of inter-state clubs from Western Australia and Queensland. Both clubs were privately owned and composite sides comprised of ex-VFL and non-VFL players.

The VFL was renamed the Australian Football League in 1990 prior to the admission of a composite South Australian side in 1991. The AFL's new strategic five year plan of 1994 recommended the inclusion of second sides from Western Australia and South Australia and this occurred in 1995 and in 1997. The financial demise and liquidation of the Fitzroy Football Club in 1996 lead to a merger with the Brisbane Bears, to form the Brisbane Lions from season 1997 onward. Thus, since 1995 the AFL has comprised sixteen clubs.

Corporate Governance

By virtue of its national scope and consequent financial strength, the AFL has become the controlling organization in Australian football. The current AFL strategic objectives reflect these diverse responsibilities. The objectives of the AFL are to

- Effectively manage the national competition to ensure it is the most successful national elite sports competition for the benefit of our key stakeholders—our AFL clubs, the players and the public;
- Promote high levels of player participation in well-managed programs at all levels of community football to ensure Australian football is the pre-eminent national football code;
- Promote public interest in the game by building the strongest consumer brand position in Australian sport;
- Maximise the economic benefits of Australian football to our member clubs, our players, the supporters, the football fraternity and the community at large. (Australian Football League, 2002, 8–14)

The essential component of the corporate governance structure of the AFL is the AFL Commission—an eight-member body that includes the AFL chief executive officer who is appointed by the commission. AFL clubs retain the right to appoint AFL commissioners other than the CEO. Clubs may overturn a commission decision to admit, relocate, or merge AFL clubs with a two-thirds majority vote, whereas a decision to expel a club must be approved by a simple majority of the AFL clubs. The AFL Commission has all other powers to run the national competition.

Basketball

League History

Basketball was invented in the United States by Dr. James Naismith in 1891 and was introduced to Melbourne and Australia by the Young Men's

Christian Association in 1905. Local competitions subsequently developed in each Australian state and the first quasinational league, the South Eastern Conference, existed between 1965 and 1971 before collapsing due to the traveling costs involved in interstate competition (Harris, 1992).

The National Invitational Basketball League, later renamed the National Basketball League (NBL), commenced with a ten-club competition in the winter of 1979. Reflecting both the traditional power base of basketball and a desire for a national competition, league administrators invited two clubs each from Adelaide, Melbourne, and Sydney, along with one club each from Brisbane, Canberra, Newcastle, and Wollongong for the inaugural NBL season.

NBL expansion was rapid. Ten cities hosted NBL clubs by 1982, and a two-division format was utilized in 1983 and 1984 to support a sixteen- and then seventeen-club competition. The NBL stabilized as a one-division competition with thirteen or fourteen clubs between 1985 and 1996, and basketball entered a golden era, during which all Australian capital cities (excluding Darwin) hosted at least one NBL club. Attendance growth was driven by a public fascination with basketball and American culture in general, and commentators generally agreed that basketball was "hot" (Stickels, 1994). However, match attendance peaked in 1994, and television audiences and time slots deteriorated from 1992 onward. By 1996, a strategic redirection was necessary, and two crucial decisions were made to arrest the decline. The first decision was to drop clubs in the small markets of Hobart, Geelong, and the Gold Coast after the 1996 season, and the NBL has been an eleven-club competition ever since. Two clubs each are currently located in both Melbourne and Sydney, and NBL clubs are also based in Adelaide, Brisbane, Cairns, Canberra, Perth, Townsville, and Wollongong.[3] The second, more radical decision saw the NBL become a summer competition, with the 1998–1999 NBL season being the inaugural season played between October and April. This switch was intended to avoid product market competition from the AFL and National Rugby League and to provide the Australian national basketball team (the Boomers) with an enhanced opportunity to prepare for international tournaments such as the Olympics and the International Basketball Federation (FIBA) Basketball World Championships.

Corporate Governance

The legal structure of the NBL involves a Participant Agreement between the NBL league administration (NBL Management Ltd.), Basketball Australia (BA)—the governing body for Australian basketball and Australian national teams—and the various clubs competing in the NBL. League strategy is formulated by an eight-member board of directors, which includes the NBL CEO and four directors elected from the ranks of the participants. The NBL clubs and BA ("the participants") are equal shareholders in NBL

Management Ltd., and the Participant Agreement specifies the principles governing the operation of the NBL:

- The NBL will be conducted on the basis of a national high-class home and away competition, and specifically:
- To provide the highest possible level of competition between basketball teams in the large towns and cities of Australia.
- To provide regular home and away Australia-wide competition during each NBL season.
- To provide a competition acceptable to the public and the media, so that basketball gains prominence and recognition as a major sport in the Australian community.
- To provide a National League competition on substantially the same basis as National League competitions operated in other countries in the world.
- To provide a standard of competition which will assist in the preparation of the Australian National Team for World Championships, Olympic Games and other major international competitions.[4]

Fifteen percent of NBL Management Ltd. was sold to the Sportsworld Media Group in 2001 for $3.5 million. As part of this deal, Sportsworld also purchased the marketing rights to the NBL for the sum of $3 million per annum; however, Sportsworld went into receivership in April 2002 and the NBL canceled the marketing agreement, which has now been taken over by the Australian sports marketing company Sporting Frontiers (Howell, 2002).

Rugby League

League History

The sport of rugby league split from rugby union on the issue of professionalism in Northern England in the 1890s. The rules of the fifteen-a-side rugby union game were modified over the next decade, and the thirteen-a-side sport of rugby league was clearly different from rugby union by the time the NSWRL was born of similar concerns in 1907. The inaugural NSWRL season was contested in 1908 by nine clubs, with South Sydney winning the first NSWRL Premiership.[5]

The NSWRL was an exclusively Sydney-based competition from 1910 until the expansion of the league into Wollongong and Canberra in 1982.[6] New South Wales Rugby League Limited (NSWRL Ltd.) was incorporated as the formal legal entity to manage the NSWRL, and the Newtown club was dropped from the league after the 1983 season. Subsequent expansion with the entry of clubs from Brisbane, Newcastle, and the Gold Coast saw only eleven of sixteen NSWRL clubs based in Sydney between 1988 and 1994.[7] The largest expansion in the history of rugby league occurred in 1995. Four clubs from Brisbane, Perth, Townsville, and Auckland, New

Zealand, were admitted, resulting in a twenty-team competition. The competition was renamed the Australian Rugby League (ARL) after the national governing body, the Australian Rugby Football League Ltd. (ARFL Ltd.), assumed responsibility for the expanded competition. This period also saw the genesis of the "Super League war," which ultimately led to two rival competitions in 1997, before the formation of the National Rugby League (NRL) in time for the 1998 season.

The Super League concept first emerged in 1994 as a proposal for an "elite competition" with twelve privately owned teams from Australia and New Zealand, and the concept was quickly adopted by News Limited (the Australian subsidiary of News Corporation) as a device for gaining television rights to rugby league, particularly pay-television content for the fledgling Foxtel network. Super League kicked off with ten clubs—including the eight defectors and two new franchises in Adelaide and Newcastle—in direct competition with the twelve-club ARL competition. The ARL reverted to a competition based in rugby league heartland, with eight clubs based in Sydney and four other clubs located in Newcastle, Wollongong, Brisbane, and on the Gold Coast. Community dissatisfaction, low attendance (down 18% between 1995 and 1997), cost pressures caused by the interleague competition for players, duplication of administrative expenses, and the prohibitive costs of litigation created impetus for a merger of the rival competitions. After months of negotiation, a series of agreements were executed in 1998 that resulted in the merger of the ARL and Super League competitions.

The new NRL competition commenced in 1998 with twenty clubs, including eleven ARL clubs, eight Super League clubs, and a new Melbourne-based club that had been established by News Limited. After mergers, dropping of clubs, and the court challenge by South Sydney to the legality of its exclusion from the competition, the NRL currently has fifteen teams.[8]

Corporate Governance

The NRL has a two-tier corporate structure, with ARFL Ltd. and News Limited subsidiary National Rugby League Investments Pty. Ltd. (NRLI Pty Ltd) having entered into a 50–50 partnership (the NRL Partnership) "for the purpose of owning and operating the NRL Competition."[9] That agreement also established the National Rugby League Ltd.; the objectives of which are to

- Organize and conduct a national rugby league competition [meaning the competition rounds and the finals series] in Australia ("NRL Competition");
- Foster and develop the NRL Competition;
- Take such action as may be considered conducive to the best interests of the NRL Competition; and
- Encourage and promote rugby league players, coaches, and administrators in the NRL Competition.[10]

The NRL Partnership has entered into a Services Agreement with NRL Ltd., whereby NRL Ltd. would manage the NRL competition subject to the provisions of the Services Agreement and a further Members Agreement among the members of NRL Ltd. Under the complex two-tier structure, NRL Ltd. has responsibility for the management of the national competition, although the NRL Partnership retains authority with respect to major strategic issues facing the NRL competition. Representative football and junior development are managed by ARFL Ltd. in conjunction with the state organizations (NSWRL Ltd. and Queensland Rugby League Limited).

REGULATORY STRUCTURE OF LEAGUES AND COMPETITIONS

Sports leagues may be characterized by the degree of economic freedom given to clubs and athletes (employers and employees) by the nature of the labor and product market regulations imposed by the central league administration. For each sport, we begin with an examination of the labor market regulations governing clubs and players, including an overview of collective bargaining and the role of player associations in the sport.[11] This is followed by a discussion of product market regulations, including those governing the sharing of revenue generated from the sale of television and broadcasting rights, sponsorships, and general admission tickets.

Australian Football

Labor Market

The VFL/AFL labor market has historically been one of the most heavily regulated in Australian sports, after introducing a system of residential zoning in 1915. Under this system, individuals living in metropolitan Melbourne and Geelong were "zoned" to a particular VFL club based upon their place of residence. The counterpart to the zoning system was the player transfer system, under which players were bound to a club and required a transfer clearance from that club before being allowed to play for a different club. The VFL zoning-and-transfer system operated until 1983, when it was declared to be an unreasonable restraint of trade by the Victorian Supreme Court in *Foschini v. Victorian Football League*,[12] following a similar earlier ruling in *Hall v. Victorian Football League*.[13] Following the Foschini case, all players were effectively entitled to free agency if not actually contracted to a VFL club, although transfer fees were not abolished by the VFL until 1988.

The VFL sought a new regulatory system that would both restrain player wages and create a degree of competitive balance in the league while avoiding another player- or club-motivated legal challenge to the league regulations. After extensive analysis of the North American major leagues, the VFL introduced a team salary cap, or total player payments (TPP), and a player drafting system to replace the old zoning and transfer/clearance system. The TPP cap was introduced for the 1985 VFL season, and the first VFL national draft was held in November 1986. Maximum club player lists were also introduced.

The TPP cap initially varied in line with existing contractual commitments and the capacity of clubs to pay; however, the cap was standardized at $1.3 million per club in 1989. Table 2 shows the value of the TPP cap between 1991 and 2003, along with the value of the base financial distribution from the AFL to each AFL club. The TPP cap for 2003 was set at $5.937 million, representing a 357% increase in fifteen years. The size of club player lists has steadily declined from fifty-two players in 1989 to the current level of thirty-eight. Although the specifics of the AFL draft have regularly changed, the principle of a reverse-order draft has been sustained throughout the national draft's fifteen-year history. The VFL/AFL national draft was first held in November 1986, with the twelve VFL clubs and the Brisbane Bears each selecting five players in reverse order to the 1986 VFL league ladder. Clubs were allowed to trade players for draft picks beginning in 1988, and trading rules were further liberalized to allow player-for-player trades in 1994, although cash sales of players or draft picks are prohibited.

The Australian Football League Players Association (AFLPA) (originally known as the Victorian Football League Players Association, or VFLPA) was formed in 1973, and apart from isolated cases of minor industrial unrest, highlighted by the initiation of an industrial dispute under the provisions of the Industrial Relations Act 1988 in 1993,[14] the AFL and the AFLPA have enjoyed a harmonious relationship. The two parties first negotiated a standard playing contract in 1988 and common law collective bargaining agreements spanning the 1994–1995, 1996–1998, and 1999–2003 AFL seasons (Dabscheck, 1996). The AFL bargains on behalf of the AFL clubs, and the AFLPA has enjoyed a membership rate of over 99% of AFL players for at least the past decade.

Product Market

The AFL has an extensive revenue-sharing system. Centralized revenue streams, including the sale of national television broadcasting and Internet rights, league sponsorships, and revenue from the AFL finals series, enter AFL consolidated revenue, and after league administration expenses are deducted, they form the basis for the equal distribution to AFL clubs each season.

Table 2
Australian Football League Player Payments, 1992–2003

Season	1992	1993	1994	1995	1996	1997	1998	1999	2000	2001	2002	2003
Gross Player	$26.558 m	$28.277 m	$32.061 m	$39.830 m	$47.961 m	$55.674 m	$62.189 m	$71.985 m	$80.951 m	$88.958 m	n.a.	n.a.
Total Player Payments	$24.000 m	$26.200 m	$27.700 m	$36.800 m	$40.000 m	$46.400 m	$52.400 m	$68.000 m	$76.000 m	$83.000 m	$89.000 m	$95.000 m
TPP per Club	$1.600 m	$1.747 m	$1.847 m	$2.300 m	$2.500 m	$2.900 m	$3.275 m	$4.250 m	$4.750 m	$5.188 m	$5.562 m	$5.937 m
Total Senior Grade	554	533	530	569	573	576	583	576	568	539	n.a.	n.a.
Average Salary of	$47,940	$50,910	$58,609	$70,005	$77,698	$91,448	$101,957	$117,398	$140,295	$165,062	n.a.	n.a.
Base AFL	$1.303 m	$1.222 m	$1.402 m	$1.402 m	$1.480 m	$1.700 m	$1.870 m	$2.220 m	$2.720 m	$3.157 m	n.a.	n.a.
Base Distribution as	.814	.700	.759	.610	.592	.586	.571	.522	.573	.609	n.a.	n.a.

Note: Includes only those players who played senior grade football in that AFL season.
Source: AFL (2000, 2002).

Basketball

Labor Market

The Australian labor market for basketball players has always been small, with only 120 to 220 hoopsters having played in the NBL each season. NBL clubs have used an average of 138 players (eleven clubs) per season since the NBL shifted to summer play for the 1998–1999 season. The NBL clubs are theoretically able to draw from a large pool of playing talent. The Australian Basketball Association (ABA), with six conferences and sixty-three clubs from all states and Territories excluding Western Australia and the Northern Territory, is the next level of semiprofessional basketball in Australia below the NBL. Similarly, the international dimension of basketball means the potential labor pool is immense, although NBL salaries are low relative to international alternatives in the October to April season.

The combination of local financial conditions and the international pressures of the basketball labor market have largely shaped labor market regulation in the NBL. A salary cap was first introduced in the 1989 NBL season, and, following a major review, the supporting web of salary cap regulations was revamped for the 1993 season. The value of the salary cap has quadrupled from $260,000 to $1,050,000 for the twelve-man active player roster in the fourteen seasons between 1989 and 2002.[15] However, the salary cap figure may be even more illusory in the NBL than in the AFL or NRL for two reasons. First, available data suggest minimal or negative growth in average salaries over the past decade (Macdonald, forthcoming). This trend is primarily due to many clubs restricting salary expenditure due to financial difficulty. Second, the NBL administration has insufficient resources (and expertise) to effectively police the salary cap. The other major labor market regulation the NBL is the "two import rule." Foreign-born players (primarily from the United States) have long been a feature of the NBL. Clubs were allowed to employ four "imports" (foreign nationals) in the 1979 inaugural NBL season, but by the mid-1980s, the generally higher skill level of such imports had created a degree of resentment because Australian players were not getting enough court time, and this disparity had negative implications for the general development of Australian basketball. The two import rule went into effect in the 1990 NBL season, and it limits NBL clubs to employing no more than two players "who are not eligible to represent the Australian National Team in the Main Official Competition of FIBA, pursuant to all FIBA regulations as determined from time to time."[16]

The National Basketball League Players' Association (NBLPA) was formed in 1989 and has enjoyed a membership rate of over 75% since the mid-1990s (Dabscheck, 1996; Dempsey, 1998). The NBLPA has successfully engaged in collective bargaining with the NBL since the first Collective Bargaining Agreement (CBA) was signed to cover the two years between April 1996 and March 1998. The first NBL-NBLPA CBA established a minimum salary of $7,500 in 1996 and $10,000 in 1997. In addition, the NBL agreed to fund NBLPA administrative costs and a player welfare and retirement fund.

Product Market

The NBL quickly established a philosophy of balance between the central authority of the NBL and the free enterprise of individual (privately owned) clubs (Harris, 1992; NBL Management Ltd., 1995). This philosophy is reflected in the fact that NBL clubs retain 100% of regular season home gate revenue and local television broadcasting revenue as the reward for direct club responsibility over marketing and development in local markets. There have been three major product market deviations from this philosophy. The first was an early decision to equalize the costs of air travel. The second is revenue sharing. Revenue from the sale of national television broadcasting rights and sponsorship of the NBL is distributed equally between all clubs after NBL administration costs are deducted (Palmer, 1998). The NBL also deducts 50% of merchandising sales (Stewart and Smith, 1999) and a percentage of the admission price for each attendee at playoff games (Buti, 1994) for equal distribution to all clubs.

Rugby League

Labor Market

Rugby League administrators have experimented with at least six different general systems of labor market regulation since 1960, when the "retain-and-transfer" system replaced the former residential zoning system that had required players to reside in the local district or zone of their NSWRL club. The NSWRL retain-and-transfer system was similar to that in English soccer and the VFL, and it required clubs to lodge a list of players the club wished to retain and a list of players they were willing to transfer to another club. Players on the transfer list were only allowed to play for a different club if that club was willing to pay the nominated transfer fee for that player. The retain-and-transfer system lasted until 1971, when it was defeated in the High Court of Australia in the case of *Buckley v. Tutty*.[17]

Buckley v. Tutty effectively granted out-of-contract players free agency, and the NSWRL responded by changing the labor market regulations governing both player transfers and salaries in the NSWRL. In order to curb rising player salaries, the league introduced limits in October 1972 on the maximum value of individual sign-on fees ($2,000, later increased to $4,000 for those who had played fifty senior games with a club) and bonuses for match victories ($200 per win). The wage maxima survived only eighteen months, with most clubs disregarding them altogether before they were abolished in May 1974 (see Dabscheck, 1993). The "thirteen import rule" was subsequently introduced in 1975, lasting until the reintroduction of transfer fees in 1983. Under the import rule, clubs were only allowed to employ (or "import") thirteen players from outside of their residential zones.

In late 1982, the NSWRL sought to introduce a standard playing contract and reintroduce transfer fees. Fearing another restraint of trade action, the NSWRL negotiated with the Association of Rugby League Professionals (ARLP) to draft a scale of fees, where the maximum transfer fees were fixed at 80% of the average sign-on fee for players of different experience levels. The NSWRL[18] and the ARLP negotiated such scales in 1983, 1986, and 1988, by which time they ranged from $2,000 for an individual who had played fewer than twenty senior games, up to a maximum transfer fee of $50,000 for those who had played more than three rugby league tests matches (Dabscheck, 1993, 258–262).

By the late 1980s, the transfer system had again proven to be unsuccessful, with the wealthy clubs using their financial strength to acquire good players from less well-off clubs. This trend was both creating a competitive imbalance in the competition and destroying the financial stability of NSWRL clubs as they spent beyond their means to acquire or retain key players (Masters, cited in Khoshaba, 1998, 92). League administrators saw the combination of a salary cap and draft as the solution to these related problems (Dabscheck, 1993). The salary cap was introduced in 1990, and the initial payment ceilings ranged from $800,000 to $1.5 million, depending upon the financial position of each club.[19] By 1995, the cap had risen to $1.8 million per club, and rugby union players were declared to be exempt from salary cap calculations for one season (Middleton, 1995, 137). In practice, the 1995 salary cap was disregarded when the Super League player raids sparked a bidding war for the services of rugby (league and union) players. The salary cap did not return until the 1999 NRL season and was set at $3.25 million per club for the four seasons between 1999 and 2002. The second major change to the NSWRL labor market in 1990 was the introduction of the internal draft. Modeled on the AFL preseason draft, the NSWRL internal draft was introduced to act as the player transfer mechanism for current players who were out of contract. Players were immediately concerned with the effect of the internal draft rules, and a legal challenge was mounted in the Federal Court of Australia.[20] In September 1991, the full court of the Federal Court ruled the internal draft rules were void as an unreasonable restraint of trade.[21] Rugby league players have since enjoyed free agency subject only to the salary cap and conditions of their standard playing contracts.

The NRL merger and resultant reduction of clubs from twenty-two in 1997 to fifteen in 2002 has shrunk the rugby league labor market by roughly 30%. This reduction, combined with the introduction in 1999 of the $3.25 million NRL salary cap (calculated on the twenty-five-player senior grade squad), has had a deflationary effect upon rugby league salaries. Implementation of the NRL salary cap was complicated by the long-term contracts signed during the Super League war, and as a result, many NRL clubs have been penalized for breaching the cap.

Collective player representation has an unusual history in Australian rugby league. The NSWRL required the support of the ARLP when transfer fees were reintroduced after the 1982 NSWRL season. Dabscheck (1993) notes that at the time, the ARLP had an approximate coverage of 70% of all rugby league players and that by 1991 (the time of the Adamson case) the membership rate had grown to around 95%. The ARLP had initially supported the internal draft, but after a bitter dispute and election of a new chief executive, the ARLP became the first player association in Australian sports to initiate (and subsequently win) legal action challenging the labor market regulations of a league (Dabscheck, 2000). In 1993, the ARPL merged with the Media, Entertainment and Arts Alliance (MEAA). The MEAA and ARFL Ltd. subsequently negotiated a standard playing contract that has now been replaced by the NRL standard playing contract.

Product Market

Under current arrangements, the NRL Partnership retains the ultimate right to all revenue from "key revenue rights" (media, sponsorship, and merchandising) contracts.[22] Such revenue is retained by ARFL Ltd. and News Limited or distributed to NRL Ltd. and the NRL clubs for operational purposes (as with the annual $2 million club grants). Clubs retain 100% of gate revenue for regular season home games and the sale of season tickets, and NRL Ltd. collects the revenue from finals series matches. In the period of the Super League war, and subsequently, there has been substantial funding of clubs by media organizations. For example, at least $23 million was committed to achieve a fourteen-club NRL competition in 2000, including outright grants of between $5 million and $8 million to each joint venture club (St. George–Illawarra; Wests Tigers, and the Northern Eagles) as an incentive to merge.[23]

PERFORMANCE

The governing principles of the sports competitions under review essentially identify two main dimensions of performance: (1) consumer demand for sports, and (2) the relative and absolute quality of the sports product. Hence, in this section we focus on performance indicators for each competition related to those dimensions: match attendance; television; and the long run and seasonal competitive balance of each sporting competition.

Match Attendance

In terms of annual aggregate match attendance, Table 3 indicates that the AFL is by far the most popular sports competition in Australia, although the

Table 3
Australian Professional Sporting Competitions: Attendance, 1990–2001

Season	Australian Football League			National Basketball League			National Rugby League		
	Aggregate Attendance	Average Attendance	Games (H&A + F)	Aggregate Attendance	Average Attendance	Games (H&A + F)	Aggregate Attendance	Average Attendance	Games (H&A + F)
1970	3,310,768	24,344	132 + 4				1,630,630	11,990	132 + 4
1971	3,326,436	24,459	132 + 4				1,562,338	11,488	132 + 4
1972	3,522,848	25,344	132 + 7				1,469,899	10,808	132 + 4
1973	3,338,648	24,193	132 + 6				1,390,810	10,006	132 + 7
1974	3,245,550	23,518	132 + 6				1,278,823	9,267	132 + 6
1975	3,206,016	23,232	132 + 6				1,529,415	10,924	132 + 8
1976	3,288,470	23,829	132 + 6				1,594,183	11,552	132 + 6
1977	3,304,080	23,770	132 + 7				1,440,765	10,365	132 + 7
1978	3,478,069	25,203	132 + 6				1,582,914	11,307	132 + 8
1979	3,574,281	25,901	132 + 6	196,000	2,154	90 + 1	1,500,369	10,872	132 + 6
1980	3,770,836	27,325	132 + 6		n.a.		1,498,634	10,860	132 + 6
1981	3,830,234	27,755	132 + 6		n.a.		1,312,977	9,514	132 + 6
1982	3,681,556	26,678	132 + 6		n.a.		1,716,490	9,130	182 + 6
1983	3,638,017	26,362	132 + 6		n.a.		1,458,144	7,715	182 + 7
1984	3,394,571	24,598	132 + 6	242,022	1,158	200 + 9	1,379,655	8,464	156 + 7
1985	3,113,255	22,560	132 + 6	317,372	1,697	182 + 5	1,450,162	8,897	156 + 7
1986	3,323,759	24,085	132 + 6	394,685	2,088	182 + 7	1,705,156	10,461	156 + 7
1987	3,419,269	21,370	154 + 6	483,467	2,518	182 + 10	1,658,354	10,237	156 + 6
1988	3,528,878	22,055	154 + 6	536,493	3,232	156 + 10	1,966,658	10,747	176 + 7
1989	3,581,822	22,386	154 + 6	662,439	3,897	156 + 14	2,040,375	11,150	176 + 7
1990	4,063,385	25,238	154 + 7	887,443	4,551	182 + 13	2,209,363	12,073	176 + 7
1991	4,178,884	24,296	165 + 7	825,645	4,256	182 + 12	2,413,318	13,188	176 + 7
1992	4,814,271	27,990	165 + 7	945,117	5,463	156 + 17	2,282,194	12,540	176 + 6
1993	4,657,489	29,666	150 + 7	1,083,490	5,445	182 + 17	2,625,467	14,426	176 + 6
1994	5,237,398	30,100	165 + 9	1,127,033	5,692	182 + 16	2,732,389	15,013	176 + 6
1995	5,712,693	30,879	176 + 9	1,097,678	5,461	182 + 19	3,352,927	14,642	220 + 9
1996	5,694,921	30,783	176 + 9	1,019,988	5,075	182 + 19	2,743,516	12,303	214 + 9
1997	6,402,997	34,611	176 + 9	896,349	5,064	165 + 12	2,747,817	11,594	222 + 15
1998	6,691,897	36,172	176 + 9	771,364	4,408	165 + 10	2,921,264	11,546	240 + 13
1999	6,243,586	33,749	176 + 9	645,073	4,511	143 + 13	3,156,483	14,819	204 + 9
2000	6,307,373	34,094	176 + 9	714,017	4,636	154 + 14	2,902,227	15,195	182 + 9
2001	6,447,560	34,838	176 + 9	814,918	4,738	154 + 18	2,682,210	14,043	182 + 9
2002	6,097,739	32,961	176 + 9	840,074	4,641	165 + 16	2,656,198	14,054	180 + 9

Note: Attendance results include both home and away (H&A) season and finals/playoffs (F) games. NBL results from 1999 and 2000 include home and away season attendance only. NRL season attendance for 1997 is calculated as the combined attendance at both ARL and Super League home and away and finals games.
Sources: AFL (2002); Meadows (2002); NBL (1995); Shilbury and Deane (2001); http://stats.rleague.com

vast majority of this attendance occurs in Melbourne, where ten of the sixteen AFL clubs are located. The NRL exhibits a similar attendance pattern due to the popularity of rugby league in New South Wales and concentration of NRL clubs in Sydney.

Attendance at AFL matches was relatively steady between the early 1970s and late 1980s. During the 1990s, both aggregate and average per match attendance expanded rapidly, and although there has been some decline in recent years, both remain significantly above levels of a decade ago. NRL attendance declined from the early 1970s to the mid-1980s, but then grew until the mid-1990s. The Super League war caused a dramatic fall in attendance, but in the ARL era the level of aggregate and average per match attendance have returned to levels of the mid-1990s. Attendance at NBL matches grew spectacularly between the mid-1980s and mid-1990s, but since that time have declined—between 1994 and 2002 both aggregate and average per match attendance have declined by about 20%.

Television

There are three free commercial television networks (the Seven, Nine, and Ten Networks) and two free state-owned networks (the Australian Broadcasting Corporation [ABC] and the Special Broadcasting Service in Australia). These networks cover the Australian capital cities and have affiliate relationships with broadcasters that cover rural and regional Australia. The Australian pay-television system emerged in the 1990s, and a duopoly of cable-based content providers currently exists in the metropolitan markets (Foxtel and Optus Vision).

Broadcasting schedules vary considerably among different cities and regions, but in general, sports dominate the Australian airwaves. The winter months are dominated by live and delayed AFL and NRL coverage from Friday night to Sunday night. Only limited television ratings data are available without cost to the general public; however, available data for 2001 and 2002 show the AFL and NRL Grand Finals to be among the nation's ten highest rated television programs in both years.[24] Ratings patterns reflect the geographic variations in the popularity of each sport, with the estimated audiences in Sydney and Melbourne representing only 24% to 28% of the television audience in the natural home of each sport.[25]

Australian Football

The AFL had a forty-five-year relationship with the Seven Network between 1957 and 2001. VFL/AFL football was shown on Seven for every year except 1987 (ABC), with Seven first securing exclusive rights as part of a five-year, $3-million deal in 1976 and then regaining exclusive rights in 1988 with a five-year, $30-million agreement (Turner and Shilbury, 1997). Seven renegotiated the exclusive rights several times during the 1990s. Stensholt and Way (2001) suggest $80 million was paid for the period between 1993 and 1996 and a further $150 million for the AFL rights between 1997 and 2001 (see Turner and Shilbury, 1997, 57). For 2002 onward, the

AFL subsequently announced a five-year, $500-million agreement with a consortium including the Nine, Ten, and Foxtel and Australia's largest telecommunications company, Telstra (for Internet rights).

Basketball

The NBL has been televised ever since the inaugural 1979 NBL season, with local broadcasts in all cities except Melbourne and Sydney by 1986 (Way, 1989). In 1984, Network Ten offered the NBL $1 for national broadcasting rights. Network Ten experimented with nationally televised games in a late-night Tuesday time slot. These games rated poorly, and former NBL general manager Bill Palmer noted, "We never even got that dollar" (cited in Harris, 1992, 214) after Network Ten experienced financial difficulties. After several seasons during which some clubs had local television deals with Network Ten and others with the Seven Network, all clubs had contracts with the Seven Network by the end of 1988, hence it became the sole NBL broadcaster from 1989 to 1991. This agreement was worth over $500,000 in addition to the revenue generated by each club in its local television contract (Harris, 1992). The NBL returned to prime time on Friday and Saturday nights in 1992, after Network Ten secured free television rights to the NBL for five seasons. Low ratings caused Network Ten to relegate NBL games to variable late-night time slots midway through the 1992 season, and no commercial broadcasters were interested in a national broadcast agreement when the rights were again available in 1998. The NBL eventually negotiated a zero-dollar agreement with ABC, which televised the national game of the week on Sunday afternoons. This agreement lasted four seasons between 1998 and 2001. The NBL did not have free-television coverage for either the 2001–2002 or the 2002–2003 season, although some clubs (particularly Perth and Brisbane) have had local broadcasting agreements since 1998.

Rugby League

The most interesting era in the history of televised rugby league began in 1989, when Network Ten paid around $48 million for a five-year deal to broadcast the NSWRL rugby league State of Origin and Kangaroo tests (Shoebridge, 1989). After being placed into receivership, Network Ten was unable to make a scheduled payment at the end of the 1990 season, and the NSWRL terminated this contract. The Nine Network subsequently purchased the rights to the NSWRL and the State of Origin games at around $6.5 million per annum for three years, with the NSWRL rights, from 1991 on, sold back to Network Ten for around $4 million, while Nine retained the marquee State of Origin games (Masters, 1990). Nine Network broadcast both the NSWRL and the State of Origin series in 1992, and in 1993 secured the rights to the NSWRL, State of Origin, and international rugby

Table 4
League Premiers/Champions and Long-Run Competitive Balance

Australian Football League (1897 – 2002)				
Clubs	Premierships	% T	Seasons	% E
Essendon	16	.151	104	.154
Carlton	16	.151	106	.151
Collingwood	14	.132	106	.132
Melbourne	12	.113	103	.117
Richmond	10	.094	105	.105
Hawthorn	9	.085	78	.115
Fitzroy *	8	.075	100	.080
Geelong	6	.057	103	.058
Kangaroos	4	.038	78	.051

National Basketball League (1979 – 2002)				
Clubs	Championships	% T	Seasons	% E
Perth Wildcats	4	.167	21	.190
Adelaide 36ers	4	.167	21	.190
Canberra Cannons	3	.125	24	.125
Melbourne Tigers	2	.083	19	.105
Brisbane Bullets	2	.083	24	.083
North Melbourne Giants *	2	.083	19	.105
Southern Melbourne Saints *	2	.083	13	.154
South East Melbourne Magic *	2	.083	7	.286
Wollongong Hawks	1	.042	24	.042

Rugby League (1908 – 2002)				
Clubs	Premierships	% T	Seasons	% E
South Sydney	20	.211	90	.225
St. George *	15	.158	76	.197
Sydney Roosters	12	.116	92	.122
Balmain *	11	.116	89	.124
Bulldogs	7	.074	67	.106
Manly-Warringah *	6	.063	53	.113
Brisbane	5	.053	15	.357
Parramatta	4	.042	56	.073
Western Suburbs *	4	.042	89	.045

AFL

	T	% T		% E
Sydney	3	.028	105	.029
Adelaide	2	.019	12	.167
West Coast	2	.019	16	.125
Brisbane	2	.019	16	.125
Western	1	.009	78	.013
St. Kilda	1	.009	104	.010
TOTAL	**106**			

AFL	P	GF
1983 – 1992	5/14	7/14
1993 – 2002	6/18	11/18
1983 – 2002	8/18	12/18
History	15/19	15/19

NBL

	T	% T		% E
Launceston *	1	.042	3	.333
West Adelaide *	1	.042	6	.167
TOTAL	**24**			

NBL	P	GF
1983 – 1992	6/20	9/20
1993 – 2002	6/17	9/17
1983 – 2002	8/24	13/24
History	11/27	16/27

NRL

	T	% T	T	% T		% E
Canberra	3	.032	3	.032	21	.150
Newtown *	3	.032	3	.032	73	.041
Newcastle	2	.021	2	.021	15	.143
North Sydney *	2	.021	2	.021	89	.022
Melbourne	1	.010	1	.010	5	.250
Penrith	1	.010	1	.010	36	.029
TOTAL **	**96**					

NRL	P	GF
1983 – 1992	6/17	8/17
1993 – 2002	7/26	11/26
1983 – 2002	9/27	14/27
History	15/32	20/32

Note: % T = Premierships/Total number of league seasons. % E = Effectiveness: Premierships/number of seasons contested by club.

* Club is no longer competing in league.

** 96 NRL/ARL/NSWRL/Super League premierships have been won in ninety-five seasons due to the 1997 split between the ARL and Super League.

Table 5
Seasonal Competitive Balance, 1970–2002

Season	Australian Football League		National Basketball League		National Rugby League	
	SD / ISD	Range	SD / ISD	Range	SD / ISD	Range
1970	1.732	.636			1.303	.614
1971	2.164	.727			1.339	.682
1972	2.275	.795			1.464	.614
1973	1.857	.682			1.324	.568
1974	1.846	.636			1.191	.636
1975	1.670	.682			1.133	.636
1976	1.384	.477			1.177	.591
1977	1.966	.636			1.636	.773
1978	1.510	.500			1.407	.636
1979	2.009	.727	1.931	.666	1.339	.682
1980	2.071	.568	1.868	.637	1.139	.568
1981	2.355	.727	1.414	.500	.990	.432
1982	2.268	.682	2.273	.731	1.291	.654
1983	1.557	.500	2.285	.750	1.296	.615
1984	1.624	.591	2.329	.725	1.386	.750
1985	2.013	.727	2.287	.692	1.344	.584
1986	1.850	.727	1.956	.731	1.237	.396
1987	1.616	.591	2.321	.693	1.422	.521
1988	1.665	.682	2.020	.792	1.815	.568
1989	1.775	.636	1.819	.542	1.696	.727
1990	1.809	.591	2.040	.654	1.846	.659
1991	1.878	.727	1.851	.654	1.627	.682
1992	1.875	.568	1.695	.750	1.329	.568
1993	1.671	.625	1.851	.654	2.028	.727
1994	1.408	.545	2.137	.654	1.862	.636
1995	1.839	.818	1.864	.577	2.187	.818
1996	1.854	.705	1.815	.577	1.752	.636
1997	1.156	.500	1.401	.500	1.547	.545
1998	1.312	.477	1.670	.567	1.904	.604
1999	1.714	.636	1.282	.384	1.716	.625

Table 5   (*continued*)

2000	1.796	.864	2.424	.715	1.297	.500
2001	1.859	.682	2.674	.679	1.554	.539
2002	1.610	.682	1.090	.400	1.571	.500
Mean	1.787	.647	1.929	.634	1.489	.615
St. Dev.	.269	.096	.375	.106	.280	.090

Notes: SD/ISD: Standard deviation of all clubs H&A season WPCT/idealized standard deviation of all clubs H&A season WPCT. ISD calculated using Quirk and Fort (1992) method. *Range*: Range of WPCT on league ladder at conclusion of the H&A season.

league matches in a seven-year, $70-plus-million deal (Stephens, 1993). The Nine Network has broadcast NRL games on Fridays and Sundays since the inaugural NRL season in 1998 and also broadcasts the State of Origin series and Kangaroo tests. Foxtel and Optus shared the pay-television rights between 1998 and 2000, and Foxtel subsequently paid $400 million for the pay-television rights between 2001 and 2006 (Middleton, 2001). The true value of rugby league broadcasting rights is clouded by the effect of Super League and the massive investments by Nine Network, Optus, News Limited, and Telstra in player salaries, payments to clubs, the NSWRL, ARL, and NRL as well as (part) ownership of several clubs by News Limited.

Competitive Balance

Competitive balance, or the evenness of sporting competition, is generally regarded by the managers of Australian sporting competitions as a key operational objective, for the measurement of competitive balance represents an evaluation of both the absolute and relative quality of a team and the sports competition in which that team participates. Three general types of competitive balance may be identified: (1) the closeness of individual match results, (2) the evenness of seasonal results, and (3) the long-run (or multiseasonal) evenness of a league or sports competition. In this chapter, we focus on presenting descriptive information on the latter two dimensions for each competition. One set of measures of competitive balance—reported in Table 4—shows the degree of concentration of seasonal results; that is, the different number of clubs to win the Premiership and contest the Grand Final or championship playoff in different eras. It is evident that over the past two decades the degree of long-run competitive balance has been higher in the AFL than NRL or NBL. Comparing the period 1983 through 1992 against 1993 through 2002, it seems that long-run competitive balance has been relatively stable in the AFL, has increased in the NBL, and has tended to decline in the NRL. A second set of measures—reported in Table 5—shows the seasonal competitive balance of each competition. The first measure is the ratio of the actual standard deviation (SD) of regular-season winning percentage ($WPCT$) or competition points (PTS) to the "idealized" standard deviation (ISD) for that season.[26] A second measure is the annual range of home and away season league ladder performance—the difference in the home and away season performance of the best and worst ranked club in each competition—for each competition. It is notable that in each competition there is a high degree of volatility across time in seasonal competitive balance. Using the standard deviation measure it appears that the AFL and NBL became more even in the 1993 to 2002 period than in the 1983 to 1992 period, whereas the NRL became less even; but this pattern is not evidence from the range measure.

NOTES

1. This chapter draws extensively on material prepared by Macdonald (forthcoming).

2. See, for example, Sport 2000 Task Force (1999, 74–78).

3. The current NBL clubs (year of debut in parentheses) include the Adelaide 36ers (1982), Brisbane Bullets (1979), Cairns Taipans (2000), Canberra Cannons (1979), Melbourne Tigers (1984), Perth Wildcats (1982), Sydney Kings (1988), Townsville Crocodiles (1993), Victoria Giants (1999), West Sydney Razorbacks (1999), and Wollongong Hawks (1979).

4. National Basketball League Participant Agreement, part 6: Principles for Operation of the NBL, clause 6.2.

5. The original nine NSWRL clubs included Eastern Suburbs (now the Sydney Roosters), Balmain, Cumberland, Glebe, Newcastle, Newtown, North Sydney, South Sydney, and Western Suburbs.

6. The 1982 NSWRL clubs (year of league entry in parentheses) included Balmain (1908), Canberra Raiders (1982), Canterbury (1935), Cronulla (1967), Eastern Suburbs (1908), Illawarra Steelers (1982), Manly-Warringah (1947), Newtown (1908), North Sydney (1908), Parramatta (1947), Penrith (1967), St. George (1921), South Sydney (1908), and Western Suburbs (1908).

7. The Brisbane Broncos, Gold Coast Seagulls/Chargers, and the Newcastle Knights entered the NSWRL in 1988.

8. *South Sydney District Rugby Football Club Ltd v. News Ltd. and Ors* (2001) FCA 862 (July 6, 2001) (Heerey, Moore, and Merkel JJ).

9. *South Sydney District Rugby Football Club Ltd. v. News Ltd.* (2000) FCA 1541 at [50] [109] (November 3, 2000) (per Finn J, discussing the execution of the Partnership Agreement and citing the Members Agreement (clause 1.1) definition of "NRL Partnership").

10. National Rugby League Limited, Memorandum of Association, clause 2.1.

The six members of NRL Ltd. include ARFL Ltd., NRLI Pty. Ltd., and two nominees of each company (National Rugby League Limited, Memorandum of Association, clause 8).

11. The collected works of Braham Dabscheck provide a comprehensive review of industrial relations issues and labor market regulations in Australian sports (see, for example, Dabscheck, 1996).

12. Unreported judgment, Supreme Court of Victoria, Crockett J, April 15, 1983.

13. (1982) VR 64.

14. *Anderson and Ors v. Adelaide Football Club and Ors* (1993) 48 IR 440.

15. Clubs may also have a development squad of twelve players aged fifteen to eighteen. These players are not contracted but may play in NBL matches (National Basketball League Rules and Regulations, 12.0: Player Transfers, Clearances, Contracted Players and Waivers, clause 12.16 [as of December 1998], copy on file with author).

16. National Basketball League Rules and Regulations, 10.0: Team Content, clause 10.1.2 (as of December 1998, copy on file with author). Clause 3.3.1 of the FIBA Internal Regulations permit only those players holding legal nationality of a country to play for the national team of that country. Under clause 3.3.3, national teams are only allowed to have one team member who acquired legal nationality by naturalization.

17. (1971) 125 CLR 353.

18. The league was an unincorporated association until December 1983 and the formation of NSWRL Ltd.

19. *Adamson and Ors v. New South Wales Rugby League Ltd. and Ors* (1991) 27 FCR 535, 543 (Hill J).

20. *Adamson and Ors v. New South Wales Rugby League Ltd. and Ors* (1991) 27 FCR 535 (Hill J).

21. *Adamson and Ors v. New South Wales Rugby League Ltd. and Ors* (1991) 31 FCR 242 (Sheppard, Wilcox, and Gummow JJ).

22. *South Sydney District Rugby Football Club Ltd v. News Ltd. and Ors* (2000) FCA 1541 (November 3, 2000) (Finn J) at [124]...[128].

23. Perrine (2000) suggests the "joint venture grant" was $8 million per club, whereas Hely J in *South Sydney District Rugby Football Club Ltd v. News Ltd. and Ors* (1999) FCA 1710 (December 9, 1999) at (41) quotes the figure as only $5 million per joint venture.

24. Responsibility for official television ratings shifted from ACNielsen to the OzTam company in 2001. The AFL Grand Final was ranked four and three, and the NRL Grand Final ranked ten and seven in the national program rankings for 2001 and 2002 (see http://www.oztam.com.au).

25. Calculated from the OzTam *Top 20 Progam Ranking Reports* for 2001 and 2002.

26. This is the Noll-Scully approach, as popularized by Quirk and Fort (1992). The idealized seasonal standard deviation of seasonal *WPCT* equals $(.500)/\sqrt{N}$. N is the number of home and away season games played by each club, and .500 is the mean seasonal *WPCT* of a league, where all clubs are assumed to have an equal playing strength.

19

Labor Market Intervention, Revenue Sharing, and Competitive Balance in the Australian Football League, 1897–2002

Ross Booth

INTRODUCTION

A long-running debate in sports economics has centered on whether labor market devices and revenue-sharing rules are effective in increasing competitive balance in sports leagues comprising either profit-maximizing or win-maximizing clubs. This chapter examines the levels of competitive balance in a league comprising win-maximizing clubs under a variety of labor market devices and revenue-sharing rules that make for interesting comparisons with competitive balance levels achieved in other professional sports leagues.

Formed in 1897, the Victorian Football League (VFL) expanded nationally to become the semiprofessional Australian Football League (AFL) now comprising sixteen member-owned clubs playing a unique brand of Australian rules football. Analysis of the clubs' finances and stated objectives suggests that the clubs are win-maximizers (subject to breaking even), rather than profit maximizers.

This chapter traces the history of labor market devices and revenue-sharing rules the VFL/AFL has used to try to increase competitive balance. Six different periods between 1897 and 2002 are identified, and the different levels of competitive balance are calculated for each year and then matched against the devices and rules used in each period.

The levels of competitive balance achieved in the VFL/AFL are compared with major leagues in North America. It is suggested that the high levels of competitive balance achieved in the VFL/AFL in the most recent period result from the introduction of both a player draft and a team salary cap.

LEAGUE HISTORY, CLUB OBJECTIVES, AND OWNERSHIP

From the VFL to the AFL

The Victorian Football Association (VFA) was formed in Melbourne in 1877 in the state of Victoria, Australia. In 1896, eight of the original VFA clubs broke away to form the Victorian Football League, and the first season of competition was played in 1897. Over time, the number of VFL clubs in Melbourne grew, and in the 1980s and 1990s clubs from cities outside Victoria were admitted. This necessitated an official name change at the end of 1989 to reflect the expansion of the former Victoria-based competition into a truly national competition. Since 1990, the competition has been known as the Australian Football League (AFL).

The VFL began with eight clubs: Carlton, Collingwood, Essendon, Fitzroy, Geelong, Melbourne, St. Kilda, and South Melbourne. University and Richmond were admitted in 1908, but University disbanded before the start of the 1915 season. During WWI, the number of clubs fell to four in 1916, increased to six in 1917, to eight in 1918, and to nine in 1919. In 1925, Footscray, Hawthorn, and North Melbourne joined to make a twelve-team competition that continued until 1987, except for Geelong's withdrawal during WWII in 1942 and 1943. South Melbourne moved to Sydney for the 1982 season and became the Sydney Swans in 1983. National expansion continued with the inclusion of Brisbane and West Coast (Perth) in 1987, Adelaide in 1991, and Fremantle in 1995, making a league of sixteen teams. In 1997, Port Adelaide was admitted, but the Brisbane Bears' merger with Fitzroy to become the Brisbane Lions kept the number of clubs at sixteen, and Footscray began trading as the Western Bulldogs. In 1999, North Melbourne commenced as the Kangaroos.

Objective Function of VFL/AFL Clubs

Dabscheck (1973) analyzes the objectives of VFL clubs in the early 1970s. These findings, which the author also summarizes later (1975a, 1975b), make a distinction between the football club and the parent club. The football club is a subunit within the parent club and makes on-field decisions such as training, coaching, and selection of teams. The parent club is concerned with financial decisions that affect the ability of the football team, such as raising money to pay players. According to Dabscheck (1975a, 178–179) when interviewed:

Football and "parent club" officials state that their major objective is to see their football team win as many premierships as possible. These officials also add that extra revenues which come into the club are either used to purchase and pay players or to improve ground and spectator facilities, and it is quite apparent that "parent clubs," in an effort to acquire a winning football team, are prepared to pay out more money for players in terms of wages and transfer fees than they expect to gain from increases to gate receipts and football club membership income.

Stewart (1985, 7) concurs with Dabscheck's general view on the objective of clubs, arguing that the overriding goals of clubs are winning and team success: "Profits are seen as a secondary goal: a premiership is ranked more highly than an operating surplus. A club is therefore prepared to go into debt if it means high calibre coaches and players can be secured, motivated and integrated into a winning team. To this end, clubs are continually in search of new means of expanding their revenue base (and wage fund) in order to attract premiership players." Thus, both Dabscheck and Stewart conclude that VFL/AFL clubs are utility maximizers, specifically wanting to maximize the number of matches their team wins. The suggestion that clubs are prepared to go into debt does not alter the fact that a club has a budget constraint with which it must ultimately comply in the longer term.

More recently, Shilbury (1994), in a study of the strategic planning practices of AFL clubs, finds that financial trading performance and on-field performance are the two most important aspects of football club management. Whereas general managers tend to be employed to manage the financial affairs of the club, the focus of club presidents upon on-field success tends to reflect the responsibilities to club members of the elected board of management. Shilbury (1994, 257) describes this as "the utility maximising effect of voluntary administration by the president and board of directors."

Ownership of VFL/AFL Clubs

Member-Owned Clubs

Most clubs in the history of the VFL/AFL have been member-owned. The traditional emphasis on success on the field no doubt stems from the nature of a VFL/AFL club, which traditionally has been run by a board of directors elected by "financially paid-up" club members. The aim of club members has not been to achieve a financial return on their membership, but rather to assist with and to enjoy the playing success of their club. In other words, the clubs have not been profit-maximizers but win-maximizers subject to a budget constraint; that is, breaking even financially. During the 1980s and 1990s, VFL/AFL clubs (and their directors in particular) seemed to become much more conscious of the need for financial viability, both in the short and long term, given a world where clubs were fearful of their capacity to survive.

Evidence for this view is supported by a survey conducted by the Institute of Chartered Accountants in Australia (2002) of the sixteen AFL clubs' financial reporting. Over the three-year period from 1999 to 2001, average annual club membership was 27,658, with Adelaide having the highest (42,343) and the Western Bulldogs the lowest (19,211). Average club membership for 2002 was 28,096, with the highest being Adelaide (46,620) and the lowest St. Kilda (17,696). Over the three-year period from 1999 to 2001, the largest average annual profit was that of Essendon, AU$1 million on average annual operating revenue of around AU$15.88 million (excluding financial distributions from the AFL). The largest average annual loss over the same three-year period was Fremantle's AU$1.125 million on average annual operating revenue of around AU$12.24 million (excluding AFL distributions). The average annual loss of the three-year period was just AU$2,000 in a league where the clubs' three-year average annual operating revenue (excluding AFL distributions) was AU$14.89 million a year. The club with the largest average annual operating revenue over the three-year period was West Coast (AU$19.12 million) and the club with the lowest was the Kangaroos (AU$11.41 million).

Other Forms of Ownership

In 1987 North Melbourne issued AU$3 million worth of shares on the (now defunct) second (junior) board of the Stock Exchange, primarily as a fund-raising exercise. Also, beginning in 1987, St. Kilda issued unlisted shares, ostensibly for the same reason.

State League Ownership

The West Australian Football Commission (WAFC), formed in 1989 to oversee football in Western Australia, owns the West Coast (in Perth) and Fremantle licences.[1] Originally, the West Australian Football League (WAFL) bought the West Coast license to compete in the VFL/AFL beginning in 1987 and then struck a sublicense agreement with Indian Pacific. Indian Pacific aimed to raise capital through a public share float but the float failed, and eventually Indian Pacific was forced to offer equity to the WAFL in lieu of its royalty payment. West Coast and Fremantle must return 75% of any profits to the WAFC.

Adelaide and Port Adelaide have sublicence agreements with the South Australian National Football League (SANFL), which appoints the South Australian Football Commission (SAFC) to administer football in South Australia. Adelaide and Port Adelaide make a royalty payment of 80% of any profits to the SANFL.

Each of these four clubs has a large membership base. The only practical difference for members is that they do not directly elect the board of directors. That state's Football Commission appoints each club's board.

Private Ownership

The VFL/AFL's experiment of private ownership with the expansion teams in the northern states of New South Wales and Queensland proved to be brief and financially unsuccessful.

In response to growing financial pressures, South Melbourne played eleven games in Sydney in 1982. In May 1983, the VFL agreed that it would subsidize the club and appointed an eight-person board to run the club, whose name was changed to the Sydney Swans. At the end of July 1985, the VFL sold the Sydney Swans to private owners led by Geoffrey Edelsten. In May 1988, the Sydney club license was sold back to the VFL until December 1988, when the VFL announced that a new private consortium led by Mike Willesee had taken over for a period of five years. This group proved unsuccessful in turning the club's finances and on-field performance around, and eventually, in May 1993, a restructuring was announced that included the return to a traditional membership-based club.

A syndicate headed by Paul Cronin won the battle for the VFL/AFL license for a team in Brisbane and together with Christopher Skase were founders of the Brisbane Bears in October 1986. The Bears quickly ran into debt, and when Skase's Qintex Corporation collapsed, Reuben Pelerman bought the license from the ANZ Bank in February 1990, but lost money before eventually transferring the license back to a traditional membership-based structure in November–December 1991. The Brisbane Bears became the Brisbane Lions in 1997, after a merger with Fitzroy in July 1996.

In summary, the member ownership of clubs, the research on club objectives, and the analysis of clubs' finances all strongly suggest that win maximization (subject to breaking even) is a more accurate reflection of the true objective function of VFL/AFL clubs than is profit maximization.

HISTORY OF LABOR MARKET DEVICES AND REVENUE-SHARING RULES

The six periods between 1897 and 2002 chosen for analysis are identified depending on the various combinations of different labor market devices and revenue-sharing rules in operation at the time. The labor market devices varied from no intervention at all (in which case players are complete free agents) to other devices such as geographical (territorial) zoning of metropolitan Melbourne, maximum limits on an individual player's wage (the Coulter Law), various player payment schemes, and geographical zoning of country (rural) Victoria. More recently, a team salary cap (and then minimum team salary), a national player draft, and a minimum wage have been adopted. Aside from these labor market devices, rules regarding the sharing of gate revenue and league revenue have also been used to influence the ability of clubs to recruit and pay players.

Period 1 (1897–1914) was one of strong competition for new players, described as a period of free agency. Officially, the VFL was an amateur competition until 1911, although there was very strong suspicion that under-the-table payments were being made. Transfer rules applied to current players, but uncertainty remains as to how effectively these transfer rules were enforced and whether signing-on fees and/or transfer fees were common.

Period 2 (1915–1929) was one in which each club was allocated a geographical zone of metropolitan Melbourne from which players could be recruited. However there was keen competition between VFL clubs for country, interstate, and VFA players. The period ended with the introduction of the Coulter Law.

Period 3 (1930–1944) was one of metropolitan zoning, with free agency for country and interstate players. Transfer fees and signing-on fees, although illegal, were not uncommon for country and interstate recruits. Employment was also a strong inducement. The Coulter Law, a uniform maximum imposed on each individual player's wage, was imposed in 1930. Despite this maximum wage being adjusted through the period, it became much more difficult to enforce with the passage of time.

Period 4 (1945–1967) began with the introduction of what the AFL describes as a "modified-form of gate sharing" in 1945. Television coverage began in 1957, the income from which was shared equally between the clubs. Metropolitan zoning and the Coulter Law remained the major labor market devices in use.

Period 5 (1968–1984) included the addition of country zoning to complement metropolitan zoning, a transfer fee system, and various schemes to control player payments. Country zoning was introduced for the 1968 season. In 1970, transfer fees, signing-on fees, and contracts were allowed for each club's two permissible interstate recruits. At the end of 1971, transfer payments were allowed for exchanges of players between VFL clubs. Player contracts became increasingly common, and transfer fees were prevalent into the early 1980s. An interstate player draft was introduced in time for the 1982 season. Concern was raised over the validity of the VFL's zoning, transfer, and player payment rules, which culminated in the courts declaring the regulations an unreasonable restraint of trade in the 1983 Foschini case. To complement 50–50 gate revenue sharing, in 1981 an equalization levy was charged against all cash-paying spectators, paid into an equalization fund, and then redistributed equally among all clubs. Beginning in 1982, a contribution from each adult club membership ticket was also made to the VFL Club Membership ticket pool.

Period 6 (1985–2002) began with the introduction of the team salary cap in 1985. The appointment of an "independent" VFL Commission in 1984, which replaced the old VFL board of directors, comprising a delegate from each of the clubs, heralded a new policy direction. Zoning was phased out during this period, with country zoning ending in 1986 and metropolitan zoning in 1991. The first national player draft was held in time for the 1987 season, with drafted players initially being "bound" for three years, later reduced to two. A preseason draft began in 1989. The sale of player contracts was banned, and apart from a midseason draft from 1990 to 1993, players and draft selections could only be traded between clubs during specified times during the off-season. Senior player lists (rosters) were also introduced at the time of the player draft. A minimum wage was introduced in 1994 as part of the first of a series of collective bargaining agreements (CBAs) between the AFL and the Australian Football League Players' Association (AFLPA). Recruiting concessions were given to new clubs (Brisbane, West Coast, Adelaide, Fremantle, and Port Adelaide) to help them form their player lists. In 1993, special draft concessions were given to the three bottom teams with competitive difficulties, but beginning in 1998, one priority selection prior to round one of the national draft was given to any team that won fewer than 25% of its matches in the season. Beginning in 1999, the team salary cap was replaced by a total player payments cap, which included injury payments and payments for preseason matches and finals. Moreover, the equivalent of a minimum team salary was introduced, requiring a club to spend at least 95% of the total player payments cap on player payments. Genuine marketing and promotional activity was excluded from the new payments cap. The 1999 season was the first under the CBA for seasons 1999–2003. New minimum base payments (for first-, second-, and third-round draft selections) and new senior match payments were negotiated. A long-term injury list, a rookie list, and a veterans list were also introduced. Fifty-fifty gate revenue sharing was abolished beginning in 2000, with net gate revenue after deduction of match costs going to the home team. The equalization levy (a levy on all matchgoers paid into a central fund and distributed equally among the clubs) and the "blockbuster levy of AU$25,000 were retained and adjusted for inflation." The major change for 2002 was the reduction of the minimum team salary to 92.5% of the total player payments cap.

COMPETITIVE BALANCE IN THE VFL/AFL

Following the approach suggested by Noll (1988) and first applied by Scully (1989), competitive balance ratios have been used in the United States by Quirk and Fort (1992), Vrooman (1995), Berri (2001), and others to compare the closeness of competition within seasons. These ratios compare the actual performance of the league with the performance the league would have achieved if all teams were of equal playing strength by measuring the dispersion of teams' win percents over a season relative to the "idealized" dispersion when all teams are assumed to have equal playing strengths. The lower the deviation of the actual league performance from the ideal league value, the greater is the degree of competitive balance.

In a league of teams with equal playing strength, the probability of winning any game is .5. The value of the idealized standard deviation depends on the number of games (rounds) in a league season. Quirk and Fort (1992) point out that it follows from the properties of a binomial distribution that the idealized value of the standard deviation for the season-long win percent is equal to $(.5)/\sqrt{N}$, where N is the number of league games (rounds) in a season. The competitive balance ratio for each year can be calculated by dividing the actual standard deviation by the idealized standard deviation. The lower the ratio is, the more competitive balance there is in the league.

Table 1 and Figure 1 show the competitive balance ratios for the VFL/AFL based on the teams' win percent data for the home and away seasons between 1897 and 2002. An interesting feature of Figure 1 is the very high level of unevenness in the competition at the end of each of period, with two exceptions. The first is during WWII at the end of period 3 (1930–1944), before a "modified-form of gate sharing" was introduced. Perhaps the evenness during WWII was thought to be an aberration, and one impact of the war was to change the ideology of VFL administrators to a more egalitarian one. The other exception is at the end of period 6 (1985–2002) with the player draft and team salary cap, in which there is a noticeable downward trend in competitive balance ratios (improvement in competitive balance). One possible explanation for the various changes to different combinations of labor market devices and revenue-sharing rules is that the VFL/AFL perceived whatever system at the time to be ineffective, as evidenced by the very high competitive balance ratios (unbeknownst to these administrators) at the end of several periods. Club administrators and players might just have needed enough time to work out how to circumvent the particular devices and rules in operation at the time.

At the end of period 1 of free agency (1897–1914), the competition was very uneven. In each of the five years from 1910 to 1914 the competitive balance ratio was greater than 2 (with the exception of 1912, when it was 1.9322). At the end of period 2 of free agency and metropolitan zoning (1915–1929), the competitive balance ratio was above 2 for four successive years from 1926 to 1929. However, the introduction of the Coulter Law in 1930 did little to redress imbalance in competition, with the ratio remaining at 2 or above from 1931 until 1936, after an initial fall to 1.8659 in 1930. In all the years after 1936 until the end of period 3 in 1944, only once in 1941 was the competitive balance ratio above 2. As mentioned earlier, this result would suggest some motivation other than addressing perceived competitive imbalance as the reason for the introduction of a "modified-form of gate sharing" in 1945.

Table 1
Competitive Balance Ratios and Season Length (Rounds): VFL/AFL, 1897–2002

Year	Rds	CB Ratio	Year	Rds	CB Ratio	Year	Rds	CB Ratio
1897	14	2.1339	1933	18	2.0344	1969	20	1.6758
1898	17	2.2262	1934	18	2.2215	1970	22	1.7321
1899	17	2.1004	1935	18	2.1731	1971	22	2.1638
1900	17	1.6977	1936	18	2.0000	1972	22	2.2747
1901	17	2.1386	1937	18	1.8782	1973	22	1.8566
1902	17	2.0580	1938	18	1.7743	1974	22	1.8464
1903	17	2.1454	1939	18	1.9555	1975	22	1.6697
1904	17	1.4297	1940	18	1.3472	1976	22	1.3844
1905	17	1.8981	1941	18	2.0184	1977	22	1.9656
1906	17	1.9852	1942	15	1.9343	1978	22	1.4902
1907	17	1.1632	1943	15	1.2411	1979	22	2.0094
1908	18	1.8738	1944	18	1.9100	1980	22	2.0707
1909	18	1.9293	1945	20	1.9770	1981	22	2.3549
1910	18	2.0028	1946	19	1.7622	1982	22	2.2680
1911	18	2.1499	1947	19	1.8918	1983	22	1.5570
1912	18	1.9322	1948	19	1.7547	1984	22	1.6237
1913	18	2.2336	1949	19	1.6490	1985	22	2.0132
1914	18	2.0385	1950	18	1.9508	1986	22	1.8505
1915	16	2.0242	1951	18	1.8733	1987	22	1.6157
1916	12	1.5679	1952	19	1.8353	1988	22	1.6652
1917	15	1.2383	1953	18	1.9603	1989	22	1.7707
1918	14	1.7321	1954	18	1.2693	1990	22	1.8091
1919	16	1.9543	1955	18	2.0638	1991	22	1.8781

(*continued*)

Table 1   (*continued*)

Year	Rds	CB Ratio	Year	Rds	CB Ratio	Year	Rds	CB Ratio
1920	16	2.0000	1956	18	1.7533	1992	22	1.8749
1921	16	1.5855	1957	18	0.9813	1993	20	1.6713
1922	16	1.3123	1958	18	1.4011	1994	22	1.4078
1923	16	1.3070	1959	18	1.5546	1995	22	1.8387
1924	16	1.3693	1960	18	1.6415	1996	22	1.8540
1925	17	1.9225	1961	18	1.4561	1997	22	1.1555
1926	18	2.2132	1962	18	2.0548	1998	22	1.3121
1927	18	2.0794	1963	18	1.9413	1999	22	1.7139
1928	18	2.0367	1964	18	2.1731	2000	22	1.7678
1929	18	2.2812	1965	18	1.7213	2001	22	1.8586
1930	18	1.8659	1966	18	2.2751	2002	22	1.6096
1931	18	2.1257	1967	18	1.8810			
1932	18	2.1452	1968	20	2.0656			

At the end of period 4 (1945–1967), there is another period of significant competitive imbalance in the years before the introduction of country zoning in 1968. In the six years from 1962 to 1967, on three occasions the ratio is above 2, and two other years have ratios above 1.88. Finally, near the end of period 5 (1968–1984), just before the introduction of the team salary cap in 1985, there are four successive years (1979–1982) when the ratio is above 2. Indeed, 1981 (2.3549) and 1982 (2.2680) have the highest competitive balance ratios (the lowest levels of competitive balance) in the history of the VFL/AFL.

The most even year of competition in the home and away season based on the competitive balance ratios is 1957 (0.9813), but this observation is an outlier. The 1997 season (1.1555) is the second most even competition, followed closely by 1907 (1.1632), another outlier. As mentioned above, unevenness of competition peaked in the early 1980s, but since then there appears to have been a general downward trend in these competitive balance ratios.

Table 2 shows the average ratios for the six different identified periods. The average competitive balance ratio over the whole history (as of this

Figure 1
Competitive Balance Ratios: VFL/AFL, 1897–2002

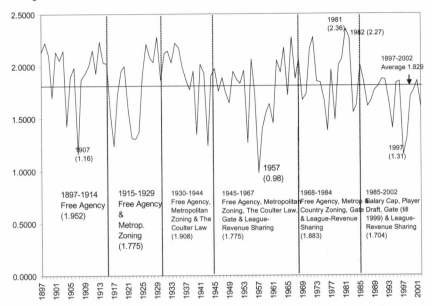

Table 2
Average Competitive Balance Ratios: VFL/AFL, 1897–2002

Periods of Labour Market Intervention and Revenue Sharing	CB Ratio
1. (1897-1914) Free Agency	1.9520
2. (1915-1929) Free Agency and Metropolitan Zoning	1.7749
3. (1930-1944) Free Agency, Metropolitan Zoning & the Coulter Law	1.9083
4. (1945-1967) Free Agency, Metropolitan Zoning, The Coulter Law, 'Modified Form' of Gate-Revenue Sharing and League-Revenue Sharing	1.7749
5. (1968-1984) Free Agency, Metropolitan Zoning, Country Zoning, 50-50 Gate-Revenue Sharing and League-Revenue Sharing	1.8829
6. (1985-2002) Team Salary Cap, National Player Draft (from 1987), 50-50 Gate-Revenue Sharing and League-Revenue Sharing. (Total Player Payments Cap and Minimum Team Salary from 1999, 50-50 Gate-Revenue Sharing abolished in 2000)	1.7037
(1897-2002) Average	1.8291

writing) of the VFL/AFL (1897–2002) is 1.8291. Period 6 (1985–2002) with the player draft, team salary cap, 50–50 gate revenue sharing (until the end of 1999), and league revenue sharing is the most even of any with the lowest average competitive balance ratio (1.7037).[2]

The most uneven period was that of free agency in period 1 (1897–1914), which has the highest ratio (1.9520). Moreover, the decline in competitive balance ratios (evening up of the competition) over time is evident, with two exceptions. Historically, period 2 (1915–1929) was one of a relatively high level of competitive balance (1.7749). Perhaps metropolitan zoning was accepted and effective until at least seasons 1926 to 1929, all of which have ratios above 2, indicating a relatively uneven competition at the end of this period prior to the introduction of the Coulter Law in 1930. Period 5 (1968–1984) was characterized by the introduction of country zoning to combine with free agency, metropolitan zoning, 50–50 gate revenue sharing, and league revenue sharing. Given the prevalence of transfer fee payments and interstate recruiting, this period had a lower competitive balance ratio (1.8829) than might have been expected. But, by the end of this period, the VFL/AFL was most concerned about what it perceived to be a very uneven competition, one in which the financial health of some of its member clubs was in jeopardy. This problem led the VFL Commission to reemphasize "financial equalisation" among the clubs and to introduce the team salary cap and then the national player draft.

COMPETITIVE BALANCE COMPARISONS WITH U.S. LEAGUES

Table 3 shows competitive balance ratios calculated by Vrooman (1995) for Major League Baseball (MLB), the American League (AL), the National League (NL), the National Basketball Association (NBA), and the National Football League (NFL) between 1970 and 1992. Table 4 shows Berri's (2001) ratios calculated for the same leagues for the years 1991 to 2000.[3]

Considering Vrooman's (1995) data first, the evenness of competition in the VFL/AFL between 1970 and 1992 compares not unfavorably with that in U.S. leagues. The VFL/AFL's average competitive balance ratio over the period from 1970 to 1992 was 1.858. The average ratios in the AL and the NL for the same period were only slightly lower, 1.826 and 1.761, respectively. The NBA was the most uneven with a ratio of 2.621, and the NFL was the most even with a ratio of 1.568. These ratios show the NBA to be a much more unevenly competitive than the VFL/AFL, which in turn is not quite as even as the NFL.

Berri's (2001) data reveal a similar pattern. The average ratio in the VFL/AFL over the period from 1991 2000 is 1.647, which again compares favorably with the AL (1.610) and the NL (1.701) over the same period. The NBA ratio (2.998) indicates an increase in unevenness in competition

Table 3
Vrooman (1995) CB Ratios: AL, NL, NBA,
and NFL, 1970–1992

Year	AL	NL	NBA	NFL
1970	2.410	1.564	2.182	1.537
1971	2.128	1.641	2.655	1.403
1972	1.744	2.103	3.400	1.701
1973	1.718	1.641	3.600	1.724
1974	1.154	1.974	2.418	1.478
1975	1.897	1.897	2.145	1.873
1976	1.564	2.051	1.909	1.873
1977	2.513	2.051	1.782	1.590
1978	2.231	1.615	2.018	1.376
1979	2.333	1.821	1.873	1.392
1980	2.051	1.590	2.764	1.496
1981	1.949	2.179	2.927	1.392
1982	1.769	1.590	2.782	1.704
1983	1.872	1.564	2.927	1.392
1984	1.487	1.385	2.091	1.680
1985	1.872	2.231	2.655	1.568
1986	1.410	1.923	2.618	1.672
1987	1.641	1.513	2.800	1.400
1988	1.949	1.949	2.873	1.344
1989	1.667	1.513	2.945	1.440
1990	1.462	1.462	3.164	1.624
1991	1.564	1.564	2.873	1.744
1992	1.615	1.692	2.891	1.656
Ave	**1.826**	**1.761**	**2.621**	**1.568**

Table 4
Berri (2001) CB Ratios: AL, NL, NBA, and
NFL, 1991–2000

Year	AL	NL	NBA	NFL
1991	1.49	1.49	2.81	1.71
1992	1.55	1.61	2.83	1.63
1993	1.34	2.29	2.81	1.26
1994	1.40	1.49	3.15	1.38
1995	1.93	1.51	2.87	1.20
1996	1.70	1.37	3.05	1.45
1997	1.53	1.42	3.40	1.43
1998	1.97	2.17	3.37	1.68
1999	1.88	1.94	2.83	1.47
2000	1.31	1.72	2.86	1.55
Ave	**1.61**	**1.701**	**2.998**	**1.476**

in this period, whereas the lower NFL ratio (1.476) suggests an improvement in competitive balance.

The ratios calculated by Vrooman (1995) and Berri (2001) for the period from 1970 to 2000 for the AL and the NL are plotted in Figure 2 with those of the VFL/AFL. In the 1970s, there was considerable volatility in the levels of competitive balance in the AL, but much less volatility in the 1980s and 1990s. During the 1970s, there were five years in which the ratios were well above 2, with 1980 being the last time the ratio was above 2. By contrast, the NL generally appears to have experienced less volatility than the AL, although there are four individual years in the 1980s and 1990s in which the competitive balance ratios have been well above 2. The VFL/AFL also experienced high levels of competitive imbalance in the 1970s and early 1980s with ratios above 2 in 1971, 1972, 1979 to 1982, and 1985. Since 1985, the year the team salary cap was introduced in the VFL/AFL, the ratio has not risen above 2.

The Vrooman (1995) and Berri (2001) ratios for the NBA and the NFL are plotted in Figure 3 with those of the VFL/AFL. Figure 3 reveals the consistently high levels of imbalance in the NBA with ratios above 2 in all

Figure 2
Competitive Balance Ratios: VFL/AFL, AL, and NL, 1990–2002

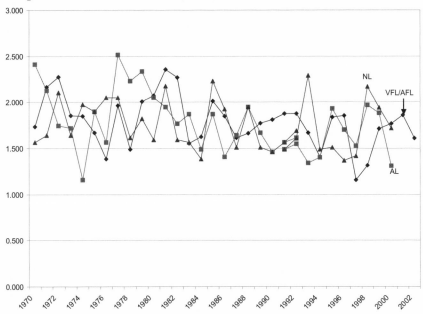

Figure 3
Competitive Balance Ratios: VFL/AFL, NBA, and NFL, 1990–2002

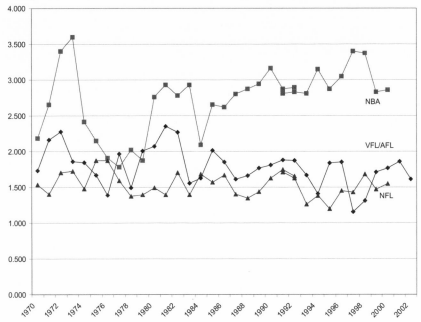

years except 1976, 1977, and 1979. If anything, there appears to be a long upward trend in these ratios from the late 1970s until at least the late 1990s. In stark contrast, the NFL seems to have a consistently high level of competitive balance, with the highest competitive balance ratio in any of the years between 1970 and 2000 being 1.873 in both 1975 and 1976. The VFL/AFL's improved levels of competitive balance since the mid-1980s are now at levels not too dissimilar to that achieved in the NFL.

CONCLUSION

We conclude this chapter by comparing labor market devices and revenue sharing used in the U.S. leagues, as outlined by Fort (2003), with those in the VFL/AFL in its most recent period. This is in addition to the different types of ownership resulting in profit-maximizing "teams" in the U.S. leagues and win-maximizing "clubs" in the VFL/AFL.

Competitive balance ratios between MLB and the VFL/AFL are not vastly different. MLB has had player drafts, but since 1976 players are eligible for free agency after six years of major league experience. Team salary caps have not been used, and media revenues vary enormously among teams, mainly because of local TV revenues not being shared.

There is more in common in terms of labor market devices and revenue sharing between the NFL and the VFL/AFL than there is between the NBA and the VFL/AFL, so it is not surprising that the levels of competitive balance achieved in the VFL/AFL are more akin to those of the NFL than of the NBA. The NFL has had a player draft, but since 1994 has had limited free agency, first for players with four years of NFL experience and later for players with five years of experience. There has been a team salary cap (and minimum team salary) since 1993, and with no local TV revenue and nearly all other revenues shared, revenues among clubs are the most equal of any of the leagues. The NBA has a player draft and had restricted free agency for players with four years of experience until 1988, and since then unrestricted free agency after four years of experience. There has been a so-called "soft" team salary cap in the NBA since the early 1980s, and with no gate or local TV revenue sharing, there is much more revenue variation than in the NFL, but not as much variation as in MLB.

The high levels of competitive balance achieved in the VFL/AFL from 1985 on appear to be highly correlated with the introduction first of the team salary cap in 1985 and then the player draft in 1987. These two labor market devices tend to reinforce one another, since a player cannot be drafted unless it can be demonstrated to the VFL/AFL that his anticipated salary can fit under the team salary cap. Although cash sales of player contracts are not permitted in the AFL, the trade of players and draft selections can partially undo the effects of the player draft. However, if the player draft is combined with a "hard" and enforceable team salary cap, and teams have the revenue to actually pay the team salary cap, in a win-maximizing world there appears to be little incentive for a club to trade away (net) player talent. Nor are there any financial incentives for (net) player talent to change clubs.

Club revenues have typically been large enough to allow even those with the lowest revenues to pay the team salary cap. If not for 50–50 gate revenue sharing over the years and league revenue sharing of key income streams from national broadcast rights (there is no local TV revenue), corporate sponsorship, and finals, the revenues of the smaller clubs might not have been sufficient to pay the team salary cap.[4] The team salary cap has been strongly enforced in recent years, with Essendon and Melbourne in 1999, Fremantle in 2001, and Carlton in 2002 having incurred especially large fines and national draft selection losses following team salary cap breaches.

In conclusion, these competitive balance ratios lend strong support to the view that in the VFL/AFL, a league comprising win-maximizing clubs, revenue sharing, a player draft, and the team salary cap have all played their part in helping to achieve a satisfactory level of competitive balance.

NOTES

1. The WAFC held 79% of the stock in Indian Pacific in 1998.

2. In Booth (2000), a hypothesis test was conducted to determine whether the mean competitive balance ratio (1.6940) for the period 1985 to 1998 was significantly lower than the mean competitive balance ratio (1.8547) for periods 1 to 5 (1897–1984) without the player draft and team salary cap. With a t statistic of 1.8889, there is a significant difference between the mean competitive balance ratio in the two periods at the 5% level. Alternatively, the p-value of the t test value is .03090.

3. Note the slight discrepancy in the estimates for the common years 1991 and 1992. One possible explanation for the discrepancy could be that one author assumed a sample and the other author assumed a population when calculating the actual standard deviation.

4. Fitzroy was an exception and was merged with Brisbane at the end of 1996. Although there is agreement that revenue-sharing arrangements in general have no impact on competitive balance in a league of profit-maximizing clubs, revenue sharing improves competitive balance in a league of win-maximizing clubs (see Késenne, 2001). In any case, 50–50 gate sharing was abandoned in 2000 in favor of the home team keeping the net gate receipts (after deduction of match expenses). Generally speaking, VFL/AFL clubs have kept their own home membership, reserved seat, and corporate box income. Increasingly, this meant that teams playing in small stadia filled mostly with members, reserved seat holders, and corporate boxes had little room for a cash-paying crowd, thus providing a poor return to the visiting team. Moreover, the practice of deducting match costs from the gate meant that only with a large cash-paying crowd were there any proceeds left to share with the visiting club. In

other words, the home team was not paying for its share of match expenses. With the home team keeping the net gate receipts beginning in 2000, there is also now more incentive to move home games to larger stadia with larger cash crowds.

20

Australian Professional Team Sports in a State of Flux

Braham Dabscheck

INTRODUCTION

Over the last quarter of a century, especially in the 1990s and continuing into the new millennium, major changes have occurred in the operation of Australia's leading professional team sports. Traditionally, with the exception of cricket, Australia developed city-based competitions. Respective leagues have transformed themselves from city to national leagues—in the case of rugby union to a bifurcated international competition—in seeking to maximize revenue from broadcasting rights, sponsorship, and merchandising, a process that intensified with the emergence of pay and cable television in the 1990s. Associated with this change, various sports have experienced "wars" between and/or have been subject to the threat of competition from rival leagues. The major labor market change in this period has been the "coming of age" of player associations. The 1990s witnessed the formation of such bodies in soccer (1993), rugby union, and cricket (both in 1995). Organizations had been previously formed in Australian rules football (1973) and rugby league (1979). With the exception of rugby league, these player associations have negotiated lengthy, complicated, and more or less sophisticated collective bargaining agreements with their respective leagues. Labor market rules in Australia were modeled on, or variations of, English, or world, soccer's transfer system. Beginning in the 1980s, Australian sports interchanged the transfer system for salary caps, drafts, and, in the case of soccer, free agency after a player has played for six years—labor market arrangements found in North America.

The major product and labor market changes that have occurred in cricket, Australian rules football, rugby league, rugby union, and soccer will be examined here. The chapter will draw on earlier work of the author (Dabscheck, 1989, 1991, 1993, 1996, 1998, 1999, 2000). Three peculiarities associated with the operation of Australian sports should be noted. First, respective sports have different "architectures." Australian rules football, rugby league, and soccer operate leagues that are similar to those in North America. Although cricket has a domestic competition, it is essentially an international sport—especially in terms of revenue generation—in which Australia competes against other nations, home and abroad. Rugby union, which only turned professional in 1995, comprises three state teams playing in an international league against teams from New Zealand and South Africa—the Super 12—and a national team (the Wallabies) in a regular Tri-Nations series, as well as intermittent matches against other nations. Soccer and rugby league also field international teams, and rugby league has a very popular State of Origin series between New South Wales and Queensland, whose implications are ignored here.

Second, different sports, despite their transformation into national competitions, are popular in different regions. Australian rules football holds sway in the southern states—Victoria, South Australia, Western Australia, and Tasmania. The two rugby organizations are dominant in the northern states of New South Wales and Queensland. Soccer does not enjoy the market appeal of other football games. Since 1989, it has been played in summer to avoid clashes with Australian rules football and rugby league. Cricket is the nation's summer sport. Third, with the exception of soccer, the leagues of respective sports perceive themselves as having a pastoral role for the development of community or grassroots sports. Resources are channeled from central cash cows to the periphery for administrative, coaching, and other purposes. Leagues seek to ensure both a ready supply of future playing talent and consumers to purchase various products associated with the production of their respective games.

CRICKET

Teams from different states compete against each other in a regular league format and against touring, usually national, teams. The Australian Cricket Board (ACB) instituted a residential rule for state selection and provided states with a right of veto against players who had represented their state, even in underage competitions, transferring to another state. In 1991, the Supreme Court of Victoria in *Nobes v. Australian Cricket Board* (no. 13613 of 1991, unreported) found such rules constituted an unreasonable restraint of trade.

The best state players are selected to represent Australia. Up until the late 1970s and early 1980s, players—Australian representatives, and more especially, state players—received low salaries. They were forced to supplement their income from other sources and/or retired prematurely. In the late 1960s, continuing into the 1970s, players became increasingly critical of inadequate payments and the poor treatment they received from the ACB. For example, in the 1974 to 1975 Ashes series against England, they received $200 a game. The gate revenue for the Melbourne test exceeded $250,000, with, of course, extra income from other sources. The sum of payments to all players was $2,400. Although it is unclear what the appropriate share of player income should be, and at the risk of putting words into their mouths after the fact, they thought 1% was somewhat small! Representations resulted in the ACB retrospectively increasingly payments by $357 per match. Nonetheless, a strong residual of player discontent remained.

Following the introduction of television in Australia in 1956—for the Olympic Games—cricket was shown on the publicly owned Australian Broadcasting Commission (ABC). In 1976, media magnate Kerry Packer sought exclusive rights for his Nine Network. The ACB demurred, having recently "shaken hands" on a new three-year deal with the ABC. Packer responded (retaliated) by signing virtually all the best players in Australia, West Indies, and other countries to form a rival competition known as World Series Cricket (WSC) (Haigh, 1993, provides the best account of this dispute). Players received salaries in the range of $16,500 to $35,000; on average, $25,000 plus incentives. In *Greig v. Insole* ([1978], 1 WLR 302), an attempt by the English cricket establishment to ban Packer players was found to be an unreasonable restraint of trade. (For a later case concerning "rebel" tours to apartheid South Africa see *Hughes v. Western Australian Cricket Association* [1986] ATPR 40-676.) In 1977, Australian Packer players formed the Professional Cricketers' Association of Australia (PCAA) to pursue their collective interests. It enjoyed a cordial relationship with WSC.

League wars end when rivals reach an agreement and merge, or the league with the deepest pockets destroys its opponent. The fly in the ointment, in this case, was the ABC. Following the expiration of its contract with the ABC, the ACB granted broadcasting rights to Packer's Nine Network. Per the arrangements that had operated during WSC, the top twenty to twenty-five players were offered contracts by the ACB, which provided them with "high-ish" incomes. The PCAA sought to continue operations after peace was restored, but it effectively folded in 1982 due to internal organizational problems associated with limited income and an inability to find leadership. The net effect of the WSC venture was to provide (future) leading players "decent" incomes.

In the 1980s, and continuing into the 1990s, there was occasional talk of establishing a new players' association. A major concern was the plight of state players. For the 1996–1997 season, it was estimated that 60% of players received less than $20,000. In September 1995, a new players' body was formed, the now-named Australian Cricketers' Association (ACA). In the latter part of 1997, it threatened strike action in attempting to gain recognition from the ACB and negotiate a collective bargaining agreement. The threat proved successful. The ACB eventually granted recognition, with an agreement being reached, after many months of negotiation, in September 1998.

The cornerstone of this agreement, which covered the 1997–1998 to 2000–2001 seasons, was a salary cap. Players would receive 20% of Australian cricket revenue, up to $60 million per annum, and 25% of any income over $60 million. For the 1998–1999 season, 57.5% of the players' share was allocated to twenty-five ACB contracted players and 42.5% to (approximately) 120 state players, resulting in an approximate doubling of income for state players. For administrative purposes, assumptions would be made about total payments to players for subsequent years, with such payments guaranteed by the ACB. If actual income exceeded estimates, players would receive a "top-up" bonus on a pro rata basis. For the 1999–2000 season, players received an additional $3.9 million (Ray, 2000).

A second four-year deal was completed in May 2001, which stated that players would receive a 25% share, "smoothed" over the life of the agreement. Provisions would be made for adjustment, up or down, if there were substantial variations in actual, from estimated, income. ACB contracted players would receive 55% of player income, state players 45%. The agreement contains minimum payments—retainers—for both ACB contracted and state players. Twenty-five players ultimately will be contracted to the ACB. Each state has between sixteen and twenty contract players and between two and five rookie players (less than twenty-three years old), providing state squads with approximately twenty-one players. Taking account of various caveats contained in the 2001 to 2005 agreement, it is possible to estimate annual earnings for ACB contracted and state players. Such information is contained in Table 1, together with minimum retainers. Compared to a quarter of a century ago, current, and future players can earn healthy incomes from their cricketing careers.

AUSTRALIAN RULES FOOTBALL

Australian rules football has, is, and will probably always be Australia's most popular team sport. The Victorian Football League (VFL), which commenced operations in 1897, was the sport's powerhouse. In the early 1980s, the VFL began the process of creating a national competition by moving a Melbourne-based club to Sydney. In 1997, the Australian Football League (AFL), the name change occurring in 1989, comprised sixteen teams—nine based in Melbourne plus one in Geelong (regional Victoria), two each in Perth and Adelaide, and one each in Sydney and Brisbane. This transforma-

Table 1
Minimum Retainer and Estimated Average Income for Australian Cricket Board and State Contracted Players, 2001–2002 to 2004–2005

Year	Australian Cricket Board Contracted Player		State Contracted Player	
	Minimum Retainer $	Estimated Average Income $	Minimum Retainer $	Estimated Average Income $
2001/02	95,000	456,000	22,500 (10,000)	74,000
2002/03	110,000	498,000	27,500 (12,000)	81,000
2003/04	125,000	539,000	32,500 (15,000)	88,000
2004/05	140,000	582,000	37,500 (17,000)	94,000

Note: Figures in parentheses are payments for rookie players.
Source: Memorandum of Understanding between Australian Cricket Board and Australian Cricketers' Association (2001).

tion witnessed the demise of Fitzroy in 1996, a foundation member of the VFL.

Since the mid-1990s, the AFL Commission has produced a variety of documents and discussion papers to strategically enhance the growth and commercial success of the sport. The AFL Commission champions equalization as the key to achieving such goals. In 2001, the AFL allocated slightly less than $3.2 million (plus variable additional amounts concerning other arrangements) from centrally raised revenue streams to each club. The AFL also provides hardship payments to clubs in financial difficulties to ensure that they remain competitive on the field, subject to such difficulties being unavoidable and said clubs developing business plans to overcome such problems. For the 2002 to 2006 seasons, the AFL has a broadcasting deal, with a consortium of News Limited, the Nine and Ten Networks, and Fox Sports, worth $500 million—approximately 10% being in contra.

Up until the 1980s, the labor market for players combined zoning with a transfer system (and, at various times, individual wage maxima). In the late 1970s and early 1980s, the courts, in a raft of decisions, found such rules to be unreasonable restraints of trade. See *Adamson v. West Perth Football*

Club ([1979] 27 ALR 475); *Hall v. Victorian Football League* ([1982] VR 64); *Foschini v. Victorian Football League* (Supreme Court of Victoria, no. 9868 of 1982, unreported); and *Walsh v. Victorian Football League* ([1983]) 74 FLR 207). In the 1980s, some clubs included an option clause in players' contracts. The option received endorsement from the courts in *Buckenara v. Hawthorn Football Club* ([1988] VR 39); also see *Hawthorn Football Club v. Harding* ([1988] VR 49).

During the second half of the 1980s, the VFL/AFL substantially revised its employment rules. It introduced a common roster for clubs (initially set at fifty-two players), a salary cap, and drafting. The salary cap originally varied among clubs, given contractual agreements with players, but eventually becoming a common monetary amount. Clubs can trade current players for draft picks. The draft comprises two elements. The external draft, per arrangements in North American sports, involves the selection of new players. The internal draft, a unique contribution of Australia to the myriad labor market rules, involves the selection of current players who have been unable to settle on terms with their clubs and/or have not been traded.

The Victorian Football League Players' Association (VFLPA) formed in December 1973, changing its name to "Australian" (AFLPA) in 1989. For the first two decades of its operation it found it difficult to obtain concessions from the league. In late 1992 it sought to negotiate a collective bargaining deal with the AFL. The AFL refused, and withdrew recognition of the AFLPA. The AFLPA responded by seeking an award from the Australian Industrial Relations Commission (AIRC). To avoid external scrutiny and the possible imposition of a quasijudicial body, the AFL, in an Australian version of what is known in North America as "labor exemption," decided to negotiate with the AFLPA, and an agreement for the 1994 and 1995 seasons was completed. It established a minimum wage of $7,500, with deductions for board and lodging, as well as various welfare, security, and leave benefits and a grievance procedure.

A second agreement was negotiated for the 1996 to 1998 seasons. It contained a clause whereby the AFLPA agreed that the AFL's draft(s) and salary cap were "necessary and reasonable for the proper protection and legitimate interests of the AFL." Other changes included increases to various minima, rules for players' intellectual property rights, and allocation of funds for second career training and for creating a player welfare advisory service. The 1998 to 2003 agreement built on many of these provisions. Payments to players, both global and minima, were increased—between 1998 and 2003 the former increased by 52.7%. Information supplied to the author by the AFLPA reveals that the players' share of (broadly defined) income for 2001 was 26.9% (remember the league's pastoral role). The salary cap has become "softer," with greater scope for earnings from servicing agreements and licensing arrangements. For 2001, such payments were in the order of $5 million. Several millions of dollars have been earmarked, for each year of the

Table 2
Total Player Payments, Club Salary Caps, Estimated Average Salaries, and
Minimum Payments: Australian Football League, 2000 to 2003

Year	Total Player Payments (million) $	Club Salary Caps (million) $	Estimated Average Salary $	Minimum Payment $
2000	76	4.75	103,261	24,000 (12,000)
2001	83	5.1875	117,898	25,000 (12,500)
2002	89	5.5625	126,420	36,000 (18,000)
2003	95	5.9375	134,943	37,000 (18,500)

Note: Figures in parentheses are payments for rookie players.
Source: Australian Football League and Australian Football League Players' Association
Collective Bargaining Agreement (1998–2003).

agreement, for player education and welfare, to be administered by the players' association. Table 2 provides information on total player payments, club salary caps, estimated average salaries, and minimum payments for seasons 2000 to 2003. Rosters for 2000 were forty-six; forty-four thereafter. The forty-four roster has two components—thirty-eight to forty primary players and four to six rookies. Rookies can be used to replace injured players, and their minima is half that for drafted, primary players.

RUGBY LEAGUE

In 1907, rugby league developed as an offshoot from the amateur game of rugby union over issues associated with recompensating players for lost time from playing and injuries/medical expenses (Cunneen, 1979). A similar development had occurred in 1895 in England with the formation of Northern Union. The professional rugby league historically recruited players from the amateur rugby union. We will see later that this story has a certain sting in its tail. The New South Wales Rugby League (NSWRL) commenced operations in 1908. By 1967, it had grown to twelve teams in a Sydney-based competition. In the early 1980s, the NSWRL embarked on expansion into regional New South Wales, Canberra, Queensland, other states, and New Zealand. In 1995, the now-named Australian Rugby League (ARL) had expanded to a twenty-team competition.

In 1995, with pay and cable television on the horizon, Rupert Murdoch's News Limited announced it intended to establish a new competition called Super League. The ARL's broadcaster was Kerry Packer's Nine Network. Australia's two leading media moguls locked horns. The ARL, in a bid to forestall clubs jumping to Super League, requested that they sign five-year commitment agreements to play exclusively in the ARL, and later on, loyalty deeds, confirming such commitments. A bidding war erupted for clubs, coaches, and, especially, leading players, with a concomitant increase in their income (see McCracken, 1996, 112–123, for details). Super League challenged the commitment agreements and loyalty deeds as breaching the Trade Practices Act 1974 and corporation law. The Federal Court of Australia found in favor of Super League (*News Limited v. Australian Rugby Football League* [1996] [64 FCR 410; *News Limited v. Australian Rugby Football League* [1996] 58 FCR 447; litigation involving players has been ignored here).

The 1997 season witnessed the now twelve-team ARL competing against the ten-team Super League. Both leagues bled to death. At the end of 1997, they announced a truce and the creation of a merged competition called the National Rugby League (NRL). It would comprise twenty teams in 1998, to be reduced to fourteen by 2000. South Sydney, a foundation member of the NSWRL, found itself excluded from the competition at the end of 1999. It initiated court action, claiming its exclusion breached the Trade Practices Act 1974. The Federal Court of Australia ruled for South Sydney (*South Sydney District Rugby League Football Club v. News Limited* [2001] FCA 862; *South Sydney District Rugby League Football Club v. News Limited* [2000] FCA 1541; *South Sydney District Rugby League Football Club v. News Limited* [1999] FCA 1710), which resumed playing in the now fifteen-team NRL in 2002.

Rugby league's "network wars" have not come to an end. In 2001, the NRL, which is 50% owned by News Limited, entered into a broadcasting deal with Fox Sport, in preference to Channel Seven's C7. On the surface, C7's offer appears to have been more attractive than Fox Sport's (although both contained caveats concerning subscription levels). C7 offered a seven-year deal of $70 million plus $10 million contra per year, compared to Fox Sport's six-year, $400-million offer, which included high levels of contra. C7 was forced to withdraw. Its parent, Channel Seven, has commenced proceedings against the NRL and Fox Sport.

Prior to 1960, the NSWRL operated a zoning, or residential, system that required local players to have lived in their zone for a year, with twenty-eight days' residency for country or interstate players. In 1960, it introduced a transfer system. In 1971, the High Court of Australia in *Buckley v. Tutty* ([1971] 125 CLR 353) (also see *Tutty v. Buckley* [1970] 3 NSWR 463), found the NSWRL's transfer system to be an unreasonable restraint of trade.

Following this, the NSWRL developed individual wage maxima, which it discontinued because of problems associated with enforceability. In 1975, the NSWRL introduced the "thirteen-import rule." Clubs would be allowed to "import" thirteen players from outside their residential zones; with adjacent clubs "married," or sharing zones. In late 1981, these rules were relaxed to allow an import who had played three consecutive years with a club to be regarded as a local, and players who had been with a club for five consecutive years could freely move to other clubs.

In May 1979, a players' association, in recent years known as the Rugby League Players' Association (RLPA), was formed. It initially experienced difficulties in gaining concessions for members. At the end of 1982, the NSWRL wanted to reintroduce a transfer system. Given the Tutty case, such fees could be conceivably protected from legal attack if endorsed by the players' association. The NSWRL and RLPA entered into a piecemeal bargaining relationship. Issues of concern would be discussed and considered. The RLPA never attempted to establish a comprehensive collective bargaining agreement. A formula based system of transfer fees, linked to levels of player proficiency, was introduced in 1983, with revisions, upward, in 1986 and 1988.

At the end of the 1980s, the NSWRL announced its intention to introduce a salary cap and drafting, following models earlier developed by the AFL (discussed earlier). The salary cap, introduced in 1990, varied among clubs, given existing contractual arrangements with players. The NSWRL introduced both an external and internal draft. Fears by existing players concerning the internal draft, fueled by leading coaches, resulted in a palace revolution within the RLPA and a new leader committed to mount a legal challenge to the internal draft. The Federal Court of Australia eventually found the internal draft to be an unreasonable restraint of trade (*Adamson v. New South Wales Rugby League Limited* [1991] 31 FCR 242; *Adamson v. New South Wales Rugby League Limited* [1990] 27 FCR 535). The NSWRL abandoned both versions of the draft.

This was the first time in the history of Australian sports that a players' association had initiated action against a league's labor market rules—and the RLPA had been successful to boot. It might be thought that such success would have helped to consolidate the RLPA's position, but events did not turn out that way. The RLPA failed in an attempt to negotiate a collective bargaining deal in 1992. In 1993, in an apparent move to increase its organizational effectiveness, it merged with the 35,000-strong Media, Entertainment and Arts Alliance (MEAA). The next three years were devoted to disputes over members between principals of the "old" and "new" unions. Moreover, after 1995, players were more concerned with cashing in on the bounty thrown up by the Super League war than worrying about player associations. In 1997, the MEAA negotiated a bare bones consent award with the ARL, under the auspices of the AIRC. It contained a minimum wage of

$36,000 for a club's first seventeen players (Australian Rugby League Players Award 1997, AIRC, A2491 A S Print P5383, September 25, 1997). In August 2000, this minima was increased to $37,245, applying only to ARL clubs in the NRL—including South Sydney, which had been excluded—to expire in August 2001 (Australian Rugby League Players Award 1997, AIRC, A2491 Print S9850, September 7, 2000). In 2001, the RLPA severed its relationship with the MEAA. Although the RLPA has access to the NRL, it has been unable to negotiate a collective bargaining agreement.

Since its formation, the NRL has imposed a salary cap of $3.25 million. With a squad of twenty-five players this translates into an average of $130,000. The NRL provides clubs with a $2.5 million annual grant from its revenue sources. Most clubs also receive grants from "parent clubs" (known as leagues' clubs) that provide food and entertainment, including poker machines, for patrons—that is, from poker machine income. In 2000, they ranged from $1.4 million to $4.5 million (McGuire, Dunne, and Ramsay, 2001). In recent years, rugby union has become increasingly successful (see the next section). It has begun the process of cherry picking leading rugby league players—well, three as of this writing—to join union. (In addition, an increasing number of players have signed with English clubs.) Despite squeals by clubs, especially those losing players, to loosen up the salary cap, the NRL has declined to do so, not wishing to enter into a bidding war for such players. Rugby league is still licking its wounds from the Super League war.

RUGBY UNION

Rugby union has traditionally been an amateur sport (with increasing elements of "shamateurism"). It has been historically vulnerable to player raids from rugby league, a fear that intensified during the Super League war. To overcome this problem, South Africa, New Zealand, and Australia formed a consortium and announced that they had signed a ten-year agreement (with a five-year option), worth U.S.$550 million, with Murdoch's News Limited (see Fitzsimons, 1996). Rugby union turned professional in August 1995.

The new consortium had not informed players of this development and, more important, had not signed them to contracts—after all, the players were amateurs. To add to the confusion, a newly formed organization called the World Rugby Corporation entered the market for players, offering "generous" contracts. A bidding war for players ensued, and the Australian players made a crucial decision. They would *collectively* decide on which of the rival organizations they would join. The Australian Rugby Union (ARU), in endeavoring to ensure that players signed with it, in what has become known as the Ferrier letter (Ian Ferrier being a member of the ARU board), agreed that 95% of Australia's share of Murdoch's television revenue would be distributed in accordance with a yet-to-be-formed players' association "direction," and $10,000 would be advanced by the ARU to this body to aid it in its organization. In what can only be regarded as a freak of nature, the Rugby Union Players' Association (RUPA) achieved recognition before its formation. The players signed with the ARU. The World Rugby Corporation disintegrated.

Once the dust of rugby union's rival league war had settled, RUPA experienced problems in enforcing its power of "direction," per the Ferrier letter. RUPA decided to test the contractual validity of the Ferrier letter in the courts. At approximately the same time, the ARU indicated its preparedness to enter into a collective bargaining agreement. Tentative bargaining commenced. After RUPA achieved an initial victory on security of costs (*The Rugby Union Players' Association v. Australian Rugby Union*, Supreme Court of New South Wales, no. 50225 of 1996, unreported), bargaining proceeded in earnest. An agreement was reached in October 1997, covering the next three years.

Like cricket, this agreement was based on a salary cap, or revenue sharing (being negotiated prior to the cricket deal). The players, 111, thirty-seven from each of three "states" (New South Wales, Queensland, and Canberra) would receive total guaranteed payments of a set monetary amount, or 25% of player-generated revenue, whichever was higher. Minimum payments of $55,000 to $67,000 were established, increasing over the life of the agreement, for the first twenty-one of the thirty-seven players on states' rosters, and $26,250 to $28,900 for players twenty-two to thirty-seven. The agreement contained clauses that said states could not collude in negotiating with players, and that there could not be any transfer, draft, or assignment rules introduced without the written consent of RUPA.

Rugby union has become increasingly popular with spectators and sponsors. This popularity, no doubt, has been aided by the success of the Wallabies in the 1999 Rugby World Cup. A second collective bargaining agreement was completed in April 2001, this author being part of RUPA's bargaining team. The 2001 to 2004 agreement increased players' share of player-generated revenue to 30%, with a more generous definition of such revenue. The bifurcated wage minima were abolished. A flat figure of $45,000 for 2002, adjusted each year for changes in the consumer price index, was established. State rosters were increased from thirty-seven to forty. To cover for injuries, players could be employed on casual contracts for up to four games in Super 12 games. If they played more than four games (including being a reserve), they had to be offered a full-time contract, at least equal to the minimum wage. Provision was also provided for each state to give up to three prospective players trials for three months, at a salary of $12,500, which could be repeated twice. Rules were introduced concerning the use of players' images and intellectual property rights, and $550,000 per annum was allocated to vocational and second career education as well as player welfare. Taking account of various caveats in the agreement, estimates of average player income are $135,000 for 2001; $145,000 for 2002; $155,000 for 2003, and $160,000 for 2004.

SOCCER

Soccer, the world game, the beautiful game, a game that in Australia, seems to be forever doomed, lurching from one self-inflicted crisis to the next. The National Soccer League (NSL) was formed in 1977, and it has proved to be a most unstable league. It has varied from twelve to twenty-four teams—forty teams have competed in the league. Clubs forever in financial straits, on the verge of insolvency, owe monies to players and creditors. Their survival has often been dependent on transfer fees from overseas for a star player (most of Australia's leading players well in excess of 100 ply their trade in overseas, mainly European, leagues) or on rich benefactors bailing them out. The NSL attracts small crowds. In recent years, it has averaged 5,000 or so spectators.

In addition, there has been much disquiet concerning the general operation of Australian soccer. During 1993 and 1994, there were rumors concerning maladministration, if not malfeasance, by officials, coaches, and agents in the transfer and selection of players; coaches demanding payments from players to be selected; and secret commissions and significant proportions of transfer fees from overseas clubs being directed to other, or unknown, parties. In June 1994, Soccer Australia announced the appointment of the Honorable Donald Gerald Stewart, a former judge of the Supreme Court of New South Wales and a former head of the National Crime Authority, to conduct an inquiry into Australian soccer.

Stewart's report was not published by Soccer Australia; it feared that those named would initiate proceedings to defend their reputations. The Australian Senate published the report (Stewart, 1995) under parliamentary privilege. Stewart said that soccer required a "sea change" to realize its potential and recommended that certain persons should not be involved with the sport. Most of those named stayed put. Different leadership teams have come and gone, with disputes occurring within the board. Soccer Australia has experienced financial problems, operating at a loss in recent years. It sold commercial exploitation of its rights to International Entertainment Corporation (IEC). In mid-2002, IEC began proceedings for an order stating Soccer Australia was insolvent. The matter was put on hold pending negotiations between the parties (*International Entertainment Corporation v. Soccer Australia* [2002] FCA 879). They reached an undisclosed settlement whereby the agreement was terminated. To overcome its financial problems Soccer Australia has imposed increases in levies for the registration of junior and adult players in local, invariably amateur, competitions. Soccer has the distinction of being the only Australian sport that is redirecting income away from the grass roots, rather than encouraging its development, to pay for errors and decisions of those at the top.

In April 1993, a players' association was formed, the now-named Australian Professional Footballers' Association (PFA). It merged with the MEAA in that year and went its own way in 1998. During 1994 and 1995, it proceeded with a case before the AIRC, seeking abolition of soccer's transfer system. In June 1995, the AIRC did not accede to this request. However, and this is quite a big however, the AIRC expressed disquiet concerning the transfer system's operation and gave the parties time to negotiate an alternative, as part of a comprehensive collective bargaining agreement. The AIRC indicated that if they could not reach an agreement it would, in all probability, abolish the transfer system in arbitrating the dispute (*Media, Entertainment and Arts Alliance v. Marconi Fairfield Soccer Club*, AIRC, Dec 1285/95 S Print M2565, June 9, 1995).

This labor exemption type of decision considerably strengthened the hand of the PFA. Two collective bargaining agreements have been negotiated since the AIRC's decision, and they contain two provisions that enhance the economic position of players. First, players who do not receive an offer of employment from their current club thirty days prior to the expiration of their contract, on "terms and conditions no less favourable than their previous contract," automatically become free agents. Second players who are twenty-six, or have played six seasons, automatically become free agents for the balance of their Australian careers—fees are still payable for overseas transfers. The former clause models developments in English soccer, after *Eastham v. Newcastle United Football Club* ([1964] Ch 413), and the latter, North American baseball, following Peter Seitz's 1975 private arbitration that brought about the end of the reserve/option clause.

Soccer has a minimum training list of eighteen players. For 2002, the minimum wage was $22,432, the same as the minimum adult wage determined by the AIRC (*Living Wage Case*, AIRC, PR002002, May 9, 2002). There were modest payments—$100 a week and $200 a game—for part-time players. In 1996, the average income of players was $20,000. By 2000, it had increased to $42,000; by 2001, to $43,000. The PFA believes that the major constraint limiting its ability to enhance members' welfare is the poor state of the game and/or Soccer Australia's lack of business and commercial acumen. Frustrated by Soccer Australia's lack of progress, the PFA, in 2000, obtained rights to the name Australian Premier League and in 2001, created PFA Management Limited to explore commercial opportunities for the sport (see the PFA Web site: http://info@pfa.net.au). In 2002, the PFA was searching for financial backers to establish a new league. This is the first time a players' association has embarked on such a venture since the 1890 attempt by the Brotherhood of Professional Baseball Players in North America.

SUMMARY AND CONCLUSION

In the last quarter of a century, especially since the 1990s, Australian professional team sports, with the obvious exception of soccer and question marks concerning rugby league, have become increasingly successful. Cricket, Australian rules football, and rugby union have enjoyed increasing revenue streams from spectators, sponsors, and broadcasters. The Super League war of the 1990s set back rugby league, an episode from which it has yet to recover. For its part, soccer has found itself in a sporting black hole. Leading players, particularly of cricket, Australian rules football, and rugby union can earn substantial incomes from pursuing careers in their respective sports. Rugby league players have seen their incomes decline from the heady heights of the Super League war. Despite soccer's problems, players' income has doubled over the last five years, admittedly from a low base. With the exception of rugby league, player associations are assuming an increasingly important role in the governance of their respective sports. They have combined threats of industrial action and various legal maneuvers in enhancing the rights, incomes, and other entitlements of players. It will be interesting to observe how product and labor market forces will intertwine in these respective sports as they compete with each other for their place in Australia's sporting sun.

Bibliography

Aidar, A. C., J. J. Oliveira, and M. P. Leoncini. 2002. *A Nova Gestão do Futebol.* Rio de Janeiro: Editora FGV, 2d edição.

Akers, C., and G. Miller (eds.). Various Editions. *The Rugby Almanac of New Zealand.* Auckland: Hodder Moa Beckett.

Andreff, W. 2000. "L'évolution du Modèle Européen de Financement du Sport Professionnel." In *Reflets et Perspectives de la Vie Economique 2–3.* Bruxelles: De Boeck Université.

Andreff, W. 2001. "The Correlation Between Economic Underdevelopment and Sport." *European Sport Management Quarterly*, 1 (4), December: 251–279.

Andreff, W. 2002a. "Sport Underdevelopment in Developing Countries and the 'Muscle Drain.'" Paper presented at the 4th Conference of the International Association of Sport Economists, Columbia University, New York, July 11–12.

Andreff, W. 2002b. "FIFA Regulation of International Transfers and the Coubertobin Tax: Enforcement, Scopes and Return. A Rejoinder to B. Gerrard." *European Sport Management Quarterly*, forthcoming.

Andreff, W., and P. D. Staudohar. 2000. "The Evolving European Model of Professional Sports Finance." *Journal of Sports Economics*, 1 (3), August: 257–276.

Antonioni, P., and J. Cubbin. 2000. "The Bosman Ruling and the Emergence of a Single Market in Soccer Talent." *European Journal of Law and Economics*, 9: 157–173.

Arnaud, P. 2000. *Le Sport en France: Une Approche Politique, Économique et Sociale.* Paris: La Documentation Française.

Arthurson, K. 1997. *Arko: My Game.* Sydney: Ironbark.

Australian Football League. 2000. *103rd Australian Football League Annual Report*. Melbourne.

Australian Football League. 2002. *105th Australian Football League Annual Report*. Melbourne.

Australian Football League and Australian Football League Players' Association Collective Bargaining Agreement, 1994–1995. Mimeo.

Australian Football League and Australian Football League Players' Association Collective Bargaining Agreement, 1995–1998. Mimeo.

Australian Football League and Australian Football League Players' Association Collective Bargaining Agreement, 1998–2003. Mimeo.

Australian Rugby Collective Bargaining Agreement, 1997–2000. Mimeo.

Australian Rugby Collective Bargaining Agreement, 2001–2004. Mimeo.

Baimbridge, M., S. Cameron, and P. Dawson. 1995. "Satellite Broadcasting and Match Attendance: The Case of Rugby League." *Applied Economics Letters*, 2 (10): 343–346.

Baimbridge, M., S. Cameron, and P. Dawson. 1996. "Satellite Television and the Demand for Football: A Whole New Ball Game?" *Scottish Journal of Political Economy*, 43 (3): 317–333.

Baker, D. 2001. "Why Do We Avoid Financial-Transactions Taxes?" *Challenge*, May–June: 90–96.

Ball, D. 1976. "Ascription and Position: A Comparative Analysis of 'Stacking' in Professional Football." In *Canadian Sport: Sociological Perspectives*, ed. Richard Gruneau and John Albinson. Boston: Addison-Wesley.

Barnes, J. 1983. *Sports and the Law in Canada*. Toronto: Butterworths.

Barnes, J. 1996. *Sports and the Law in Canada*, 3rd ed. Toronto: Butterworths.

Barnett, S. 1990. *Games and Sets: The Changing Face of Sport on Television*. British Film Institute.

Bernard, A. B., and M. R. Busse. 2000. "Who Wins the Olympic Games: Economic Development and Medal Totals." Mimeo, October 20. http://www.andrew.bernard.org

Berri, D. 2001. "The Short Supply of Tall People: Explaining Competitive Imbalance in the National Basketball Association." Paper presented at the 76th Annual Conference of the Western Economic Association International, San Francisco. Betriebswirtschaft, 72: 163–180.

Blainey, G. 1995. *A Shorter History of Australia*. Port Melbourne, Victoria: Mandarin.

Boardman, A. E., and S. P. Hargreaves-Heap. 1999. "Network Externalities and Government Restrictions on Satellite Broadcasting of Key Sporting Events." *Journal of Cultural Economics*, 23: 167–181.

Bolotny, F. 2002. "Les Clubs de Football—Ouel Modèle Économique Pour le Football Français?" Mimeo. Eurostaf/Centre de Droit et d'économie du Sport, Limoges.

Booth, R. 1997. "History of Player Recruitment, Transfer and Payment Rules in the Victorian and Australian Football League." *Australian Society for Sports History Bulletin*, 26: 13–33.

Booth, R. 2000. "Labour Market Intervention, Revenue Sharing and Competitive Balance in the Victorian Football League/Australian Football League, 1897–1998." Unpublished Ph.D. Dissertation, Monash University, Melbourne.

Borland, J., and J. Lye. 1992. "Attendance at Australian Rules Football: A Panel Study." *Applied Economics*, 24: 1053–1058.

Bourg, J. F. 1989. "Le Marché du Travail Sportif." In *Economie Politique du Sport*, ed. W. Andreff. Paris: Dalloz.

Bourg, J. F. 2000. "L'Economie du Sport." In *Le Sport en France*, ed. P. Arnaud. Paris: La Documentation Française.

Bourg, J. F. 2002. "Les Ligues Sportives Professionnelles aux Etats-Unis." In *Encyclopaedia Universalis*. Paris: Universalia.

Bourg, J. F. 2003. "L'avenir du Modèle Sportif Européen." In *Encyclopaedia Universalis*. Paris: Universalia.

Bourg, J. F., and J. J. Gouguet. 1998. *Analyse Économique du Sport*. Paris: Presses Universitaires de France.

Bourg, J. F., and J. J. Gouguet. 2000. *Economie du Sport*. Paris: La Découverte.

Bourg, J. F., and J. J. Gouguet. 2001. *Economie du Sport, Collection Repères*. Paris: La Découverte.

Bourguinat, H. 1987. *Les Vertiges de la Finance Internationale*. Paris: Economica.

Brown, A. 1996. "Economics, Public Service Broadcasting, and Social Values." *The Journal of Media Economics*, 9 (1): 3–15.

Brown, A., and M. Cave. 1992. "The Economics of Television Regulation: A Survey with Application to Australia." *The Economic Record*, 68: 377–394.

Bruggink, T. H., and J. W. Eaton. 1996. "Rebuilding in Major League Baseball: The Demand for Individual Games." In *Baseball Economics*, ed. E. Gustafson and L. Hadley. Westport, CT: Praeger.

Buchanan, M., and D. Slottje. 1996. *Pay and Performance in the NBA*. Greenwich, CT: JAI Press.

Burkitt, B., and S. Cameron. 1992. "Impact of League Restructuring on Team Sport Attendances: The Case of Rugby League." *Applied Economics*, 24, February: 265–271.

Buti, A. 1994. "Players' Associations: An Examination of Players' Associations and the Sporting Industry They Operate Within: Utilizing the National Basketball League Players' Association as a Case Study." Unpublished Masters of Industrial Relations Thesis, Department of Organizational and Labor Studies, University of Western Australia.

Cairns, J. 1988. "Uncertainty of Outcome and the Demand for Football." Discussion Paper 88-02, University of Aberdeen.

Cairns, J. 1990. "The Demand for Professional Team Sports." *British Review of Economic Issues*, 12 (28): 1–20.

Canadian Football League. Various Editions. *Facts, Figures & Records*. Toronto: Canadian Football League.

Canes, M. E. 1974. "The Social Benefits of Restrictions on Team Quality." In *Government and the Sports Business*, ed. R. G. Noll. Washington, D.C.: Brookings Institution.

Carmichael, F., J. Millington, and R. Simmons. 1999. "Elasticity of Demand for Rugby League Attendance and the Impact of BSkyB." *Applied Economics Letters*, 6: 797–800.

Carroll, G. R. 1984. "Organizational Ecology." *Annual Review of Sociology*, 10: 71–93.

Cashman, R. 1995. *Paradise of Sport: The Rise of Organised Sport in Australia.* Melbourne: Oxford University Press.

Cashmore, E. E. 1994. *And Then There Was Television.* London: Routledge.

Cave, M., and R. Crandall. 2001. "Sports Rights and the Broadcast Industry." *Economic Journal*, 111: F4–F26.

Cave, M., and R. W. Crandall. 2000. "Sports Rights and the Broadcast Industry." Paper presented at the SAL GROUP MEETING, December 1, Imperial College, London.

Cazeneuve, B. 2001. "Sittin' Pretty." *Sports Illustrated*, June 11, 94.

Cheffins, B. 1998. "Sports Teams and the Stock Market: A Winning Match?" *UBC Law Review*, 32: 271–291.

Chester, N. 1968. *Report of the Committee on Football.* London: Department of Education and Science.

Chester, N. 1983. *Report of the Committee of Enquiry into Structure and Finance.* London: The Football League.

Cockerill, I. 1998. "Leagues of Their Own: The National Obsession." *The Sunday Age*, February 22, 27.

Coffin, D. A. "If You Build It, Will They Come? Attendance and New Stadium Construction." In *Baseball Economics*, ed. E. Gustafson and L. Hadley. Westport, CT: Praeger.

Coleman, M. 1996. *Super League: The Inside Story.* Sydney: Ironbark.

Combe, E. 2002. *La Politique de la Concurrence, Collection Repères.* Paris: La Découverte.

Conn, D. 1998. *The Football Business: Fair Game in the '90s?* Edinburgh: Mainstream.

Cosentino, F. 1995. *A Passing Game.* Winnipeg: Bain and Cox.

Cowie, C., and M. Williams. 1997. "The Economics of Sports Rights." *Telecommunications Policy*, 21 (7): 619–634.

Cunneen, C. 1979. "The Rugby War: The Early History of Rugby League in New South Wales, 1907–15." In *Sport in History: The Making of Modern Sporting History*, ed. R. Cashman and M. Mcernan. Brisbane: University of Queensland Press.

Czarnitzki, D., and G. Stadtmann. 2002. "Uncertainty of Outcome Versus Reputation: Empirical Evidence for the First German Football Division." *Empirical Economics*, 27: 101–112.

Dabscheck, B. 1973. "The Labour Market for Australian Footballers." Unpublished Master's of Economics Dissertation, Monash University, Melbourne.

Dabscheck, B. 1975a. "Sporting Equality: Labour Market versus Product Market Control." *Journal of Industrial Relations*, 17 (2): 174–190.

Dabscheck, B. 1975b. "The Wage Determination Process for Sportsmen." *Economic Record*, 51 (133): 52–65.

Dabscheck, B. 1989. "Abolishing Transfer Fees: The Victorian Football League's New Employment Rules." *Sporting Traditions*, 6: 63–87.

Dabscheck, B. 1991. "The Professional Cricketers' Association of Australia." *Sporting Traditions*, 8: 2–27.

Dabscheck, B. 1993. "Rugby League and the Union Game." *Journal of Industrial Relations*, 35 (2): 242–273.

Dabscheck, B. 1996. "Playing the Team Game: Unions in Australian Professional Team Sports." *Journal of Industrial Relations*, 38 (4): 600–628.

Dabscheck, B. 1998. "Trying Times: Collective Bargaining in Australian Rugby Union." *Sporting Traditions*, 15: 25–49.

Dabscheck, B. 1999. "Running to the Same End: The Australian Cricket Pay Dispute." *A Q Journal of Contemporary Analysis*, 71: 52–56.

Dabscheck, B. 2000. "Sport, Human Rights and Industrial Relations." *Australian Journal of Human Rights*, 2: 129–159.

Daly, G. G. 1992. "The Baseball Player's Labor Market Revisited." In *Diamonds Are Forever: The Business of Baseball,* ed. P. M. Sommers. Washington, D.C.: The Brookings Institution.

Davies, B., P. Downward, and I. Jackson. 1995. "The Demand for Rugby League: Evidence from Causality Tests." *Applied Economics*, 27, October: 1003–1007.

Dawson, A., and P. M. Downward. 2000. "Measuring Habit Persistence Effects in Attendance at Professional Team Sports Encounters: A Cautionary Note." *Economic Issues*, 5 (1): 37–40.

de Brie, C. 1996. "L'Afrique Sous la Coupe." In *Le Sport C'est la Guerre*, ed. I. Ramonet and C. de Brie. Le Monde Diplomatique, Manière de Voir no. 30, Mai.

Deloitte & Touche. 2000. *Annual Review of Football Finance.* Manchester: Deloitte & Touche.

Deloitte & Touche Sport. 2002. *Annual Review of Football Finance.* Manchester: Deloitte & Touche.

Demmert, H. G. 1973. *The Economics of Professional Team Sports.* Lexington, KY: Lexington Books.

Dempsey, T. 1998. "The Role of Players' Associations in Professional Sport." In *Seminar Paper—Big Bucks in Sports Law: Volume 1.* Sydney: Continuing Legal Education Department, NSW College of Law.

Depken, C. A. 1999. "Free Agency and the Competitiveness of Major League Baseball." *Review of Industrial Organization*, 14: 205–217.

Dobson, S., and B. Gerrard. 2000. "Testing for the Rent Sharing in Football Transfer Fees: Evidence from the English Football League." In *The Economics of Professional Team Sport*, ed. P. M. Downward and A. P. Dawson. London: Routledge.

Dobson, S., and J. Goddard. 1995. "The Demand for Professional Football in England and Wales, 1925–1992." *The Statistician*, 44: 259–277.

Dobson, S., and J. Goddard. 1998. "Performance and Revenue in Professional League Football: Evidence from Granger Causality Tests." *Applied Economics*, 30: 1641–1651.

Dobson, S., and J. Goddard. 2001. *The Economics of Football.* Cambridge, UK: Cambridge University Press.

Donzel, J. 1999. *Rapport Sur le Recrutement, L'accueil et le Suivi des Jeunes Étrangers (hors Union Européenne) Dans les Centres de Formation de Football Professionnels en France*, 30 November. Paris: Ministère de la Jeunesse et des Sports.

Downward, P. M., and A. Dawson. 2000. *The Economics of Professional Team Sports.* London: Routledge.

Drever, P., and J. McDonald. 1981. "Attendance at South Australian Football Games." *International Review of Sport Sociology*, 16: 103–113.

Dunnett, P. 1990. *The World Television Industry: An Economic Analysis.* London: Routledge.

Eastham, J. 1999. "The Organisation of French Football Today." In *France and the 1998 World Cup*, ed. H. Dauncey and G. Hare. London: Frank Cass.

Eckard, E. W. 2001. "Free Agency, Competitive Balance, and Diminishing Returns to Pennant Contention." *Economic Inquiry*, 39: 430–443.

The Economist. 2001. "Charlemagne: UEFA's Gerhard Aigner." May 26: 52.

Eichengreen, B., J. Tobin, and C. Wyplosz. 1995. "Two Cases for Sand in the Wheels of International Finance." *Economic Journal*, 105, January: 162–172.

El Hodiri, M., and J. Quirk. 1971. "An Economic Model of a Professional Sports League." *Journal of Political Economy*, 79, November/December: 1302–1319.

Elmandjra, M. 1984. "Médailles Olympiques et Développement." *Futuribles*, October: 67–82.

Ericson, T. 2000. "The Bosman Case: Effects on the Abolition of the Transfer Fee." *Journal of Sports Economics*, 1 (3), August: 203–218.

Ericsson Cup [Soccer] Collective Bargaining Agreement, 1996–1999. Mimeo.

European Commission. 1998. "The European Model of Sport." Consultation paper of DGX.

Eurostaf. 1998. *Les Clubs de Football, Collection Dynamique des Marchés.* Paris: Les Echos.

Fama, E. F., and R. Roll. 1968. "Some Properties of Symmetric Stable Distributions." *Journal of American Statistical Association*, 63: 817–836.

Fama, E. F., and R. Roll. 1971. "Parameter Estimates for Symmetric Stable Distributions." *Journal of American Statistical Association*, 66: 331–338.

Fatès, Y. 1994. *Sport et Tiers Monde.* Paris: Presses Universitaires de France.

FIFA. 2001. *Règlement de la FIFA Concernant le Statut et le Transfert des Joueurs.* August 30.

The Financial Times. 2002.

Fishwick, N. 1989. *English Football and Society, 1910–1950.* Manchester: Manchester University Press.

Fitzsimons, P. 1996. *The Rugby War.* Sydney: Harper Collins.

Flynn, A., and L. Guest. 1994. *Out of Time: Why Football Isn't Working.* London: Simon and Schuster.

Football Association and Other English Football Authorities. 2001. "The Football Transfer System, an Interim Briefing Paper." September 25.

Forrest, D., and R. Simmons. 2002. "Outcome Uncertainty and Attendance Demand in Sport: The Case of English Soccer." *Journal of the Royal Statistical Society, Series D (The Statistician)*, 51 (2): 229–241.

Fort, R. 2000. "European and North American Sports Differences (?)" *Scottish Journal of Political Economy*, 47 (4): 431–455.

Fort, R. 2003. *Sports Economics.* Upper Saddle River, NJ: Prentice-Hall.

Fort, R., and J. Quirk. 1995. "Cross Subsidization, Incentives and Outcomes in Professional Team Sports Leagues." *Journal of Economic Literature*, 33 (3), September: 1265–1299.

Fort, R., and R. Rosenman. 2001. "Attendance and Uncertainty of Outcome in Major League Baseball." Unpublished Manuscript, Department of Economics, Washington State University, Pullman.

Fougere, G. 1989. "Sport, Culture and Identity: the Case of Rugby Football." In *Culture and Identity in New Zealand*, ed. D. Novitz and B. Willmott. Wellington: GP Books.

Franck, E. 1995. *Die Ökonomischen Institutionen der Teamsportindustrie: Eine Organisationsbetrachtung*. Wiesbaden: Gabler.

Frick, B. 1999. "Kollektivgutproblematik und Externe Effekte im Professionellen Team-Sport: 'Spannungsgrad' und Zuschauerentwicklung im bezahlten Fußball." In *Professionalisierung im Sportmanagement*, ed. H.-D. Horch, J. Heydel, and A. Sierau, 144–160. Aachen: Meyer & Meyer.

Frick, B. 2003. "Market Size and Survival in Professional Team Sports Leagues: Empirical Evidence from the German Bundesliga." Mimeo, Department of Economics, University of Witten/Herdecke.

Frick, B., A. Dilger, and J. Prinz. 2002. "Signing Bonuses and Team Performance." *Zeitschrift fq´r*.

Garland, J., D. Malcolm, and M. Rowe (eds.). 2000. *The Future of Football: Challenges for the 21st Century*. London: Frank Cass.

Gaustad, T. 2000. "The Economics of Sports Programming." *Nordicom Review*, 21: 101–113.

Gerrard, B. 2002. "The Muscle Drain, Coubertobin-Type Taxes and the International Transfer System in Association Football." *European Sport Management Quarterly*, 2: 47–56.

Getúlio Vargas Foundation. 2001. "Consulting Study for Confederação Brasileira de Futebol." Unpublished Manuscript, Rio de Janeiro, Brazil.

Goff, B. L., R. E. McCormick, and R. D. Tollison. 2002. "Racial Integration as an Innovation: Empirical Evidence from Sports Leagues." *American Economic Review*, 92 (1), March: 16–26.

Goff, B. L., W. F. Shughart, II, and R. D. Tollison. 1997. "Batter Up! Moral Hazard and the Effects of the Designated Hitter Rule on Hit Batsmen." *Economic Inquiry*, 35, July: 555–561.

Goff, B. L., W. F. Shughart, II, and R. D. Tollison. 1998. "Moral Hazard and the Effects of the Designated Hitter Rule Revisited." *Economic Inquiry*, 36, October: 688–692.

Gouguet, J. J., and D. Primault. 2001–2002/2003. "Analyse Économique du Marché des Transferts dans le Football Professionnel." *Revue des Affaires Européennes Law and European Affairs*, Mys and Breesch Editeurs, 305–323.

Grimes, A. R., W. J. Kelly, and P. H. Rubin. 1974. "A Socioeconomic Model of National Olympic Performance." *Social Science Quarterly*, 55: 777–782.

Guttman, A. 1994. *Games and Empires*. New York: Columbia University Press.

Haigh, G. 1993. *The Cricket War: The Inside Story of Kerry Packer's World Series Cricket*. Melbourne: Text Publishing Company.

Hall, S., S. Szymanski, and A. Zimbalist. 2002. "Testing Causality Between Team Performance and Payroll: The Cases of Major League Baseball and English Soccer." *Journal of Sports Economics*, 3: 149–168.

Hamil, S., J. Michie, and C. Oughton. 1999. *The Business of Football: A Game of Two Halves*. London: Mainstream Publishing.

Hamil, S., J. Michie, C. Oughton, and S. Warby (eds.). 2000. *Football in the Digital Age*. Edinburgh: Mainstream.

Harding, John. 1991. *For the Good of the Game: The Official History of the Professional Footballers' Association.* London: Robson Books, Ltd.

Harris, B. 1992. *Boom! Inside the NBL.* Sydney: Pan Macmillan.

Hart, R. A., J. Hutton, and T. Sharot. 1975. "A Statistical Analysis of Association Football Attendance." *Journal of the Royal Statistical Society; Series C (Applied Statistics)*, 24 (1): 17–27.

Hess, R., and B. Stewart (eds.). 1998. *More Than a Game: An Unauthorised History of Australian Rules Football.* Carlton South, Victoria: Melbourne University Press.

Hill, J. R., J. Madura, and R. A. Zuber. 1982. "The Short-run Demand for Major League Baseball."*Atlantic Economic Journal*, Summer: 31–35.

Hoehn, T., and S. Szymanski. 1999. "The Americanization of European Football." *Economic Policy*, 28: 205–240.

Horrie, C. 2002. *Premiership: Lifting the Lid on a National Obsession.* London: Simon and Schuster.

Houlihan, B. 1997. *Sport, Policy and Politics: A Comparative Analysis.* London: Routledge.

Howell, S. 2002. "NBL to Buy Media Group's $3.5m Share." *The Age*, Sport, April 12, 4.

Humphreys, B. R. 2002. "Alternative Measures of Competitive Balance in Sports Leagues." *Journal of Sports Economics*, 3: 133–148.

Hutchinson, G., and J. Ross (eds.). 1998. *The Clubs: The Complete History of Every Club in the VFL/AFL.* Ringwood: Penguin Books.

ICAA Annual Survey of AFL Clubs Financial Reporting. 2002. Melbourne: The Institute of Chartered Accountants in Australia (Victorian Branch).

The Independent. 2002.

Inglis, S. 1988. *League Football and the Men Who Made It.* London: Willow Books.

Japan Baseball Organization. 2000. *Japan Baseball Record Book.* [In Japanese].

Jeanrenaud, C., and S. Késenne (eds.). 1999. *Competition Policy in Professional Sports: Europe after the Bosman Case.* Antwerp: Standaard Editions, Ltd.

Jennett, N. 1984. "Attendances, Uncertainty of Outcome and Policy in Scottish League Football." *Scottish Journal of Political Economy*, 31 (2): 175–197.

Johnsen, H. 2000. "The Economics of the Listed Events." Unpublished Paper, Centre for Media Economics. Norwegian School of Management.

Jones, J.C.H., J. A. Schofield, and D.E.A. Giles. 2000. "Our Fans in the North: The Demands for British Rugby League." *Applied Economics*, 32: 1877–1887.

Kagan World Media Ltd. 2000. *European TV Sports Databook.* London: Kagan World Media, Ltd.

Kahane, L., and S. Shmanske. 1997. "Team Roster Turnover and Attendance in Major League Baseball." *Applied Economics*, 29 (4): 425–431.

Kahn, L. M. 1993. "Managerial Quality, Team Success, and Individual Player Performance in Major League Baseball." *Industrial Labor Relations Review*, 46, April: 531–547.

Kaldor, N. 1950. "The Economics of Advertising." *Review of Economic Studies*, June: 87.

Kawaura, A., and S. J. La Croix. 2002. "The Designated Hitter Rule and Pitcher Behavior: New Evidence from Japanese Baseball." Working Paper, Department of Economics, University of Hawaii.

Késenne, S. 1996. "League Management in Professional Team Sports with Win Maximizing Clubs." *European Journal for Sport Management*, 2 (2): 14–22.

Késenne, S. 1997. "L'affaire Bosman et L'économie du Sport Professionnel." Problèmes Économiques 2503, La Documentation Française, Paris.

Késenne, S. 1999. "Player Market Regulation and Competitive Balance in a Win Maximizing Scenario." In *Competition Policy in Professional Sports: Europe after the Bosman Case*, ed. C. Jeanrenaud and S. Késenne. Antwerp: Standaard Editions.

Késenne, S. 2000. "Revenue Sharing and Competitive Balance in Professional Team Sports." *Journal of Sports Economics*, 1: 56–65.

Késenne, S. 2001. "The Different Impact of Different Revenue Sharing Systems on the Competitive Balance in Professional Team Sports." *European Sport Management Quarterly*, 1 (3): 210–218.

Khoshaba, T. 1998. "Employment Contracts in Rugby League: 1907–1997." Unpublished Thesis, Masters of Industrial Relations and Human Resource Management (Honors), University of Sydney.

Kidane, F. 1996. "Le Gouvernement: Premier Commanditaire Dans les Pays en Développement." In *Sources de Financement du Sport*, Message Olympique. July–September: 96–98.

Kipker, I. 2000. "Determinanten der Zuschauernachfrage im Professionellen Teamsport: Wie Wichtig ist die Sportliche Ausgeglichenheit?" Unpublished Chapter of Ph.D. Dissertation.

Knowles, G., K. Sherony, and M. Haupert. 1992. "The Demand for Major League Baseball: A Test of the Uncertainty of Outcome Hypothesis." *The American Economist*, 36: 72–80.

Koninklijke Nederlandsche Voetbalbond. 2000. *Financial Development of Dutch Professional Football from 1995 till 1999*. Holland.

Korean Baseball Organization. 2001. *Korean Official Baseball Guide*. Seoul. [In Korean].

Kuypers, T. 1996. "The Beautiful Game? An Econometric Study of Why People Watch English Football." Discussion Papers in Economics 96-01, University College, London.

La Croix, S. J., and A. Kawaura. 1999. "Rule Changes and Competitive Balance in Japanese Professional Baseball." *Economic Inquiry*, 37, April: 353–368.

Lavoie, M. 1997. *Avantage Numérique: L'argent et la League Nationale de Hockey*. Hull: Editions Vents d'ouest.

Lavoie, M. 2000. "La Proposition d'invariance Dans un Monde où les Équipes Maximisent la Performance Sportive." In *Reflets et Perspectives de la Vie Economique 2–3*. Bruxelles: De Boeck Université.

Lavoie, M., G. Grenier, and S. Coulombe. 1987. "Discrimination and Performance in the National Hockey League." *Canadian Public Policy*, 13 (4): 407–422.

Lee, Y. H. 2002. "Decline of Attendance in Korean Baseball League: Economic Crisis or Competitive Imbalance." Unpublished Manuscript, Department of Economics, Hansung University, Seoul, Korea.

Levine, N. 1974. "Why Do Countries Win Olympic Medals? Some Structural Correlates of Olympic Games Success: 1972." *Sociology and Social Research*, 58: 353–360.

Levitt, S. D. 1998. "The Hazards of Moral Hazard: Comment on Goff, Shughart, and Tollison." *Economic Inquiry*, 36, October: 685–687.

Longley, N. 1995. "Salary Discrimination in the NHL: The Effects of Team Location." *Canadian Public Policy*, 2 (4): 413–422.

Los Angeles Times. 2000. Figures reported August 3: B2.

Macdonald, R. Forthcoming. "League Structures, Labour Markets and Competitive Balance: A Study of Australian Professional Sporting Leagues." Unpublished Ph.D. Thesis, University of Melbourne.

Manssur, J. C., and M. A. Neto. 2002. "As Recentes Slterações Na Lei Pelé." In *A Nova Gestão do Futebol*, ed. Antônio C. Aidar, João J. Oliveira, and Marvio P. Leoncini. Rio de Janeiro: Editora FGV, 2 edição.

Marcum, J. P., and T. M. Greenstein. 1985. "Factors Affecting Attendance in Major League Baseball: A Within-Season Analysis." *Sociology of Sport Journal*, 2: 314–322.

Mason, T. 1980. *Association Football and English Society, 1863–1915.* New York: Harvester Press.

Masters, R. 1990. "Packer's TV Deal on Rugby League Will Have a Heavy Knock-on Effect." *Sydney Morning Herald*, November 10, 27.

Masters, R. 1997. *Inside Out: Rugby League under Scrutiny.* Sydney: Ironbark.

McCaw, M. 2001. "Chairman's Speech to 'Annual General Meeting 10 April 2001.'" Wellington: NZRFU.

McCracken, J., with D. Lane. 1996. *A Family Betrayal: One Man's Super League War.* Sydney: Ironbark.

McGill, C. 2001. *Football Inc: How Soccer Fans Are Losing the Game.* London: Satin.

McGuire, M., J. Dunne, and A. Ramsay. 2001. "Clubs Drop the Ball on Profit Goals." *The Australian*, August 4.

McMillan, J. 1997. "Rugby Meets Economics." *New Zealand Economic Papers*, 31: 93–114.

Meadows, S. 2002. Personal communication from National Basketball League Competitions Manager regarding NBL attendances. September 12.

Megalogenis, G. 2002. "Salary Cap Cannot Fit a Competitive Team." *The Australian*, 6.

Memorandum of Understanding between Australian Cricket Board and Australian Cricketers' Association. 1998. Mimeo, September 15.

Memorandum of Understanding between Australian Cricket Board and Australian Cricketers' Association. 2001. Mimeo, May 24.

Middleton, D. (ed.). 1995. *Rugby League 1995.* Sydney: HarperSports.

Middleton, D. (ed.). 2001. *Rugby League 2001.* Sydney: HarperSports.

Mignon, P. 2002. "L'argent du Football." *Pouvoirs*, 101, 2d semester.

MINTEL Report. 1997. *The Football Business.* London: Mintel International Group, Ltd.

Moorhouse, G. 1995. *The Official History of Rugby League.* London: Hodder and Stoughton.

Moorhouse, H. F. 1999. "Football Post-Bosman: The Real Issues." In *Competition Policy in Professional Sports: Europe after the Bosman Case*, ed. C. Jeanrenaud and S. Késenne. Antwerp: Standaard.

Moorhouse, H. F. 2000. "The Redistribution of Income in European Professional

Football: Past, Present and Future." *Reflets et Perspectives de la Vie Economique*, 309: 2, 3.

Moorhouse, H. F. 2002. "The Distribution of Income in European Football: Big Clubs, Small Countries, Major Problems." In *Transatlantic Sport*, ed. C. Baros, M. Ibrahimo, and S. Szymanski. Camberley: Edward Elgar.

Morrow, S. 1999. *The New Business of Football: Accountability and Finance in Football*. London: Macmillan.

Mulgan, J. 1947. *Report on Experience*. London: Oxford University Press.

Musgrave, R. 1959. *The Theory of Public Finance*. New York: McGraw-Hill.

Nadel, D. 1998. "The League Goes National, 1986–1997." In *More Than a Game: An Unauthorised History of Australian Rules Football*, ed. R. Hess and B. Stewart. Melbourne: Melbourne University Press.

The National Soccer League Collective Bargaining Agreement. 1999–2003. Mimeo (as extended).

NBL Management Ltd. 1995. *The National Basketball League*.

Neale, W. C. 1964. "The Peculiar Economics of Professional Sport." *Quarterly Journal of Economics*, 78 (1), February: 1–14.

Noll, R. G. 1988. "Professional Basketball." Paper presented at the Stanford University Studies in Industrial Economics.

Noll, R. G. 1999. "Competition Policy in European Sports after the Bosman Case." In *Competition Policy in Professional Sports: Europe after the Bosman Case*, ed. C. Jeanrenaud and S. Késenne. Antwerp: Standaard Editions.

Noll, R. G. 2002. "The Economics of Promotion and Relegation in Sports Leagues: The Case of English Football." *Journal of Sports Economics*, 3 (2): 169–203.

Noll, R. G. (ed.). 1974. *Government and the Sports Business*. Washington, D.C.: The Brookings Institution.

NZRFU. 2000. "NZRFU 2000 Annual Report." Wellington: NZRFU.

NZRFU. 2001. "NZRFU 2000 Annual Report." Wellington: NZRFU.

NZRFU. 2002a. "Air New Zealand NPC Media Guide 2002." Wellington: NZRFU.

NZRFU. 2002b. "Air New Zealand NPC Player Eligibility." Special Circular to Unions, no. 2002/31. Wellington: NZRFU.

Obel, C. 2001. "Unions, Leagues and Franchises: The Social Organisation of Rugby Union in New Zealand." Unpublished Ph.D. Thesis, University of Canterbury, Christchurch.

The Observer. 2002.

Owen, P. D., and C. R. Weatherston. 2002a. "Uncertainty of Outcome and Super 12 Attendance: Application of a General-to-Specific Modelling Strategy." Economics Discussion Paper 0211, University of Otago.

Owen, P. D., and C. R. Weatherston. 2002b. "Professionalization of New Zealand Rugby Union: Historical Background, Structural Changes and Competitive Balance." Economics Discussion Paper 0214, University of Otago.

Palley, T. 2001. "Destabilizing Speculation and the Case for an International Currency Transactions Tax." *Challenge*, May–June: 70–89.

Palmer, B. 1998. *National Basketball League General Managers Report*.

Pascoe, R. 1995. *The Winter Game: The Complete History of Australian Football*. Melbourne: The Text Publishing Company.

Peel, D., and D. Thomas. 1988. "Outcome Uncertainty and the Demand for Football: An Analysis of Match Attendances in the English Football League." *Scottish Journal of Political Economy*, 35 (3): 242–249.

Peel, D. A., and D. A. Thomas. 1992. "The Demand for Football: Some Evidence on Outcome Uncertainty." *Empirical Economics*, 17: 323–331.

Perrine, J. 2000. "Conflicts in Australian Traditional Professional Sports Leagues: Rationalisation of Individual Clubs in the National Rugby League." *Competition & Consumer Law Journal*, 7: 266–280.

Pollard, R. 2002. "Evidence of a Reduced Home Advantage When a Team Moves to a New Stadium." *Journal of Sports Sciences*, 20: 969–974.

Pommerehne, W., and B. Frey. 1993. *La Culture a-t-elle un Prix ? Essais sur Paris*. Paris: Plon.

Portuguese National Sports Ministry. 2002. Personal communication.

PricewaterhouseCoopers. 2000. *Financial Review of Scottish Football for Season 1998/99*. Edinburgh: PricewaterhouseCoopers.

Primault, D. 2001. "De la Nécessaire Régulation Économique des Sports Collectifs Professionnels." *Revue d'administration Publique*, 97.

Primault, D., and A. Rouger. 1999. "How Relevant Is North American Experience for Professional Team Sports in Europe?" In *Competition Policy in Professional Sports: Europe after the Bosman Case*, ed. C. Jeanrenaud and S. Késenne. Antwerp: Standaard Editions Ltd.

Quirk, J., and R. D. Fort. 1992. *Pay Dirt: The Business of Professional Team Sports*. Princeton: Princeton University Press. (Paperback edition, 1997.)

Quirk, J., and R. D. Fort. 1999. *Hard Ball: The Abuse of Power in Pro Team Sports*. Princeton: Princeton University Press.

Rasmussen, Eric. 2001. *Games and Information. An Introduction to Game Theory*. Oxford, UK: Blackwell Publishers.

Ray, M. 2000. "$4m Bonus for Top Players." *Sydney Morning Herald*, September 15.

Ross, S. 1989. "Monopoly Sports Leagues." *University of Minnesota Law Review*, 73: 643.

Ross, S. 1999. "Restraints on Player Competition That Facilitate Competitive Balance and Player Development and Their Legality in the United States and in Europe." In *Competition Policy in Professional Sports: Europe after the Bosman Case*, ed. C. Jeanrenaud and S. Késenne. Antwerp: Standaard Editions.

Ross, S., and S. Szymanski. 2002. "Open Competition in League Sports." *Wisconsin Law Review*, 3: 625–656.

Rottenberg, S. 1956. "The Baseball Players' Labor Market." *Journal of Political Economy*, 64 (4), June: 242–260.

Rouger, A. 2000. "La Régulation des Championnats de Sports Collectifs Professionnels: Entre Équilibre Compétitif et Équilibre Concurrentiel." Thèse de Doctorat en Sciences Économiques, Université de Limoges, France.

Rousseau, J.-J. 1915. "Considerations on the Government of Poland and on Its Proposed Reformation." In *The Political Writings of Jean-Jacques Rousseau*, Vol. 11, by C. E. Vaughan. Cambridge: Cambridge University Press.

Sandercock, L., and I. Turner. 1981. *Up Where, Cazaly?* Sydney: Granada.

Sanderson, A., and J. Siegfried. 1997. "The Implications of Athlete Freedom to Contract: Lessons from North America." *Economic Affairs*, 17: 7–12.

Schofield, J. 1983a. "The Demand for Cricket: The Case of the John Player League." *Applied Economics*, 15: 283–296.

Schofield, J. 1983b. "Performance and Attendance at Professional Team Sports." *Journal of Sports Behavior*, 6: 196–206.

Schulze, G. G. 2000. *The Political Economy of Capital Controls.* Cambridge: Cambridge University Press.

Scully, G. 1989. *The Business of Major League Baseball.* Chicago: University of Chicago Press.

Scully, G. 1995. *The Market Structure of Sports.* Chicago: University of Chicago Press.

Seners, P. 1999. *L'EPS, Son Histoire, sa Genèse.* Paris: Editions Vigot.

Sévilla, J.-J. 1997. "En Huit Ans, 2004 Footballeurs Brésiliens Ont Choisi l'exil." *Le Monde*, July 31.

Sévilla, J.-J. 1998. "Au Brésil, les Footballeurs ne Roulent Pas sur l'or." *Le Monde*, July 4.

Seymour, H. 1971. *Baseball: The Golden Age.* New York: Oxford University Press.

Shilbury, D. 1994. "A Study of the Strategic Planning Practices of the Australian Football League Clubs." Unpublished Ph.D. Dissertation, Monash University, Melbourne.

Shilbury, D., and J. Deane. 2001. *Sport Management in Australia: An Organisational Overview.* East Bentleigh, Victoria: Strategic Sport Management.

Shishkin, P. 2001a. "Europe Soccer Faces Shootout in Transfer Fees." *Wall Street Journal*, January 3, B5B.

Shishkin, P. 2001b. "Europe's Soccer Clubs Can't Stop Belgian Lawyer." *Wall Street Journal*, January 22, B1.

Shoebridge, N. 1989. "League's New Tack Wins Converts." *Business Review Weekly*, October 12, 164.

Siegfried, J., and A. Zimbalist. 2000. "The Economics of Sports Facilities and Their Communities." *Journal of Economic Perspectives*, 14: 95–114.

Siegfried, J. J., and J. D. Eisenberg. 1980. "The Demand for Minor League Baseball." *Atlantic Economic Journal*, 8: 56–69.

Simmons, R. 1996. "The Demand for English League Football: A Club-Level Analysis." *Applied Economics*, 28 (2): 139–155.

Simmons, R. 1997. "Implications of the Bosman Ruling for Football Transfer Markets." *Economic Affairs*, 17: 13–18.

Sloane, P. 1971. "The Economics of Professional Football: The Football Club as a Utility Maximizer." *Scottish Journal of Political Economy*, 17, June: 121–145.

Sloane, P. J. 1969. "The Labour Market in Professional Football." *British Journal of Industrial Relations*, 7: 181–199.

Sloane, P. J. 1976. "Restrictions of Competition in Professional Team Sports." *Bulletin of Economic Research*, 28: 3–22.

Sloane, P. J. 1997. "The Economics of Sport: An Overview." *Institute of Economic Affairs*, 17 (3): 2–6.

Solberg, H. A. 2002a. "The Economics of Television Sports Rights. Europe and the U.S.—A Comparative Analysis." *Norsk Medietidsskrift*, 9 (2): 57–80.

Solberg, H. A. 2002b. "The European Commission's Listed Events Regulation—Over Reaction?" *Culture, Sport, Society*, 5 (2), Summer: 1–28.

Solberg, H. A., and C. Gratton. 2000. "The Economics of TV-Sports Rights—With

Special Attention on European Soccer." *European Journal for Sport Management*, 7 (special issue).

Souchaud, Y. 1995. *Situation Sportive Dans les Pays Moins Avancés d'Afrique: Bilan.* Division de la Jeunesse et des Activités Sportives, UNESCO, Juillet.

Spahn, P. 1996. "La Taxe Tobin et la Stabilité des Taux de Change." *Finances et Développement*, 33 (2): 26–27.

Spence, M., and B. M. Owen. 1977. "Television Programming, Monopolistic Competition, and Welfare." *Quarterly Journal of Economics*, 91: 103–126.

Sport and the Law Journal. 2002. 10 (1): 118–121.

Sport 2000 Task Force. 1999. *Shaping Up: A Review of Commonwealth Involvement in Sport and Recreation in Australia.* Canberra: Commonwealth of Australia.

Sports Illustrated. 2001. "Go Figure." May 14, 29.

Staudohar, P. 1999. "The Scope of Pro Football's Antitrust Exemption." *Labor Law Journal*, 50: 1.

Staudohar, P. D. 1996. *Playing for Dollars: Labor Relations and the Sport Business.* Ithaca, NY: Cornell University Press.

Staudohar, P. D. 2000. *Diamond Mines: Baseball and Labor.* Syracuse, NY: Syracuse University Press.

Stensholt, J., and N. Way. 2001. "Football's King Hit." *Business Review Weekly*, April 12, 46–52.

Stephens, T. 1993. "Kerry's Coup: League on Nine until 2000." *Sydney Morning Herald*, October 8, 1.

Stewart, B. 1985. "The Economic Development of the Victorian Football League, 1960–1984." *Sporting Traditions*, 1 (2): 2–26.

Stewart, B., and A. Smith. 1999. "The Road to Competitive Balance in Australian Professional Team Sports: Regulation or Free Market?" Unpublished Manuscript, Victoria University of Technology.

Stewart Report. 1995. Report by the Hon. D. G. Stewart, Senate Environment, Recreation, Communications and the Arts References Committee, January 10.

Stickels, G. 1994. "Basketball's Star Status: It's Just Not Cricket." *Business Review Weekly*, October 16, 72.

Strutt, J. 1801. *The Sports and Pastimes of the People of England, London.* London: J. White.

Szymanski, S. 1998. "Hermetic Leagues, Open Leagues and the Impact of Revenue Sharing on Competitive Balance." Mimeo, Imperial College, London.

Szymanski, S. 1999. "The Market for Soccer Players in England after Bosman: Winners and Losers." In *Competition Policy in Professional Sports: Europe after the Bosman Case*, ed. C. Jeanrenaud and S. Késenne. Antwerp: Standaard Editions.

Szymanski, S. 2000. "Sport and Broadcasting." Paper presented at the Institute for Economic Affairs, October 18.

Szymanski, S. 2001. "Income Inequality, Competitive Balance and the Attractiveness of Team Sports: Some Evidence and a Natural Experiment from English Soccer." *Economic Journal*, 111: F69–F84.

Szymanski, S. 2003. "Statistical Dribble That Never Hits Goal." *Times Higher Educational Supplement*, January 24, 32–33.

Szymanski, S. 2003. "The Economic Design of Sporting Contests." *Journal of Economic Literature*, forthcoming.

Szymanski, S., and T. Kuypers. 1999. *Winners and Losers: The Business Strategy of Football*. London: Penguin Books Ltd.

Szymanski, S., and S. F. Ross. 2000. "Open Competition in League Sports." Law and Economics Working Paper Series No. 00-07, College of Law, University of Illinois.

Szymanski, S., and R. Smith. 1997. "The English Football Industry: Profit, Performance and Industrial Structure." *International Review of Applied Economics*, 11: 135–153.

Taylor, Lord Justice. 1990. "The Hillsborough Stadium Disaster (15 April 1989)." Inquiry by the Rt. Hon. Lord Justice Taylor, Final Report, Cm. 962, London: HMSO.

Thomas, D. 1997. "The Rugby Revolution: New Horizons or False Dawn?" *Economis Affairs* 17 (3): 19–24.

Tobin, J. 1978. "A Proposal for International Monetary Reform." *Eastern Economic Journal*, 4: 153–159.

Trandel, G. A., L. H. White, and P. G. Klein. 1998. "The Effect of the Designated Hitter Rule on Hit Batsmen: Pitcher's Moral Hazard or the Team's Cost-Benefit Calculation? A Comment." *Economic Inquiry*, 36, October: 679–684.

Tshimanga, B. E. 2001. *Le Commerce et la Traite des Footballeurs Africains et Sud-Américians en Europe*. Paris: L'Harmattan.

Turner, P., and D. Shilbury. 1997. "Sport on Television: A Study of the Australian Football League Television Rights." *Sport Marketing Quarterly*, 6 (3): 55–62.

UEFA. 2000a. "Final Report of the Task Force Set Up by the UEFA Executive Committee on the Subject of Salary Caps." UEFA Administration, December 14.

UEFA. 2000b. "The Football Transfer System: Report of the Task Force Sub-Committee on Economic Matters." Nyon, Switzerland: UEFA.

Utt, J., and R. Fort. 2002. "Pitfalls to Measuring Competitive Balance with Gini Coefficients." *Journal of Sports Economics*, 3: 367–373.

Vamplew, W. 1988. *Pay Up and Play the Game: Professional Sport in Britain 1875–1914*. Cambridge: Cambridge University Press.

Victorian Football League. 1985. *Establishing the Basis for Future Success*.

Vierne, J. J. 1998. "France Football." *Saga Africa*, 3, February.

Vrooman, J. 1995. "A General Theory of Professional Sports Leagues." *Southern Economic Journal*, 61 (4): 971–990.

Vrooman, J. 2000. "The Economics of American Sports Leagues." *Scottish Journal of Political Economy*, 47: 364–398.

Walker, B. 1986. "The Demand for Professional League Football and the Success of Football League Teams: Some City Size Effects." *Urban Studies*, 23 (3): 209–220.

Way, N. 1989. "Why Business Is Playing Ball." *Business Review Weekly*, August 31, 48.

Whannel, G. 1992. *Fields in Vision: Television Sport and Cultural Transformation*. London: Routledge.

Williams, G. 1994. *The Code War*. Middlesex: Yore Publications.
Zimbalist, A. 1992. *Baseball and Billions*. New York: Basic Books.
Zimbalist, A. 2002. "Competitive Balance in Sports Leagues: An Introduction."
    Journal of Sports Economics, 3: 111–121.

Index

About the Editors and Contributors

ANTÔNIO CARLOS KFOURI AIDAR is Professor of Economics at Escola de Administração de Empresas de São Paulo da Fundação Getúlio Vargas-(FGV-EAESP). He is the author of *A Nova Gestão do Futebol* (2002), now in its second edition. He is the author of several sports business articles and a regular speaker on radio and TV and at conferences and seminars in Brazil. Recently, he was an invited speaker at the London Conference on Football in the Americas, jointly organized by the Football Industry Group, School of Management, University of Liverpool, the Institute of Latin American Studies in London, and the Centre for Brazilian Studies in Oxford. In addition, Professor Aidar has testified before the Brazilian Congress Comissão Parlamentar de Inquérito on Brazilian Football management and the political and legal measures needed to bring transparency to the whole process.

WLADIMIR ANDREFF is Professor of Economics at the University Paris 1 Panthéon Sorbonne, Honorary director of the research team ROSES (CNRS), and the incumbent President of the International Association of Sport Economists. He is the author of dozens of articles and the co-author of four books (in French) on sports economics. He serves on the editorial boards of the *Journal of Sports Economics, European Sport Management Quarterly* (UK), and *Revue Juridique et Economique du Sport* (France). For years, he has advised and reported to the Committee for the Development of Sport and the meeting of Ministers for Sports of the Council of Europe, and he is still advising the French Ministry for Sports in developing a national economic accounting of sports.

ROSS BOOTH is Lecturer in Economics at Melbourne's Monash University. His PhD dissertation concerned the effectiveness of labor market and revenue-sharing devices in achieving competitive balance in the Australian Football League. Booth is a regular media commentator on the economics of Australian sporting leagues. In 2002, he taught sports economics at Monash, the first subject of its kind to be offered in Australia. He has helped administer amateur football in Melbourne since 1986 and from 1988 has broadcast football on ABC TV's coverage of the Victorian Football League and been the VFL columnist for Melbourne's *Sunday Age* newspaper.

JEFF BORLAND is Professor of Economics at the University of Melbourne. He has written on a variety of topics relating to the economics of Australian professional sporting competitions, and is on the editorial board of the *Journal of Sports Economics*.

JEAN-FRANÇOIS BOURG is Researcher at the Centre for the Law and Economics of Sports and professor at the University of Limoges. He is the author of ten books and sixty articles on sports economics. Professor Bourg serves on the editorial board of the *Journal of Sports Economics* and is a member of the International Association of Sports Economists. He serves as an expert for the Committee for the Development of Sport of the Council of Europe. Most recently, he has published two books with Jean-Jacques Gouguet, *Analyse économique du sport* and *Economie du sport*, which has been translated into Portuguese.

BRAHAM DABSCHECK is Associate Professor, School of Industrial Relations, University of New South Wales, Sydney, Australia. He has published more than forty articles on economic, industrial relations, legal, human rights, and historical aspects of professional team sports in Australia and overseas. He is on the editorial board of *Sporting Traditions* and a number of industrial relations journals. He is a past editor of *The Journal of Industrial Relations* and past president of The Australian Society for Sports History. Professor Dabscheck has been an expert witness in a number of sporting cases in Australia, a consultant to a number of Australian player associations, and a member of the Professional Footballers' Association Advisory Board since 1999. In 2001 he was part of the team that prepared FIFPro's submission to the European Commission on soccer's international player transfer system. He is a long-suffering supporter of St. Kilda in the Australian Football League.

CLARISSA BUENO DE AMEIDA has a bachelor degree from Escola de Administração de Empresas de São Paulo da Fundação Getulio Vargas (FGV-EAESP). In 2001, she worked as an assistant to professors Antônio Carlos Kfouri Aidar (FGV-EAESP) and Rogan Taylor (University of Liverpool Management School) on a project related to fan equity of Clube

Internacional de Porto Alegre, one of the biggest fan clubs of football teams in Brazil.

STEPHEN DOBSON is Senior Lecturer in Economics at Otago University, New Zealand. He has published numerous articles on the economics of professional team sports as well as being co-author with John Goddard of *The Economics of Football*. He serves on the editorial board of the *Journal of Sports Economics*. His other research interests are in industrial and development economics.

PAUL DOWNWARD is Professor of Economics at Staffordshire University Business School and the author of a large number of articles on sports, leisure, and tourism economics. He is the co-author of *The Economics of Professional Team Sports* and serves on the editorial boards of the *Journal of Sports Economics* and *Tourism and Hospitality Planning and Development*. As well as academic research, Professor Downward regularly provides research for public and private agencies working in the sports, leisure, and tourism industries. Professor Downward also has an interest in political economy and methodology and has published widely in these areas.

JOHN FIZEL is the Director of Pennsylvania State University's online MBA program, the *iMBA*. He co-edited (with Elizabeth Gustafson and Lawrence Hadley) *Baseball Economics* and *Sports Economics* and contributed a chapter on competitive balance in *Stee-rike Four! What's Wrong with the Business of Baseball?* and a chapter (with Randall Bennett) on college sports in Walter Adam's *The Structure of American Industry*. Professor Fizel has also published papers on a variety of sports economics topics.

DAVID FORREST is Senior Lecturer in Economics at the University of Salford, UK, and has published extensively in his fields of current interest, the economics of sport, the economics of gambling, and valuation issues in cost benefit analysis. He directs a major research project on state lotteries and is a frequent media commentator on sports and on gambling policy. His practical involvement with sport is as a keen cricketer.

RODNEY FORT is Professor of Economics at Washington State University, the author of dozens of articles and monographs on sports economics, serves on the editorial board of the *Journal of Sports Economics* and is a Vice President of the International Association of Sports Economists. He is a regular speaker and panel participant on sports issues both in the United States and Europe, as well as a frequent contributor to media discussions on the topic. His recently published textbook, *Sports Economics* (2003), follows two well-known books with James Quirk, *Pay Dirt* (1992) and *Hard Ball* (1999). Professor Fort also has testified before the U.S. Senate on competitive balance issues and often renders expert opinion in legal cases in the United States.

BERND FRICK is Professor of Personnel and Organization Economics at the University of Witten/Herdecke. His research includes the analysis of alternative remuneration systems, the impact of mandated codetermination on firm performance, the economics of superstars in the wine and restaurant industry as well as in rock music, the allocation and remuneration of professional athletes, and the organization of professional team sports leagues. He has published widely in these areas in dozens of refereed journals. Professor Frick is a committed marathon runner with a personal best of 2:39:24 and a 10k best of 33:25.

BILL GERRARD is Professor of Sport Management and Finance at Leeds University Business School in the UK. He has published articles on many aspects of the economics and finance of professional team sports including the transfer system in soccer, the measurement of player quality, coaching efficiency, media ownership of teams, and the dynamics of sport sponsorship. He is a regular speaker at both academic and industry conferences and frequently appears in the national and local media as an expert on sport finance. He is Acting Editor of the *European Sport Management Quarterly* and a member of the editorial boards of the *Journal of Sport Management* and the *Journal of Sports Economics*. Professor Gerrard has developed player wage and transfer valuation systems used in professional soccer, regularly consults for teams and governing bodies, and provides expert evidence in legal cases. He is a soccer fan of Celtic (Scotland) and Leeds United (England) and a fully paid-up member of the Tartan Army (the "Braveheart" fans of the Scottish national soccer team).

JOHN GODDARD is Reader in Economics at University of Wales Swansea, UK. He is co-author with Stephen Dobson of *The Economics of Football* (2001). He has published numerous articles on the economics of professional team sports and participates in radio and TV discussions on the economics of professional football in England and Scotland. He is a member of the editorial board of *Journal of Sports Economics*. His other research interests are in industrial economics and the economics of the banking sector.

JEAN-JACQUES GOUGUET is Senior Lecturer in economics at the University of Limoges (France) and a member of two research centers (CDES and CRIDEAU). He mainly studies Regional Science, Sport, and the Environment. In the field of sport economics, he is the author of three books and many articles and has contributed numerous book chapters. He serves on the editorial board of the *Journal of Sports Economics* and the *Revue Juridique et Economique du sport*. He is General Secretary of the International Association of Sports Economists.

CHRIS GRATTON is Professor of Sport Economics and Director of the Sport Industry Research Centre (SIRC) at Sheffield Hallam University. He is a specialist in the economic analysis of the sport market. He is co-author (with Peter Taylor) of six books specifically on the sport and leisure industry and together they have published over 100 articles in academic and professional journals in the area of the economics of sport and leisure.

IAN JACKSON is Senior Lecturer in Economics at Staffordshire University Business School and the co-author of several articles on sports economics. The articles include demand forecasting in professional team sports and an economic analysis of spectatorship. He is also an industrial economist whose academic and commercial research focuses upon a number of industries including aerospace, brewing, and ceramics.

AKIHIKO KAWAURA is Professor of Economics at the Otaru University of Commerce, Japan. Previously, he was a staff economist at the United Nations Economic and Social Commission for Asia and the Pacific (ESCAP) and the World Bank, and Fulbright Visiting Scholar at the George Washington University. His publications include professional articles comparing competitive balance in Japanese and North American baseball and analyzing discrimination in the market for baseball cards.

SUMNER J. LA CROIX is Professor, Department of Economics, University of Hawaii at Manoa, and a Senior Fellow at the East-West Center. His research focuses on the economic history, development, and current state of economies in the Asia-Pacific region with an emphasis on issues pertaining to institutional change, property rights, and organization and regulation of industry. He is the co-editor of *Japan's New Economy: Continuity and Change in the Twenty-First Century* (2001). His publications include professional articles comparing competitive balance in Japanese and North American baseball and analyzing discrimination in the market for baseball cards.

YOUNG HOON LEE is an Associate Professor of Economics at Hansung University. His research interests are in sports economics and econometrics including productivity measurement. His recently published book, *Sports and Money* (written in Korean) introduces the economics of sports to the public. He also serves as an advisor for the Korean Professional Baseball Players Association (KPBPA).

NEIL LONGLEY is Professor of Administration at the University of Regina, Saskatchewan, Canada. In addition to sports economics, his research interests include public choice and international trade policy. His work on discrimination in the National Hockey League was reprinted in Andrew Zimbalist's *The International Library of Critical Writings in Economics: The Economics of Sport* (2001). He has published in a wide range of scholarly journals, including *Contemporary Economic Policy, Public Choice, American Journal of Economics and Sociology, Canadian Public Policy, Columbia Journal of World Business,* and the *Journal of Sports Economics.*

ROBERT D. MACDONALD is the Managing Director of the sports management consultancy Premiership Strategies International Pty Ltd. He is also completing an LLB and a PhD, "League Structures, Labour Markets and Competitive Balance: A Study of Australian Professional Sporting Leagues," at the University of Melbourne. Macdonald has authored several articles on competitive balance and collective bargaining in professional team sport and developed courses on labor relations and human resource management in the sports industry for two Australian universities.

RENATO GIOSA MIRALLA graduated from Escola de Administração de Empresas de São Paulo da Fundação Getúlio Vargas (FGV-EAESP) and is a consultant for retail companies and utilities in Brasil. He was the vice-president of the FGV-EAESP Student's Athletics Association in 2000. He worked with Antônio Carlos Kfouri Aidar on fan equity research for a professional football team in Brazil.

H. F. MOORHOUSE is Director of the Research Unit in Football Studies at the University of Glasgow, Scotland. He is the author of around forty academic articles and consultancy reports on most aspects of European professional football (soccer). He has also written a book analyzing American hot rodding and drag racing. In the 1990s he acted as a consultant on various economic aspects of football for the Scottish Sports Council, the European Commission, the Scottish Football Association, the British Office of Fair Trading, and the Federation Internationale des Associations de Footballeurs Professionnels.

P. DORIAN OWEN is Professor of Economics at the University of Otago, New Zealand. He has previously been a faculty member at the University of Reading (UK) and the University of Canterbury (NZ) and also editor of *New Zealand Economic Papers* (1995–1997). His research interests include empirical modeling of economic growth, applied monetary economics, and economics of sport.

DIDIER PRIMAULT is an economist and member of "Centre de Droit et d'Economie du Sport" at the Limoges University (France). He is the author of dozens of articles on sports economics. He also specializes in labor law. He has been treasurer of the International Association of Sports Economics since its foundation, in Limoges in 1998. Between 1989 and 1997, he was director of the French Basketball Player Association and General Secretary of the European Basketball Union.

JOACHIM PRINZ is research assistant at the University of Witten/Herdecke and a sports economist particularly interested in the field of team sports and race cycling. He currently works on the wage-tenure profile puzzle using a ten-year database that covers NBA player performance statistics and player salaries. With his analysis on the determinants of prize money won from the German TV show "Who Wants to Be a Millionaire" he has drawn much attention in the German media.

ROBERT SIMMONS is Lecturer in Economics in The Management School, Lancaster University, UK, and the author of a large number of journal articles and book chapters in the fields of labor economics, sports economics, and the economics of gambling. He is a member of the editorial board of the *Journal of Sports Economics* and is also active on the pitch as a soccer referee.

HARRY ARNE SOLBERG is associate professor at Trondheim Business School, Sør-Trøndelag University College, Norway, where he teaches microeconomics, welfare economics, and sports economics. His research has concentrated on analyzing economic impacts from sports activities with special attention on sporting events. He has published a number of articles about the markets for TV sports rights and also on tourism impacts from sporting events.

PAUL D. STAUDOHAR is Professor of Business Administration at California State University, Hayward. He is the author or editor of twenty books, including his most recent, *Diamond Mines: Baseball and Labor* (2000). Professor Staudohar is a member of the National Academy of Arbitrators, cofounder of the *Journal of Sports Economics*, and past President of the International Association of Sports Economists.

STEFAN SZYMANSKI is Professor of Economics at The Business School, Imperial College London. He is the author of numerous academic articles on the economics and business of sport and co-author (with Tim Kuypers) of *Winners and Losers: The Business Strategy of Football* (1999). He also appeared as an expert witness for the UK Office of Fair Trading on the collective selling of the FA Premier League's broadcasting rights. His athletic talents are, however, sadly limited.

CLAYTON R. WEATHERSTON is a postgraduate student faculty member at the University of Otago, New Zealand. Before that, he worked at the New Zealand Treasury. His current research interests include empirical modelling of economic growth, econometric methodology, issues in tertiary education, and the economics of sport.